Rein Tideiksaar

Falling
in
Old
Age

Prevention
and Management

Second Edition

Springer Publishing Company

Springer Publishing Company, Inc.
536 Broadway
New York, NY 10012-3955

Cover design by Margaret Dunin
Production Editor: Pamela Lankas

97 98 99 00 01 / 5 4 3 2 1

Library of Congress Cataloging-in-Publication-Data

Tideiksaar, Rein.
    Falling in old age : its prevention and management / Rein
Tideiksaar. — 2nd ed.
      p.   cm.
    Includes bibliographic references and index.
    ISBN 0-8261-5291-0
    1. Falls (Accidents) in old age—Prevention.   2. Falls (Accidents)
in old age—Treatment.   I. Title.
    RC952.5.T53   1996
    613'.0438—dc20   96-30179
                                                CIP

Printed in the United States of America

Contents

Preface

Since *Falling in Old Age* first appeared in 1989, the subject of falls in older people has advanced immensely. Although many of the general principles concerning the phenomena of falling remain the same, numerous specifics have changed. Both fall-related research and the number of investigators involved has increased substantially. As a result, the risk factors for falls and injury have been clarified and several potential preventive interventions, many of which are currently under investigation, have been proposed. This has allowed for better treatment of older persons who fall or are at risk for falls. That is the good news. With respect to clinical practice, however, attention to the problem of falls has not kept pace with research efforts. There are still too many health care professionals who either find themselves ill-prepared to deal with falls in older persons, or who fail to address the problem at all. Several recent episodes help illustrate this point.

The first concerns an invitation to me from the chairman of neurology of a well-known teaching hospital in the New York metropolitan area, asking me to lecture to his house staff on the etiology and treatment of falls in the elderly. When I asked why he wanted me to speak, he stated that "Many of our elderly patients—both in the hospital and community—are falling. And to put it quite frankly, I am embarrassed when my residents ask about falls. Beyond the neurologic explanation, I have nothing to offer—specifically with respect to prevention."

The second is a case history. DL is an 83-year-old gentleman with a long-standing problem of diabetes mellitus who was being followed in the diabetic management clinic. He was referred to my outpatient falls and mobility clinic for an evaluation of multiple falling episodes. His problems started 6 months prior to this visit, when he tripped and fell while walking outdoors. Following this episode he fell several times again under similar circumstances. Subsequently he developed a fear of falling, which led to a restriction of outdoor activities. He became housebound. Unfortunately, his "strategy" did not eliminate his falls. He quickly developed muscle weakness from disuse and began to fall from the toilet and bathtub. As a result, he became depressed. I determined

that his falls were most likely due to a combination of peripheral neuropathy, impaired vision, and decreased muscular strength. Based on
these findings, he was furnished with a cane for balance support and his
bathroom equipped with grab rails and a tub bench for mobility assistance. Finally, he was started on a program of muscle-strengthening
exercises. I called his attending physician in the diabetic clinic to convey
my recommendations.

His physician was pleased with the management plan. He said that
he had never inquired about the patient's falls, nor would he have if
not for the insistence of a fourth-year medical student assigned to the
diabetic clinic (interestingly enough, this medical student had previously
spent time with me in the falls clinic during a geriatric rotation). Subsequently, the patient did quite well. He stopped falling, his depression
and fears subsided, and he was able to leave his home.

The last incident concerns a long-distance telephone call I received
from a frustrated woman seeking advice concerning her 86-year-old
mother, who lived by herself. Her mother recently had experienced a
number of falls that resulted in a fear of falling that significantly compromised her everyday activities. As a consequence, the daughter was
quite concerned about her mother's safety, and brought her to a family
physician for evaluation.

The physician found that her mother had bilateral "drop foot," which
probably caused her to fall, and he instructed her to be more careful
around the house. Of course, this did not solve the problem, as she continued falling. In frustration, the daughter called a number of medical
centers and schools located in the state for help. They told her that "we
don't have a geriatric program," and thus were "unable to offer any
assistance." The daughter subsequently asked if I would evaluate her
mother, and was prepared to travel a considerable distance for me to
do so. Rather than subjecting the daughter to any further burden, I suggested an alternative approach. First, I told her that the condition of
"drop foot" was due to a number of underlying neuromuscular disorders
that needed to be identified, and referred her to a neurologist located
near where she lived. Secondly, I advised her that if the problem was
not amenable to medical or surgical treatment, there were a number of
specific rehabilitative strategies (i.e., exercise, gait training, and ambulation devices) that could be attempted, and I referred her to a physiatrist.
She called me back 2 months afterwards to tell me that her mother's
condition had improved.

These instances should make it obvious that as the population of
older persons continues to increase—and in particular, of those individuals most susceptible to falls and their untoward effects—it becomes

even more crucial that health professionals become involved in the prevention of falls. But in order to do so, they need to become more knowledgeable about fall prevention.

When I wrote *Falling in Old Age,* it was my intention that the book would serve as an introduction to the phenomena of falling. The book was an attempt to provide community- and institutional-based health care professionals with an understanding of the extent and consequences of falls, the numerous factors involved in fall causation, and the management strategies available to prevent falls. Reviews indicated that I had achieved this goal. Therefore, I have not changed this approach in the second edition.

I have tried to organize an enormous body of fall-related research into easy, digestible information for health professionals, which hopefully has direct clinical applications to the prevention and management of falls. Aside from updating the information, I have expanded several topics and introduced a number of new ones, such as rehabilitative strategies to reduce the risk of falls and issues surrounding the use of mechanical restraints, in order to reflect the current state of research in this area. Also, patient cases have been included throughout the book, which hopefully will help to emphasize the discussion.

I wish to especially thank Barbara Fletcher, who generously gave of her time in order for me to write this book and who amazingly put up with my Zenlike attachment to the word processor. Second, I would like to thank the literally hundreds of older people whom I have cared for over the years. They have taught me a great deal about the prevention and management of falls.

CHAPTER 1

An Overview of the Problem

INTRODUCTION

This century has witnessed a dramatic increase in the number and proportions of older persons. In the United States alone, the percentage of older persons in the population has tripled. In 1900, there were a little over 3 million persons, or 4% of the population, aged 65 years and older (Rabin & Stockton, 1987). Today, that number has increased to about 32 million, or 12% of the population. Between the years 1960 and 1985 alone, the population aged 65 and older increased by 71%, almost three times faster than the rate of increase for those under 65 (National Center for Health Statistics [NCHS], 1989). Much of this growth is due to advances in medical technology and improved treatment of acute and chronic illness. As a result, by the year 2000, it is expected that there will be 35 million Americans aged 65 or older, and as many as 40 million by 2010.

Within the older population, the proportion of those individuals in the 75-to-84 and 85-and-older age groups have shown the greatest growth (Rabin & Stockton, 1987). Together, these age groups comprise about 40% of the older population. More striking, however, is the growth in the numbers of persons 85 years and over, which is increasing at the fastest rate. Since 1960, this group of very old persons has grown almost sixfold compared with that of the population as a whole, and is expected to nearly double by the turn of the century (NCHS, 1989). Of even greater significance, this very old population is the most vulnerable segment of the older population. Currently they have the highest rates of chronic diseases, functional disabilities, hospitalization,

1

and institutionalization, which will continue into the future (Schneider & Guralnik, 1990). Most industrialized countries in the world—the Scandinavian nations, Canada, Japan, and Great Britain, for example—are experiencing similar trends for the older population in both their demographics and health care utilization (Schieber, Poullier, & Greenwald, 1992). Consequently, health care professionals must deal with a number of problems that occur most frequently in the older population, and especially in the oldest age groups. One of the most common and often critical problems is that of falling.

FREQUENCY OF FALLING

Over the past several decades, the extent to which older people fall in different clinical settings has been extensively studied worldwide. Data from several of these studies on the incidence of falls in the community, acute care hospitals, and long-term care facilities is reviewed in Table 1.1. Overall, the lowest incidence rates (0.2 to 0.8 per person annually) are reported as occurring in the community, and the highest rates in the hospital and long-term care facility—0.6 to 2.9 and 0.6 to 3.6 per bed annually, respectively (Rubenstein et al., 1988). Although the rates of falls vary considerably, a certain agreement about the magnitude of falls among older people can be arrived at from looking at survey data.

Among community-residing populations, up to one quarter of persons aged 65 to 74 and a third or more of those aged 75 and older fall annually (Hale, Delaney, & McGaghie, 1992; Tinetti, Speechley, & Ginter, 1988; Vetter & Ford, 1989). Up to 50% of these individuals experience multiple falling events every year (Blake et al., 1988; Nevitt, Cummings, Kidd, & Black, 1989; Tinetti et al., 1988; Vetter & Ford, 1989). About 20% of older persons who fall will experience another fall within 6 months (Vellas, Garry, Wayne, Baumgartner, & Albarede, 1992).

Most studies have shown that the frequency of falls increases with advancing age (Blake et al., 1988; Cwikel, 1992; Downton, 1987; Lord, Ward, Williams, & Anstey, 1993; Nevitt et al., 1989; Shepherd, Lutz, Miller, & Main, 1992; Tinetti et al., 1988). For instance, in their survey of a community population of older people reporting falls, Prudham and Evans (1981) found that 22.4% of persons aged 65 to 69 years reported falling, with the percentage of respondents increasing in the following way on the basis of age: 70 to 74 years (27.9%), 75 to 79 years (31.4%), and 80 to 84 years (39.6%). Beyond the age of 85, however, the number of persons reporting falls decreased to 35.2%. Similar trends have been

TABLE 1.1 Incidence of Falls in Different Settings and Countries

Community-Based Surveys

Annual incidence per 1,000 persons at risk

Great Britain:
224 (Gabell, Simons, & Nayak, 1985)
677 (Graham & Firth, 1992)
424 (Downton & Andrews, 1991)
280 (Vetter & Ford, 1989)
350 (Blake et al., 1988)

Finland:
368 men
611 women (Luukinen et al., 1994)

New Zealand:
683 (Campbell, Borrie, et al., 1990)

United States:
300 (a) (Lach et al., 1991)
625 (Perry, 1982)
609 (Sorock & Shimkin, 1988)
809 (Tinetti et al., 1988)
279 (Robbins, Rubenstein, Josephson, et al., 1989)
217 (Teno, Kiel, & Mor, 1990)

Sweden:
410 (a) (Svensson, Rundgren, & Landahl, 1992)

Institutional-Based Surveys

(a) Annual incidence per 1,000 beds; (b) per 1,000 patients at risk;
(c) per 1,000 admissions

Hospital Surveys

Canada:
840 (a) (Morse, Prowse, Morrow, & Federspiel, 1985)

Denmark:
2805 (a) (Sehested & Severin-Nielsen, 1977)

Great Britain:
620 (b) (Scott, 1976)
422 (b) (Morris & Isaacs, 1980)
645 (c) (Odetunde, 1982)

United States:
1900 (a) (Catchen, 1983)
1400 (a) (Morgan, Mathison, Rice, & Clemmer, 1985)
3700 (a) (Poster, Pelletier, & Kay, 1991)
1590 (a) (Caley & Pinchoff, 1994)

3

TABLE 1.1   *(Continued)*

Nursing Home Surveys

Canada:
   668   (b) (Ashley, Gryfe, & Amies, 1977)
   650   (a) (Gryfe, Amies, & Ashley, 1977)
   730   (a) (Pablo, 1977)
   1559 (a) (Berry, Fisher, & Lang, 1981)

Great Britain:
   3061 (b) (Woodhouse, Briggs, & Ward, 1983)
   3600 (a) (Blake & Morfitt, 1986)

Sweden:
   350   (a) (Svensson et al., 1991)

United States:
   784   (b) (Rodstein, 1964)
   2400 (a) (Cacha, 1979)
   1400 (a) (Miller & Elliott, 1979)
   2600 (a) (Colling & Park, 1983)
   760   (a) (Louis, 1983)
   1292 (b) (Venglarik & Adams, 1985)
   2000 (a) (Berryman, Gaskin, & Jones, 1989)
   1200 (a) (Rubenstein et al., 1990)

reported by several other researchers (Downton, 1987; Hornbrook, Wingfield, Stevens, Hollis, & Greenlick, 1991). The decline which occurs in fall rates beyond age 85 is not well understood, but may reflect a limitation of activities in the old-old population, or the survival of a fit cohort (Tideiksaar, 1989).

Some investigators have also shown the frequency of falls to increase with age, but here the incremental relationship between increasing age and the prevalence of falls (Blake et al., 1988; Downton & Andrews, 1991), and the decline in fall rates for those persons beyond 85 years (Askham et al., 1990; Blake et al., 1988) has not been consistently demonstrated. Nor do we really know why falls in the old-old continue. Aside from an increase in frailty in this population, falls may reflect their social circumstances; that is, persons of extreme old age may not have the assistance of other persons such as family members, friends, or formal caregivers to help with activities.

The majority of community-based studies have found that older women tend to fall more frequently than older men (Blake et al., 1988; Campbell, Borrie, et al., 1990; Campbell, Spears, & Borrie, 1990; Downton

& Andrews, 1991; Hornbrook et al., 1991; Tinetti et al., 1988). Overstall (1985), in an examination of community-dwelling persons, reported that in the 65-to-69-year age group, the prevalence of falls is approximately 13% for males and 30% for females, which increases in the 80-to-84-year age group to about 33% and 44%, respectively. These sex differences in the frequency of falling remain constant, even after age adjustments are made to account for the greater number of women than men in the older population.

There are several possible explanations for this discrepancy. First of all, women may report falls more often than men. A national survey conducted in 1985 by the Israel Bureau of Statistics found that among community-dwelling persons over the age of 65 years, older women reported falling twice as often as older men (Cwikel, 1992). This is supported by Campbell, Spears, and Borrie (1990), who reported that men were more likely than women to deny having fallen. In their study, after obtaining a history of falls from the man's spouse or an observer, or after close questioning, they found that the fall rates for the sexes were equal. Social factors may also be responsible in part for the difference in falls between men and women. For instance, Cwikel (1992) found that older persons living alone (i.e., single, widowed), and particularly women, reported falls at a greater rate than their married counterparts. Second, Campbell, Spears, and Borrie (1990) suggested that older men and women may differ in both the circumstances in which they fall and the risk factors for falls. Regardless, the divergence of fall rates begins to disappear after the age of 75 (Luukinen, Koski, Hiltunen, & Kivela, 1994), and by age 85, the prevalence of falls in men and women is nearly equal (Woodhouse et al., 1983). Svensson, Rundgren, and Landahl (1992) in a study of 741 community-residing persons aged 84 to 85 showed no gender difference in fall incidence.

Within institutional settings, falls are of equal importance for older people, and the frequency of falls is considerably higher than that among those living in the community. In the acute care hospital, falls account from 40% to 80% of all incident reports (Jones & Smith, 1989; Maciorowski et al., 1988). The majority of fall incidents occur among patients 65 years and older (Raz & Baretich, 1987). It is estimated that one out of every five older patients falls during their hospital stay (Falbe, 1990). As many as 50% of these individuals fall repeatedly (Caley & Pinchoff, 1994; Gaebler, 1993; Hernandez & Miller, 1986).

In the nursing home, into which older people are often admitted for safety reasons, falling is even more of a problem. Up to 50% of residents fall each year; over 40% experience more than one fall (Clark, Lord, & Webster, 1993; Gurwitz, Sanchez-Cross, Eckler, & Matulis, 1994;

Rubenstein et al., 1988; Svensson, Rundgren, Larsson, & Landahl, 1992; Tinetti, 1987; Wright, Aizenstein, Vogler, Rowe, & Miller, 1990). The probability of falling, in both hospitals and nursing homes, increases with advancing age, with the highest incidence of falling occurring in the 80-to-89-year-old age group (Luukinen et al., 1994; Rubenstein et al., 1990). Some studies have found falls to decrease in the eighth and ninth decades (Morris & Isaacs, 1980). This decline in falls in the very old may be due to the presence of living in protected institutional settings, or else represents a self-imposed restriction of activities or an increase in restraint use by staff to guard against falls. The frequency of falls in men and women is inconstant. Some studies report a higher incidence in men (Catchen, 1983; Morgan et al., 1985; Sehested & Severin-Nielsen, 1977), others in women (Caley & Pinchoff, 1994; Haga, Shibata, Shichita, Matsuzaki, & Hatano, 1986; Hernandez & Miller, 1986), or else no sex difference in fall rates (Gaebler, 1993; Morse, Tylko, & Dixon, 1987).

As one can readily see, an extraordinary amount of data on the incidence and prevalence of falls has been collected over the years. This epidemiological information has at least two important functions. First of all, it provides a heightened awareness of the magnitude of the problem; secondly, it helps to target subgroups of older persons for interventions. Thus, the accuracy in determining the incidence and prevalence of falls, particularly with respect to the community and institutional population, becomes critical. However, a number of gaps and weaknesses exist in many of these epidemiological studies. These studies may, as a result, lead to erroneous conclusions with respect to the extent of falls, and perhaps an inappropriate utilization of preventive resources.

For instance, from the data it appears that falls are more frequent as older people pass from the community to the institutional setting. This might imply that the problem of falls is of greater concern for persons residing in the institution, due in part to greater frailty, than for those in the community; and hence, institutionalized elderly could be seen as deserving greater attention. However, there are other factors that come into play, which can account for the differences in fall rates between the two populations. Notice in Table 1.1 (p. 3) for example, that even between comparable community and institutional population-based studies, the rates of falls vary widely. These variations, in part, can be explained by methodological problems consisting of differences in reporting and defining falls, and in part by the selection of target populations.

Community fall studies are mostly based on surveys that rely on older persons to recall their falls. But this method may not always provide the most accurate data. For instance, these events may not be easily remembered or recorded accurately. In one community-based population study, Cummings, Nevitt, and Kidd (1988) found that 13% of older people who reported a fall failed to recall any falls when questioned after one year. However, as the authors state, this data may not be representative of the problem, or actually may underestimate the tendency of older persons to forget falls, since their population underwent intensive surveillance which may have reinforced recall of falls. In another study, Hale, Delaney, and Cable (1993) surveyed a group of geriatric family practice outpatients with falls and found that after a 3- and 6-month period, respectively, only 31% and 44% of subjects were able to recall falls. Suggested reasons for poor recall include memory deficits and a reluctance by older people to admit to falls (Cummings et al., 1988; Hale, Delaney, & McGaghie, 1990). At the other extreme, falling events may be overreported by older people. In their study, Cummings and colleagues (1988) found that 10% of the falls reported by the subjects did not meet the study definition of a fall. As most falls are unwitnessed events, the accurate reporting of falls by older people residing in the community becomes a critical issue. Furthermore, the almost threefold higher incidence of falls found in nursing home dwellers as opposed to community-dwelling persons may be related in part to a more accurate reporting of falls in institutions (Rubenstein, Josephson, & Robbins, 1994).

Another method of capturing information about falls in the community is through health care records that generally contain information about those individuals known to have fallen (e.g., physician practice lists, emergency room records, acute and nursing home admissions registers, etc.). The accuracy of this data is questionable because most falls experienced by older persons are not injurious and, as a result, they do not typically receive medical attention. Furthermore, health professionals may not always document those patient falls that occur. Hale et al. (1993) found that fewer than one-fifth of reported falls were noted by physicians in the patient's medical record. Therefore, the detection of falls is dependent upon older people reporting noninjurious falls, and health professionals inquiring about falls. Both of these sources may be highly unreliable.

Secondly, community researchers may utilize different definitions to describe what constitutes a "fall." For instance, some studies have utilized a standard fall definition that has been proposed by a recent consensus report on the subject (Gibson, 1987). This report defines a fall as

an event which results in a person coming to rest inadvertently on the ground or other lower level, and other than a consequence of the following:

sustaining a violent blow, loss of consciousness, sudden onset of paralysis, as in a stroke, or an epileptic seizure. (p. 4)

Others, however, may either use a definition that includes those
medical conditions excluded by the aforementioned definition, or else
develop their own definition, or even fail to specifically define falls.
Instead, they rely on the older person's interpretation of the event.
Any inconsistency of fall definitions can lead to the over- and underreporting and recording of falls.

Hospital and nursing home studies for the most part rely on data
obtained from incident reports recording falls. As opposed to community studies, the documentation of falls in institutional settings has one
major advantage: falls are routinely recorded by nursing staff and are
required to be tracked by incident reports. However, any research that
relies solely on incident report data to record the rate of falls may
underestimate the extent of the problem. Incident reports can be completed carelessly or erroneously, or else may be ignored altogether by
staff. Sutton, Standen, and Wallace (1994), in a hospital-based survey,
found that up to 35% of accidents were not documented on incident
reports by the nursing staff. Falls accounted for the majority of these
unreported accidents. Similarly, in the nursing home, up to 15% of falls
may be missed by relying on incident reports alone, as opposed to
examining both incident reports and medical charts for fall occurrences (Buchner et al., 1993). On the other hand, there is a general tendency within institutional settings to sometimes overreport falls. This
is related to both a fear of legal liability by staff members, and a failure
to provide staff with specific definitions as to which events constitute
a fall. Any lack of consistency in fall definitions can influence the accuracy of incident report data, as the decision to fill out an incident
report is left to the interpretation of the individual staff member.
Subsequently, the accuracy of hospital and nursing home fall rates can
be affected.

Lastly, epidemiological studies are not always comparable with
respect to the extent of falls. First, the incidence and prevalence rate
of falls are often used erroneously in the literature (Cumming, Kelsey,
& Nevitt, 1990). "Incidence" refers to the number of falls occurring during a specified time period, while "prevalence" refers to the number of
falls—new and old—that are present during a given point of time. An
inability to distinguish the difference between these terms makes it difficult to evaluate the findings of various researchers. Furthermore,
some studies are retrospective, while others are prospective and use a
variety of different observation periods, and express fall rates in

numerous ways (i.e., falls per bed day, falls per 10,000 patient days, falls per bed, fall rate per 1000 admissions or persons) which leads to confusion (Downton, 1987). Also, researchers may target or study different populations. For example, some community-based studies survey all persons over age 65 with falls, while others confine their attention to those aged 75 and older. Some researchers study all falls occurring in the community; others may investigate falls occurring in the home, or limit their research to injurious falls that come to medical attention (e.g., a physician's office, emergency room, etc). Similarly, among hospital-based studies, some researchers include all inpatient units in their investigation, while others confine their study to examining specific services (e.g., general medical, neurological, geriatric, surgical, psychiatry, or rehabilitation units). This makes comparisons difficult. In summary, the methodological differences between studies can lead to both an under- or overestimation of falls among older people in the community and institutional setting, and a misrepresentation of the actual extent of falls.

A HISTORICAL PERSPECTIVE

Although an abundance of epidemiologic information on falls in older people exists today, most of our knowledge has been gathered only during the last 15 years. During that period, it has evolved appreciably. As a result, our understanding and concepts of how to manage falls in older persons are changing rapidly, and will undoubtedly continue to do so during the years ahead. To provide insight into the progress and present state of the art, it is helpful to briefly review the history of our knowledge regarding falls in older persons.

Scientific study directed towards eliminating injury and, specifically, addressing the problem of falls in older persons has occurred very late in relation to other health issues. Several explanations suggest themselves. First of all, at the turn of the century, the importance of falls in older persons never reached the critical mass necessary to attract the attention or investigation that such issues are given today. At the time, only a small percentage of persons reached old age. Recall that the average life expectancy at birth was only 49 years. Most persons died as a result of infectious diseases (i.e., tuberculosis, influenza, and pneumonia). In 1910 the mortality rates in the aged from these infections were far greater than were death rates from falls. Consequently, the problem of falls was overshadowed by the prominence of infectious diseases. The "practice" of medicine (e.g., its clinical focus and scientific research) concentrated largely on eradicating these infectious diseases, developing public health stratagems (i.e., better sanitation, improved hygiene practices, and producing vaccines and antibiotics), and controlling their spread where possible.

By the 1940s, because of the great strides made in disease control and public health, mortality rates began to decrease dramatically. At the same time, the numbers of older persons began to grow, as did their longevity. The life expectancy at birth increased to about 68.2 years. This newfound longevity, however, was accompanied by an increase in the frequency of falls, and the complications of these falls began to take a toll. During the latter years of this century, the age-specific mortality rates for falls began to increase and medical interest in the care of older people as a separate group began to flourish. However, the problem of falls and injury, and the need for injury prevention in older people, failed to generate the kind of interest as had infection control. Much of this had to do with our attitudes toward the conception of falls.

Historically, falls have been viewed as "accidental" occurrences, events attributable to bad luck—unpredictable and therefore unavoidable. As a consequence, the burden of falling has, for the most part, been borne by the host as an act of individual carelessness, and not considered a public health problem. There was also another, perhaps more insidious view: that falls were an unfortunate consequence of the aging process. That is, the onset of falling was considered as being a part of the "normal" phenomenon of aging—an irreversible manifestation of expected organ system decline, which occurred with advanced age. Another misconception, held by the medical community for many years, was that in the older person with multiple medical problems, the problem of falling was just another "hopeless" outcome of a "hopeless" state in which one disorder after another leads inexorably (and literally) to a downhill course.

As a consequence of these misconceptions, our perceptions of falls in older people were oriented toward host-related factors and focused on individual error or fault, negligence, and carelessness as the cause. This orientation had two main consequences. First, rather than investigating possible causative factors, such as medical diseases, fall investigation chiefly concentrated on identifying factors in the environment that led to injuries as well as cataloguing the nature of the injury following the fall itself. As a result, the bulk of preventive efforts concentrated on teaching older persons how to avoid accidental falls. These efforts consisted of modifying behavioral factors, appealing for individuals to "be more careful" (as they were "accident-prone"), and educational measures, such as pamphlets on home safety. Secondly, much of the research at the time was directed toward examining the consequences of injury, rather than uncovering the potential host-related factors that might have been responsible.

In short, during most of the first half of this century, falls in older persons were attributed to "fate" or "bad luck," which inhibited progress towards the scientific examination of falls and injury causation. A shortage of data about both the extent and causes of falls in older people resulted. However, these misconceptions and our view of the problem of falls in older people have greatly changed.

Hugh De Haven, a World War I pilot turned physiologist, in 1942 was one of the first to recognize that the occurrence of injury per se was not due solely to the shortcomings of the people involved (DeHaven, 1942). De Haven reported on eight individuals who fell from heights of 50 to 150 feet without sustaining injuries. He examined the estimated deceleration forces, characteristics of the structure the falling person impacted, and the manner in which the body landed. He concluded that the surface of the environment is the dominant cause of injury, and that the surface can be modified to reduce the probability of mechanical injury in the event of falling. These findings were later expanded upon by John E. Gordon, a Harvard epidemiologist who in 1949 considered that "accidents" were a problem in medical ecology; that is, a relationship existed between the host—the person susceptible to injury—an agent, the specific causal factor, and the environment (Gordon, 1949). He suggested using an epidemiological approach to injury control that included analysis of risk factors, implementation of preventive measures, and the evaluation of the effectiveness of these measures.

The contributions of De Haven, Gordon, and others helped to shift injury prevention away from blaming the person. The idea of looking at falls in older people with the same spirit of scientific inquiry was first advanced in 1948 by J.H. Sheldon, a noted British physician. Up until then, information about the frequency of falls in the older population was generally not available. Sheldon noted a high incidence of falls—40%—among older persons in the town of Wolverhampton, England. Subsequently, he wrote a landmark book, *The Social Medicine of Old Age,* in which he discussed the importance of falls in older persons and questioned the lack of attention to the problem (Sheldon, 1948). He remarked that

> The fact that old people are liable to tumble and hurt themselves is a matter of common knowledge. . . . Not only may the injuries resulting from

these falls be of great severity, but in really old people a fall may have the effect of precipitating a senile decay. Apart altogether, however, from its social importance, the liability of old people to fall represents problems of the greatest clinical interest. It is odd that this has attracted so little curiosity, and it is greatly to be hoped that a more intensive study of the question may be made in the future. (p. 105)

In the United States, one of the first reports to appear in the medical literature that addressed the problem of "accidental" falls and the physician's responsibility in preventing falls was written by Frederic D. Zeman, a physician affiliated with the Home for Aged and Infirm Hebrews in New York City (Zeman, 1948). He stated that

The increasing interest of physicians in the social and medical problems of old age leads directly to the question of prevention. Accidents may often be avoided if the physician appreciates what a great contribution he can make by studying the factors involved. In his dealing with older patients . . . he will make every effort to detect ocular, auditory, cardio-vascular, musculoskeletal, neurological and mental abnormalities that may predispose to accidental injury. (p. 24)

Hence, the writings of Sheldon and Zeman marked the beginning of a change of focus in the medical literature. In the 1950s, a number of physicians and epidemiologists began to write about the problem of falls in both the community and institutional setting (Boucher, 1959; Exton-Smith, 1959; Fine, 1959; Howell, 1955; Parrish & Weil, 1958; Scott, 1954; Seiler & Ramsay, 1954; Snell, 1956). More than likely this flourish of activity was stimulated by a number of factors. With an increase in life expectancy, the number of older people, particularly those most susceptible to falling, began to increase rapidly. As a consequence, an increase in both the frequency of falls and accidental mortality (mainly due to falling) began to be recognized by geriatric physicians as a serious situation.

In 1960, Sheldon followed up his original work and wrote a seminal paper on the natural history of falls in old age. He was apparently critical of much of the literature to date, and addressed the need for greater attention towards the problem of falling. He stated that

The liability of older people to tumble and often to injure themselves is such a commonplace of experience that it has been tacitly accepted as an inevitable aspect of aging and thereby deprived of the exercise of curiosity. The literature, in fact, on what has always been a trial for the elderly and now is becoming a problem for the community is very meager, and bears little relation to either the practical importance or the intrinsic interest of the subject. An essential preliminary to further investigation is a knowledge of what actually happens . . . (p. 1685)

Sheldon proceeded to describe his own survey of 500 falls in 202 older individuals living in the community, which he described as "the natural history of falls." He suggested that these falls were caused by a combination of medical problems—"difficulty in maintaining erect posture once balance has been disturbed" (p. 1686) and "sudden collapse of postural controlling mechanisms leading to drop attacks"—and environmental conditions—"an increased liability to trip over trivial objects" (p. 1687).

While Sheldon's original observations, now four decades removed, remain largely on target, new interest as well as research on the subject of falling has changed the clinical perception of these events. We have been able to confirm Sheldon's findings and elaborate upon them to a great degree.

Starting in the 1960s, epidemiologists and geriatricians began to study (en masse) and write about the epidemiology, consequences, and underlying factors responsible for falls in older persons (Agate, 1966; Berfenstam, Lagerberg, & Smedby, 1969; Gray, 1966; Rodstein, 1964). Although, many of these early studies were primitive—retrospective and descriptive in nature, using readily available populations of older patients, such as those visiting emergency rooms, hospital patients in geriatric wards, and residents in long-term care institutional settings—they started to define the problem. These research efforts continued throughout the 1970s and 1980s, and have increased exponentially into the present. Researchers began in earnest to address the epidemiology of falls in older people, and to design preventive approaches (Campbell, Borrie, & Spears, 1989; Campbell, Borrie, et al., 1990; Hogue 1982 a, b; Nevitt et al., 1989; Tinetti et al., 1988; Waller, 1974, 1978). More importantly, as opposed to earlier research efforts, several studies, particularly over the past ten years, have been much more carefully designed. Many of these studies, which will be discussed in detail in the succeeding chapters, are population based (unlike the earlier work done with restricted groups) and therefore their findings can be generalized. They are prospective rather than retrospective; and they measure risk factors, including the subject's health status, activities, and the state of their environmental conditions. They adequately measure the type of injury, the sequelae, and long-term consequences as well. As a result, this research has greatly contributed to our knowledge of falls.

Thus, since 1960, fall-related research has advanced from estimating the consequences of the problem of falls to studies that are now predicting the risk of falling and identify potential intervention strategies for preventing falls. A more recent development includes a shift from focusing not only on the older individual with falls, but also to examining groups or distinct populations of older people with falls. That is, attention is focused on the universal effects of specific age-related factors and disease states, such as neuromuscular and cardiovascular conditions, and their relationship to fall causation; and on suggesting interventions.

In the United States, the National Institute of Aging (NIA) has been a driving force behind this research effort. In 1984, the NIA held a workshop titled "Falls in the Elderly: Biological and Behavioral Aspects" and subsequently initiated a number of research projects relevant to the epidemiology, etiology, and prevention of falls. This body of work was ultimately published in a separate monograph (Radebaugh, Hadley, & Suzman, 1985). This experience prompted the NIA, in conjunction with the National Center for Nursing Research (NCNR) and the Centers for Disease Control (CDC) to convene a workshop on frailty and fall-related injuries in 1988. Its purpose was to explore strategies for testing interventions aimed at reducing frailty and falls. This effort resulted in a series of clinical multicentered trials, collectively known as FICSIT (Frailty and Injuries: Cooperative Studies of Intervention Techniques). The FICSIT trials are designed to study the interactions among biomedical, behavioral, and environmental factors contributing to frailty and fall-related injury, and offer possible solutions (Ory et al., 1993).

Interest in the study of falls in older people has not been limited to the United States, but has extended worldwide. In the United Kingdom, a Home Accident Surveillance System (HASS) has been in place since 1977 (Askham et al., 1990). The HASS is designed to estimate the overall numbers, types, and circumstances of falls. This effort has lead to a clearer understanding of the epidemiology of falls, and the development of several intervention programs. The HASS has been duplicated by several other European countries as well (Askham et al., 1990). In 1987, the Kellogg International Program on Health and Aging, in association with the World Health Organization (WHO), convened an international work group to study how to prevent falls by the elderly and make recommendations to WHO member countries (Gibson, 1987). Similar initiatives have recently taken place during the European Congress of Gerontology, Madrid, Spain (Vellas, Toupet, Rubenstein, Albarede, & Christen, 1992) and in association with the Department of Health, University of Tampere, Finland (Jantti, 1993).

As a result, and contrary to popular myth, falls, to a large degree, are no longer regarded as normal consequences of aging or "accidental" and random events, but are now considered as predictable events, the outcome of a multitude of host-related and environmental factors. As a mark of change, the term "accident" has been abandoned as a description of falling events, and has been replaced by the term "unintentional injuries." More importantly, many of the determinants that contribute to falls, as we are beginning to discover, are potentially amenable to interventions. By minimizing or eliminating antecedent risk factors, falls can be prevented or reduced.

Further steps are still necessary. In order to implement preventive measures, health professionals need to first change their attitudes with regards to looking at falls as "accidental" occurrences; secondly, they need to understand the conditions under which falls occur, and the factors associated with fall risk. Additionally, they must have a sound approach to the clinical assessment of falls and fall risk as well as intervention strategies.

My intent is to help health care professionals approach the prevention and treatment of falls in older people. This book attempts to take a tremendous amount of research and interpret the results into clinical practice. Chapter 2 examines the outcome of falls with respect to individual consequences, and their effects on families, and health professionals. Chapter 3 reviews the causes of falls with respect to age-related, pathological disorders, medications, and extrinsic or environmental factors in community and institutional setting. Chapter 4 provides a discussion of fall and injury risk factors. Chapter 5 provides a description of medical strategies that reduce falls, and includes a discussion of the clinical approach to the assessment of both falls and fall risk. Chapter 6 is a discussion of psychosocial problems and strategies to reduce fall risk. Chapter 7 is a description of the rehabilitative strategies to reduce fall risk, and includes exercise programs, the prescription of ambulation devices, and footwear. Chapter 8 is a description of environmental fall hazards and obstacles and the design of modifications (i.e., lighting, ground surfaces, furnishings, etc.) aimed at reducing falls and injury. Included is a discussion of device technology and compliance. And finally, chapter 9 addresses the issues surrounding the use of mechanical restraints in the management of falls.

While falls that occur in the community, hospitals, and nursing home settings are somewhat different in terms of the causative and risk factors, the intervention strategies within each setting are, for the most part, similar. However, when it becomes necessary to consider the specificity of each setting in the discussion that follows, it will be noted and a distinction appropriate to each will be set forth.

CHAPTER 2

Complications of Falling

INTRODUCTION

Falls represent a major source of death and disability in older people, posing a serious threat to their physical health and psychological well-being. The consequences of falls are not solely confined to the older person themselves. They place a burden on family members, make demands on health care professionals, and strain the economic resources of health care institutions as well.

MORTALITY

Fall-related mortality is a critical problem in the older population. While the majority of falls among older persons do not result in death, falls experienced by this age group are a leading cause of mortality. According to data from 1984, the overall death rate in the United States from falls was 5.1 per 100,000; however, in those persons 65 and older the death rate increased to 31.3 per 100,000 (Devito et al., 1988). Depending on the country, mortality from falls among older persons ranges from 10 to 35 per 100,00 among those aged 65 to 74, to 65 to 240 per 100,00 among those aged 75 and over (World Health Organization, 1986). It is estimated that in the United States, falls account for up to 10,000 deaths each year in older persons (National Center for Health Statistics [NCHS], 1987; Tinetti & Speechley, 1989; United States Department of Health and Human Services [USDHHS], 1990). Almost one-third (32%) of all deaths from falls occur among people greater than age 85, although this group represents 1% of the population as a whole. Fifty-nine percent of fall deaths occur to persons 75 and older, or 5% of the population. There are more deaths from falls among people 85 and older than motor vehicle occupant deaths among males aged 18 to 19 (3,800 versus 3,000), and the death rate per 100,000 population is more than twice as high (Baker, O'Neill, Ginsburg, & Guohua, 1992). Overall, falls represent the sixth leading cause of death in persons 65 years and older (Baker, O'Neill, & Karpf, 1984; Baker et al., 1992). With respect to unintentional injury, in those persons 65 to 75 years falls represent the second leading cause of mortality (motor vehicle accidents are the leading cause), and in those persons over age 75 falls are the leading cause of death (National Safety Council, 1990). Rice, Mackenzie, Jones, et al. (1989) reported that the death rate from falls in persons 75 years and older is almost 12 times greater than the rate for all ages combined. The risk of mortality appears to be greater in those individuals with a clustering of falls (i.e., multiple events occurring over a short time period). Wolinsky, Johnson, and Fitzgerald (1992) examined data from the Longitudinal Study on Aging and found a positive association between repetitive falls, rapid deterioration of health status, and increased mortality in older persons.

The actual number of deaths in which a fall is a contributing factor is likely to be much higher, as some argue that the number of fall-related deaths occurring in older people may be underestimated (Fife, 1987; Hongladarum, 1977; Waller, 1978). The contention of these researchers is that the mortality data, which is derived mostly from death certificates, may underreport the number of fall-related deaths, as these certificates usually do not include falls as a cause of death, or as a contributing factor. Rather, common death-related complications of falling, such as pneumonia or septicemia, may be more likely to be listed instead. This is supported in part by an earlier British study (Wild, Nayak, & Isaacs, 1981a) that reported a 1-year mortality rate of 26% in a group of community-dwelling older people with falls. They found that none of the deaths were reported as fall-related.

Nonetheless, the available data on fall-related mortality remains impressive. The risk of mortality increases with advancing age. For example, the death rates from falling for both men and women combined at age 65 to 69 are 16.4 per 100,000 persons, increasing to 59.4 per 100,000 between the ages of 75 to 79, and progressing to 338.2 per 100,000 over age 85 (USDHHS, 1986). Older men, especially those over the age of 75, have greater fall-related mortality than older females without any increase in falls (Kohn, Sinoff, Strulov, Ciechanover, & Wei, 1991). Sattin et al. (1990) found that men were nearly twice as likely as women to die following a fall injury. Several explanations have been suggested. First, older men tend to experience a greater number of falls from excessive heights, such as stairways and ladders, and as a result may be at increased risk for mortality-related injury (Baker et al., 1992). Second, older men who fall may be more frail and far less capable of full recovery from major medical events than older women (Campbell, Borrie, & Spears, 1989; Kohn et al., 1991). As well, death rates from falls have been found to be twice as high for whites as for Blacks (Baker et al., 1992). In part, this may be related to an increased inci- dence of osteoporosis and the risk of hip fractures in whites (Cummings, Kelsey, Nevitt, & O'Dowd, 1985; Griffin, Ray, Fought, & Melton, 1992), or else it may represent an underreporting of fall-related deaths for non- whites (Sorock & Shimkin, 1988).

Fall mortality rates are, for the most part, higher in urban than rural areas (Baker et al., 1992), and in Northern states, particularly for whites, regardless of seasonal variations. States with the highest age-adjusted mortality rates are those located in the New England area; Southern states, such as Mississippi, have the lowest rates (Hogue, 1980). Several explanations may account for these findings and may challenge the notion that seasonal variation plays a minor role. One premise may, in part, relate to the location of falling, i.e., whether falls occur indoors versus outdoors. For example, a recent study that examined injuries suffered by a northern inner-city population of older persons found that almost 40% of outdoor falls occurred during December and January (Grisso et al., 1990). This may imply that persons in urban set- tings are perhaps more ambulatory than those in rural settings and, during winter months when conditions are hazardous, these persons may be prone to fall injuries, i.e., hip fractures. Furthermore, Campbell, Spears, Borrie, and Fitzgerald (1988) found that older women experi- enced an increased rate of falls during the winter when temperatures dropped to 1 degree Celsius or below. They attributed the increased risk of falls to defects in thermoregulatory mechanisms and hypother- mia. However, Baker, O'Neill, Ginsburg, and Guohua (1992) contend that geographic differences could be due to variations in describing and coding deaths. As well, the underlying circumstances are not spec- ified in records of 80% of falls that occur, and particularly those associ- ated with injury (Baker et al., 1992).

In those older persons residing in the community, up to 60% of fatal falls occur in the home (Sattin, 1992). Moreover, the likelihood of a fatal fall at home increases with age; 35% in the 65-to-74 age group, and

61% in persons over age 75 (Askham et al., 1990). More than likely, heightened mortality is related to the increased prevalence of chronic diseases in the oldest-old age group. Some community studies indicate that falls associated with "long lies" (that is, the person is unable to get up following a fall and remains on the floor for an hour or more) are related to increased mortality, independent of physical injury (Tinetti, Liu, & Claus, 1993; Vellas, Cayla, Bocquet, de Pemille, & Albarede, 1987). Of those individuals admitted to the hospital after a fall, only about one-half will be alive a year later (Gyrfe, Amies, & Ashley, 1977; Overstall, 1985). Within the hospital setting, about 10% of older patients who have fallen die before discharge (Lucht, 1971). In nursing homes, approximately 1800 fatal falls occur annually (Baker et al., 1992). For those aged 85 and older, it is estimated that one in every five falls ends in death (Baker et al., 1992). Fall-related mortality appears not to be a direct result of the fall, as the majority of deaths occur weeks to months after the fall (Morfitt, 1983; Waller, 1978; Wild, Nayak, & Isaacs, 1981a). Rather, mortality is the end result of fall-related complications (i.e., immobility) and the presence of both acute (i.e., pneumonia, heart failure, pulmonary embolism, decubitus ulcers) and chronic comorbid conditions. Dunn, Rudberg, Furner, and Cassel (1992) examined the relationship between falls and mortality in a nationally representative population of persons aged 70 and over, and found a significant association between falls and 2-year mortality, largely due to the presence of multiple chronic diseases and disabilities.

Hip fractures are a leading cause of fall-related mortality in older people. In fact, the event has become so ordinary as to give rise to an often quoted saying: "We come into the world under the brim of the pelvis and go out through the neck of the femur" (DeLee, 1984, p. 1211). Although this assessment is somewhat pessimistic, it helps underscore the ominous consequences associated with hip fractures in older persons. As a result, mortality following hip fractures is one of the most frequently studied and documented outcomes of falling. Early studies showed a mortality rate as high as 50% one year following a hip fracture. More recently, however, the overall mortality rate in older persons 12 months after a hip fracture varied from 14% to 36% (Ions & Stevens, 1987; Jette, Harris, Cleary, & Campion, 1987; Magaziner et al., 1989; Weatherall, 1994). Variance may be due to several factors. First, differences in the populations studied (e.g., older age, poor mental status and mobility, number of comorbid conditions) may influence mortality. Secondly, some argue that hip fracture mortality is underreported (Pemberton, 1988). Donaldson, Parsons, and Cook (1989) compared national mortality data against a large cohort of older patients admitted to hospitals with the diagnosis of fractured neck of the femur. They found that 930 deaths occurred within the cohort, but only 52 were listed on death certificates as dying from fractured hips.

Regardless of whether the reported declines in mortality are real or not, death associated with hip fractures in older persons remains a significant problem. In general, the mortality rate in older persons remains about 12% to 20% higher than in older persons of similar age and gender who have not suffered a fracture (Kenzora et al., 1984). Most of this excess mortality occurs within the first 6 months following fracture (Holmberg, Conradi, & Falen, 1986; Magaziner et al., 1989), after which mortality rates approach those for non-hip fracture patients. As a result, it is estimated that hip fractures lead to an overall 5% to 20% reduction in life expectancy for older persons (Cummings et al., 1985).

Many studies have attempted to identify factors responsible for the excess mortality following hip fractures. The presence of chronic diseases, such as congestive heart failure, diabetes mellitus, and chronic obstructive pulmonary disease, and their acute exacerbations at the time of injury, has been found to increase mortality after injury (Parker & Anand, 1991). Kenzora et al. (1984) reported that four or more medical comorbidities significantly increased the mortality rate. In their series of 406 patients who had a hip fracture and who were followed for at least 1 year, the mortality rate was 11% for those patients with less than three medical conditions, compared with a rate of 25% for those who had more than four concurrent conditions. Several investigators have found that poor cognitive status (e.g., dementia, psychosis) is an important determinant of survival after a hip fracture (Ions & Stevens, 1987; Magaziner et al., 1989). The length of the perioperative period following hip fracture also influences mortality. Sexson and Leher (1987) found that patients who had three or more comorbid medical problems had a poorer rate of survival when hip fracture repair was completed within 24 hours of injury, as opposed to those individuals who had surgery after 24 hours. Likewise, Zuckerman, Skovron, Fessel, Cohen, and Frankel (1992–1993) reported that a delay in surgery for those patients with three or more medical problems reduced mortality. Presumably, patients who are medically ill benefit from a delay in surgery, allowing for the treatment and control of unstable medical conditions. Other factors that have been shown to have a negative effect on survival include postoperative complications, such as decubitus ulcer, urinary tract infection, and malnutrition (el Banna, Raynal, & Gerebtzof, 1984; Verluysen, 1985). Persons who are institutionalized following a hip fracture, as opposed to those persons who return home, have greater mortality. Holmberg et al. (1986) reported that, in a series of 3002 patients who had been followed for 6 years, persons who had been institutionalized had a 1-year mortality rate of 46%, a level that was almost three times that of those living at home (16%).

The mortality associated with hip fractures also varies by gender. While both older women and men are at risk for death, men appear to experience greater mortality rates than women. Approximately 83% of women with hip fractures are still alive 1 year after injury, compared with only 63% of men (Magaziner et al., 1989). Several reasons have been suggested. Older men may have more coexisting chronic diseases and cognitive dysfunction that can lead to poor functional status, and have access to less social support to provide mobility assistance post-hip fracture (Magaziner et al., 1989). However, it is unclear whether the presence of illness and disability in men leads to this excessive mortality. For example, Baker et al. (1992) argue that even when serious concurrent illness is controlled for, white men hospitalized for hip fracture still have greater death rates than women. They suggest that alcohol may contribute to higher death rates in men, because severe injuries are more likely to involve its consumption than are minor injuries. Alcohol abuse has been shown to be associated with loss of bone density (Felson, Kiel, Anderson, & Kannel, 1988; Spencer, Rubin, Rubio, Indreika, & Seitam, 1986), which could contribute to both the likelihood of osteopenia and balance impairment and, as a result, to severe injuries.

While the fall-related mortality figures presented here are disturbing, there are encouraging developments. In recent years, most developed nations have reported a decline in the rate of mortality from falls (World Health Organization, 1984). Riggs (1993), for one, studied the fall-related mortality rates per 100,000 persons from 1962 through 1988 in the United States. He discovered that deaths from falling declined by 63.5% (from 165.6% to 60.4%) among men at age 83.4 years, and declined 76.3% (from 86.2% to 20.4%) among women at age 77.5 years. The decline was attributed to a general improvement in trauma care. Others have postulated that since the incidence of hip fractures has remained constant over the years, the decline in mortality reflects an increase in the survival of hip fracture patients due to improved surgical and postoperative procedures, such as early ambulation following surgery (Lu-Yao, Baron, Barrett, & Fisher; 1994; Rodriguez et al., 1987; Sorock & Shimkin, 1988). This is supported by a British study that showed a reduction in hip fracture mortality from 40% in 1975 to 28% in 1985 (Evans, 1987). The decline in mortality was largely attributed to improvements in surgical management and subsequent rehabilitation. Reductions in fall-related mortality appear to be greater in older women than in men (Sorock & Shimkin, 1988). In the United States, the death rate from falls in persons aged 75 years and older between 1960 and 1980 declined more for women than men: 67%, versus 49% (Sorock & Shimkin, 1988). Again, the gender difference may reflect, in part, the fact that older men have greater severity of injuries from falls. While mortality rates from falls have declined, it is unknown whether the rate of falls has changed correspondingly.

MORBIDITY

In contrast to the study of fall-related mortality, the study of morbidity following falls in the older population has not received equal attention. In fact, the rate of morbid complications may be greater than supposed because, on the one hand, fall-related mortality rates are declining, while on the other hand, the numbers of older persons who are at fall risk are increasing.

PHYSICAL INJURY

While most falls experienced by older persons do not result in physical injury, the risk is real and potentially crippling. During a 1-year prospective study of 336 community-residing persons 75 years of age or older, 32% fell at least once. Of those who fell, 24% sustained serious injuries; more than 5% experienced fractures (Tinetti, Speechley, & Ginter, 1988). Approximately 15% of falls experienced by older persons, regardless of the clinical setting, result in physical injury serious enough to warrant medical attention (Tinetti & Speechley, 1989). Of these, about 3%–5% result in bone fractures (Nevitt et al., 1989; Rubenstein et al., 1988; Tinetti & Speechley, 1989), and the remaining 5%–10% lead to other serious injuries (e.g., head and soft tissue trauma) (Tinetti & Speechley, 1989). Although any bone may be broken, distal forearm and hip fractures are among the most common to occur due in part to osteoporosis (i.e., trabecular bone loss and diminished strength) (Crilly et al., 1987; Kelsey & Hoffman, 1987). Between 0.2%–1% of falls result in hip fractures (Nevitt et al., 1989; Sattin, 1992; Tinetti et al., 1988). Other fractures occur frequently as well, such as those of the pelvis, rib, hand, foot, head, and ankle, but their precise estimates with regards to falls are unknown. Poor reporting of fractures by older people, in part, may contribute to the lack of epidemiological data. In a population of community-dwelling older women, Nevitt et al. (1992)

found that with the exception of hip, wrist, and humerus fractures, the individuals tended to overreport hand, finger, rib, and face or skull fractures. A history of falls and osteoporosis was associated with greater inaccuracy. Conversely, Jonsson, Gardsell, Johnell, Redlund-Johnell, and Sernbo (1994) found a considerable underreporting of fractures of the hand, foot, and distal end of the radius by men and women.

The risk of fall-related injury increases with age. Sattin et al. (1990), in a community-based surveillance system in Miami Beach, Florida, found that the rate of nonfatal fall injury events increased steadily after the age of 65, reaching a high of 138 per 1000 for men and 159 per 1000 for women aged 85 years and older. Covington and colleagues (1993) analyzed a statewide trauma registry in North Carolina and reported that 86% of the registry injuries to those 85 and older were due to falls. A Swedish study analyzed falls in a population of persons aged 84 to 85 living at home, and found that in 80% of falls an injury occurred, of which every fourth (25%) was a fracture (Svensson, Rundgren, & Landahl, 1992). It appears that older women are more likely to suffer serious injury following a fall than men (Sattin et al., 1990; Sjorgen & Bjornstig, 1991), possibly due to the presence of osteopenia.

Distal Forearm Fractures

Distal forearm or wrist fractures, particularly among white women, are a common cause of injury following a fall. The usual mechanism of this injury follows a fall onto an outstretched arm and hyperextension of the wrist (Melton, Chao, & Lane, 1988). The incidence of distal forearm fractures rises at or near the menopause, and then reaches a plateau by age 65–70, when their frequency is surpassed by hip fractures (Melton et al., 1988; Nevitt, Cummings, & Study of Osteoporotic Fractures Research Group, 1993). The lifetime risk of a distal forearm fracture at age 50 for a white woman is estimated to be 15% (Cummings, Black, & Rubin, 1989).

As only about 18% of distal forearm fractures result in any hospitalization and require little rehabilitation (Garraway, 1979), this injury has generally been considered free of any long-term disability. This assumption, however, is not entirely correct. About one-fifth to one-third of persons with distal forearm fracture have a poor to fair functional outcome (de Bruijn, 1987). Common problems include persistent pain, diminished range of motion, neuropathies, and postsurgical arthritis (deBruijn, 1987), problems that can significantly impact the person's activities of daily living. Madhok and Green (1993) surveyed a cohort of older patients with upper limb fractures, the majority of which were due to distal radius fractures, and found that up to 26% of the patients reported residual disabilities (i.e., difficulty with bathing, getting in and out of bathtubs, shopping, etc.). As a consequence, many older people recovering from distal forearm fractures rely on the support of caregivers to maintain their mobility (Madhok & Bhopal, 1992; Nankhonya, Turnbull, & Newton, 1991). For those frail older individuals who may not have social support to help with activities, the consequences may be significant.

> RS is an 82-year-old woman who suffered a distal forearm fracture following a fall at home. As a consequence she experienced great difficulty with seat transfers (i.e., from chairs and toilets) and getting into and out of her bathtub, as she was dependent upon armrest support. Because she lived alone and was without help with mobility assistance, she required admission to a nursing home until her wrist healed.

> CJ is a 79-year-old woman with Parkinson's Disease and, as a result, was dependent on a walker for her ambulation. She fell at home and fractured her wrist. She was then unable to use her device properly and ambulate, and required nursing home placement. There, she needed nursing assistance to perform her ADL activities, which she resisted. Subsequently, while attempting toileting on her own, she fell and fractured her hip. CJ never went home.

Hip Fractures

In the United States, about 220,000 hip fractures occur annually among persons 65 and older (National Center for Health Statistics, 1988). The overall annual incidence rate is 660 per 100,000 older persons (Jacobson, 1990). Up to 90% of hip fractures are directly related to falling (Melton, 1988); the remaining 10% occur spontaneously on weight-bearing, a result of severe osteopenia. The incidence rate of hip fractures increases dramatically beyond the age of 50 years, approximately doubling with each additional decade (Cummings et al., 1985).

Older women are two to four times more likely to fracture a hip than older men (Cummings et al., 1989; Jacobson et al., 1990). An earlier study estimated that among those persons who survive to 90 years of age, 33% of women and 17% of men will have suffered a hip fracture (Gallager, Melton, & Bergstrath, 1980). Although men have lower hip fracture rates, they show as great a rate of increase with age (Hedlund & Lindgren, 1987). White women experience the highest incidence of hip fracture, followed by white men (Farmer et al., 1984; Vogt, 1995). The rate of hip fracture in white women at age 85 and older is almost

10 times the rate at ages 65 to 74. Blacks experience relatively low rates of fracture, whereas Hispanics and Asians appear to be at intermediate risk (Jacobson, 1990; Silverman & Madison, 1988). The significance of these numbers is better appreciated by noting that the lifetime risk of a hip fracture, 15% in white women and 5% in men (Cummings et al., 1985), is equivalent to the lifetime risk of breast and uterine cancer in women, and about the same as the lifetime risk of prostate cancer in men (Cummings et al., 1985).

In those older persons who survive a hip fracture, considerable morbidity is likely to occur. Following a hip fracture, many older persons experience a substantial decline in physical function and never regain their premorbid level of ambulation. Up to three-quarters of patients who are independent in ambulation prior to hip fracture become functionally dependent in walking at 6–12 months after fracture (Jette et al., 1987; Magaziner et al., 1990; Marottoli, Berkman, & Cooney, 1992). Thereafter, these persons experience little improvement in walking, and often require canes, walkers, or human assistance to maintain their mobility. Mossey, Muhran, Knott, and Craik (1989) studied community-dwelling, ambulatory, white females and found that 74% could walk outside the home at 12 months, although only 28% returned to their prefracture ambulatory status. Older persons who fracture their hip while residing in a long-term facility experience similar problems. Folman, Gepstein, Assarof, and Liberty (1994) examined the functional outcome of femoral neck fractures in a group of institutionalized older persons with an average age of 81 years; of these individuals, 94% were women. They found that only 12.9% of the patients regained their preinjury level of ambulatory status. Seventy-five percent of the population studied had preexisting neurological or cardiovascular disease that may have interfered with their rehabilitation.

Poor recovery following a hip fracture has been found to be associated with advanced age over the age of 75, female sex, prefracture dependency, longer hospital stays (increased risk of iatrogenic problems), cognitive dysfunction (dementia, depression), post-surgical delirium, and lack of social supports (Magaziner et al., 1990; Mossey et al., 1989, 1990; Shamash, O'Connell, Lowy, and Katona, 1992). Sometimes prefracture dependency on assistive devices is associated with poor outcomes, as individuals who rely on them may have a number of existing chronic diseases that may interfere with ambulation. However, Meadows, Zuckerman, Sakales, and Frankel (1991) in a study of 250 community-residing persons following hip fracture found that those individuals who used a cane or walker before injury were more likely to regain their prefracture walking ability than those persons who had not required the need of an assistive device. Possibly, these individuals may have found using the device more acceptable, or may have experienced a previous successful outcome following hip fracture, as opposed to the others, who may have refused to use the device. This theory is partially supported by Borkhan and Quirk (1992), who reported that older hip fracture patients with greater previous experience with major illness or injury who expect to recover will more likely improve their ambulatory status faster and more completely than others.

Many persons may require nursing home care on a temporary or permanent basis because of poor recovery and decreased mobility after a hip fracture. It is estimated that between 30% and 60% of patients with hip fractures are discharged from the hospital directly to nursing homes (Borkhan & Quirk, 1992; Fitzgerald, Moore, & Dittus, 1988; Sattin et al., 1990). Up to 40% continue to reside in the nursing home 6 months later (Bonar, Tinetti, Speechley, & Conney, 1990; Fitzgerald, Fagen, Tierney, & Dittus, 1987; Palmer et al., 1989), and as many as 57% after a 1-year period (Fitzgerald & Dittus, 1990; Fitzgerald, Moore, & Dittus, 1988). The factors contributing to permanent institutionalization are similar to those associated with poor recovery immediately following injury, consisting of age greater than 80 years, disorientation, decreased ambulatory and transfer status, and lack of social supports in the community (Bonar et al., 1990). In addition, the availability of rehabilitation services in the nursing home, that is, the extent of physical therapy received by the patients post-hip fracture, influences recovery (Bonar et al., 1990).

The prospective payment system for U.S. acute care hospitals and its effect on hip fracture recovery has been examined as well. Fitzgerald et al. (1987) compared hip fracture patients before and after implementation of the current reimbursement system and found that after implementation of the new system individuals had a decreased length of hospital stay and, at the same time, an increase in nursing home admissions. They suggested that the shift of patients from the hospital to the nursing home setting for rehabilitation may negatively influence hip fracture recovery. While it is usually assumed that immediate discharge from the acute hospital to the home is associated with better prognosis or more rapid recovery than discharge to a nursing home, this has not been demonstrated. Williams, Oberst, and Bjorklund (1994) recently studied the outcomes after hip fracture among older women discharged home and to the nursing home, and showed no difference in regaining mobility between short-stay nursing home patients (less than 1 month) and those who were returned to their homes. Palmer et al. (1989) showed that the proportion of older patients who were discharged to a nursing home and remained in the nursing home after 6 months did not change significantly after the introduction of the prospective payment system.

For those older persons discharged from the hospital to the community, the ability to walk is crucial for independent function. Any persistent loss of mobility following a hip fracture often results in increased dependence on others. Ceder, Throngren, and Wallden (1980) have shown a greater propensity of caregivers to take over certain tasks for hip fracture patients when returning home. If support is not available or is insufficient to meet the individual's functional requirements, there is an increased probability of admission to a long-term care facility on a permanent basis. Poor ambulation, along with the absence of caretakers in the home, has been shown to be a strong predictor of nursing home placement (Bonar et al., 1990; Ceder et al., 1980).

Both the incidence and morbidity associated with hip fracture is expected to increase as the population becomes older. In the United States, the national projections for the annual number of age-related fractures of the hip for the year 2000 range from 260,000 to more than 325,000 (Brody, Brock, & Williams, 1987; Schneider & Guralnik, 1990). A similar increase has been projected for many industrialized nations that are already faced with an increased hip fracture incidence (Ho, Bacon, Harris, Looker, & Maggi, 1993; Lauritzen, Schwarz, Lund, McNair, & Transbol, 1993; Rockwood, Horne, & Cryer, 1990).

HEAD TRAUMA

Falls have been found to be a leading cause of head injury in older persons (Pentland et al., 1986), and occur equally in both older men and women (Galbraith, 1987; Sattin et al., 1990). Most head injuries in older persons that result in acute hospitalization are sustained as a result of falling (Saywell, Woods, Rappaport, & Allen, 1989). In older men with head injury, the use of alcohol has been ascribed as a cause in up to 50% of cases (Galbraith, 1976). Aside from bruises and lacerations, the most critical head injury is that of subdural hematoma. Noltie and Denham (1981) found that up to two-thirds of older patients with subdural hematoma report a recent history of falls or head injury, and older men showed a greater incidence of subdural hematoma. More recently, Curtis, Wofford, and Branch (1995) found that 54% of older persons hospitalized with subdural hematoma experienced a fall shortly before admission. Older people are at increased risk for subdurals because of certain age-related changes in the older brain (i.e., reduced cerebral reserve). As a result, older people are less able to withstand even minor trauma, such as might occur from hitting a bed headboard, wall, or floor. As a clinical rule, any time a person suffers mental confusion following a fall, a subdural hematoma should be suspected and ruled out by a neurologic evaluation. Any lingering subdural hematoma that is not evacuated within a relatively short period of time can lead to permanent cognitive dysfunction.

> WW is a 93-year-old woman who was admitted to the hospital with a history of multiple falls and confusion. The patient's falls occurred during ambulation; she experienced episodes of instability and fell backwards, striking her head. A CT scan was ordered to rule out a subdural hematoma as the cause of her confusion. The scan revealed the presence of an old subdural that was not previously reported; unfortunately, it was too late to evacuate the clot. As a result of her confusion, she required permanent institutionalization.

MUSCULOSKELETAL AND OTHER INJURIES

About 5%–10% of falls result in serious soft tissue injuries such as hematomas, sprains, and joint dislocations requiring medical care (Tinetti & Speechley, 1989). Another 30%–50% of falls result in minor soft tissue injuries that do not receive medical attention (Nevitt et al., 1989). A variety of other injuries occur following falls, although their extent is not known. Several reports describe rhabdomyolysis (skeletal muscle injury) in older persons resulting from falls (Marcus, Rudensky, & Sonnenblick, 1992). Most of these cases are subclinical, and quickly resolve. However, rhabdomyolysis has been associated with acute pressure sores (Levine, 1993).

Another complication associated with falls is skin tears, a separation of the dermis from the epidermis caused by minor trauma. Skin tears occur commonly within the institutionalized population (Gurwitz et al., 1994; White, Karam, & Cowell, 1994). Many take place when persons either fall against or bump into furnishings with sharp edges, such as dressers, tabletops, chair frames, and other objects. One study conducted in the nursing home found that 18% of skin tears in the resident population were due to falls and near-falls (i.e., bumping into objects) (Malone, Rozario, Garinski, & Goodwin, 1991). This can be a particular problem in persons with friable skin. For example:

> LN is a 92-year-old woman who resides in the nursing home. Her medical problems consist of dementia, visual impairment, chronic obstructive pulmonary disease (treated for many years with steroids), and multiple falling and near-falling episodes. As a consequence of the steroid therapy,

her skin was extremely friable (i.e., almost peeling to the touch). She also had multiple skin tears covering both her upper and lower extremities. When I observed the patient walking, it was easy to see why she had skin tears. Because of her impaired balance, she consistently bumped into sharp-edged furnishings that were in her path. More than likely, the patient's visual impairment exacerbated the problem. The patient was provided with a walker, which not only supported her balance but also served as a protective barrier against the furnishings.

Lastly, falls can lead to long lies (an inability to get up from the floor) even in the absence of physical injury (Cummings & Nevitt, 1991; Ryynanen, Kivela, Honkanen, & Laippala, 1992; Tinetti et al., 1993). About half of fallers require help getting up, with most resulting in a lie less than an hour long (Campbell, Borrie, et al., 1990; Nevitt, Cummings, & Hudes, 1991). Some falls are associated with prolonged lies. It is estimated that between 8.2% and 20% of falls among community-dwelling older persons result in lies greater than an hour or more in a length (Campbell, Borrie, et al., 1990). The morbidity following prolonged lie times can be considerable. These persons are at risk for dehydration, pressure sores, and rhabdomyolysis (Marcus et al., 1992). Furthermore, prolonged lies can lead to a fear of further falls, a restriction of activity, functional decline, and increased family burden (Tinetti et al., 1993).

RESTRICTED ACTIVITY

Falls in older persons are commonly associated with a restriction of activities and, subsequently, a loss of functional status. Wild and colleagues (1981a) reported that fallers residing in the community were twice as likely as non-fallers to become functionally dependent 1 year after falling. Kosorok, Omenn, Diehr, Koepsell, and Patrick (1992), utilizing data from the *1984 Supplement on Aging* of the National Health Interview Survey, found that falls in the noninstitutionalized United States population were associated with about 18% of all restricted activity days experienced per year. When compared with other chronic health conditions associated with restricted activity, such as arthritis, cerebrovascular disease, diabetes, etc., falls accounted for the highest proportion of restricted activity days. Kiel, O'Sullivan, Teno, and Mori (1991), using similar resource data from the *Study of Aging* (1984 to 1986), examined the relationship between falls and functional status. They found that, compared to non-fallers, one-time fallers and multiple fallers experienced a greater decline in their functional status over a 2-year period. Those persons who experienced multiple falls experienced the greatest decline in their activities of daily living. Similar findings have been reported by Dunn et al. (1992) and Wolinsky et al. (1992) who showed that, compared with single fallers, persons with multiple falls demonstrated greater functional disabilities. Comparable changes in functional status following falls occur in the institutional setting as well (Rubenstein et al., 1994). Clark, Dion, and Barker (1990) examined the reasons for taking to bed among a population of independently ambulating older individuals residing in an intermediate-care facility. They found that 58% of the residents who took to bed did so after a fall, and that this activity was associated with worsening of functional abilities.

Falls can lead to restrictions in activity and functional decline through a variety of pathways. The most obvious is that of physical injury. Aside from the functional problems associated with hip fractures previously discussed, any type of musculoskeletal trauma can lead to a restriction of activity. The extent of the restriction, of course, will be dependent upon the duration of the trauma suffered, which can be extensive. For example, Grisso, Schwarz, Wolfson, et al. (1992) found that over 40% of persons who visited the emergency room for fall injuries continued to report pain or a restriction in their usual activities after 2 months. Remarkably, in 40% of these individuals, complaints persisted on average for 7 months. Additionally, falls may be caused by any acute illness, exasperation of comorbid medical conditions, or adverse medication effects that can lead to a restriction of activities and, depending on the duration, interfere with the individual's function.

Even in the absence of physical injury, once an older person has fallen, there is a tendency for the individual to reduce the level of activity, even if only for a few days. At other times, falls may be more ominous, leading to a fear of further falls, which in turn, may cause the person to become depressed and restrict their activities for longer periods of time. About one-quarter of falls in the community result in activity limitations because of a fear of falling (Nevitt et al., 1989; Tinetti et al., 1988). Sometimes family members, formal caregivers, and institutional health professionals may become fearful for the safety of the older person (particularly after a fall) and become overprotective, restricting their activities. At times, institutional policies, procedures, and nursing levels may govern the level of independent function that older patients are permitted. The more restrictive the policy and the greater the number of nurses available to enforce it, the greater the effect on patient mobility. Lastly, certain features of the home and institutional environment can lead to a restriction of activities and functional impairment. For example, elevated bed heights and side rails may be prohibitive. Low-seated chairs and sofas may be difficult to rise from.

Floor surfaces that are excessively glossy may appear dangerous to walk upon. Any disability and loss of independence associated with falling is likely due to a combination of these factors. In one early study, MacDonald and Butler (1974) found that nursing home residents who have the potential to walk but who may be at fall risk are instead encouraged to ride in wheelchairs due to the following: (1) staff expectations of helplessness; (2) residents accepting the "sick role"; (3) lack of staffing and rehabilitation programs; and (4) hazardous environmental conditions, such as slickly waxed floors or hallways without benches and chairs to provide rest periods.

IMMOBILITY

As a consequence, older persons with any restriction of activity following a fall are at risk for immobility and a host of morbid complications. Virtually each system of the body can be affected. The most dramatic effects occur in the musculoskeletal system. First of all, immobilization of muscles and lack of weight-bearing on bone causes bone demineralization (i.e., osteoporosis) and may increase the risk of fractures. The long bones of the lower extremities and the vertebrae are the most susceptible to mineral loss. The loss of calcium increases rapidly from the first to third week of immobility, and thereafter begins to plateau at a lower level. Therefore, just a few weeks of bedrest is sufficient to allow a significant loss of bone. In a study of hospitalized patients, Krolner and Toft (1983) found that lumbar bone mass decreased by 0.9% per week during recumbency, that is, at a rate of about 45% per year. The loss of bone calcium may also lead to calcium deposits in soft tissues and joints, causing ankylosis, or fixation of the joint, which interferes with mobility.

Some of the most visible changes associated with a restriction of activity occur in the muscles. Prolonged immobility results in muscle atrophy (i.e., loss of muscle mass), and as a result, in decreased muscle strength. A completely rested muscle will lose approximately 10% to 15% of strength per week, and as much as 1% to 3% for each day of immobility (Halar & Bell, 1988). Leg muscles lose strength about twice as fast as those of the arm (Harper & Lyles, 1988). Muscles that remain in a shortened or fixed position can also become contracted quickly. Eventually, much of the muscle tissue is replaced by fibrous components, and normal function becomes difficult to restore. Contractures of the joint capsule and surrounding muscle can cause a restriction in the range of motion of the joint. This follows prolonged periods of recumbency (i.e., lying in bed or sitting in a chair), as a full range of motion is difficult in these positions. As flexor muscles are stronger than extensor muscles, contractions usually follow a pattern of flexion. Although all joints can be affected, the hip, knee, and ankle are the most susceptible. Sometimes ankle flexion contractions can occur from the weight of bed covers on the feet during bed rest. The lack of joint movement results in decreased synovial fluid, which may eventually lead to degenerative changes in the joint cartilage. Taken together, these changes greatly impact on the older individual's mobility and ability to maintain a safe level of gait and balance.

The skin or dermal system can become involved as well. Any restriction of activities that results in bed or chair rest is strongly associated with the development of pressure sores or decubitus ulcers (Allman, 1989). Any direct pressure on the skin or bony prominences that exceeds capillary perfusion pressure (usually 32 mm Hg), sometimes for as little as 2 hours, can lead to reduced tissue blood flow. In turn, this can result in skin breakdown or ulcers. Age-related changes in the skin include thinning of the epidermis and dermis, reduction in vascularity, and loss of subcutaneous fat in thin persons hastens the development of pressure ulcers (Allman, 1989).

Periods of immobility may have profound effects on the respiratory system by (1) interfering with chest expansion; (2) reducing the movement of secretions; and (3) causing decreased ventilation. Full expansion of the alveoli occurs in the upright position and is compromised while lying in bed or sitting in a chair. In these positions, maximum contraction of the intercostal, diaphragm, or abdominal muscles during expiration and inspiration is not achieved. As a result, the lungs do not completely expand, and the normal flow of air into and out of the lungs is inhibited. Subsequently, the individual's vital capacity is reduced, and respiratory secretions become more difficult to remove. Eventually, this can lead to a pooling of secretions in the alveoli, causing inflammation and infections, such as hypostatic pneumonias.

Deterioration of the cardiovascular system is especially dramatic with extended immobility, resulting in hemodynamic changes and orthostatic hypotension or low blood pressure. This occurs when a person moves from a reclining to a sitting or standing position and experiences a marked drop in blood pressure that results from a pooling of blood in the lower extremities and a decrease in circulating blood volume. After a period of prolonged bedrest, recovery of orthostatic function may take several weeks. Also, immobility diminishes muscle contractions in the legs, a mechanism that promotes venous return of blood to the heart. The resulting venous stasis can lead to edema of the lower extremities. Furthermore, any pressure of the legs against the bed or chair may additionally impede circulation. All these can cause thrombus formation and the risk of pulmonary embolism.

The urinary system is subject to several adverse effects arising from the recumbent position. In the upright position, gravity plays an essential role in assisting the proper drainage of urine. In the recumbent position, urine flow from the kidneys occurs against gravity, but this is insufficient. Thus, either lying or sitting down, positions which play against the forces of gravity, can lead to retention of urine and increase the risk of urinary tract infections. The loss of calcium from the bones is also great in the supine position, leading to hypercalciuria (calcium in the urine) and the risk of renal calculi (stones). Furthermore, older persons can develop urinary incontinence secondary to problems of restricted activity. Ehrman (1983) reported that patients with restrictions of activity are six times more likely to be incontinent than those who were mobile. Most often this is related to functional incontinence, that is, the urinary mechanisms are intact, but the patient either cannot get to the bathroom in time, or is dependent in toileting.

In addition, inactivity affects the gastrointestinal system. It commonly causes constipation and fecal impaction. The mechanisms involved appear to be decreased bowel activity, or peristalsis, which results in slowed movement of feces into the descending colon and sigmoid. The muscles of fecal expulsion—the abdominals, diaphragm, and levator ani—are particularly susceptible to atrophy with prolonged immobility, resulting in constipation. Also, a failure to assume the optimal defecation position (sitting erect or squatting), such as using a bedpan, also contributes to constipation.

Functional inactivity can affect the neurological system as well. Vestibular dysfunction can occur quite rapidly and is marked by decreased postural stability and the risk of balance loss. After several days of activity, balance usually returns to normal, although the significance and extent of any vestibular change is more likely to be dependent on premorbid conditions affecting the neurological system.

Finally, older persons who are immobilized are subject to a number of altered psychological and behavioral responses. At one extreme, individuals can experience periods of lethargy, passivity and social withdrawal, and depression. At the other, persons may exhibit anxiety, fear and panic, paranoia, and even hostility. Immobility can also lead to sensory deprivation, which can result in delirium and confusion. These behavioral responses are usually variable from person to person, both in pattern and degree, and their expression is largely dependent upon the individual's underlying personality and premorbid psychiatric status.

Perhaps the best way to summarize and emphasize the negative effects of immobility is to paraphrase Dr Richard Asher, a British physician, who in 1947 characterized the patient at prolonged bedrest:

> Look at the patient lying long in bed. What a pathetic picture he makes. The blood is clotting in his veins, the lime draining from his bones, the scybala stacking up in his colon, the flesh rotting from his seat, the urine leaking from his distended bladder, and the spirit evaporating from his soul (Asher, 1947, p. 967).

On a more serious note, the risk of morbid complications, in general, increases with the duration of immobility, such as extended confinement in a bed or chair. In frail persons (i.e., those with diminished physiologic reserve), the likelihood of multiple complications increases. Any long-standing loss of functional status resulting from the combined effects of inactivity and immobility is strongly associated with a "spiral" response (Tinetti, 1986), a rapid deterioration that is associated with a further risk for falls, injury, institutionalization, and even death (Tinetti, Williams, & Mayewski, 1986; Wolinsky et al., 1992).

PSYCHOLOGICAL EFFECTS

Following falls, many older persons may experience one or more emotional problems including depression, shame, loss of confidence, anxiety, and fears of diverse nature. Depending on the specific manifestations of the fall—whether they are self-limiting or recurrent in duration—the severity or consequent morbidity, and their premorbid psychological makeup, older persons react in highly variable ways. Furthermore, those falls associated with physical injury, prolonged lies, and/or functional decline are likely to increase the risk of these psychological complications. Individuals suffering from other chronic illness and their emotional impairments may suffer a additive effect.

For some older persons, the onset of falling can represent an initial confrontation with frailty and for persons with multiple chronic diseases and disabilities, falls may represent a further threat to autonomy and functional ability. In both instances, the capacity for maintaining a customary level of independent activity is endangered. Significant lifestyle changes and emotional distress often result.

Some older persons become increasingly depressed over their present situation and future prospects. Fear of helplessness, loss of self-sufficiency, and dependency are often dominant. As a result, the person may conclude that life will not get any better, only worse. Loss of motivation, discouragement, and depression are often the result. Additionally, individuals may voice great anxiety about what impact their frailty will have on spouses and other family members, and may worry about who in the family will care for them if they are further disabled. Of course, issues related to caregiving become more critical to persons without available family support. Some individuals respond by becoming apathetic and withdrawn. Others become angry, expressing bitterness and rage over the situation and what has happened to them. Sometimes this anger is directed at others, such as family members and health professionals. At other times, the anger is more self-directed, as these people may blame themselves for the fall (for example, feeling they were not cautious enough) or for other subsequent fall-related complications. These responses, at least on a short-term basis, may be appropriate, since they are reactions to a loss of mobility and autonomy which, for some, can occur quite suddenly. Accepting these losses without experiencing a decrease in self-worth may be difficult, especially for people who have been independent and in control for the last 70 or 80 years of their lives. However, failure to resolve these feelings or adapt to changes in function often leads to further emotional distress. Any additional falls or decline in function and autonomy are likely to increase the individual's agitation.

Aside from these problems, older persons with repetitive falls frequently feel great shame. After all, they have been independent for many years, and don't want to appear frail or to fall in front of others, and especially their peers. Also, they may be humiliated at the prospect of needing help with activities, and sometimes needing help getting up after a fall.

It is not uncommon for health professionals and families to become overprotective of these individuals and thus often discourage independence unintentionally, and attempt to restrict these elders' activities and, hence, their autonomy. As a result, persons often become overly insistent on maintaining a set level of activities and their own self-sufficiency. These concerns mask fears of loss of freedom, mobility, decisionmaking power, abandonment, and a return to a childlike state of dependence (i.e., role reversal) on their children and other caregivers. For similar reasons, some persons are reluctant to visit a physician for evaluation, as they have a general fear that the doctor may restrict their autonomy, that is, that the doctor will recommend a limitation of activities, relocation to sheltered housing, etc.

The threat of a fall can also alter an individual's self-image and self-confidence, and create feelings of increasing frailty and incompetence. In those persons with recurrent falling episodes, the threat of a future fall may intensify these feelings, creating a situation somewhat analogous to the Greek myth about a courier who was forced to sit through a banquet under a sword suspended overhead by a single horsehair. Persons with multiple falls do not know when the next falling event will occur, or what will follow the fall: whether they will be injured, whether they will be able to get up off the floor, or what to do about the whole of the event. This uncertainty elicits increased anxiety during the performance of everyday activities (getting out of bed, transferring from the toilet, climbing stairs, etc.), as concern about whether or not the tasks can be accomplished safely is always present. This anxiety may be heightened when persons are attempting an activity that previously resulted in a fall. These persons can become increasingly apprehensive, and their sense of vulnerability to falling and self-injury may be sharpened. The presence of one or more underlying chronic neuromuscular diseases that interfere with the safe performance of activities can often exacerbate these concerns.

Some older people may develop a fear of falling. Tinetti and Powell (1993) defined "fear of falling" as a lasting concern about falling that leads to an individual avoiding activities that he/she remains capable of performing. It is estimated that between 10%–50% of community-dwelling older persons with a recent history of falls express a fear of falling (Arfken, Lach, Birge, & Miller, 1994; Baraff et al., 1992; Downton & Andrews, 1990; Nevitt et al., 1989; Tinetti et al., 1988; Walker & Howland, 1991). However, falling is not a prerequisite for fear of falling to occur. About one-third of persons without recent falls admit to a fear of falling (Downton & Andrews, 1991; Tinetti & Speechley, 1989). Arfken et al. (1994), studying a cohort of community-dwelling older persons, reported that half of those individuals who were very fearful had not fallen in the prior 12 months. In the nursing home population, Franzoni, Rozzini, Boffelli, Frisoni, and Trabucchi (1994) reported that nearly 50% of residents report a fear of falling. The prevalence of fear of falling has been shown to increase with age (Arfken et al., 1994). Some studies have found that fear of falling is more prevalent in women than men (Arfken et al., 1994; Cwikel, Fried, & Galinisky, 1989, 1990; Walker & Howland, 1991) while others report no gender difference (Downton & Andrews, 1991). However, in spite of its reported prevalence, the true extent of fear of falling is probably underestimated. There are several reasons for this. First, until quite recently the problem has not been widely appreciated by researchers and health professionals, and therefore has not been inquired about. And secondly, older persons themselves, particularly males, out of embarrassment are often reluctant to admit to a fear of falling.

The most obvious explanation for fear of falling is that its expression represents a rational response to danger. In an older person with a history of falling, a certain degree of fear may be protective if it motivates the person to avoid activities to which they are no longer equal, to recognize their limitations, and to become more cautious. In this sense, a fear of falling can help maintain safety and may protect the individual from further falling episodes. Too little can lead to carelessness and the risk of falls.

However, fear of falling can also be detrimental, adversely affecting an individual's mobility and independence (Clark et al., 1990). Some older people can become so frightened and preoccupied with fall avoidance that they limit their everyday activities because they fear additional falls and injury. Tinetti and co-workers (1988) found that 26% of fallers admitted to avoiding activities, as did 13% of non-fallers. In a prospective study conducted by Nevitt et al. (1989), 10% of recurrent fallers reported avoiding activities because of fear of falling. Vellas et al. (1987) described a 41% decline in activity over a 1-year period among fallers compared with a 23% decline among non-fallers. They attributed this decline largely to fear of falling. Tinetti, Mendes de Leon, Doucette, and Baker (1994), in a cohort of community-dwelling persons, reported that 24% acknowledged a fear of falling but denied that this fear had an effect on their activities, while another 19% stated that they avoided activities because of fear.

Some persons with a fear of falling develop a phobic reaction that is excessive or unreasonable in a particular situation. Several investigators have attempted to characterize this phobia. Marks and Bebbington (1976) described the appearance of a space phobia in a group of older women. The hallmark of this syndrome is an intense fear of falling in association with open spaces and an absence of visuospatial support in the environment. For example, sufferers may be unable to cross a room except by going on their hands and knees, unless they are able to skirt the walls. At least in the early stages, actual physical support is not needed, only visual evidence that such support is close by. When no visual support is available, persons begin to experience an intense fear of falling.

For instance, the authors presented the case of one person who was able to dance on a crowded dance floor—the other dancers served as visual support—but had to leave if the crowd left. Balaha and colleagues (1982) used the term ptophobia to describe this phobic reaction to falls in a group of older persons. These individuals exhibited a fear of sitting and standing without the evidence of environmental or human support. In some of the persons, walking was not feasible because of their intense fear of falling, where as in others, maximal assistance in walking was required. Murphy and Isaacs (1982) described the post-fall syndrome in a group of hospitalized patients who expressed a great fear of falling and were unable to walk without support after suffering a fall. When attempting to walk, many of these individuals tended to "clutch and grab" onto environmental objects within their view for support. Common features contributing to the fear of falling in these persons included having been housebound prior to falling; having lain for more than 1 hour on the floor after falling (prolonged post-fall lie time); and having expressed marked anxiety and fear while walking. Moreover, one-third of the patients died within 4 months of hospital admission. Death was mainly due to bronchopneumonia, myocardial infarction, and pulmonary embolism, conditions associated in part to the complications of immobility. However, the relationship between fear of falling and mortality has not been fully examined.

Tideiksaar and Kay (1986) coined the word "fallaphobia" to describe the abnormal reaction to the fear of falling. Fallaphobia commonly occurs in older persons who live alone and have poor gait and balance, and is particularly noticeable in women. This phobic reaction is typically triggered by a cluster of falls (although isolated falls and near-falls are not uncommon), and physical injury and/or prolonged post-fall lie times. Some older hospital patients with severe fear of falling or fallaphobia may delay or eventually refuse discharge back to the community, because they fear an inability to live alone and function safely by themselves.

There are a number of other situations that may commonly result in excessive fear of falling. Sometimes older women who learn that they have severe osteoporosis, or who become knowledgeable about the effects of aging on bone density and their dire consequences (i.e., hip fracture) can develop an intense fear of falling. Rubin and Cummings (1992) compared a group of women with below-normal and normal bone density and found that 38% of the women with low bone density become more fearful of falling, whereas 2% of women with normal results had increased fear of falling. Furthermore, 24% of the women with abnormal results, but only 2% with normal results limited their activities to avoid falling.

Some older persons with a friend or neighbor who may have recently fallen, fractured a hip, and ended up in the nursing home, may view themselves in a similar situation and as a result, begin to exhibit a profound fear of falling. Both situations, knowing one's risk of fracture and poor outcome following injury, can lead individuals to significantly restrict their mobility.

PM is a 74-year-old woman who developed a fear of falling after attending a lecture on osteoporosis at the local senior center. Although she had not experienced any previous falls, she developed an intense fear of fracturing her hip subsequent to the talk. As a result, she refused to leave her home, even in only mildly inclement weather. She frantically insisted on scheduling all her medical and other business appointments before November because she was fearful of leaving her home during the winter months.

RN is a 90-year-old woman who was living alone. She had not suffered any falls, nor had she experienced any problems with her gait and balance. However, her best friend fell in the street, broke a hip, and required permanent long-term institutionalization. Shortly afterwards, RN developed a fear of falling. She began to restrict her outdoor activities and started to use an umbrella as a cane for support when walking.

Any restriction of activities that occurs as a result of a fear of falling can lead to a host of morbid outcomes that can further increase one's fall risk. Arfken et al. (1994), in an examination of fear of falling, found that moderate fearfulness was associated with an increased dissatisfaction with life, depressed mood, increased frailty, and recent falls. Being very fearful was associated with all of the above, as well as decreased mobility and social activities. Franzoni et al. (1994) showed that fear of falling in nursing home residents was positively associated with repetitive falls and functional decline. However, Tinetti et al. (1994) found that fear of falling in community-dwelling older persons was only marginally related to ADL-IADL functioning and was not predictive of social or physical functioning.

The gait and balance of persons with fear of falling has also been shown to be impaired (Franzoni et al., 1994; Maki, Holliday, & Topper, 1991). Typically, their gait becomes hesitant and irregular and ambulation is accompanied by a great deal of anxiety. While attempting to walk, these individuals often "clutch and grab" onto furnishings for support, a strategy which may in itself lead to loss of balance and further fear of falling. Moreover, the use of assistive walking devices (canes, walkers) to help maintain safe mobility is often rejected, as these persons may be reluctant to project an image of frailty and suffer social rejection by their peers. Other persons with fear of falling and gait and balance impairments may resist independent ambulation at all costs, and only walk while accompanied by another person. Eventually, this pattern of behavior may lead to the individual's becoming totally dependent in function, to the point of becoming housebound, and even chair- or bed-bound. For instance, Marks and Bebbington (1976) described several persons with "space phobia," who ultimately progressed to a state of being confided to their homes and to a wheelchair. Persons in this category not only are at risk for social isolation from friends and family, but also for nursing home placement, particularly if the assistance of others to help with activities is not available. Even with assistance, some persons can develop an additional fear of being dropped by caregivers in the course of chair, bed, toilet, and tub transfers.

And lastly, older persons with reduced mobility, who ultimately require the assistance of others (i.e., spouses, family members, neighbors, home attendants, and nursing staff) to help with everyday mobility tasks, may respond emotionally. Asking others for help with routine activities is difficult, as the fear of loss of privacy and autonomy is realized. Sometimes, older persons who are dependent on caregiver support become increasingly anxious over the burden that they may be imposing on others. In particular, becoming both a physical and financial burden to family members (i.e., to spouses and adult children) is of great concern. These feelings are further intensified if the relationship between the older person and caregiver is strained to begin with. Additionally, requiring assistance from caregivers often implies frailty, an image that older people would rather not project. This concern can extend to the avoidance of assistive mobility devices (bathroom grab rails, bathtub benches/chairs, etc.) as well.

In response, some older persons may reject all attempts of help, preferring to maintain autonomy despite their functional dependence. In an effort to decrease the risk of falls, these people will often restrict their spheres of activity. For example, the person may avoid walking to the bathroom toilet, but instead use a bedside commode. Likewise, they may limit going outdoors if this activity proves hazardous. Instead, they spend more time indoors, in the safety of their home. While this behavioral response may be beneficial for limited time periods, eventually it can work against the older person. The person may become homebound, or even worse, keep to a chair or a bed, all behaviors that can lead to social isolation and great despair. Other persons in response may be more adventurous, and continue to attempt physical activities on their own. As a result, they may experience additional falls, which may lead to further activity limitations.

Consequently, these individuals may be left with little option other than to accept help, even though this can be emotionally damaging. Under these circumstances, some persons may require relocation to either their grown childrens' homes, an assisted-living facility, or long-term nursing home. This move in itself might be disconcerting and met with resistance by an older person if attempted against that individual's will. As well, any change in living arrangements may involve separation from spouses, family members, and neighbors, that can result in loneliness and feelings of depression.

CAREGIVER PROBLEMS

Family members of the older person with falls or at fall risk can be affected as well. Children who live apart from their parents may blame themselves for not being there to prevent a fall. Likewise, spouses or adult children residing with the older person and observing the fall take place may blame themselves for not being able to prevent it. Naturally, family members have a legitimate fear of further serious falls and hip fracture and, consequently, often consider making safer living arrangements for the parent. This may include having the older person (and their spouse, if available) move in with the children.

Such a change in living arrangements can be problematic for the older person and the family member alike. In order to prevent additional falls, families may attempt to restrict the person's activities and attend to all ADL tasks. The older person may resent their loss of autonomy which, in turn, may increase the family member's guilt. Moreover, the reversal of the traditional parent–child role can lead to further resentment and stress by both parties; i.e., rather than the parent caring for the child, the opposite occurs; when the child cares for the parent.

The responsibility for the daily care of the older person may create additional burdens for family members, interfering with their own personal lives—fulfilling their own family responsibilities, working, socializing, and maintaining leisure activities. Women are especially affected, as they usually assume the major share of parent care. For daughters, this may involve caring for several older parents simultaneously. In her study of three generations of women, Brody (1981) pointed out that older people still expect more care from daughters than sons and that women also expect to provide this care themselves. These women may also be responsible for their own families and children. Such women are often called "women-in-the-middle" or the "sandwich generation."

The demands of caregiving do not diminish because of job responsibilities outside the home. Approximately half of all daughters providing care for older parents work outside the home (Wykle, 1994). Providing care for both the older parent and the family, and trying to hold down a job at the same time can often create conflicts. Either the older parent or the husband and children may feel neglected at times, or the woman's career may suffer as a consequence. Sometimes, a deterioration of immediate family ties may occur. This may affect the marriage relationship. Small children may also resent the time their mothers spend away from them. Attempting to balance multiple caregiving roles may cause women to feel inadequate and guilty because they are unable to spend equal time with all their care recipients.

Testing the patience of the caregivers to such an extent often elicits rage. Many caregivers may become angry with both themselves and the older parent. In some instances, the caregiver may lose patience with the parent, particularly if they find themselves being unable to manage the demands of the caring role. The potential for "elder abuse" in these situations is real, as the adult child can lose complete control. If any ill-treatment occurs, caregivers often feel remorse and guilt afterwards. The result is often a love-hate relationship with the older person. On the one hand, adult children may feel an affection and "parental obligation" to care for their older parent, but at the same time they find the caregiving role to be stressful and resent the responsibility. All this, of course, can lead to a deteriorating relationship between the family and older person.

Moreover, the strain of caregiving may, in some instances, lead to physical and psychological deterioration. Most studies have shown that caregivers suffer more medical illness, anxiety and depressive disorders, and utilization of health services than do noncaregivers (Schulz, Visintainer, & Williamson, 1990). Even when positive aspects of the task are recognized, providing care on a daily basis can be stressful. This may become a particular concern for adult children and spouses who are old themselves. It is estimated that about 35% of caregivers of older adults are themselves aged 65 and older (Wykle, 1994). Older family caregivers often report that the task of caring is physically exhaustive and tiring. Many of these individuals have health problems of their own. As a result, caregivers may become worried about their ability to provide continuing care, another situation that may negatively affect the relationship between the caregiver and older person. The extent of any physical and/or psychological sequelae are to a large degree dependent upon availability of resources (home attendants, day care centers, etc.), and the type and extent of illness of the care recipient.

In addition to the physical and emotional strain, the economic burden of caring for the older person (buying medical equipment for walking, toileting, and bathing; providing home attendants; giving up their employment, etc.) may be more than the caregiver can handle financially. Often, spouses and adult children in this position begin to consider placement in sheltered long-term care housing, even if they find this option repugnant. A study conducted in France found that 39% of persons over age 70 who had fallen were institutionalized upon their families' request (Albarede, Lemiux, Vellas, & Grouix, 1989). The themes of constant care demands and their effects on caregivers' health are often cited as predictors of institutionalization (Stevens, Walsh, & Baldwin, 1993).

Nursing home placement of the spouse or older parent is usually described as a family crisis. The move is often a last resort, after all other resources—personal, social, and economic—are exhausted. Although nursing home placement culminates with caregivers relinquishing active caregiving duties, institutionalization may not relieve their anxiety. Caregivers may feel guilt and ambivalence about the decision. At times, this stress may be greater than that produced by keeping the older person at home. Also, if the older person is against the move and/or is unhappy with their new environment, family members become more frustrated.

When older persons fall while in the hospital and nursing home, family members often suffer emotional stress as well. They may feel guilty; or they may blame the nursing staff. In response, families become concerned for the older parent's safety, and may insist on the use of physical restraints. This is especially likely if the older person is at increased risk for further falls. While family members often become upset at the sight of restraints, for safety reasons, they accept their use. Others will insist on their removal—even if it places individuals at fall risk—and then suffer guilt if a fall occurs. Moreover, families often question whether the older hospital patient at fall risk should return home, particularly if the patient lives alone. Subsequently, some families may conclude that the patient is better off living in the protective surroundings of the nursing home. Other families may choose to have the older parent move in with them instead. Hawe, Gebski, and Andrews (1986) reported that older persons living independently prior to hospitalization are less likely to return home alone and are more likely to live, at least temporarily, with family and friends. Unfortunately, both options are likely to increase family burden. As previously mentioned, long-term institutionalization is often a displeasurable decision. On the other hand, older patients discharged from the hospital to the custody of families may require care that is too complex for the family to manage.

Finally, health professionals may be affected as well, although studies examining the consequences are scarce. First, health professionals may find the responsibility of constantly deciding the balance between the patients' desire for autonomy, the families' requests for safety, and guarding against the risk of falls emotionally demanding. On the other hand, health professionals can easily become discouraged when an older person continues to fall and suffer complications, despite the professionals' best attempts to reduce falls. Furthermore, health professionals such as home attendants and nursing aides may "burn out," particularly if they are constantly held responsible for the safety of the older individual at risk for further falls.

CI is a 79-year-old woman who lives at home by herself. She has Parkinson's disease and, as a result, falls. Her family hired a 24-hour home attendant to help with her mobility problems and safety. However, CI fell on two separate occasions while getting out of bed at night when the attendant was asleep. The family was infuriated with the attendant, blaming her completely for the fall, and threatening to dismiss her if the patient fell again. Subsequently, the attendant slept with "one eye open" to prevent the patient from leaving her bed unattended. Eventually the attendant became exhausted. One night, when the attendant inadvertently dozed off, the patient fell again. Not wanting to face the family, the attendant literally ran away, from the area and, undoubtedly, from the home health care profession.

HEALTH CARE UTILIZATION

Falls and their sequelae are associated with an increased utilization of health care services (Sattin et al., 1990; Shapiro, 1988; Sjorgen & Bjornstig, 1989). The number of falls requiring medical treatment increases exponentially with age for both men and women (Sattin et al., 1990). This increase varies from lows of 24.5 and 36.5 per 1000 person-years, respectively, for men and women aged 65 to 69, to highs of 138.5 and 158.8 per 1000 person-years, respectively, for men and women aged 85 and older. Fall-related fractures are the most common reason for medical treatment (Ryynanen et al., 1992a). However, many older persons are treated by health professionals for less severe injuries as well.

Examining data from the *Longitudinal Study of Aging,* Kiel et al. (1991) reported that one-time fallers and, especially, repeated fallers (those experiencing 2 or more falls in the preceding year) were at greater risk of subsequent hospitalization, nursing home admission, and frequent physician contact than were non-fallers in the subsequent 2-year period. Wild, Nayak, and Isaacs (1981b) compared the use of institutional resources by a group of fallers and non-fallers residing in the United Kingdom. At 3 and 12 months following the index fall, fallers had three times the number of hospitalizations than did non-fallers. In contrast, Wolinsky et al. (1992) studied the relationships between falling and the use of health services both 2 and 4 years after the initial fall and found that falling just one time did not significantly affect health status or health services utilization, and that repetitive falling was related to a decreased likelihood of visiting a physician. However, they did report that repetitive falling was related to an increased likelihood of hospitalization and nursing home placement, and that falling just one time was positively associated with nursing home placement.

Falls represent a leading cause of emergency room visit among persons 75 years and older (Lowenstein, Crescenzi, Kern, & Steel, 1986). Denman et al. (1989), in a study of emergency room use by older people, found that fall-related injuries accounted for 14% of the visits. Similar findings have been reported by Lowenstein et al. (1986). In one community-based surveillance study, 85% of older persons with falls living in Miami Beach, Florida were seen in the emergency room (DeVito et al., 1988). More than 40% of injured fallers cared for in the emergency room are hospitalized (Sattin et al., 1990).

Falls in older persons are a leading cause of acute hospital admission in older persons (Kiel, O'Sullivan, Teno, & Mor, 1991). Alexander, Rivara, and Wolf (1992) reported an annual hospitalization rate of 13.5 per 1000 persons aged 65 and older, a rate that was five times that for nonfall trauma. One British study estimated that 20% of hospital admissions of older persons are directly attributable to falling (Naylor & Rosen, 1970). A Danish study (Lucht, 1971) surveyed falls treated in the casualty department of a hospital serving a population of 210,000. This researcher found that on average throughout a year, 16 hospital beds were occupied by older persons who had been admitted following a fall in the home; more recently, Kiel et al. (1991) reported that within a 1-year period, 16 older persons out of a population of 210,000 people will occupy a hospital bed as a consequence of falls. Among a population of older people residing in Florida, DeVito et al. (1988) reportedly that 42% of those who sought medical attention for a fall were hospitalized. Massachusetts, one of the few states in the U.S. that distributes hospital utilization data, reported that 74.2% of all hospital discharges in 1983 for persons 65 years and older were due to falls (Massachusetts Department of Health, 1987). Moreover, the likelihood of being hospitalized following a fall increases with age. Up to 10% of persons aged 65 to 74 years and 23% of those persons over the age of 75 are admitted to the hospital after a fall (Askham et al., 1990). Lord (1990) reported that the incidence of fall-related hospital admissions reaches 4% per annum for men and 7% per annum for women aged 85 years and older. Once in the hospital, fallers have an average length of stay of 11.6 days (Sattin et al., 1990), almost twice the length of stay of non-fallers (Maguire, Taylor, & Stout, 1986). Naylor and Rosen (1970) estimated that 47% of older patients admitted to the hospital become long-stay patients. About 10% of older persons require increased home care services following acute hospitalization for fall-related trauma (Tinetti, 1994).

Fall-related hip fractures are a primary cause of hospital admission in older people. Baker et al. (1992) estimated that hip fractures result in more acute hospital admissions than any other injury in the aged. After age 75, hip fracture in both sexes outnumbers all other types of fractures combined as a cause of hospitalization (Baker et al., 1992). Each hip fracture results in an average stay of 13.5 to 21 days in a short-term hospital (Baker & Harvey, 1985; Graves, 1990), compared with 8.9 days for all other causes of hospital admission in the aged (Graves, 1990). Approximately 50% of acute orthopedic beds are occupied by patients with hip fractures (Griffin, 1990). An earlier study estimated that a hospital serving a population of 210,000 might expect an average of 16 beds to be occupied by persons 60 years of age and older who have been admitted with a fall (Lucht, 1971). Aside from hip fractures, Sattin et al. (1990) reported that even minor fall-related injuries lead to hospital admissions, presumably the result of increased comorbidity (i.e., cardio- and cerebrovascular conditions).

Acute hospitalization often leads to significant functional declines in older persons. McVey, Becker, Saltz, Feussner, and Cohen (1989) estimated that up to 36% of older patients suffer a decline in function between admission and discharge. Similarly, Hirsch, Sommers, Olsen, Muller, and Winugrad (1990) found that almost half of hospitalized older persons required help in walking at discharge, compared to only one-quarter needing assistance prior to hospitalization. Presumably, the effects of acute and chronic illness, treatments rendered, and inactivity (e.g., remaining in bed or chair rest) contribute to the loss of function. As a consequence, the period immediately following hospitalization is associated with increased risk of falls and subsequent rehospitalization. Mahoney, Sager, Dunham, and Johnson (1994), in a study that examined the incidence of falls in patients 70 years and older after hospitalization, found that 13.6% of the patients fell within 1 month after discharge. Major risk factors for falls included declines in mobility, use of assistive devices, and cognitive impairment. One British study that examined reasons for hospital readmission of older persons found that 59% of patients had recurrent problems, mainly due to falls (Andrews, 1986). Many of these patients required permanent long-term institutional care as a result.

It is estimated that in the United States, up to 40% of nursing home admissions are precipitated by a history of falls and instability (Gibson, 1987; Tinetti & Speechley, 1989). Alexander and co-workers (1992) reported that community-dwelling older persons injured in falls are discharged to nursing homes three times more often than are persons hospitalized for non-trauma causes. Approximately up to 50% of fall injuries that require hospitalization result in discharge to nursing homes (Alexander et al., 1992; Sattin, 1990). Once in the nursing home, about one-fourth of older residents will fracture a hip at some time during their stay (Strain et al., 1991).

HEALTH CARE COSTS

The health care costs associated with falls and injury in older people are considerable. In 1984, nearly $10 billion was spent on the treatment of falls in the older population (Rice, Mackenzie, Jones, & Associates, 1989) in the United States alone. Based on data extrapolated from the 1977 National Center for Health Services Research and Health Care Technology Assessment, Bernstein and Schur (1990) estimated that in 1984, $3.7 billion was spent on injury-related medical care—and the majority on falls—in the noninstitutionalized older population. The current costs for acute care associated with fall-related fractures alone has been estimated at $7–$10 billion annually (Cummings & Nevitt, 1989; Kelsey & Hoffman, 1987). The yearly cost of nursing home care related to fall injuries is estimated to be $2.5 billion (Baker et al., 1992). Sjorgen and Bjornstig (1991) studied 621 injury events occurring in the home over a 1-year period among a population of persons aged 60 years and older residing in Northern Sweden. Fall injuries accounted for 76% of the events. Compared with nonfall injuries, fall injuries resulted in a greater number of outpatient visits and rates of hospitalization. The overall costs for these 621 injuries was calculated to be $1.3 million, with fall injury events accounting for 92% of the costs. On average, each fall injury cost almost four times more than a nonfall injury. The cost of fall injury in women nearly doubled that of men, on average costing 1.3 times more. In a study that examined the use of hospital resources to treat injured older persons at North Carolina Trauma Centers, Covington, Maxwell, and Clancy (1993) found that over a 2-year period, 68% of the older individual's injuries were caused by falls, generating a total hospital cost of $17.6 million. In part, prolonged hospital and intensive care unit lengths of stay contributed to their high costs. The mean hospital charge for fall-related injury for persons between 65 and 74 years of age was $11,800. The authors suggested that a 10% reduction in falls could save approximately $2 million in hospital charges over a 2-year period. In a study examining hospital discharge data in Washington State for the year 1989, Alexander and colleagues (1992) reported that fall-related trauma accounted for 5.3% of all hospitalizations of older adults, accounting for $53 million in hospital charges. The authors calculated that the annual per capita cost of fall-related hospitalization was $92 per person. The costs of such hospitalization were higher for women and increased with age, ranging from a low of $30 for persons 65 to 69 years of age to a high of $178 for persons aged 80 to 84 and $279 for persons 85 and older. Bates and co-workers (1995) examined the correlates of serious falls in hospitalized older patients and the resource utilization associated with such falls. They reported that falls were associated with increases in length of stay and total charges. Fallers stayed 12 days longer and had charges $4,233 higher than control patients without falls.

However, for several reasons it is likely that the costs depicted by these studies are conservative figures, and underestimate the financial consequences associated with falls in older people. First, most studies examining the cost of falls have focused on the direct expenditures associated with injuries and not on their long-term complications. For example, the figures just cited, for the most part, represent immediate post-injury costs (i.e., outpatient visits, emergency room use, and acute hospital charges) but exclude the costs of long-term complications arising from fall-related injuries (e.g., long-term rehabilitation, home and nursing home care, loss of function, disability days, fear of falling, family support, etc.) which, generally, have not been taken into account. Also, most studies do not include the costs associated with noninjurious falls and their sequelae, such as the major changes in lifestyle and loss of autonomy that commonly ensue.

Conversely, a uniform analysis of fall-related costs is often difficult to perform. For example, one fall might be trivial and without significant sequelae; thus the associated dollar cost is either inconsequential or nil. At the polar opposite, however, another fall might be much more serious, associated with hip fracture and accompanying morbidity. The costs here will obviously be greater and add to the difficulty in attempting to quantify them. Lastly, falls are associated with a wide range of indirect and direct costs that can further drive up the price tag (Table 2.1). These costs have not been studied to any extent, with the exception of the following.

A Canadian study reported that pain after a fall accounted for up to 46% of problems precipitating resident transfers between the nursing home and emergency room (Bergman & Clarfield, 1991). These transfers may be expensive in terms of transportation, emergency room evaluation, hospital admission, and readmission to the nursing home (Kayser-Jones, Wiener, & Barobaccia, 1989). In one Swedish study, transportation from the nursing home to the emergency hospital and

TABLE 2.1   Fall-Related Health Care Costs

DIRECT:

Patient transportation costs (to and from physician's office, outpatient departments, emergency room, etc.)

Costs associated with diagnostic work-up and laboratory examination of falls and/or injury

Hospital injury costs other than surgical-related fees (increased hospital length of stay, legal fees, litigation costs, etc.)

Post-fall/injury costs:

Treatment/care of physical consequences (immobility, pressure sores, etc.)

Treatment/care of psychological consequences (fear of falling, depression/anxiety, family distress, etc.)

Labor costs:

Inpatient/outpatient health professional services (physicians and other subspecialists, nurses, social workers, physical therapists, etc.)

Administrative costs (completing institutional incident reports, documenting patient/resident medical charts, attending quality assurance and safety committees, arranging for home care and related services, etc.)

Intervention costs:

Medical treatments and medications

Repeat physician visits and other health services (visiting nurse services, home physical therapy, short-term nursing home rehabilitation, long-term nursing home placement, etc.)

Paid homecare services (homemakers and attendants, etc.)

Equipment (bedrails, wheelchairs, canes and walkers, durable medical equipment, environmental modifications, personal emergency response systems, restraints/restraint alternative devices, etc.)

INDIRECT:

Family caregiver costs:

Lost earnings (time spent caring for/visiting older parent and loss of employment, etc.)

Medical and psychological treatment/care associated with caregiver stress (increased sick days, physician visits, etc.)

Patient costs:

Decreased quality of life (restriction of mobility, decreased ADL/IADL activities, fear of falling, decreased socialization, etc.)

"Out of pocket" expenses not covered by health insurance (formal home attendants, durable medical equipment, etc.).

back accounted for 20% of the cost of injuries sustained by older residents (Svensson et al., 1991). Rehospitalizations of older patients are also associated with considerable costs. When compared to an initial hospitalization, the rehospitalization costs are 24%–55% higher (Zook, Savickis, & Moore, 1980). Fethke, Smith, and Johnson (1986) estimated that the rehospitalization rates for patients aged 70 years and over account for at least one-quarter of all hospital admissions. Expenditures for rehospitalized Medicare beneficiaries in 1984 were estimated to be $8 billion (Andrews & Steinberg, 1984). Moreover, falls in the hospital and nursing home can result in increased costs arising from potential liability risks. Falls frequently represent the largest category of incident reports submitted to risk management for review because of potential liability. It is estimated that up to 7% of legal claims against hospitals are due to falls (Potempa, Carvalho, Hahn, & LeSage, 1990; Quinlan, 1994). In older hospital patients, Quinlan (1994) reported that the risk of legal action was greatest in those individuals whose falls were associated with serious injury (i.e., fracture). Moreover, family members, rather than patients themselves, were more likely to file claims against the hospital, perhaps in part due to guilt over their relative's poor outcome. The institution and its employees are responsible for the individual's safety as long as a person resides in a hospital or nursing home and may be held responsible if the person falls and sustains injuries. Thus, both parties are at risk for legal liability, increased costs associated with legal fees, and settlement awards.

The following case study helps to illustrate the economic impact of a single fall.

FH, an 80-year-old white female, was ambulating with her walker when she suddenly "slipped" and pitched backwards onto the hard kitchen floor, fracturing her collarbone and hip. As FH, along with her anxious daughter, waited in the emergency room for an available hospital bed, the last thing on either of their minds was how much it was going to cost. But the meter had started to run. In the emergency room, FH immediately underwent a battery of tests to determine the extent of her injury. There were X-rays of her hip, pelvis, and shoulder ($168), a routine physical examination ($215), and a series of blood tests ($112). Once in the hospital the charges continued to mount: $3,608 for the use of the operating room (a charge that covered the cost of nurses and anesthesia), $4,300 for the surgeon, $401 for blood products, and $550 a day for the semiprivate hospital room. One month later, FH was discharged to the nursing home for rehabilitation, with a hip replacement and a bill for $29,814.52 in charges. This included a variety of charges including room and board ($17,050), house staff visits ($475), medications ($2,366.46), rehabilitation ($1,630), medical-surgical supplies ($638.56), and laboratory work ($2,219). Under the present Medicare system, the hospital only received reimbursement for half this amount because FH exceeded her predetermined length of stay due to complications that included an adverse reaction to the anesthesia that caused delirium, requiring 15 extra days.

In the nursing home the costs continued to mount. FH spent a total of 299 days in the nursing home, at a cost of $67,275 reimbursed by Medicaid. This included room and board ($225 per day) and covered medications, physician visits, and physical therapy services. Now 9 months later, FH remains in the nursing home with little hope of returning home. The total cost of FH's fall to date is $97,089.52, and the meter's still running.

Given the extent of fall-related complications which occur to both older persons and their caregivers, and the increased utilization of health care resources and associated costs following falls, it is apparent that efforts towards fall prevention must assume a high priority. In order to design and implement preventive approaches to reduce the risk of falls, it becomes necessary to discover why older people fall. Any attempt to reduce the likelihood of falls will be highly dependent upon recognizing, correcting, or modifying the underlying factors responsible. Thus, the next chapter will begin by examining the causes of falling in older persons.

CHAPTER 3

Causes of Falling

INTRODUCTION

The likelihood of falling—an event in which the person comes to rest on the ground or another lower level (chair, bed, stairs, etc.)—increases when an older person engages in an activity that results in a loss of balance and the body mechanisms responsible for compensation or stability fail. While the chances of balance loss are clearly increased during activities that greatly exceed an individual's limits of stability (e.g., standing on a chair seat to replace a light bulb or to obtain objects from shelves that are difficult to reach), it is estimated that these hazardous activities account for only about 5% of falls in the aged (Tinetti, Speechley, & Ginter, 1988). In comparison, the vast majority of falls experienced by older people in both the community and institutional setting take place during commonplace everyday activities. These consist of walking about, both indoors and outdoors; going up and down stairs; transferring on or off chairs, wheelchairs, beds, and toilets; getting in and out of bathtubs and showers; and reaching up or bending to retrieve or place objects.

Any subsequent fall that occurs may be precipitated by a multiplicity of underlying factors. Typically, these factors are grouped into categories that are either intrinsic or extrinsic to the host or person. Intrinsic factors encompass age-related physiologic changes, pathological conditions, and adverse medication effects; extrinsic factors consist of such problems as hazardous environmental conditions, faulty devices, and unsuitable footwear. In addition, there are a number of situational factors, such as the length of stay in institutional settings, time of falling, and availability of caregivers that influence the likelihood of falling. The purpose of this chapter is to examine the intrinsic, extrinsic, and situational causes of falls; to describe under which conditions they take place; and, lastly, to place the etiology of falls into a clinical perspective.

INTRINSIC FACTORS

AGE-RELATED CHANGES

To a great extent, the ability to avoid falling is contingent upon maintaining one's mobility: the capacity to walk about and transfer effectively in one's environment. The achievement of mobility is dependent upon the operation and integrity of several systems, primarily the visual, neurological, musculoskeletal, and cardiovascular systems. With advancing age, these systems decline gradually in function, affecting an individual's gait and balance and influencing the risk of falling.

VISUAL FUNCTION

A number of age-related physiologic changes occur that can affect visual performance and lead to fall risk. To start with, visual acuity—the ability to detect subtle differences in shapes—declines as a function of age. There is a gradual decline in visual acuity, or the resolving ability of the eye, prior to the sixth decade of life, followed by a more rapid decline between the ages of 60 to 80 years. Acuity may decline as much as 80% by the ninth decade. Moreover, visual acuity is closely related to contrast sensitivity—the ability to perceive spatial detail and object contrast—that also declines with age (Higgins, Joffe, Caruso, & de Monasterio, 1988). As a result, healthy older persons require about three times as much contrast as younger persons for the detection of objects in the environment. Contrast sensitivity also seems to be closely related to the ability to detect and discriminate objects in a naturally cluttered environment (Owen, 1985). An increased thickening and loss of elasticity and a reduction in retinal illuminance have all been suggested as possible factors responsible for a decrease in visual acuity and contrast sensitivity (Elworth, Larry, & Malmstrom, 1986). Moreover, the loss of acuity and contrast sensitivity is more evident under conditions of low illumination (Lampert & Lapolice, 1995). Together, these changes can lead to problems with the visual perception of objects in the environment. Typically, persons will complain of not being able to see well in poor lighting. In particular, the ability to detect subtle differences in shapes and figures, such as steps' edges that are disguised in detailed and patterned stairway coverings, may be difficult. Also, low-contrast objects, such as grab bars, extended chair and table legs, door thresholds, and carpet edges of a color similar or indistinguishable from their surrounding background can be problematic. Ground surface objects that are not easily visualized can unexpectedly lead to tripping. Transfer surfaces (chair and toilet seats, the bed mattress, etc.) that are difficult to perceive may interfere with transfer activities—obtaining a stable and secure seating position—which can increase the likelihood of balance loss and falls (Werner, Peterzell, & Sheetz, 1990).

An age-related decline in color sensitivity—the ability to discriminate between certain colors—has been found by some (Eisner, Fleming, Klein, & Mauldin, 1987) to be the result of a thickening and yellowing of the lens. This decline may further exacerbate one's ability to visually detect objects, as cool colors—especially blues, greens, and violets—are particularly difficult to distinguish. Warm colors—reds, oranges, yellows—are much easier to differentiate and are sometimes used to enhance the contrast of objects such as step edges from their backgrounds. Errors in color discrimination are more noticeable when the amount of illumination is decreased.

HB is an 82-year-old female with Parkinson's Disease who required a rolling walker for ambulation. When HB was observed walking, she caught her walker leg against a chair leg despite having sufficient space to ambulate within. As a result, the patient lost her balance and fell. The shape and color of the chair leg was visually indistinguishable from the surrounding environment. Her manuverability markedly improved after the application of brightly colored yellow strips around the chair legs.

WK is an 84-year-old male who complained of balance loss while toileting. Just after sitting on the toilet, half of the patient's buttocks would be off the seat to the side. In an effort to regain a stable sitting position, the patient attempted to shift the weight of body onto the seat. But in doing so, he experienced a loss of balance, and would have fallen if he hadn't supported himself against the wall. It was felt that a lack of contrast sensitivity (an inability to distinguish the position of the toilet seat) in part contributed to the patient's poor sitting balance. The toilet seat was replaced with one that was in direct contrast to the color of the toilet and surrounding area, which led to an improvement in the patient's ability to sit down properly.

A decline in depth perception—the ability to judge distances and relationship among objects in the visual field—can develop as a consequence of age as well (Christenson, 1990). The perception of depth is aided by a variety of visual cues, which include object height and contour, placement of shadows and brightness, and accommodation. Any change in depth perception can make the detection of ground and step surfaces (patterned or checkered linoleum, carpet/rug designs, etc.) appear, to the older eye, as elevations or depressions on the ground. As a result, older people sometimes prefer to step around or over, or else, avoid walking on these surfaces entirely.

RJ is an 82-year-old female nursing home resident with dementia and bilateral knee osteoarthritis. While her gait was mildly impaired, she was able to ambulate without a cane or walker. The patient was relocated to another building in the facility, and shortly afterwards, experienced several falls. She was found on the floor in the hallway by the nursing staff, but was unable to recount what happened. In observing the patient's gait, it was clear that she would momentarily come to a halt in the hallway whenever she encountered a design embedded in the floor (a 12-inch dark strip running every 20 feet along the width of the floor), and would attempt to step "over" the design. However, in doing so, she exceeded her gait capacity and lost her balance. It was felt that she had a decline in depth perception and perceived the floor design as an obstacle. The patient was provided with a rolling walker. While she continued to step over the floor design, she was able to maintain her balance with the walker.

In addition, the loss of depth perception makes it exceedingly difficult to perceive hazardous objects that lie in shadows and in areas of low illumination or excessive brightness. Older persons with decreased depth perception may also have difficulty in estimating the correct heights of curbs and steps, which can lead to improper foot placement.

Declines in light sensitivity—the ability of the eyes to adjust to varying levels of dim and bright light—are also noticeable with advancing age (Eisner et al., 1987). Consequently, older people generally require more time to adjust to environmental lighting changes, such as walking from areas of low to high illumination and vice versa. Dark adaptation—the ability to adjust to low levels of illumination—is especially affected (Christenson, 1990). A decline in the diameter of the pupil (i.e., senile miosis), which limits the amount of light reaching the retina, and an inability of the lens to focus properly accounts for much of this change. As a result, the person's visual capacity, particularly under conditions of low illumination, may be compromised, placing individuals at fall risk. Older persons who commonly get up in the middle of the night to toilet under existing ambient light may especially be at risk. On the other extreme, the ability of older persons to distinguish objects under conditions of excessive brightness is impaired as well. This may occur when the individual, after getting up at night, enters the bathroom and turns on the light, which may be very bright. Also, persons can experience difficulty seeing low-contrast objects against bright backgrounds.

> LC is an 87-year-old male who tripped and fell while walking up a short flight of steps located outside his home. He complained that he was unable to visualize the step edges due to the presence of bright sunlight radiating on the steps. The contrast of the steps was increased by painting each step edge in a bright yellow color, a modification that allowed the patient to visualize the steps.

Older persons also display a greater sensitivity to glare—a dazzling effect associated with a source of intense illumination—and a decline in glare recovery (Christenson, 1990). Both effects can lead to visual dysfunction. A thickening or opacity of the lens (which diffuses incoming light) and degenerative changes in the cornea have been suggested as a primary cause of glare sensitivity. Sources of glare can either be direct or indirect. Common sources of direct glare include sunlight shining through windows, bright light from exposed or unshielded light, and fluorescent bulbs directed toward the eye. Indirect glare can result from sunlight shining off concrete sidewalks, or indoors, from light reflecting off waxed floors or glossy table tops, plastic chair seats, and stainless steel ambulation devices (canes, walkers) and grab bars. Floor glare may be particularly troublesome. It can hide potential ground surface hazards, such as low-lying objects or changes in ground elevation.

> MO is an 83-year-old woman who tripped and fell in her hospital bedroom. She stated that while attempting to walk to the side of her bed, she stumbled against the feet of the overbed table that she didn't see, and lost her balance. The feet of the overbed table were surrounded in glare emanating from sunlight shining through the window.

> SG is an 89-year-old woman who fell in the hallway. The patient stated that she was walking along without incident, when all of a sudden the level of the flooring sloped downward unexpectedly, causing her to lose

her balance. The patient was unable to visually detect a change in the floor surface (level to downward gradient) due to sunlight glare disguising the change.

As well, glare can produce visual distortions in older people that may result in their perceiving floor surfaces as excessively slippery. Sometimes persons deal with glare emanating from floors by avoiding walking on the surface altogether. This type of protective behavior is often observed within the institutional setting, where floor glare is frequently problematic, either due to ceiling lighting or sunlight shining directly on highly waxed linoleum floor surfaces. At other times, persons may alter their gait to compensate. They walk slower, more flat-footed, and with a wider base of support, a pattern reminiscent of the type of gait people adopt when walking on icy surfaces. However, this change in gait may not always be safe, depending on the individual and their underlying neuromuscular condition, as it may lead to unsteadiness and falls.

An age-related decline in the extent of the visual field (Christenson, 1990) can have important consequences as well. Johnson and Keltner (1986) reported a prevalence of visual field loss of 3% to 3.5% for persons between 16 and 60 years of age. The prevalence doubled for people aged 60 to 65, and nearly redoubled for individuals over 65. The peripheral and upper visual fields are most affected. Much of the restriction of visual fields is due to optical factors (senile miosis or decreased pupil size), and mechanical problems, such as relaxation of the upper eyelid and loss of retrobulbar fat, which results in the eyes sinking deeply into the orbits. Any loss of peripheral vision makes it difficult to detect low-lying objects and furnishings in the pathway that lie outside the lateral view of vision. The likelihood of a slip or trip may occur as a result. A decrease in upward gaze may cause older persons to miss warning cues located above their line of vision, such as street lights and signage, which can lead to the risk of hazardous activities (for example, crossing the street against the light in heavy vehicular traffic, and walking in areas that are marked unsafe).

Lastly, visuospatial function—the ability to match and integrate the positions of stimuli and objects in space—has been shown to deteriorate with age. Wahlin, Backman, Wahlin, and Lindblad (1993) studied a population-based sample of 219 healthy older persons ranging in age from 75 to 96, and examined their visuospatial ability (modified Block Design Test) and spatial orientation (Clock Setting and Clock Reading Tests). They found an age-related decline in both visuospatial abilities and spatial orientation, which can continue into the 10th decade of life.

A decrease in visiospatial abilities can lead to dysfunction in the area of spatial orientation.

BALANCE

The basic task of balance is to position the body's center of gravity (COG) over its base of support (BOS) or limits of stability: the area surrounding or contained within the feet while standing (about 5 to 10 cm in size) (Figure 3.1). Balance or postural control is maintained through a complex process involving the coordinated efforts of sensory components (visual, vestibular, and proprioceptive inputs) and motor or musculoskeletal responses. Both are organized through a variety of central nervous system or central mechanisms. When the body's COG extends beyond its BOS, such as might occur when a person attempts to stand still on a moving bus, the limits of stability or postural control

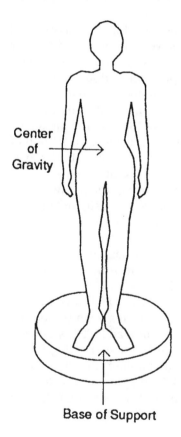

Center of Gravity

Base of Support

FIGURE 3.1 The center of gravity (COG) in relationship to the base of support (BOS) when standing. Reprinted with permission of Tactilitics, Inc.

are exceeded, and instability or balance loss ensues. At this point, to guard against falling, the resulting imbalance is detected by the sensory system—the visual, vestibular, and proprioceptive components—which sends signals to stretch receptors located in the joints and muscles of the body, which in turn initiates a set of coordinated postural motor responses. There interaction culminates in postural sway (small low-frequency movements of the COG) that is designed to realign the COG and BOS. Postural sway is characterized by a continuous process of anteroposterior (from heel to toe) and lateral (from side to side) motion of the erect body that controls stability and protects against the forces of gravity. Readers can appreciate postural sway by reducing their own BOS; stand in place for several minutes with the feet together or in a tandem position (i.e., placing one foot in front of the other). The body normally will begin to sway like a pendulum rotating about the ankle joints.

Postural control, an alignment between the COG and BOS, is similarly maintained during other activities, such as when transferring, walking, climbing stairs, reaching up and bending down. For example, when in the seated position, the COG is positioned or aligned over some portion of the BOS, the buttocks (Figure 3.2). When rising from the seated position, the COG falls outside the BOS, leading to instability. In response, this displacement is detected by the body's sensory components, and through integration of sensomotor information within the

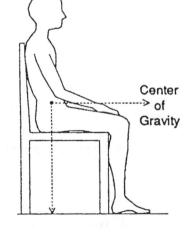

Center of Gravity

Base of Support

FIGURE 3.2 The center of gravity (COG) in relationship to the base of support (BOS) when seated. Reprinted with permission of Tactilitics, Inc.

central nervous system, the execution of appropriate motor responses take place, reestablishing the relationship between the COG and BOS and permitting safe egress. Likewise, when an individual takes a step forward, the COG stretches beyond the BOS and limits of stability (Figure 3.3), and comparable postural control strategies are called into action to prevent falling. However, any inability of the older person to obtain accurate sensory feedback and generate appropriate musculoskeletal responses during displacing activities significantly increases their risk of balance loss and falls.

Corrective postural responses may be either anticipatory adjustments that are preparatory to an imminent and predictable loss of balance (a feedforward activation) or compensatory reactions that restore equilibrium after an unexpected disturbance of balance (a feedback activation). For example, the feedforward strategy is used in those situations when a person may expect a loss of stability, such as might occur while standing on a moving bus, walking on a street covered by ice, or else reaching up on one's tiptoes for an object on a high shelf. In these instances, the individual will attempt to preserve balance by spacing

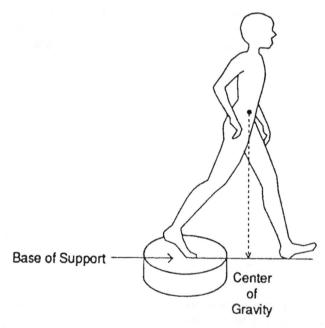

Base of Support

Center
of
Gravity

FIGURE 3.3 The center of gravity (COG) in relation to the base of support during ambulation. Reprinted with permission of Tactilitics, Inc.

their feet wider apart, a response that increases the BOS. Another example of this strategy is seen when an older person may seek the additional support of a handrail or chair armrest to increase their BOS
while climbing or descending a flight of stairs and rising from a chair.
Often, feedforward strategies reflect prior learning experiences from
situations that have led to instability. Conversely, the feedback strategies are employed in those situations in which the person unexpectedly
experiences a loss of stability, such as might occur after slipping on a
wet floor surface or sliding rug, or tripping on an uneven sidewalk or
other ground elevation. In these circumstances, balance is regained by
taking a number of small steps either forward or backward, a response
that attempts to align the person's COG in relation to their BOS.

The central nervous system (CNS) plays an important role in the
maintenance of balance. The CNS assesses and integrates the sensory
information regarding instability provided through the visual, proprioceptive, and vestibular inputs, and in response selects the proper
corrective postural strategy that will be employed in response to unexpected and anticipatory balance loss; through the integration of motor
and sensory commands, the CNS then sends and initiates the actual
corrective response that follows. For example, if an individual is walking about in dim lighting, the CNS may rely less on information from
visual input and more on information from other sensory components,
such as proprioceptive and vestibular input. Similarly, if an individual
experiences an unexpected loss of balance (e.g., slipping on a rug) the
CNS triggers a set of corrective postural responses within a shorter time
interval than that required for an anticipatory, voluntary response, such
as reaching over to pick up a book. These components and their age-
related effects are detailed in the sections that follow.

Sensory Components

Proprioception. Proprioceptive input, which emerges from receptors
located in muscles and tendons, joint receptors, and deep-pressure
receptors in the plantar aspects of the feet, represents a primary source
of sensory input that is required for balance. Proprioceptive input provides the body with information on the immediate environment; it allows
the body to orient itself during standing and motion with respect to
the support or ground surface, and body segments (the head, trunk,
and extremities) with regard to each other.

Proprioceptive input, as evidenced by decreased joint position sense
and cutaneous vibratory sensation, has been shown to decline with
age (Kokmen, 1978; Olney, 1985; Potvin, 1980; Skinner, 1984; Whanger

& Wang, 1974). The loss of vibratory sensation and joint position has been found to be greater in the lower than the upper extremities (Brocklehurst, 1982; Kokmen, 1978; Onley, 1985; Skinner, 1984). Several investigators have found an association between declines in vibratory sense and instability (i.e., increased postural sway); however, the results vary widely among different age groups, and between older men and older women. For instance, Brocklehurst et al. (1982) reported an inverse relationship between increased postural sway and impaired lower extremity vibration sense in women aged 75 to 84 years, but not in women aged 65 to 74 or beyond 85 years. MacLennan et al. (1980) showed a significant association between vibration sense and sway in women aged 75 to 84 years, but no association in women aged 65 to 74 years or in men aged 65 to 84 years. Era and Heikkinen (1985) found a positive association between sway and vibration sense in men aged 51 to 55 years, but not in men aged 71 to 75 years. In an effort to explain these differences, Olney (1985) postulated that despite the fact that vibration and proprioception are mediated via similar peripheral pathways, it is possible that the neurons involved in vibration sense decline or degenerate independently from proprioceptive function, and hence do not necessarily demonstrate age-related declines in a given individual.

With respect to joint position sense and postural sway, the results are equally contrary. MacLennan et al. (1980) measured proprioception in the toes, but did not find an association with increased body sway. Duncan, Studenski, Chandler, and Prescott (1992), in a community-based study of older persons, found a strong relationship with impaired vibration sense and sway, but not passive joint movement. Likewise, Brocklehurst et al. (1982) did not find a correlation between joint position sense and sway (although they acknowledged that this lack of association may have been due to imprecise testing methods). In contrast, Lord, Clark and Webster (1991) found that poor joint position sense of the toes was associated with increased body sway. Similarly, Woollacott et al. (1982) showed that older persons had greater postural sway when ankle proprioception was eliminated. Despite the discrepancy of findings between vibratory and joint position sense and body sway, it appears that older persons with diminished proprioceptive input are at certain risk for impaired balance.

Although healthy older persons rely to a great extent on proprioceptive feedback gained from joint and muscle receptors to maintain their balance, under conditions in which this information is reduced or missing, visual input becomes more crucial. This was demonstrated in a classic study conducted by Dornan et al. (1978). They measured postural sway (with eyes open and closed) in a group of above-the-knee amputees (limited proprioception) compared with a nonamputee group of individuals. The amputee group showed significant increases in sway. Similarly, Fernie and Holliday (1978) observed an increase in sway in both below- and above-knee amputees when their eyes were closed. Woollacott, Shumway-Cook, and Manchester (1986) found that when standing on a stable ground surface (i.e., normal proprioceptive input), older persons were able to maintain their balance; however, when proprioceptive input was eliminated they exhibited increased sway, and one-half the people lost their balance when their eyes were closed. Clinically, this is demonstrated when an older person with proprioceptive loss stands in place with their eyes closed or walks into a dark room; in both cases, balance becomes unsteady. In an effort to compensate for poor balance, persons will rely on visual input to augment proprioceptive input or counteract their loss. For example, persons will often ambulate by looking down to view the correct placement of their feet on ground and step surfaces; to ensure proper bed, chair, and toilet transfers, they constantly view the surface they are about to sit on. Subsequently, although younger persons rely heavily on proprioceptive input to maintain balance, it is felt that older persons rely more on visual information (Bohannon, 1984; Potvin, 1980), perhaps due to a decline in proprioceptive function that occurs with age. More recently, Judge, King, Whipple, Clive, and Wolfson (1995) demonstrated that balance performance in a group of community-dwelling persons 75 years and older was significantly impaired by reductions in both visual and proprioceptive input.

Vision. Vision is a mainstay of balance. The eyes provide the body with information on the placement and distance of objects in the environment, the type of surface (stable vs. unstable) on which movement will take place, the position of body parts, and the intensity of effort or degree of difficulty of the required movement. Vision also provides the information the person needs to think ahead of time and gauge the timing and control of movement. The more difficult the activity or precision and speed needed to accomplish the movement, the greater the importance of vision. Furthermore, vision plays a significant role in maintaining balance when the ground surface is unstable or compliant (Paulus, Straube, & Brandt, 1987), such as might occur when a person stands or walks on beach sand or thick absorptive carpeting. In both situations, the compliant ground surface contributes to decreased proprioceptive feedback, and instability. As a result, the person becomes more reliant on visual input in order to compensate and maintain stability.

Subsequently, when visual input is available, older people are able to adapt to a loss of stability as well as younger individuals; however, such may not be the case when visual cues are absent, particularly on compliant ground surfaces. Pyykko, Jantti, and Aalto (1990) studied a group of healthy men and women who were 85 years and older, and found that visual deprivation had a significant effect on postural stability, contributing about 50% of stability. Manchester, Woollacott, Zederbauer-Hylton, and Marin (1989) found that stability in older persons was significantly decreased under conditions in which peripheral vision was occluded and ankle proprioception was limited. Several studies have demonstrated an association between increased body sway and poor visual acuity (Dornan, 1978), particularly with near-vision (Liechtenstein, Shields, Shiari, & Berger, 1988). The effect of altered visual function, such as contrast sensitivity and visual acuity, and increased sway has been shown to be greater on compliant or absorptive support surfaces (i.e., with decreased proprioceptive feedback). More recently, Lord et al. (1991) measured visual acuity and contrast sensitivity in a group of persons aged between 59 and 97 years. They found that visual acuity and contrast sensitivity were not associated with body sway when persons were standing on a firm base; however, when the subjects were standing on a absorptive foam surface, body sway was associated with poor visual acuity and contrast sensitivity. Further research on age-related visual changes has demonstrated that diminished sensitivity to low frequency spatial information, which is mediated by the peripheral field of vision, may influence balance as well (Leibowitz, 1979). A narrowing of visual fields deprives the older person of that part of the field most sensitive to movement (Stelmach & Worringham, 1985). Paulus et al. (1984) found that decreased peripheral vision was associated with greater sway in the anteroposterior direction. However, with deprivation of visual information and altered proprioception, both anteroposterior and lateral sway increased markedly (Ring, Nayak, & Isaacs, 1989). Interestingly enough, lateral sway on eye closure alone did not increase with age.

Vestibular Input.   The vestibular system works in conjunction with the visual and proprioceptive systems to achieve balance; it helps to maintain ocular stability and head orientation (its position in space) when moving about the environment. Vestibular end organs are responsible for maintaining stability and upright posture by responding to angular and linear accelerations of the head, and by influencing tone in antigravity muscles by way of the lateral vestibulospinal tract (Sloane, Baloh, & Honrubia, 1989). The otoliths (i.e., the utricle and saccule) sense linear acceleration; the head is pulled in a sideways, backward, or forward direction, and the semicircular canals regulate angular acceleration, as might occur when a person moves from facing in one direction to facing in another. The turning of the head during any rotational or other directional movement not only stimulates postural reflexes to maintain balance, but also serves to initiate a reflexive movement of the eyes in a direction equal and opposite to the movement of the head. This vestibulo-ocular reflex serves to keep the eyes fixed on the visual field and retain balance during movement. Without this reflex, the person's visual images would be constantly changing each time the head moved even slightly, and would thus contribute to instability. For example, if this reflex were to be diminished, an activity as simple as looking down at a curb and back up to visualize the walkway might upset the control of balance. Therefore, persons with vestibular dysfunction must stop to read a street sign when walking to allow ocular fixation during body motion, because when the body is in motion, objects in the environment appear to jiggle.

In addition, during periods of body displacement or balance loss, the vestibular system contributes to postural control in other ways. Vestibular end organ receptors detect the loss of stability and prompt a voluntary response of antigravity extensor muscles that elicits compensatory head, trunk, and limb movements that serve to oppose postural sway. This body-orientating response is known as the righting reflex. An example of this reflex is displayed when the individual, following an episode of instability, raises and stretches their arms away from the side of the body to a forward-outward position, a change of body posture that is employed to regain stability (i.e., a realignment of the COG and BOS).

The vestibular system is subject to a number of age-related changes that may affect balance. Several studies that have examined the vestibular system indicate a 20% decline in hair cells in the otoliths, and a 40% reduction of hair cells in the semicircular canals (Rosenhall & Rubin, 1975). DiZio and Lacker (1990) showed a functional difference in vestibulo-ocular responses and oculomotor control between healthy young college-aged individuals and older persons. The implication is that quick movements of the head, for example, when an older person looks left and right before crossing a street, may interfere with balance. In addition, it is felt that the ability to exhibit the righting reflex diminishes with age (Cape, 1978). As a consequence, any loss of stability may result in an increased risk of falling.

Age-related vestibular changes alone and their effects on balance are uncertain. For instance, one would suspect that, similar to declines in proprioceptive and visual input, a decrease in vestibular function would also be associated with increased body sway. But their relationship has not been studied as extensively as has the relation of vision and proprioception. This is mainly due to the difficulties associated with experimental manipulation of the vestibular system, that is, our inability to selectively stimulate the vestibular receptors (Stelmach, 1985; Woollacott, 1982). For example, Brocklehurst et al. (1982) employed a seat-tilting device, which showed that persons greater than 85 years of age displayed impaired vestibular responses; however, no correlation with sway was found. They concluded that the tilt test used in this study could be affected by proprioception input from the buttock area, and thus lead to misleading information with respect to vestibular function. However, a more recent study by Lord et al., (1991) failed to find an association between vestibular testing and body sway, even though the large number of older persons studied had evidence of vestibular impairment. This agrees with Nashner (1971), who found that the otoliths are not initially involved in detection of body sway. Others suggest that there is considerable amount of plasticity in the vestibular system. As a result, the loss of cells in the peripheral structures may not exert a significant effect on balance. Despite these findings, Woollacott, Inglin, and Manchester (1988) showed that the inability of older people to stand while using primarily vestibular inputs (decreased visual and proprioceptive feedback) may, in part, indicate impaired vestibular function.

When proprioceptive and visual inputs are available, the vestibular system plays a minor role in controlling balance. This is because proprioceptive and visual inputs are more sensitive to postural sway than is the vestibular system. However, vestibular input is critical for stability when both proprioceptive and visual feedback are unavailable. Chandler, Duncan, and Studenski (1990) examined a group of persons aged 18 to 85 years with unilateral peripheral vestibular loss and found greater problems of balance when visual and proprioceptive inputs were altered. For example, Black et al. (1983) tested the postural control of persons with vestibular deficits, and found that when proprioceptive and visual input was eliminated, only those individuals with no vestibular function lost their balance. Clinically, this is exhibited when individuals with vestibular dysfunction are standing in darkness on unstable (absorptive or compliant) ground surfaces; they become more unsteady. Also, vestibular input is used to resolve conflicting information from visual images and support or ground surfaces (altered proprioceptive input). Under these circumstances, the vestibular system is quite adapt in quickly dismissing the misleading information in order to preserve balance.

Motor Components. When a person's balance is disrupted, one of a combination of three different postural control strategies is used to regain stability: an ankle strategy, a hip strategy, and a stepping or stumbling strategy. The ankle strategy is used in response to slow, small disturbance of the BOS. This strategy is accomplished while maintaining the placement of the feet, and shifting the COG backward and forward by rotating the body about the ankle joints with minimal movement of the hip and knee joints (a task that attempts to put the COG over the BOS). This movement causes the body to sway at the ankle joint, and the subsequent stretch or activation of the ankle muscles elicits contractions that return COG in alignment with the BOS. These responses are organized into muscle response synergies. The muscle sequence of activation (in the ankle strategy) occurs in a distal-to-proximal order. During an unexpected displacement in the anterior direction of the COG (for example, when an individual sways or begins to fall forward), the loss of stability triggers a distal-to-proximal activation of the plantar flexor, knee flexor, gastrocnemius-hamstring, and trunk muscles. Conversely, during a displacement in the posterior direction of the COG (for example, when an individual sways or begins to fall backward), the loss of stability activates the anterior muscles, including the dorsiflexors, knee extensors, quadriceps, and trunk flexors. These forward and backward muscle patterns are activated rapidly, about 100 milliseconds after a loss of stability—fast enough to prevent a loss of balance. The reader can experience the pattern of muscle activation involved in the ankle strategy, by standing in place with both eyes closed, and the feet positioned in tandem.

The hip strategy repositions the COG by flexing or extending the hips. This strategy is used for more forceful disturbances of the BOS, and when the BOS is compliant or reduced, such as when a person attempts to stand on a narrow beam, or to maintain balance with the feet placed in a tandem position. In this situation, the ankle strategy is inadequate to maintain balance, as the reduced size of the BOS limits the rotation that the ankle-foot can produce. In contrast to the ankle strategy, the order of muscle recruitment for the hip strategy is reversed in a proximal-to-distal sequence. For instance, during a forward displacement of balance the trunk flexors and knee extensor muscles are activated first and proceed to a triggering of the ankle dorsiflexors. The reader can experience the conditions involved in the hip strategy by standing on tiptoes and attempt to maintain balance.

The stepping strategy is used under conditions when the COG is displaced beyond the limits of the BOS. This strategy is required to regain equilibrium (for example, in a realignment of the COG and BOS) when neither the ankle or hip strategy is sufficient, such as might occur following an episode of tripping or being pushed backwards. The stepping strategy is accomplished with a series of rapid steps, hops, or stumbles that establishes the BOS under the COG.

The coordination or initiation and execution of these postural control strategies is affected by age. First, it has been shown by several investigators that the timely initiation of postural muscular responses or latency (the speed of muscle activation by the lower extremities) to balance displacements is delayed in healthy older persons (Stelmach, Phillips, DiFabio, & Tensdale 1989; Woollacott, 1990; Woollacott et al., 1986). In these studies, older persons showed slight increases (by about 20 to 30 milliseconds) in the absolute latency of distal leg muscles when compared to young persons. The delays in response latencies are reported to occur more often for the ankle flexors (anterior tibialis) than the ankle extensors (gastrocnemius) (Inglin & Woollacott, 1988; Woolacott, 1988). Secondly, occasional disruptions in the temporal sequencing of the distal and proximal muscles to balance displacements may occur as well (Woollacott, 1986). That is, in response to small disturbances of balance, some older persons exhibit a reversal of the normal distal-to-proximal muscle sequence of activation, with the proximal quadricep muscles activating in advance to the distal tibialis anterior muscles.

Similarly, voluntary postural responses to anticipatory disturbances of balance have been found to be different from those of younger persons. Mankovskii et al. (1980) studied persons of three separate age groups (20 to 29 years, 60 to 69 years, and 90 to 99 years), and asked each person to lift one leg by knee flexion, both slowly and quickly, while standing. They found that when older persons executed the maneuver at slow speeds, their latency response occurred in a timely and appropriate manner. However, when performing the task as quickly as possible, the older persons' muscle response latencies occurred later and they had greater instability. In a study by Inglin and Woollacott (1988) postural and voluntary muscle response latencies were compared for young and older persons. The individuals performed a reaction time task in which they were asked to push or pull on a handle as quickly as possible when cued. They found that the older persons showed significantly slower onset latencies of their postural muscles.

Second, the temporal sequencing or order of muscle activation of postural strategies in older persons has been found to be different from those employed by younger individuals as well (Stelmach et al., 1989; Woollacott, 1986). For example, in response to displacements of balance, rather than exhibiting a distal-to-proximal sequence of muscle activation, healthy older persons may display this distal response (i.e., ankle strategy) less often than younger persons (Woollacott, 1982). These changes have a critical influence on the ability of older persons to maintain their balance. Since postural reflexes are generally slower, it follows that older persons will be further from their BOS, and much closer to a critical area where loss of balance can occur, before corrective balance actions occur (Stelmach & Worringham, 1985).

Manchester et al. (1989) found that older people used a hip strategy significantly more often than younger persons in response to small disturbances of balance. One explanation for this is that older persons may be less able to produce sufficient ankle torque or rotation as a result of distal muscle weakness, and thus, rely more on the hip strategy for postural control. Another reason for the diminished use of the ankle strategy by older persons may have to do with decreased sensitivity at the ankle. Since the ankle joint is a major source of proprioceptive receptors controlling balance, this loss would be expected to decrease balance considerably. Further, it is possible that small and slow LOS (loss of stability) or displacement does not provide sufficient amounts of sensory information needed to detect a perturbation (Stelmach & Sirica, 1987). This appears not to be a problem with fast postural adjustments. Regardless, any sufficient delay or muscle sequency in activating lower extremity motor responses may lead to inappropriate postural responses and affect one's ability to maintain balance.

For the stepping or stumbling strategy, older persons, in comparison to younger individuals, differ as well. Luchies, Alexander, Schultz, and Ashton-Miller (1994) examined the biomechanics of stepping responses to sudden and sufficiently large backward pulls at the waist in a group of young persons compared with older persons. They found that both groups of persons were able to respond; however, whereas the younger persons took a single step, the older persons responded by taking multiple steps. Also, the steps taken by the older persons were significantly shorter, and decreased in height (clearance off the ground). The authors concluded that this more conservative approach may represent a compensatory mechanism to maintain balance. When multiple steps are taken, more balance adjustments can be made to correct any ill-chosen early postural responses, and less joint movement or rotations are required. Older persons may normally move about more slowly and more cautiously because this slow movement provides them with optimal balance.

Biomechanical factors such as strength and flexibility may preclude older persons from the ability to move faster. A decline in muscle strength and joint flexibility of the lower extremities complicates the execution of these postural strategies, making it more difficult to adjust the COG in line with the BOS, hence the risk of falls. In addition, the relative effectiveness of these strategies is dependent upon the condition of the supporting ground surface and the individual's shoe surface (slip resistance, firmness, and thickness), both of which greatly influence the postural response. For example, diminished ankle sensory input when standing on compliant surfaces (thick carpets, grass, sand) decreases proprioceptive input and decreases exhibition of ankle strategy. Wearing thick-soled footwear (running shoes) will result in a similar effect.

Effects of Age on Balance

Older persons, compared with younger individuals, exhibit more unsteadiness or postural sway when standing still (Baloh, 1994). Most studies show that postural sway increases with age (Baloh, Spain, Socotch, Jacobson, & Bell, 1995; Brocklehurst, Robertson, & James-Groom, 1982; Petera & Black, 1990). Overstall et al. (1977) studied a group of individuals aged 60 to 96 years, and found a linear relationship between age and postural sway. They also reported that women exhibited greater sway than men, although gender differences in sway have not been found by others. Colledge, Cantley, and Peaston (1994) measured sway in four healthy groups of individuals ranging in age from 20 to over 70 years, and found that sway increased linearly with age but was not affected by gender. Wolfson, Whipple, and Derby (1994), measured balance in a group of healthy community-dwelling older persons, and reported that gender differences in sway were not present during quiet standing; women initially swayed more than men when their vision was compromised, but after a period of adaptation their sway was comparable to that of the men. As well, researchers have reported that the direction of sway in older people is different from that of younger people. Lucy and Hayes (1985) found that sway in the anteroposterior direction was 52% greater in a sample of healthy subjects aged 70 to 80 years versus subjects aged 30 to 39 years, and that postural sway was greater in the anteroposterior direction than the lateral direction. Ring et al. (1989) studied 39 healthy active persons aged 17 to 79 years, and examined their body sway during standing. They found that anteroposterior sway increased with age, but lateral sway showed no change. Lee, Deming, and Saghal (1988) showed that older persons in comparison to younger individuals are more likely to experience balance instability in the posterior direction. Baloh et al. (1995) reported that, on average, velocity of sway (particularly in the anterior–posterior direction) was greater in older persons who complain of imbalance compared with age-matched controls.

Despite any increase in body sway that might occur as a consequence of age, it appears that older people have enough reserve in sensory function to maintain postural control. Healthy older persons are still able to maintain their balance while standing with both feet together (for at least 30 seconds) without the need for external supports (Potvin & Tourtellotte, 1975). If information via one system proves to be incorrect, it tends to be suppressed, and the other sensory systems are able to compensate.

However, with advancing age, this redundancy of sensory information may not be as great because of age-related changes occurring in the proprioceptive, visual, and vestibular systems. As a result, the sway of older persons begins to approach the levels of instability when both proprioceptive and visual inputs are diminished. Therefore, the older person has a reduced ability to detect and alert the CNS regarding changes in posture or balance, particularly when more than one system is challenged or when sensory information is conflicting (Woollacott et al., 1986). Of the three systems, information from the proprioceptive systems is processed the fastest, followed by that from the visual and vestibular systems, respectively. If pathology causes the processing to be too slow, the ability to maintain balance may be compromised. Normally, there is some redundancy in the sensory information necessary to maintain balance, and the failure of one source of input, such as vision, can be counteracted by feedback from an intact proprioceptive and vestibular system. However, deprivation in more than one system is likely to lower the balance threshold and increase fall risk. Teasdale, Stelmach, and Breunig (1991) compared postural sway in a group of healthy older and younger persons, and found that with the exclusion or disruption of one sensory input (i.e., visual or proprioceptive feedback) alone, body sway between the young and old did not differ significantly. However, when both visual and proprioceptive input was eliminated, the older persons exhibited substantially more sway than the young. Woollacott et al. (1986) showed that when older persons were required to balance on a platform when their ankle joint proprioceptive and visual inputs were distorted, they swayed more than younger persons, and in many cases, lost their balance.

In addition, under conditions when balance is maximally stressed, such as might occur when standing on one foot, climbing and descending steps or curbs, stepping onto a bus, and getting in and out of the bathtub (all activities performed part of the time on one foot; reduced BOS) maintaining stability becomes more difficult. For example, Bohannon et al. (1984) found that the ability of older persons to maintain balance while standing on one leg decreased significantly in comparison to younger persons. Likewise, Briggs, Gossman, Birch, Drews, and Shaddeau (1989) showed that balance decreased in older persons during one-legged stance and declined significantly as age increased.

Moreover, there are several other influences on balance. Several investigators have reported an association between certain cognitive factors and postural sway. Stelmach, Zelaznik, and Lowe (1990) studied postural sway in a group of healthy older and younger individuals, and found that following an arm-swinging task and math task (single-digit additions), performed concurrently, the older persons exhibited greater sway than the younger persons, and took longer to recover from postural instabilities. Teasdale, Bard, LaRue, and Fleury (1993) examined young and older persons performing an auditory reaction time task while maintaining an upright posture, while at the same time altering visual and surface conditions. They found that as sensory information or input decreased, the postural task became increasingly difficult for older people, and required more of their attentional demands. These studies suggest that secondary attention-demanding tasks may interfere with the control of posture in older persons. In support of this conclusion, several researchers have found that a delay in the voluntary onset of postural muscles in response to anticipatory balance disturbances may be affected by cognitive factors (i.e., decreased attention levels) (Woollacott & Manchester, 1993; Zattara & Bouisset, 1986). Also, it has been reported that older persons with a fear of falling exhibit increased sway on postural performance tests (Maki et al., 1991). The association between fear of falling and sway becomes more significant under conditions of decreased visual input (for example, eyes are closed) (Baloh et al., 1994). It is suggested that persons with poor balance and fear of falling may feel anxious about their instability and thereby display anxiety-related effects on balance, resulting in instability (Maki et al., 1991).

Balance and Falls

Several studies have reported that fallers have greater postural sway or unsteadiness than non-fallers, and that persons with multiple falls demonstrate appreciably more sway than those with single falls (Lichtenstein, Burger, Shields, & Shiari, 1990; Wolfson, Whipple, Arnerman, & Kleinberg, 1986). Kirshen et al. (1984) found that fallers demonstrate increased sway in both the anteroposterior and lateral directions. Overstall et al. (1977) found that community-residing older persons who reported falling five times or more in the previous year had more sway than those who fell one to four times or did not fall. In an institutional-based study, Fernie et al. (1982) recorded falls over a 1-year period in 205 older persons (average age 82), and found that 30% of the men and 46% of the women experienced one or more falls. Body sway was significantly greater in those individuals who fell than in those who did not suffer falls. Lichtenstein et al. (1988) in a community-based study of older women found that a history of falling in the previous year was associated with increased sway. Moreover, several researchers have demonstrated that the frequency of falls increases as sway increases (Lichtenstein et al., 1988, 1990; Ring, Nayak, & Isaacs ,1988).

There are several mechanisms by which poor balance can lead to falls. As previously stated, the slowness in detecting postural disturbances (referred to as latency and temporal sequencing) may be associated with increased sway, suggesting that the time required to detect postural changes may be a critical determinant in controlling balance. Brocklehurst et al. (1982) found a significant correlation between falls in the past year, and both postural sway and decreased proprioception.

Wild et al. (1981b) followed a group of older persons in the community for one year after a fall, and found a significant association between abnormal balance responses (i.e., external pressure applied to the sternum) and the risk of further falls. Crosbie, Nimmo, Banks, Brownlee, and Meldrum (1989) showed that in response to a single-leg stance test, older persons with falls due to idiopathic gait disorders required greater support, and displaced their COG more laterally, particularly with eyes closed, than did individuals without falls.

GAIT

Walking can be viewed as the act of falling forward and catching oneself with each step taken, or put more simply, as a series of arrested falls. However, the process of normal walking, or gait, which is defined as the manner or style of walking, is an activity that is operationally much more complex. Before examining the gait changes that occur with aging, it is important to understand normal gait. The following is a brief review of the terms used to characterize gait.

The Gait Cycle

Normal walking is usually described in terms of the gait cycle, which consists of two phases: *stance* and *swing* (Figure 3.4). The stance phase constitutes 60% of the gait cycle, and occurs when one leg is weight-

STANCE PHASE

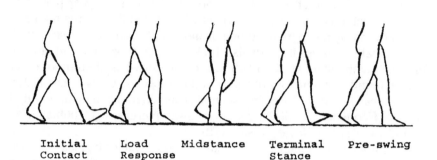

Initial   Load   Midstance   Terminal   Pre-swing
Contact   Response   Stance

SWING PHASE

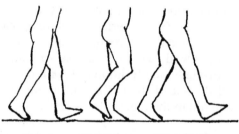

Initial   Midswing   Terminal
Swing   Swing

FIGURE 3.4   Gait cycle.

bearing and in contact with the ground. The swing phase constitutes 40% of the gait cycle, and occurs when the other non-weight bearing leg is advanced forward to take the next step. Ambulation is accomplished by a series of reciprocal leg movements alternating between stance and swing: pushing off on the leg in stance phase while, at the same time, swinging the other leg forward.

While the lower extremities are moving alternatively forward and backward, the arms swing in a direction opposite to that of the legs. For example, the right arm swings forward with the forward swing of the left lower extremity, while the left arm swings backward. This reciprocal movement of the upper extremities provides a counterbalancing action that helps to maintain balance. While arm swing is not a prerequisite to walking, it contributes to the smoothness of gait, particularly during rapid walking.

Phases of Gait

During the stance phase, five separate events take place: *heel strike, flat foot, midstance, heel off,* and *toe off. Heel strike* or *initial contact* represents the beginning of the stance phase, and occurs at the instant when the heel of the leading leg (in full extension) strikes the ground. Sometimes this stage is referred to as the *weight-loading* or *acceptance* period (of stance).

The *flat foot* or *load response* stage starts immediately after heel strike and represents the point at which the sole of the foot fully contacts the ground. At this point the body is transferring its weight to the leg in stance, and the opposite leg is preparing for the swing phase.

Midstance or *single-leg stance* is the point at which the body weight is directly over the supporting lower extremity, and the opposite leg is at the midpoint of the swing phase. At midstance—a split second of time— the knee is flexed at about 15 degrees and the foot is flat on the ground and bearing all body weight evenly. The weight immediately shifts to the ball of the foot and then to the toe. This effectively keeps the body's center of gravity low. The leg is back to full extension at the moment of heel off or terminal stance. This is the point at which the heel of the reference extremity leaves or pushes off the ground. Slight knee flexion, combined with ankle flexion, again minimizes the rise in the center of gravity, as body weight is carried forward over the stance leg. *Toe off* or *preswing* is the point at which only the toe of the ipsilateral extremity is in contact with the ground.

The *swing* phase consists of three events: *acceleration, midswing,* and *deceleration.* The swing phase begins with the *acceleration* or *initial swing* stage and occurs when the toe of the reference (ipsilateral) extremity leaves the ground and continues until, the point at which the swinging extremity is directly underneath the body. From this, the accelerating stage, the leg then enters the *midswing* or *swing-through* stage. To allow for adequate ground clearance during the swing phase, the leg is flexed at the knee and dorsiflexed at the foot.

Deceleration or *terminal* swing occurs after midswing, when the leg prepares for initial contact with the ground, or in readiness for weight-bearing at heel strike as the stance phase begins again. When the heel of the swing leg strikes the ground (a return to the stance phase), the knee becomes extended and the foot plantar flexed to provide body support. During each of these phases of gait, the coordinated effort of several muscles is critical for walking.

Gait Components

Normal patterns of gait are typically described by a series of boundaries. Time and distance are two of the basic parameters of motion, and measurements of these variables are used to describe and quantify normal gait patterns. Time or temporal variables include *single-leg stance*, *double-leg stance*, *cadence*, and *velocity*. The distance variables include *width of walking base*, *step length*, *stride length*, and *degree of toe out*. Each of these variables may be affected by such factors as age, gender, body habitus, joint mobility, muscle strength, and type of footwear.

Single-leg stance or *stance time* is the amount of time spent by the leg in stance phase. *Double-leg stance* or *double support time* is the amount of time a person spends with both feet on the ground during one gait cycle. Double support time occurs when the lower extremity of one side of the body is beginning its stance phase and the lower extremity on the opposite side is ending its stance phase. Double support increases the more slowly one walks, and decreases as walking speed increases.

Cadence or *frequency of steps* is the number of steps taken by an individual per unit of time. Cadence may be measured as the number of steps per second or minute. *Walking speed*, or *velocity*, is the distance of forward motion of the body measured over time. Increases in walking velocity are brought about by both increases in cadence and step length. *Walking base width* is the linear distance between two feet (the midpoint of the heel of one foot and the same point on the other foot).

Step length is defined as the distance between successive points of contact of opposite feet. It is usually measured from heel strike of one leg to heel strike of the opposite leg.

Stride length is defined as the linear distance between two successive events that are accomplished by the same leg during the gait cycle. Usually, stride length is determined by measuring the distance from the point of heel strike of one leg to the next heel strike of the same leg. Stride length includes two steps (a right step and a left step); however, stride length is not always twice the length of a single step, as right and left steps may be unequal. *Degree of toe out* represents the angle of foot placement during walking. The degree of toe placement decreases as the speed of walking increases.

Pelvic Movements

During walking, the body moves forward in a smooth sinusoidal curve. This is achieved through a series of pelvic movements, which to a large extent are responsible for controlling this motion. *Lateral pelvic shift* or *list* refers to the movement of the pelvis as well as the entire body in the horizontal plane—approximately 2.5 cm to the right and left, for a total of 5 cm—and represents the side-to-side movement of the pelvis during walking. This action effectively lengthens the lower extremity (the femur), thereby lengthening one's stride, allowing the foot to make contact with the floor during heel strike, and at the same time, minimize the vertical displacement of the trunk. This maneuver allows the pelvis to shift toward the weight-bearing leg, and helps to maintain balance by keeping the weight of the body, and center of gravity, over the stance leg.

At the same time, the pelvis tilts vertically downward about 5 degrees toward the weight-bearing leg, also during the stance phase, to minimize the rise in the center of gravity. *Vertical pelvic shift*, or *tilt*, is used by the body to keep the center of gravity from excessively moving up and down during normal gait.

When walking, the pelvis normally rotates a total of 8 degrees: 4 degrees forward on the swing leg, and 4 degrees posteriorly on the stance leg. Pelvic rotation lessens the angle of the femur with the ground, and allows for normal long stride during ambulation. Working together, these pelvic movements help to minimize the up-and-down and side-to-side movements of the body that occur during walking, and help to maintain balance.

Stair Gait

Climbing and descending stairs is similar to walking on level ground in that stair gait involves both swing and stance phases, in which forward progression of the body is brought about by alternating movements of the lower extremities. The stance phase is subdivided into *weight acceptance, pull up,* and *forward continuation,* and the swing phase is separated into *foot clearance* and *foot placement.* However, in contrast to walking on level ground, stair ambulation is a considerably more demanding task. First of all, successful stair ambulation requires that individuals make a transition from stepping on level surfaces to the placement of their feet on steps. Visual feedback is used initially in order to judge the position of the steps, both height and depth. This visual inspection allows the person to maximize the accuracy of foot placement. Once accomplished, individuals rely on kinesthetic cues to ensure accurate foot placement. Secondly, greater hip and knee flexion and muscle strength are required to support and accomplish normal stair gait. For instance, during the pull up phase of stair ascent, good knee extensor strength is needed, as these muscles are primarily responsible in helping the person to "pull up" the weight of their body to the next step level. In the forward continuance phase the strength and motion of ankle plantar flexors exhibit the greatest amount of energy. In addition to these intrinsic factors, extrinsic factors such as the dimensions of stairs (riser height and tread length) are important in determining stair gaits. For example, excessive riser height requires the person to exert greater knee motion during ascent and descent. Likewise, the extent of tread depth determines stability; deeper depths are associated with a more stable base upon which to step. Although many similarities exist between walking on level surfaces and stairs, the differences between the two may be significant for a given person. The fact that an individual has adequate muscle strength and joint motion for level walking does not ensure that the person will be able to walk up and down stairs.

Aging Effects on Gait

The net effect of aging on gait is variable. Some older persons show almost no changes in gait, while others display substantial alterations. As a consequence, there is considerable debate on the influence of age on gait, particularly as older persons are susceptible to certain pathological conditions that may also alter gait function. However, it is generally agreed upon that in healthy older persons, in comparison to younger age groups—and especially in those persons of advanced age beyond about 75 years—certain gait characteristics start to become evident.

The most common observable finding is that older persons tend to walk at slower speeds. For example, Himann, Cunningham, Rechnitzer, and Paterson (1988), in a study of 289 men and 149 women from 19 to 102 years of age, found that between 19 and 62 years of age there was approximately a 2.5% and 4.5% decline in normal speed of walking per decade for men and women, respectively. After the age of 62 there was an accelerated decline in walking speed for both sexes; a 16% and 12% decline in walking speed for men and women, respectively. Several studies have found similar declines in the walking velocity of older persons (Blanke & Hageman, 1989; Ferrandez, Pailhous, & Durup, 1990; Hageman & Blanke, 1986). A number of changes in the gait cycle have been associated with a decrease in walking speed. These consist of a decrease in stride length (the distance the foot travels during the swing phase) and step length (Hageman & Blanke, 1986; Larish, Martin, & Mungiole, 1988); an increase in the duration of the double support phase (when both feet are on the ground) (Gillis, Gilroy, Lawley, Mott, & Wall, 1986); and a decreased ratio of swing to stance time (Gillis et al., 1986). A slight increase in step width and decrease in steppage height (the level of ground clearance by the foot during swing phase) appears to be related to slower walking speeds as well. However, these findings are by no means universally agreed upon. For instance, Blanke and Hageman (1989) compared 12 younger men between the ages of 20 and 32 years of age with a similar number of older men between the ages of 60 and 74 years of age and found no effects of aging in regard to step length, stride length, and walking speed. The findings of Murray and co-workers (1969) failed to show a decrease in toe-floor clearance with age, but rather found an increase with advanced age. However, these gait differences may be related to gender differences, as only men were examined in both studies.

Rather than crediting age-related changes, some have suggested that slower walking speeds are self-selected, or else preferred by older persons (Ferrandez et al., 1990; Larish et al., 1988). That is, older people, particularly those with a fear of falling, walk more slowly, either as a compensatory mechanism to preserve their safety and guard against falls, or else as part of their usual and customary or habitual activity. Gabell and Nayak (1984) proposed that increased variability in stride width and double support time may be caused by a deterioration of balance mechanisms, and occur as a compensation for instability. Likewise, Wild and colleagues (1981b) suggested that balance problems are really responsible for gait abnormalities, and represent an effort to compensate. For instance, during normal walking, the COG falls outside the boundaries of the BOS for 80% of the stride length, representing an unstable condition (Winter, Patia, Frank, & Walt, 1990). Therefore, a decrease in stride length (taking shorter steps) might represent a compensation. Murray et al. (1969) proposed that this compensation does not resemble the gait of someone with nervous system pathology. Rather, it resembles that of someone walking in a restrained or guarded manner, as one might walk on a slippery surface, or in the dark. Furthermore, others have speculated that the type of footwear worn by the older person may account in part for a decrease in walking speed. Nigg and Skleryk (1988) compared the gait characteristics of two groups of healthy persons 60–69 years and 70–82 years and found that the older subjects walked more slowly and displayed less movement of the subtalar joint during the support phase of walking with personal shoes than did subjects in the younger age group. They suggested that the decrease in foot movement may be due to older persons preferring to wear shoes with more support (those that reduce the actual move-ment of the foot) in order to facilitate an increased sense of balance.

However, there are facts that support aging changes. When older persons are asked to walk quickly, they are able to do so, but rather than increasing the length of their stride, as younger persons would do to quicken their pace, older people respond by increasing the frequency of their steps. Age-related declines in stride length appear only at fast speeds of walking, although these characteristics may also manifest when the functional capacity of the older person is stressed. In some ways, this short and quick-stepped gait is similar to the festinating gait of Parkinson's Disease. It is speculated that musculoskeletal changes, such as a foreshortening of muscular collagenous structures in the anterior hip joint and declines in knee and ankle motion, may be responsible for this decrease in stride length (Larish et al., 1988).

Aside from a decline in walking speed, other age-related gait charac-teristics include a loss of normal arm swing, reduced pelvic rotations, a decrease in hip and knee rotation (Wolfson, Whipple, Amerman, & Tobin, 1990), a decrease in cadence, an increase in stride width (more stable BOS to ensure safety), and a decrease in steppage height or decrease in heel-to-floor angle (due to lack of flexibility of plantar flexor muscles).

Several of these gait changes are particular to each sex. For instance, older women have been found to walk slower and with shorter step lengths (Chao, 1983). Hageman and Blanke (1986) compared the free-speed walking of young and older women. They found that the younger women had longer step and stride lengths, greater ankle movement, pelvic tilt, and faster gait than the older women. No significant differ-ence in stride width between the two groups was found. However, oth-ers have not been able to demonstrate such gender differences (Gabell & Nayak, 1984). Jansen et al. (1982) pointed out that gender differences are only apparent as they reflect the differences in individual body weight and height, and that when these factors are taken into account, the gender differences in these gait parameters disappear.

Older women tend to develop a narrow standing and walking base, take small steps more often, and exhibit a pelvic waddle during ambu-lation (Azar & Lawton, 1964), although there is considerable variability. Azar and Lawton (1964) noted that older women have valgus changes in the configuration of their lower extremities, which is in contrast to the straight or slightly knock-kneed stance of younger women. In a population of 200 consecutive women over the age of 65, 31% manifested some degree of this change. The consequences are several and include a narrow standing and walking base of support, and waddling gait. The authors postulated that these valgus changes in many older women could alter the angulation of the neck of the femur, placing it more parallel to the ground and perpendicular to the stresses and strains of force, and thus rendering it more susceptible to fractures. Also, the decreased stepping down (less muscular control) that occurs over the age of 75 years results in feet hitting the ground more forcibly, and an increase in the force of impact. However, these early observations have not been actively pursued by others. Also, older women demonstrate decreased foot placement and clearance during the swing phase of stair descent, although under poor visual conditions they are able to significantly readjust their gait parameters (i.e., increase foot placement). This allows more space for possible perceptual errors in the location of the step edge, because the support foot is positioned further back on the step to compensate for possible errors in step location. At the same time, step cadence is decreased. All three gait patterns appear to be an adjustment to a challenging visual situation (Simoneau, Cavanagh, Ulbrecht, Leibowitz, & Tyrrell, 1991).

Conversely, older males adopt a wide standing and walking base, and assume a more stooped posture and shuffling type of gait, with increased flexion of both elbows and knees and diminished arm swing (Murray, Kroy, & Clarkson 1969). In addition, older men have been found to spend more time in stance phase and a significantly shorter time in swing phase, an increase in toe-out and stride width (increased base of support). However, these changes were described by Murray and associates in comparison to younger men (not females). The gender differences (if real) in gait are not well understood.

Whether these gait changes are truly age-associated—compensatory in nature and serving to maintain balance—or are hazardous and thus influence fall risk remains speculative. Limited information is available in most gait studies relating to the criteria used to select subjects for these observations. It is possible that the samples included persons with pathology. Other investigations reporting on subjects with declared pathology describe similar observations. For example, Imms and Edholm (1981) found that decreases in walking velocity were more strongly influenced by the onset of disease than by chronologic age. Finley (1969) compared the gait patterns of young women aged 19 to 30 years and old women aged 64 to 86 years. They found that older women had decreased velocity, shorter step lengths, and lower swing-to-stance ratio (that is, more time spent in double support). However, 78% of these older individuals had some degree of arthritis and used multiple medications that may have influenced their gait. Gehlsen and Whaley

(1990) failed to find a relationship between these other gait character-istics and falls in apparently healthy persons with the exception of a larger distance between the heels (i.e., increased width of stance and BOS). This suggests that significant changes in gait are more indicative of underlying pathological conditions.

Whether or not gait changes are hazardous is also influenced by an individual's walking requirements. For instance, slow walking in the institutional setting may not be of consequence, but is an entirely dif-ferent story for those persons in the community who need to cross a busy intersection. Therefore, persons may not have the ability to cross the street in the allotted time period (i.e., the interval between "walk" and "don't walk" signs, or green, yellow, and red lights). This factor is not insignificant. Several investigators have addressed the functional consequences of declining walking speed. Lundgren-Linquist (1983) studied the walking performance of 226 Swedish men and women, all of whom were 79 years of age. They found that women in particular were not able to achieve walking speeds sufficient enough to safely negotiate intersections. A similar study conducted by Hoxie, Rubenstein, Hoeing, and Gallagher (1994) found that older pedestrians crossing a busy intersection in Los Angeles, California took significantly longer than younger pedestrians, in part due to slower walking speeds. Of the 592 older pedestrians observed, 27% were unable to reach the opposite curb before the light changed. Whether disease processes contributed to this decline was not reported, but this research highlights the prob-lem. For example, the increased duration of the double-support phase may be compensatory mechanisms to increase stability (in the ratio between swing and stance phase).

Nevertheless, studies on the gait of older persons with falls have shown that it is clearly more compromised than that of non-fallers (Imms & Edholm, 1981). Fallers tend to exhibit decreased walking speeds, shorter stride lengths, and variability of steps. These gait alterations, to a cer-tain degree, influence fall susceptibility. Guimaraes and Isaacs (1980) showed that the gait of older hospitalized patients with falls differed significantly from that of other older persons, displaying a large vari-ability in step length, step frequency, a narrow stride width, short step length, and slow speed. Specifically, fallers demonstrate slower walk-ing speeds, shorter step length, and large variability in step length. Wolfson et al. (1990) found that stride length and walking speed differ-entiated previous fallers from non-fallers among a group of 49 nursing home residents.

Research on the relationship between age-related gait changes and stair ambulation is scant in comparison to that of gait on level ground.

This may be due to the fact that older people as a group use stairs less frequently than do younger persons (Carson et al., 1978). The avoidance of stairs by older persons may, in part, be related to a sense of vulnerability (Archea, 1985) produced by a general fear of instability when ambulating on stairs. Whatever the reason, older people continue to suffer more stair accidents per use than members of any other age group (Carson et al., 1978).

Most stair accidents and serious injuries occur during descent. Typically, the leading foot oversteps a tread and "slips" over the nosing, while the other leg collapses and is unable to support the person's balance (Archea, 1985; Svanstrom, 1974). Sheldon (1960), in a community study of falls in older people, found that one-third of falls resulted while using the stairs. The most frequent cause was missing the last step in the mistaken belief that the bottom landing had been reached. Subsequently, the majority of literature pertaining to stair ambulation in the older population, interestingly enough, has concentrated on stair descent. Simoneau et al. (1991) examined stair descent in a group of 36 healthy women between the ages of 55 and 70 and found that clearance between the foot and stair during swing phase was small under all visual conditions. While decreased visual acuity had a significant effect on cadence, foot placement, and foot clearance, visual surround conditions did not. Proper foot clearance is crucial during stair descent, since the position of the foot on the step determines the quality of the BOS for the weight-bearing phase of the gait cycle. Thus, it appears that vision plays a major role in the ability to descend steps successfully and safely. Other researchers (Pastalan, 1982; Pastalan, Mautz, & Merrill, 1973) have conducted studies in which persons wore eyeglasses to simulate the visual capabilities of persons in their seventies. These persons experienced considerable difficulty in discriminating the position of risers and treads going down a flight of stairs, and had greater difficulties when the steps were visually distracting in design (for example, those carpeted with floral print, or with treads and risers of similar colors). Archea, Collins, and Stahl (1979), using similar types of eyeglasses in a group of younger persons, found that subjects took twice as long to descend the first riser of a flight of stairs. This was attributed to problems arising from the increased time required to detect the step edge. Archea and co-workers (1979) concluded that:

> when descending a flight of stairs, a fully sighted person can usually see where to place his feet. However, because a person with diminished capability may not be able to judge the extent of the tread below, he may not be sure that his foot will have a firm footing until he has actually made contact.

Slips, Trips, and Stumbles

Age-related gait changes may contribute in part to the likelihood of slips and trips. A trip occurs when there is inadequate ground clearance during the swing phase. When the foot either fails to adequately clear the floor surface or step edge, or encounters an uneven ground surface such as a sidewalk crack, door threshold, or curled up carpet edge, the swing phase is interrupted. At that point, if uncorrected, a trip is likely to result and lead to a forward-directed loss of balance and falling. Individuals with low foot-ground clearance during the swing phase of gait may be particularly at risk.

In addition, older persons with shortened step length may experience difficulty in negotiating ground surface obstacles that are in their path. Chen, Ashton-Miller, Alexander, and Schultz (1991) studied a group of 24 young and 24 old healthy persons (mean age 22 and 71 years), and examined their ability to step over obstacles of varying heights. They found that age had no effect on swing foot clearance of an obstacle; however, older people exhibited a significantly more restrained approach to that obstacle. They stepped over it more slowly, took shorter steps, and had shorter obstacle-heel strike distance, which increases the likelihood of encountering the obstacle. The majority of older persons were able to clear the obstacle by placing their lead foot closer to the obstacle before crossing it), a strategy intended to reduce the risk of toe contact with the obstacle and a trip during the swing phase. However, as a consequence of their shortened step length, four or 17% of older persons in the study stepped directly on the obstacle. Thus, persons with decreased step length also may be at greater risk for tripping.

A slip occurs during the stance phase when friction is inadequate between the shoe/bare foot surface and ground surface. For instance, when a bare foot or shoe bottom either encounters a surface of low frictional resistance (wet/icy ground surface; sliding rug; wet leaves, etc.), dislodges an unstable object (pebbles, twigs, etc.), or approaches the ground with a change in stride length during the swing phase, a slip can occur. At this point, if an individual is unable to maintain stability, a slip is likely to result in either a back- or sideward-directed loss of balance and falling. Also at risk for slips are older persons with short stride lengths (inadequate BOS) or long stride lengths (overextension makes it difficult to recover).

The condition of the surrounding environment and visual capacity of the older person also plays an essential role in slips and trips. For instance, in the presence of decreased illumination, increased glare, and poor object contrast (resulting in poor visualization) an inability to perceive edges such as step and curb edges, or cracked and uneven sidewalk surfaces, would undoubtedly be disadvantages to the older person with poor visual function. Likewise, under similar visual conditions, an inability to detect clear liquid spills, for example, water that is lacking in contrast, can lead to slips. Whether a trip or slip results in a fall depends on the ability of the individual to initiate and execute musculoskeletal strategies or maneuvers aimed at correcting balance (realignment of the COG and BOS).

A stumble is defined as a loss of balance regained before falling to the ground. This is a postural response that attempts to correct a loss of balance occurring in either the posterior or anterior direction, characterized by taking one or two quick steps forward or backward (realignment of COG with BOS). Stumbles become falls if they fail to correct instability. Teno et al. (1990) reported that community-dwelling older persons describing two or more stumbles in the past month were at an increased risk for a fall in the following year. Grabiner, Koh, Lundin, and Jahnigen (1993) suggested that recovery from a stumble is largely dependent upon lower extremity muscle strength and the ability to restore control of the flexing trunk.

Musculoskeletal

The capacity to support independent mobility during walking and transferring in a safe manner is affected by a number of age-related musculoskeletal changes. Beginning in middle age and sometimes much earlier, most individuals experience a progressive decline in muscle strength due to a decrease in both the number and size of muscle cells and fibers (Young, 1984). Starting at the age of 25 years, muscle mass declines at an average rate of 4% per decade until the age of 50 years. Thereafter, the rate of loss becomes more significant, increasing to 10% of the remaining skeletal muscle per decade. By the age of 70 years, it is estimated that muscle mass decreases by 25% to 30% (Grimby & Saltin, 1983), declining markedly with advanced age. Such declines have been found to occur in both upper and lower extremity muscles (Vandervoort, Hayes, & Belanger, 1986), especially in those groups which are proximal in distribution. However, the greatest decline in strength occurs in lower extremity muscle groups (Grimby & Saltin, 1983). Those muscles most likely to show a decrease in strength are the active antigravity muscles such as the quadriceps, hip extensors, ankle dorsiflexors, and triceps. Lower muscle strength is crucial to many basic maneuvers such as stair climbing, transferring from seated positions, and walking (Bassey et al., 1992). There is also an association between lower extremity strength and balance. Probst (1989) found that older females with adequate hip abductor strength were more able to stand on one leg than were those individuals with poor strength. Among older persons the reserve in functional muscle capacity may be so slight that even a small additional decline in strength may render some of these basic activities impossible (Young, 1986). In addition to this decrease in strength, the ability of some muscles to provide sustained strength during repeated contractions or use may decline as well with age. A slowing of the speed of contraction may be an important factor in the ability of older persons to recover from loss of balance. In particular, the ability to break a fall may become less effective, in part, because of these changes in muscles.

One of the most noticeable musculoskeletal changes is that of posture. The typical picture of old age is one of a stooped-over woman with exaggerated kyphosis and bent knees. Two possible mechanisms for kyphosis, or stooping, have been proposed. One is a structural change in the spine, mainly the result of osteoporosis and vertebral compression fractures; second is an adaptive response to instability or fear of falling, which maximizes balance by lowering the COG in relation to BOS (Cunha, Leduc, Nayak, & Isaacs, 1987). There is great variability in the appearance of postural changes secondary to osteoporosis. In some older women with vertebral fractures there is no change in posture; in others, kyphosis occurs with no forward lean in posture; and lastly, in some, a severe kyphosis and forward lean of posture occurs (Woodhull-McNeal, 1992). The extent of postural changes is dependent upon the site of the vertebral fracture. For instance, increased kyphosis occurs more often in association with osteoporosis affecting the thoracic spine, whereas compression fractures occurring lower down in the lumbar vertebrae may have little effect on posture.

Regardless, any forward lean in posture, especially when it is severe, tends to alter the body's balance threshold. The COG is shifted forward, past the BOS (the critical point of stability) and as a result, it becomes more difficult to maintain standing balance. As well, a stooped posture can adversely influence gait. Individuals may not be able to fully extend the muscles of the hips and knees when walking, or to thrust the foot forward fast enough to preserve balance. Poor ankle muscle strength and loss of joint motion complicates the execution, making it difficult to adjust the COG in line with the BOS rapidly enough to prevent a fall. Fallers might display these abnormalities to a greater extent than normal older persons. For instance, Studenski, Duncan, and Chandler (1991) found a marked loss of ankle strength and flexibility to be more present in those persons with a history of falls when compared against non-faller controls. Adequate movement of the ankle during gait becomes important to ensure foot-ground clearance and avoid stumbles and falls. Whipple, Wolfson, and Amerman (1987) examined the strength of four lower extremity muscle groups (knee flexors and extensors, ankle dorsal and plantar flexion) between fallers and nonfallers in the nursing home setting. They found that the fallers, in comparison, had significant declines in strength for each of the muscle groups; in particular, they drew attention to poor ankle dorsiflexion function. It has been observed that ankle dorsiflexion weakness is a risk factor for posterior loss of balance and falls (Whipple et al., 1987).

A deterioration of articular cartilages in the hips and knees also becomes more prominent with age. James and Parker (1989) examined the age-associated decline in joint mobility in a group of persons aged 70 to 85 years and older recruited from senior citizens' clubs and retirement villages. When comparing the oldest age groups with the younger age groups, they found that the older age group exhibited decreased joint mobility for all hip and knee motions. Vandervoort et al. (1986) compared ankle dorsiflexion function in a large sample of middle-aged and older men and women, and found that older individuals, particularly females, exhibited greater declines in ankle flexibility. As well, they showed that the strength of the ankle dorsiflexor muscles decreased about 30% in both men and women between the youngest and oldest age groups. The increasing prevalence of degeneration of cartilage with age parallels the age-related increase in the prevalence of osteoarthritis; however, the association between the two remains poorly understood. Irregardless, these changes have been found to be associated with significant disability in the older population (Hughes, Edelman, Singer, & Chang, 1993). For instance, joint impairment may contribute to impaired transfer activity: an inability to flex the knees and hips sufficiently may impair the capacity of the legs, and a reduction of shoulder girdle strength fails to provide optimal leverage when sitting down and arising from chairs, toilets, and beds. A Swedish study that involved a small sample of 79-year-olds with self-reported joint impairment found that restricted motions of the knee joint were significantly associated with disability in getting up from a chair, climbing stairs, and using public transportation (Bergstrom, 1985). As well, declines in lower extremity muscle strength are associated with a number of gait abnormalities. Aniansson et al. (1980) found a significant relationship between gait speed and knee extension strength in healthy women. Fiatarone et al. (1990), in a study of older nursing home residents, found a relationship between decreased gait velocity and decreased ankle plantar flexor muscle strength. Murray (1967) observed that older men exhibited less ankle dorsiflexion at the beginning and end of the stance phase of the gait cycle.

Cardiovascular

Aging is associated with several physiological changes that impair blood pressure homeostasis and predispose older people to balance instability and falls. First of all, the baroreceptor reflex, consisting of stretch receptors located in large arteries that are sensitive to sudden changes in blood pressure, is an essential regulatory mechanism that maintains sufficient blood flow to the brain, despite changes in posture. It has been shown that the sensitivity of the baroreflex declines with age (Lipsitz, 1989), due to a stiffening of the arteries. Mancia et al. (1984) compared a group of persons 20 years of age with individuals that were 60 years old and found that the speed of the baroreceptor response to declining levels of blood pressure diminished with age. As a consequence, older people may display a diminished ability to adapt to sudden drops in blood pressure, such as when changing from the supine to upright position. Most often, this progressive decline in baroreflex sensitivity or stimulation becomes apparent in the diminished heart-rate response to hypotensive stimuli, such as volume loss, or to hypotensive medications. As a result, older persons are at risk for developing transient episodes of hypotension and lightheadedness. These postural changes in blood pressure can also lead to instability. For example, Overstall et al. (1977) demonstrated that older persons with a 20 mmHg drop in systolic pressure had more body sway than did persons without changes in blood pressure. Lichtenstein et al. (1988) found that a 10 mmHg drop in diastolic pressure was associated with increased velocity of sway, which was greater in older women.

Second, there is an age-related decline in cerebral blood flow (Myer & Shaw, 1984). Older persons have a resting cerebral blood flow that approaches the threshold for ischemic symptoms. Therefore, any compromise in cerebral blood flow that occurs as a result of underlying cardiovascular disease, hypotensive medications, or volume depletion may further place older persons at greater risk of cerebral hypoperfusion and transient episodes of hypotension.

Finally, older persons experience age-related changes in volume regulation and sodium conservation that may influence the control of blood pressure. Epstein and Hollenberg (1976) studied urine sodium excretion in a group of older and younger persons placed on a salt-restricted diet for five days, and found that the older individuals lost sodium at a greater rate. This tendency to lose sodium, or the ability to conserve sodium, may be due in part to an age-related loss of nephrons and reductions in basal plasma levels of renin and aldosterone (Crane & Harris, 1976). As a result, the effects of diuretics and salt restriction may be more pronounced in older persons, leading to rapid volume depletion, orthostatic changes in blood pressure in the upright position, and the risk of balance loss and falls.

PATHOLOGICAL DISEASES

Diseases and their associated impairments play a more decisive role in fall causation than do age-related physiologic changes by themselves. Older people possess considerable reserve capacity, beyond what may be needed for ordinary mobility tasks, making aging, per se, less likely to cause falls in the absence of associated diseases. Numerous community- and institutional-based studies examining the factors related to falling in older people have reported that individuals with a history of falling are more likely to show evidence of underlying medical illness (Campbell, Borrie, et al., 1990; Cwikel, 1992; Lipsitz, Jonsson, Kelley, & Koestner, 1991; Nevitt et al., 1989; Robbins et al., 1989; Rubenstein, Robbins, Josephson, Schulman, & Osterweil, 1990; Svensson et al., 1991; Tinetti, Williams, & Mayewski, 1986; Tinetti et al., 1988). Overall, it is estimated that about 55% of falls are related to medically diagnosed conditions (Rubenstein et al. 1988). Of these about 12%–17% of falls are due to acute illness and adverse medication effects, with the remainder due to chronic diseases.

ACUTE DISEASES

The falling event may be the initial sign of an underlying acute illness. Illnesses most often identified as causative of falls are those present at the time that interfere with postural stability; they include syncope, hypotension, cardiac arrhythmias, myocardial infarction, pulmonary embolism, electrolyte disorders, seizures, stroke, febrile conditions (e.g., urinary tract infections, pneumonia), and exacerbations of underlying diseases (e.g., congestive heart failure, chronic obstructive pulmonary disease, renal failure).

CHRONIC DISEASES

A fall frequently heralds a deterioration in health due to chronic disease. Disease processes that predispose to falls include any persistent physical condition that interferes with gait and balance. The most common originate in the visual, neuromuscular, and cardiovascular systems. The presence of acute and chronic or degenerative cognitive disorders by themselves, or in conjunction with organ system disease, increase the risk of further falls.

Visual Disorders

Rates of visual impairment sharply increase with age, starting at about 70 years of age (Tielsch, Sommer, Witt, & Katz, 1990), and are more prevalent among the oldest-old and the institutionalized (Salive et al., 1992). Among nursing home residents age 65 and older, nearly one-half are reported to have some problems of vision (Kirchner, 1985). The most prevalent age-related ocular diseases that affect visual function are diabetic retinopathy, glaucoma, cataracts, and macular degeneration. It is estimated that macular disease and cataracts alone account for 45% and 33%, respectively, of such visual defects (Haber, 1986). These diseases occurring in combination with age-related changes in visual function may lead to significant visual impairments. When associated with poor environmental illumination, visual function can be impaired further, to the degree that hazardous environmental ground surfaces (e.g., spills, upended rug edges, steps, door thresholds) are difficult to visualize, which predisposes to trips and slips.

Nuclear cataracts result in poor distance acuity, whereas posterior cataracts result in poor near vision. However, in advanced stages, the visual impairment resulting from cataracts is usually global. As a consequence, the individual's vision becomes "hazy," and they exhibit decreased visual acuity, contrast sensitivity, and color perception. In particular, glare disability to blinding light is a common complaint. Glaucoma in the late stages is associated with a constriction in the visual fields, with a loss of peripheral vision resulting in tunnel vision. As well, glaucoma can lead to decreased contrast sensitivity, dark adaptation, and glare tolerance. This can result in an inability to function safely, especially in dim light. Macular degeneration in the early stages may be asymptomatic. However, as the disease progresses, it is characterized by a decrease in central visual acuity, glare tolerance, contrast sensitivity, and color vision. Moreover, a loss of central vision in both eyes can result in objects appearing distorted, which may cause individuals to experience difficulty in discriminating details in the environment. Diabetic retinopathy leads to distorted or blurred vision, and is associated with a decrease in dark and light adaptation, contrast sensitivity, and glare tolerance.

A number of investigators have suggested that impaired visual function may be a predisposing factor for postural instability and falls in older persons (Felson et al., 1989). Brownlee et al. (1989) suggested that older people with falls may rely to a great extent on visual cues to both recognize and correct postural deviations, because of decreased proprioceptive input. Over (1966) proposed that a false interpretation of visual cues may be an underlying cause of falls in older people. In an effort to confirm this hypothesis, Tobis, Nayak, and Hoehler (1981) tested visual spatial perception in a group of older people with and without falls by projecting a rod on a video screen and asking the subjects to indicate the true vertical and horizontal plane. They found that fallers displayed a significant degree of error in this task of visual spatial perception. More recently, Tobis, Reinsch, Swanson, Byrd, and Scharf (1985) designed a very similar study using a portable rod-and-frame apparatus. They confirmed their earlier findings: older persons with falls were significantly more dependent on visual cues to maintain their balance. The authors suggested that this over-reliance on visual information may be in response to altered proprioceptive and vestibular feedback, a result of age or other health problems. In support, Lord and Webster (1990) examined the relationship between visual field dependence (using a static, tilted, and rotating visual field) and falls in a group of 136 persons aged 59 to 97 years. They found that 59% of the participants who had experienced one or more falls in the past year were significantly more visually dependent, compared with the 77% of individuals who had not fallen, and concluded that tilted or rolling visual stimuli may lead to postural instability and falls in older persons. Tobis et al. (1990) showed that older persons who are blind demonstrate a higher rate of falls than nonimpaired persons, suggesting that persons rely to a great extent on visual input rather than on proprioceptive and vestibular cues to maintain balance. Older persons with falls have been found to score more poorly on single-legged stance balance tests with their eyes closed than with their eyes open (Crosbie et al., 1989), a finding that supports the view that fallers rely upon visual cues to correct postural adjustments. However, others have proposed that the visual system may be too slow in responding to displacements when proprioceptive feedback is absent (Pyykko et al., 1990).

Visual loss may increase not only the risk of postural instability and falls, but injury as well. In a case-controlled study, Grisso and colleagues (1991) reported that visual impairment in older women was associated with a five-fold increase in the odds of experiencing a hip fracture. It is estimated that more than 40,000 hip fractures occur among older people each year in the United States as a result of visual impairments

(Felson et al., 1989). In addition, several cross-sectional studies have shown a positive relationship between visual impairment and altered mobility (Bergman & Sjostrand, 1992; Salive et al., 1994). For example, Havlik (1986) reported that among community-dwelling persons aged 65 to 74 years, 4.4% of those without visual impairment reported gait and balance difficulty outside the home, compared with 18.4% of those with visual impairment. Those persons reporting visual problems had greater difficulty with walking and getting in and out of a chair. Salive et al. (1994) prospectively studied 5143 older persons in three communities in the United States and examined the association of distant vision and physical function. They found that limitations in mobility such as climbing a flight of stairs, walking without help, transferring from beds and chairs, and using the toilet were significantly associated with decreased visual function. In the nursing home setting, Marx, Werner, Cohen-Mansfield, and Feldman (1992) reported that in comparison to residents having good vision, a significantly greater proportion of residents with low vision (e.g., cataracts, macular degeneration) were dependent on caregivers for toileting and transferring (from beds and chairs). These findings were independent of musculoskeletal problems and medical conditions, such as cerebrovascular accidents.

Consequently, several studies have examined visual disorders as a cause of falling (Nevitt et al., 1989; Tinetti et al., 1988). However, the extent to which specific visual deficits are responsible for falls remains poorly understood. For example, Tinetti et al. (1988) found that community-dwelling older persons with impaired near vision had a 1.7 fold increase in fall risk compared with those individuals with insignificant or no losses in near vision; those with poor distance vision had a 1.4 fold increase in fall risk. Similarly, Nevitt et al. (1989) found that a decrease in distance visual acuity was associated with a 1.5 fold increase in the risk of recurrent falls. Neither of these studies found visual acuity to be significantly related to falls when other risk factors such as gait disturbances were considered as well. Regardless of these conclusions, other factors can contribute to falls. Glynn et al. (1991) analyzed the causes of serious falls in a group of 489 ambulatory older persons receiving treatment of glaucoma. They found that ocular and systemic medications were associated with a greater risk for falls than even major visual impairments. The researchers suggested that the systemic effects from glaucoma medications (e.g., hypotension, bradycardia, and syncope) may contribute more than the ocular effects to falling. Therefore, while in some part visual impairments do contribute to falls, the relationship between visual deficits and fall risk remains an important area of future research.

Neurological Abnormalities

Gait abnormalities affect 20%–50% of older persons (Sudarsky, 1990) and represent one of the most common causes of falls (Tinetti et al., 1988). The following discussion considers some of the more common neurological disorders, their characteristic gait and balance abnormalities, and possible mechanisms for falls.

In frontal-lobe disorders (also referred to as "frontal ataxia" or "apraxia"), the gait is characterized by a wide base of support, slightly flexed posture, and small, shuffling, hesitant steps. Initiation of gait is difficult. The feet appear to be stuck or "glued" to the floor, a condition referred to as "magnetic gait." In an effort to lift the foot, the person may sway from side to side. However, any excessive sway will result in loss of balance. As well, once walking, the person may suddenly halt, come to a complete stop, be unable to move forward for several seconds, and then continue to walk. After a few small steps, the gait begins to improve. This sequence resembles the "slipping clutch" syndrome.

Similar problems arise when the person attempts to change direction. One foot may stay in place in a single spot while the other foot takes a series of small, uncertain steps. Turns are accomplished by a series of these steps, with the person pivoting on both feet in a small circle. During this period the risk of balance loss and falls is particularly great. In advanced forms of frontal-lobe disorders, the person may be unable to walk or take a step, although while lying in bed the person is capable of initiating leg motions as required and as seen in walking. Persons may walk better with assistance. Persons with Alzheimer's Disease, vascular dementia, and normal-pressure hydrocephalus typically demonstrate this type of gait disorder. In addition to gait disturbances, normal pressure hydrocephalus (NPH) is associated with mild forms of dementia and urinary incontinence, typically a late manifestation. Sometimes, the gait disturbances of NPH may be difficult to identify, since it can take on many forms, including gait apraxia—a slow, shuffling gait similar to Parkinsonism—and various balance problems (unsteady and staggering gait). The clinical response to the removal of 40–50 ml of cerebrospinal fluid may be an acceptable screening test for NPH (Sudarsky, 1990).

Dementia, especially of the Alzheimer's type, is associated with disorders of gait. Visser (1983) examined the gait and balance of eleven ambulatory older persons (mean age, 79 years) with moderately severe Alzheimer's Disease (AD) in comparison with an equal number of healthy older persons matched for age and sex. There were clear-cut differences between patients and controls on all measures of gait and balance. The persons with AD walked more slowly and took shorter steps; their frequency of steps was lower; their double support time increased; and their step-to-step variability was greater. Also, the total sway path and the degree of sway was greater. Furthermore, some persons with AD display a marked flexion of posture that appears insidiously and parallels the deteriorating course of the disease (Galasko, Kwo-on-Yuen, Klauber, & Thal, 1990) and may affect balance and increase the risk of falls. This alteration in posture may occur acutely as well. Rosenfeld, Lerman, and Habot (1993) described a series of five cases in which older persons with AD admitted to a psychogeriatric ward developed an acute onset of stooped posture. Previous to hospitalization all persons were able to walk erect; however, after the onset of stooping, the patients continued to walk but started to experience a worsening of balance and falling. This may be a reaction to fear, as these persons had moved from small apartments to the wide-open space of the psychogeriatric ward.

These observations are consistent with the view that the transcortical pathways involved in the integration of gait are damaged in AD. Proprioceptive loss and apraxia (i.e., a loss of ability to execute previous learned motor skills), visual-spatial dysfunction in object recognition, and agnosia lead to disturbances in the recognition or perception of familiar sensory information. Furthermore, older persons with moderate to severe degrees of AD exhibit apraxia (Baum, Edward, Leavitt, Grant, & DeVel, 1988), which is defined as an inability to remember how to perform routine motor tasks, such as transferring from beds, chairs, and toilets, and walking. Persons with apraxia of gait cannot process nerve impulses to perform activities correctly, even though both strength and sensation are adequate. Sometimes the person may walk in place instead of moving ahead, or the feet appear to be "glued" to the floor. Aside from this gait abnormality, at times the person will also have trouble sitting unsupported, and may slowly fall backwards. Typically, apraxia may begin with clumsiness and eventually, can progress to a profound lack of coordination and balance (Randall, Burkhardt, & Kutcher, 1990), and fall risk. These changes can lead to misinterpretation of environmental conditions resulting in trips and slips, balance loss, and a reduced ability to correct imbalance and falls.

Senile gait disorder is a milder form of frontal-lobe apraxia. It is characterized by a flexed posture, with short, shuffling steps that are especially prominent in making turns. Typically, individuals move slowly and cautiously, being uncertain of their foot placement and step. Persons with this condition use a widened stance to increase their base of support and are prone to retropulsion (toppling backward), particularly while turning. Imbalance may be elicited with a push or displacement of balance on the sternum that results in falling backwards. The cause of this gait disorder is uncertain, but it probably represents an exaggeration of the normal gait changes that accompany aging.

Sensory ataxic gait is characterized by a wide base of standing and a "foot-stamping" walk. The legs are usually flung forward and outward in a high-stepping, stamping manner. The heel touches the ground first and a "stamp" of the feet may be heard. This gait is in response to a loss of position sense so that the individual does not know where their feet are in relation to the ground or support surface. As a result, the person constantly watches the position of the legs to ensure proper foot placement. Eye closures or walking in conditions of low illumination bring out the gait abnormality, as the person is deprived of the compensatory visual information. Persons will exhibit a positive Romberg's sign. As well, the individual will manifest balance problems, often reeling from side to side. In older persons, the condition is caused by disorders affecting the posterior column, such as B12 deficiency, spinocerebellar degeneration, and cervical spondylosis. Moreover, mechanoreceptors in and around the joints in the cervical spine are of importance in providing proprioceptive information about the spatial relationships between the head and trunk (Wyke, 1979). Subsequently, any change in alignment of the cervical spine may result in disequilibrium.

Diseases of the neck joints with a loss of mechanoreceptors, such as may occur with cervical spondylosis, can also lead to abnormal gait. The condition can lead to myelopathy (disturbances in the spinal cord) and ambulation problems, such as difficulty in climbing stairs, etc.

Cerebellar ataxic gait disturbances are characterized by a widebased stance, with small, irregular, and unsteady steps. Sometimes this gait is accompanied by veering, staggering, and sudden lurching to either side, forward, or backward. In severe cases, the individual will not be able to stand unsupported, even with their eyes open. This form of gait is common in chronic alcoholism, and in degenerative conditions such as spinocerebellar atrophy and progressive supernuclear palsy. Modifiable causes of ataxia include thiamine and vitamin B12 deficiency, hypothyroidism, and sedative-hypnotic toxicity. The acute onset of this gait may be due to vascular disease (i.e., multi-infarct dementia). The person turns en bloc and shows increased unsteadiness on turning, particularly when the turn is performed quickly. Persons typically have difficulty walking on their heels and toes, or in tandem gait (i.e., on a narrow base of walking support). This disorder usually results from cerebellar dysfunction, such as nutritional and alcoholic, and certain neoplasms.

Circumduction of gait is caused by lower extremity hemiplegia or paresis due to stroke or other focal brain lesion. Here, the lower extremity is flexed at the hip and extended at the knee, and the foot is plantar flexed. As a result, the person has to swing the leg in an outward arc to ensure proper ground clearance. At the same time, the person assumes a slight lateral flexion of the trunk to the unaffected side, a posture that allows the plegic leg to complete this maneuver. This type of gait can result in a narrow, unstable standing and walking base of support (typically maintained on the good foot) and a risk of balance loss. A decrease in ankle dorsiflexion of the affected limb has two results: a diminished ability to initiate quick postural responses, and reduced foot clearance of the ground during ambulation—sometimes the toe may drag—which can precipitate tripping. In hemiplegia, the leg is usually stiff and flexion at the hip and knee joints is decreased. The foot is typically dragged along the floor, and if the shoe is examined the toe and outer side of the sole will show signs of excessive wear. The affected arm does not swing, but is flexed at the elbow and usually placed across the abdomen. Sometimes it is supported by the good hand. While walking, the person leans towards the unaffected side, compromising the base of support and balance stability. As a result, the person throws the involved leg outward from the body, a movement called circumduction, or by hip hiking to accomplish the swing phase.

Circumduction may be used as a method of advancing the leg in the absence of hip flexors, or in the case of a stiff knee. Hip hiking elevates the extremity so that the foot can clear the ground during the swing phase. Also, post-stroke patients with hemiparesis show alterations in the timing and sequence of postural muscles when balance is disturbed and in hemiplegia display altered activation of postural muscles. Instead of the normal sequence of distal-to-proximal muscle activation, DiFabio, Badke, and Duncan (1986) found that proximal muscles tended to be activated first in the paretic limb. Persons with hemiplegia have a marked increase in body sway while standing, but most individuals can maintain balance by shifting their COG towards one side, and carry most of their body weight on the intact or unaffected leg. After a hemiplegic stroke, impairment of stability commonly occurs, with a tendency to fall toward the weaker side. Studies that have investigated the reasons for this phenomenon have related it to muscle weakness or abnormal proprioception, and deficits in the ability to shift the COG sufficiently enough to counter instability (Dettman, Linder, & Sepic, 1987). Furthermore, it has been suggested that a "loss of balance" after a stroke may be related to vestibular dysfunction, an impairment of the vestibulo-ocular reflex (eye and head displacement) and righting response (Catz, Ron, Solzi, & Korczyn, 1994). Also, the appearance of visual neglect (hemianopsia) and visual-spatial impairment (hemi-inattention) following a stroke is quite common (Chen Sea, Henderson, & Cermak, 1993; Stone, Halligan, & Greenwood, 1993), and may influence the person's balance and safe mobility.

Scissoring or spastic gait leads to spasticity in pronounced cases. The person's legs are hyperextended and adducted. In the course of walking, each leg moves forward slowly and in a stiff manner, with restricted motion of both the hip and knee. As the person walks, the legs are rotated outward, and each forms a semicircle (bilateral circumduction). In severe cases, the legs may cross while the person is walking, producing what is referred to as a "scissors" gait. Typically, ankle dorsiflexors are weak, so the feet scrape the ground. Steps are shorter than normal, and walking requires a great deal of effort. With bilateral upper motor neuron lesions, the individual may manifest a scissoring gait, which is essentially a bilateral circumduction of gait. Common causes include spinal cord damage (cervical spondylosis) and lacunar infarction (multi-infarct dementia).

During steppage gait the person lifts their feet high off the ground in order to keep the toes from scraping the floor. The toes strike the floor first, followed by the heels, producing a slapping gait. This toe-to-heel slapping may be unilateral or bilateral. Steppage gait appears in association with drop foot and is caused by weakness or paralysis of the pretibial or peroneal muscles. The gait is caused by diseases affecting the peripheral nerves of the legs or motor neurons in the spinal cord, such as peripheral neuropathies (diabetes mellitus, B12 deficiency, alcoholism). In severe forms, the person has to watch their legs and the floor to determine their proper position. These individuals will often complain of tripping over trivial objects, such as cords or wrinkles in rugs. In order to walk safely, they must lift their knees high so that the foot clears the walking surface. If they don't, a fall is likely to result.

Festinating gait is a symmetrical shuffling of the feet with poor ground clearance, associated with Parkinson's Disease (PD). In this condition, the general posture of the person is that of flexion at the hips, knees, and elbows. During walking the trunk is bent forward, and the arms do not swing freely. The person walks with a series of short flat-footed shuffles that do not clear the ground (decreased steppage height). The gait may be hesitant (slow gait initiation of first few steps), and as a result, there exists the risk of balance loss in the forward direction, as the body begins to move forward before the feet. At other times the gait can "freeze"—halt immediately—particularly when approaching ground obstacles (curbs, steps, door thresholds). As movement progresses, the steps become quicker, and some persons may have diffi-culty in stopping. With a small push the person may fall in "one piece" like a log, the result of an inability to readjust the BOS and COG. Sometimes persons will rock the body from side-to-side, exhibiting an excessive path deviation away from the normal smooth sinusoidal curve. To preserve stability during walking and turning, persons typically assume a broader gait in order to increase their base of support. However, such compensation may not always be possible. For exam-ple, Weller, Humphrey, Kirollos, et al. (1992) found that persons with Parkinsonism and multiple falls had narrower foot separation than those individuals without falls. They attributed this defect to declines in striatal dopamine.

In addition, persons with PD can have certain postural defects. Park-insonism affects postural control; it institutes a loss of autonomic pos-tural reflexes—propulsion (resulting in an uncontrolled forward motion) and retropulsion (resulting in a loss of balance backward). As well, anticipatory postural and reactive postural responses are diminished, and an inability to activate upper extremity postural muscles in response to balance displacements occurs. As a result of these postural abnormalities, the risk of falls in PD is enhanced. Koller, Glatt, Vetere-Overfield, and Hassanein (1989), in a study of Parkinson's patients, found a strong relationship between postural instability and frequent falls.

Abnormal gaits associated with multisensory deficits are due to a combination of visual and proprioceptive impairment. As a result, per-sons are overreliant on vestibular input to determine the position of their feet on the ground. Typically, these persons will complain of a dizziness, unsteadiness, or light-headedness which is experienced only when walking, and sometimes is only manifest while turning around quickly. Persons often use canes, or touch walls and other furnishings while walking for both proprioceptive feedback and balance support. Diabetic patients are particularly prone to this, due to their visual and neuropathic complications.

Older persons with fear of falling may display a cautious gait. Typically, posture is flexed forward and ambulation is accomplished slowly (decreased stride length and walking speed) with the legs mildly held in a flexed position to maintain a low COG. The gait is short-stepped with feet held apart (mildly wide-based gait), a strategy that is used to maintain a greater BOS. Turning is accomplished *en bloc,* often with mild instability. Frequently, in order to maintain balance, individuals will hold onto walls and furnishings for balance support. This type of gait may be most dominant following a fall. Most persons are aware of impaired balance, even those with mild to moderate degrees of dementia, and will express the need for caution to avoid falls. Older persons with losses of visual, proprioceptive, and vestibular input may also exhibit cautious gait, because of a fear of falling. As a result, Nutt, Marsden, and Thompson (1993) suggested that cautious gait is a compensatory adaptation, "an appropriate response to real or perceived disequilibrium." In some persons, gait may improve if they are allowed to walk while holding on to others or a walker for support.

Musculoskeletal Disorders

While a cause-effect relationship between muscle strength and incidence of falls has not been established, correlative studies support this hypothesis. In one study, older nursing home residents with a history of recent falls compared with age-matched control subjects showed significant declines in muscle strength (Whipple et al., 1987). The greatest declines were found in those muscle groups associated with balance: the knee flexors and extensors, and ankle plantar and dorsiflexors. Several controlled studies have identified quadriceps muscle weakness as an important risk factor for falls (Campbell et al., 1989; Lipsitz et al., 1991; Nevitt et al., 1989; Robbins et al., 1989; Tinetti et al., 1986). Such lower-extremity weakness and disability may, in turn, lead to gait abnormalities, postural instability, and falls.

Aside from the problems of disuse, muscle atrophy, and weakness that can result from prolonged bedrest and immobility (see Chapter 2), there are a variety of diseases associated with muscle weakness and gait abnormalities. Some common conditions consist of hypo- and hyperthyroidism, polymyalgia rheumatica, polymyositis, osteomalacia, and neuropathies. Any loss of proximal muscle strength can lead to unstable, waddling gaits. A "penguin's walk" is an excellent example of this gait. Persons typically exhibit a characteristic leaning of the trunk away from the foot as it lifts. This results from gluteus medius muscle weakness and an inability to stabilize the weight-bearing hip. Generally, patients will complain of having trouble getting up from low-seated chairs and toilets, and in climbing stairs. In addition, there are a number of medications associated with muscle weakness. For example, the chronic use of diuretics can lead to depletion of skeletal muscle electrolytes. Corticosteroids exert catabolic effects on muscle tissue, leading to proximal muscle weakness and atrophy if these drugs are used for extended periods to treat conditions such as COPD and arthritis.

Arthritic conditions that result in stiff or painful leg joints are associated with unstable gait and balance. A painful hip causes an antalgic gait. The characteristics of this gait pattern consist of a reluctance by the individual to bear weight through the affected limb. In a way, this type of gait pattern may be viewed as being self-protective. The foot is placed flat on the ground, rather than with the typical heel strike, in order to reduce jarring of impact. Also, push-off is avoided to decrease transmission of forces to the involved hip. Accordingly, there is a noticeable lack of weight shift laterally over the stance leg, representing an attempt to keep weight off the involved limb. This can result in decreased stance phase of the affected leg; decreased swing phase of the uninvolved leg, which creates a shorter step length on the uninvolved side; and an overall decrease in the velocity of walking.

In osteoarthritis, the knee is flexed, and the person walks on the toes in order to minimize time spent standing or weight-bearing on the affected leg and touching the ground, leading to unsteady gaits. Sometimes this is referred to as gonalgic gait. In addition, a reduced range of motion and strength may accompany arthritic joints of the lower limbs, resulting in deviations in the usual gait cycle. Messier, Loeser, Hoover, Semble, and Wise (1992) showed that persons with symptomatic osteoarthritis of the knee have poorer flexibility and muscular strength in both the affected and unaffected legs and demonstrate significantly less range of motion of the knee when walking. Perhaps the changes occurring in the unaffected limb are due to disuse atrophy. These findings have been supported by others who have also found decreased knee range of motion in persons with osteoarthritis (Brinkman & Perry, 1985; Stauffer, 1977).

Foot pain can lead to gait impairments as well. Possible causes other than arthritic conditions of the feet include corns, calluses, toe deformities, bunions, and deformed nails. These disorders also decrease proprioceptive feedback, which further compromises both gait and balance (Kosinski & Ramcharitar, 1994). It has been shown that the toes contact the floor for about three-quarters of the gait cycle (Hughes, Clark, & Klenerman, 1990), and any foot disorder of the forefoot may interfere with safe walking. Moreover, foot disorders (toe deformities, callouses, bunions, etc.) can lead to mechanical problems during ambulation and subsequently, to unsteady gait patterns.

Leg-length discrepancies (LLD) have been associated with a number of musculoskeletal problems such as osteoarthritis of the hip (Hayes, 1982). It has been postulated that an LLD may alter a person's body posture, which in turn changes the joint mechanics of the lower extremities and spine, and increases the likelihood of balance loss (Gofton, 1971). However, any significant instability that results is often due to other comorbidities being present. Murrell (1991) found that persons with LLD, compared to individuals without LLD, did not display greater body sway, but when asked to close their eyes (decreased visual input), did exhibit more postural sway than those without LLD, thus suggesting the presence of proprioceptive loss. Persons with leg length discrepancies that commonly follow hip fracture repair demonstrate departures from the normal gait cycle. On the side of the shorter leg, as the foot prepares to make initial contact with the ground (heel strike), the pelvis drops excessively in an attempt to lengthen the leg in order to reach the ground. This results in the visual appearance of limping. In order to compensate, the joints of the unaffected leg commonly demonstrate exaggerated flexion in order to achieve swing-through, or else circumduction, of the unaffected leg.

Osteoarthritis of the knees and hips with limited joint flexibility results in similar problems. Osteoarthritic knees exhibit significantly less knee extension than do unaffected joints during gait (affecting heel strike and push-off) (Messier et al., 1992). Interestingly, Messier et al. (1992) found that persons with unilateral symptomatic osteoarthritis (OA), also demonstrated decreased flexion and extension in the unaffected leg (to a lesser extent than symptomatic knee) and relative to a control group without symptomatic OA. The authors suggested that this may indicate either asymptomatic disease, or a decrease in physical activity, which results in an overall decrease in flexibility. As a consequence, lower extremity joint impairment has been found to be associated with diminished walking ability (Gibbs et al., 1993).

Cardiovascular

There are a variety of chronic cardiovascular problems that can lead to transient reductions of blood pressure or restrictions of blood flow that may interfere with the mechanics of balance, and increase the likelihood of falls. However, direct evidence of the effect is sometimes difficult to obtain, since this necessitates prompt evaluation and measurement of cardiac abnormalities at the time of the fall.

Postural or orthostatic hypotension has been demonstrated to occur in from 6.4%–33% of older persons (Mader, 1989). It is typically associated with complaints of dizziness or unsteadiness, visual blurring, and heaviness in the legs when arising quickly. However, the relationship between orthostatic changes in blood pressure and falls is uncertain. Tinetti and co-workers (1986), in a study of falls in the nursing home, found that hypotension upon standing was present in only 3.4% of falls. Likewise, in community-residing older persons, less than 3% of falls are due to orthostatic hypotension (Campbell et al., 1981). On the other hand, Craig (1994) analyzed 50 cases of orthostatic hypotension in older people and found that falls, or mobility problems due to fear of falling, was the most common mode of presentation. Lipsitz (1991) found that 10% of fallers in a nursing home had cardiovascular abnormalities and associated hypotension as a contributing cause of falling. As a result of these findings, it was suggested that many falls in older persons are due to abnormalities in the maintenance of blood pressure. That is, many older persons are able to maintain postural control, but if challenged by pathological conditions that interfere with the regulation of blood pressure control, the likelihood of postural instability and falls is great. Some of these conditions consist of disease processes such as autonomic neuropathy, a common complication of such diseases as diabetes, alcoholism, and Parkinson's Disease; conditions causing volume depletion, such as hyperglycemia and hypercalcemia; situational circumstances that lead to deconditioning of the baroreflexes (i.e., prolonged inactivity, bed rest); and the chronic use of hypotensive medications (e.g., antihypertensives and antidepressants) (Mader, Josephson, & Rubenstein, 1987).

Additionally, hypertension raises the minimum level of blood pressure required to maintain cerebral blood flow and prevent symptoms of light-headedness (Strandgaard et al., 1973). As a result, in those older persons with chronic hypertension, cerebral blood flow can diminish markedly with mild to moderately acute decreases in blood pressure (Lipsitz, 1989). This can occur even when blood pressure changes occur within normotensive ranges. Moreover, hypertension can lead to a further loss of baroreflex sensitivity (Shimada, Kitazumi, Ogura, Sadakane, & Ozawa, 1986), and a risk of additional decreases in blood pressure. The use of antihypertensive medications may also exacerbate postural hypotension and lead to falls. For instance, Jackson et al. (1976) reported the occurrence of dizziness and falls in six older persons with hypertension soon after they received antihypertensive medication. However, others have not found an association between the chronic use of antihypertensive medications and falls (Nevitt et al., 1989; Tinetti et al., 1988). Moreover, the prevalence of postural hypotension associated with antihypertensive medications is low. One Canadian study of primarily men aged 50 and older found a prevalence of postural hypotension: 4.6% in diuretic users, compared with 3.4% in persons not taking diuretics (Myers et al., 1978). Similarly, Hulley et al., (1985), reporting on data from the Systolic Hypertension in the Elderly Program, found that symptoms of faintness on standing were described after 1 month of therapy by 3% of persons taking chlorthalidone and by 5% of those on a placebo.

Rather, the use of antihypertensives leading to fall risk may become more evident in the presence of acute hypotensive stimuli such as hypovolemia (dehydration, blood loss) and adverse drug effects, which can either lead to hypotension directly or indirectly by rendering the aging heart less capable of cardioacceleration (an increase in pulse) in order to compensate for hypotensive effects. Under these situations, the ability of the baroreflex to respond may be beyond its capacity.

A number of studies have found an age-related association between the ingestion of food and the development of postprandial hypotension in older people (Bellomo, Santucci, & Parnetti, 1988; Lipsitz & Fullerton, 1986; Peitzman & Berger, 1989). Lipsitz et al. (1983) evaluated the effects of a meal on systolic blood pressure in institutionalized older persons, and found an average decline in blood pressure of 25 mmHg. This hypotensive effect of a meal is almost immediate, and reaches a maximum decrease in blood pressure 30 to 60 minutes after eating a meal. Several possible mechanisms have been proposed to explain the pathophysiological mechanisms of postprandial hypotension. These consist of an impaired sympathetic reflex activity to splenic vasodilation; interference of insulin-induced sympathetic nervous system activation; inadequate baroreceptor sensitivity to compensate for the hypotensive effect of splanchnic blood pooling during digestion; and the involvement of vasoactive gastrointestinal peptides (Jansen & Hoefnagel, 1991; Jansen, Penterman, vanLier, Willibrord, & Hoefnagels, 1987; Jansen et al., 1989). However, the clinical significance of postprandial hypotension remains uncertain. Of 113 frail residents in one nursing home, 41 (36%) had a reduction in postprandial systolic blood pressure of greater than 20 mmHg, but only 2% of the residents experienced acute symptoms (Vaitkevicius, Esserwein, Maynard, O'Connor, & Fleg, 1991). As a result, postprandial hypotension as a cause of falls may be more likely in association with common hypotensive stimuli, such as postural changes and medications. Jonsson, Lipsitz, Kelly, and Koestner (1990) examined the frequency and magnitude of hypotensive responses to common daily activities (via blood pressure and heart rate monitoring) and their relationship to falls in a group of nursing home residents with and without recurrent falls. They found that both groups exhibited marked blood pressure reduction following meals (postprandial hypotension) and ingestion of nitroglycerin, which was significantly greater in fallers than in non-fallers, independent of the cause of the fall. In one prospective study of syncope in institutionalized older persons, postprandial hypotension in relation to postural changes and ingestion of nitrate medications accounted for 8% of syncopal falls (Lipsitz, Pluchino, Wei, & Rowe, 1986). Aronow and Ahn (1994), in a prospective study of postprandial hypotension in a nursing home, found that residents with a history of syncope or falls had a significantly greater maximal decrease in postprandial systolic blood pressure than did residents without syncope or falls. The reductions in postprandial blood pressure were greater in those residents taking angiotensin-converting enzyme inhibitors, calcium channel blockers, digoxin, diuretics, nitrates, and psychotropic drugs.

Other possible cardiovascular causes of falls include recurrent syncope, a term applied to conditions that lead to transient loss of consciousness due to failure of an adequate blood supply to the brain. Those conditions most often responsible consist of both fast and slow cardiac arrhythmias, decreased cardiac output caused by severe valvular disease (aortic and mitral stenosis) and congestive heart failure, vasovagal attacks induced by emotional distress, and micturition syncope ascribed to a failure of venous return, which sometimes occurs in older men with prostatic hypertrophy who strain while attempting to urinate (Baloh, 1992; Kapoor, 1994). Also, older persons are susceptible to carotid sinus syndrome or hypersensitivity (Lipsitz, 1985). This condition is characterized by cardiac slowing or asystole, systolic hypotension of 50 mmHg or more in the supine or standing position, or a combination of both in response to maneuvers that stimulate the carotid sinus (for example, wearing tight collars; extremes of neck-turning). As well, carotid sinus hypersensitivity is magnified by the presence of hypertension, coronary artery disease, diabetes, and some medications, such as digitalis and beta blockers (Kapoor, 1994). Also, some older persons, especially those with arthritic cervical changes or bony spikes on their cervical vertebrae that can impinge on the vertebral artery, are at increased for vertebral artery compression and dizziness during certain maneuvers that extend the neck, such as looking directly upward towards the ceiling or reaching up to get objects from high shelf heights. However, any symptoms of dizziness elicited on turning the head to the side (for example, looking over the right and left shoulder) or extending the neck backwards do not by themselves implicate carotid sinus syndrome and vertebral artery compression, as these maneuvers can cause stimulation of the neck mechanoreceptors and semicircular canals, implicating vestibular disease.

And lastly, any lower extremity edema as a result of cardiovascular disease, varicosities, or dependent positioning of the legs can be a major threat to balance. Edema is likely to distort proprioceptive feedback and kinesthesia of the feet, as persons depend on the cutaneous inputs from the soles of the feet to assist with balance reactions. Furthermore, the effects of congestive heart failure such as decreased muscle strength, poor endurance, and increased fatigue can contribute to altered gait patterns. Hausdorff et al. (1994) compared a group of older persons with compensated congestive heart failure against a group of older persons without heart failure, and found that the ability to walk at a regular and steady pace was significantly reduced in those individuals with congestive heart failure.

COGNITIVE DISORDERS

There are a number of cognitive ailments that are associated with the problem of falls in older persons. Some of these include a denial of frailty, anxiety and depression, dementia, and attention-seeking behavior (Tideiksaar, 1989, 1993b). With the exception of dementia (van Dijk, Meulenberg, van de Sande, & Habbema, 1993), and specifically Alzheimer's Disease (Buchner & Larson, 1987; Morris, Rubin, Morris, & Mandel, 1987), the epidemiologic evidence linking falls to cognitive impairment is weak (Mossey, 1985).

Denial of Frailty

Sometimes older persons who suffer multiple falls deny, or fail to appreciate, the significance of these events. They may view their falls as being commonplace, and as a result, fail to report falling episodes to health professionals. The employment of possible preventive interventions is thus prohibited in these individuals. In other instances, the older person may obtain a medical evaluation, but despite being functionally frail, reject any recommendations that are made towards preventing further falls. For example, persons may refuse to accept assistance with mobility tasks that they are incapable of performing safely, and may be reluctant to accept any modification of their usual activities. Furthermore, they may be noncompliant to corrective actions; for example, failing to remove environmental hazards or utilize durable medical equipment (canes, walkers, bath seats and benches, bathroom grab rails, etc.) to support their mobility. As a consequence, these persons remain at fall risk.

HK is a 93-year-old man who suffered a recent stroke with right-sided hemiplegia. He was prescribed a hemiwalker for ambulation assistance, but refused to use the device, and instead attempted to ambulate both indoors and outdoors by holding onto environmental objects for support. However, these supports were not always available to support his balance, and as a result, this led to several falling episodes. When HK was asked why he didn't use his device, he became quite tearful. He expressed a feeling of humiliation when using the device, stating that "the walker reminds me of my old age and frailty."

MR is a 73-year-old man who suffered a stroke that affected his balance. Despite being at fall risk, and provided with recommendations to modify his behavior, the patient continued to engage in activities that led to falls: walking outdoors without a cane, using a stepladder in the kitchen, putting his pants on while standing, etc. The patient refused to curtail such risky activities, and insisted on maintaining his autonomy and prestroke lifestyle.

GR is an 87-year-old woman with Parkinson's Disease. Although her bathtub was equipped with grab bars and she had the option of using a tub seat, she refused to use this equipment while bathing. She denied any functional impairments and the fact that her bathing activities were hazardous. As a result the patient suffered several bathtub falls, but without injury.

Much of this behavior represents a defensive reaction against viewing oneself as being frail and limiting individual autonomy. The older person may insist that they are still capable of functioning or performing activities at the same intensity as in younger years, despite the presence of gait and balance disorders that would dictate otherwise. This may particularly be the case in those persons who have been accustomed to being active and independent. Most of the time, these individuals are capable of picking themselves off the ground after falling, and do not incur any injuries as a consequence. However, there may be instances when older persons experience multiple fall-related injuries, and still refuse to accept any preventive interventions.

WG is an 82-year-old woman with severe osteoporosis and multiple falls. As a result, she had three hip and two distal forearm fractures that occurred over a 3-year period. Despite several attempts to modify her behavior, she continued to engage in activities that placed her at fall risk. She did not experience any untoward psychological or functional consequences from her injurious falls, and oddly enough, accepted surgical treatment as a quick fix for her problems.

Anxiety and Depression

Older persons commonly face a number of stressful life events, such as the loss of a spouse or other family members, friends, pets, bodily functions (urinary incontinence, memory loss, etc.), mobility and autonomy, retirement, and their homes (through moving in with adult children, relocating to sheltered housing or a nursing home, etc.). All these events can lead to episodes of anxiety and depression. Under these circumstances the person may be at greater fall risk. Episodes of emotional distress can by themselves lead to poor health and falls, or they can contribute to a worsening of comorbid medical conditions which themselves increase risk. Sometimes the occurrence of multiple falling episodes in persons with emotional problems may lead to a worsening of anxiety or depression. In particular, this becomes evident in those individuals who suffer a loss of functional independence or autonomy as a consequence. Moreover, avoiding a fall is generally not the main concern of individuals who are depressed or anxious; rather, they become emotionally consumed by their immediate problems. As a result, the person may be less alert to environmental fall hazards or unable to effectively prevent a fall in progress.

EL is a 93-year-old woman with degenerative joint disease who was admitted to the hospital following a fall that resulted in a head injury. The patient stated that she tripped over the door threshold leading into her bathroom, and hit her head on the sink edge. Despite being at fall risk as a result of bilateral knee arthritis, the patient denied any previous falls. She described feeling severely depressed since the unexpected death of her daughter following breast cancer 1 month ago. As a result, the patient often felt distracted and had great difficulty with her concentration. At the time of her fall, she stated "feeling particularly disturbed emotionally," and that she was not "paying attention" to her surrounding environment. Also, the patient stated that after losing her balance, her arms "felt very heavy," thus preventing her from grabbing hold of environmental supports.

Conversely, the treatment of emotional disorders with medications might carry a greater risk. Antidepressants and anxiolytics are commonly associated with a number of adverse effects (e.g., sedation, orthostasis, arrhythmias, and confusion) that can lead to falls (Nevitt et al., 1989; Ray, Griffin, Schaffner, & Melton, 1987; Tinetti et al., 1988).

JA is an 88-year-old woman who was treated with trazodone for her depression. Shortly afterwards, the patient began to experience increased sedation and orthostatic hypotension, and as a result, experienced several falls. Her medication was changed to fluoxetine, a selective blocker of serotonin reuptake, which produced no side effects (including falls) and resolved her depression.

MW is a 77-year-old woman with mild dementia and memory loss. As a consequence, she became depressed and was prescribed nortriptyline. About one week later, the patient was found by her housekeeper, confused and lying on the bathtub floor. Apparently, the patient was attempting to bathe by herself, a task that she had always asked her housekeeper for assistance with, as she was unable to bathe alone safely. It was felt that the nortriptyline caused the patient to be confused, which led to her attempting the activity independently.

In addition, some older persons with emotional disorders may fall in an effort to gain attention. Typically, these individuals are homebound, with few social contacts, or they may reside in a long-term care facility and have little family contact. As a consequence of their loneliness they sometimes begin to fall so as to receive attention from family members or health professionals. In these instances, the falling episode may reflect an attempt, whether conscious or unconscious, to receive help or to ensure the care and involvement of others.

MN is a 76-year-old woman who had been self-reliant and independent until the death of her spouse. She had two children who lived in the area, but they rarely visited the patient due to a poor interpersonal relationship. As a result, she became increasingly depressed and expressed feelings of abandonment, and began to experience several falls. It was felt that her falls represented in part an unconscious attempt to have her children visit more often. With family counseling, the patient was able to establish a meaningful relationship with her children, and after a while she sustained no further falls.

PD is a 73-year-old man with severe Parkinson's Disease who lived alone in a fifth floor walkup apartment. He became increasingly depressed and socially isolated, and proceeded to experience several falls. It was discovered that the patient had a close relationship with his son, and that they often had spent a lot of time together. However, the son had recently to relocate out of state, and thereby, his visits were infrequent. It was felt that the patient's falls were a form of attention-seeking behavior. After instituting a friendly visiting program for the patient, he stopped falling.

CL is an 84-year-old woman who was relocated to a nursing home because of dementia. Shortly after being admitted, she began to fall for no apparent medical reasons. It was thought that her falls represented an attempt to have her daughter visit more often. When the patient was living at home, she had had daily contact with her daughter. However, while in the nursing home, her daughter visited only on a weekly basis. The patient's falls subsided after increased visits by her daughter were arranged.

Lastly, older persons may deliberately fall in response to feelings of extreme frustration. Belfield, Young, Bagnall, and Mulley (1987) described two cases of cognitively intact older persons with severe neurological problems who began to fall repeatedly and suffered multiple face and head injuries. In both cases, the desire for self-harm was thought to be in response to extreme frustration produced by the patients' illness and disability. The authors suggested that deliberate falls are probably uncommon, but should be considered in those persons who have repeated falls producing injuries. Deliberate falls also sometimes occur as a manifestation of extreme anxiety.

IR is a 76-year-old woman who was admitted to the hospital for congestive heart failure. Her hospital course was uneventful; however, on the day of discharge to home the patient experienced two falls out of bed. Upon talking with the patient, it became evident that she was quite anxious about returning home alone. Against the judgement of the medical and nursing staff, the patient felt that she required assistance with her activities of daily living. Once the patient was assured that a home attendant would accompany her back home, her anxiety subsided almost immediately, and she didn't experience any further falls.

Dementia

Falls are an extremely common problem among older persons with dementia. Within the institutional setting, several researchers have found that older persons suffering from dementia tend to fall more often than those without cognitive impairment (Morse et al., 1987). Van Dijk et al. (1993) analyzed the number of falls in a nursing home for older persons with dementia and found a rate of about four falls per person per year. In those older persons with dementia who live in the community, falls are equally problematic. In a community-based study, Prudham and Evans (1981) surveyed all falls experienced by persons aged 65 years and older and found that fallers exhibited significantly poorer performance on a mental status test than did non-fallers. In another community study, Morris et al. (1987) compared the occurrence of serious falls in 44 older persons with Alzheimer's Disease (AD) and 56 cognitively healthy controls over a 4-year period. They found that persons with AD had three times as many falls with serious outcomes over the study period than did cognitively intact persons: 36% of AD individuals versus 11% of controls. Similarly, Teri, Larson, and Reifler (1988) examined a group of outpatients with AD, who ranged from 60 to 94 in age, and were 70% female. They found that older AD patients were significantly more likely to fall than younger AD patients. Interestingly enough, those AD patients with the onset of cognitive impairment at extreme old age were significantly more likely to fall than were AD patients with cognitive onset occurring at younger ages. Moreover, it appears that older persons with AD are at great risk for fall-related injury. One long-term care facility study found that 33% of all major injuries sustained by all residents over a 1-year period were the result of falls by residents with Alzheimer's Disease (Mass, 1988). Buchner and Larson (1987) examined fall-related fractures in older persons with AD and observed a fracture rate of 69/1000 per year, or more than three times the predicted rate. De Jaeger et al. (1994) assessed cognitive function in a population of community-dwelling older patients (mean age of 81 years) hospitalized because of fall-related fractures. These researchers found that only 12% had normal Mini-Mental State Examination scores. The authors remarked that the results of the mental status scores—a mean of 18.92—were closer to dementia scores than due to simple age-associated mental deterioration.

AD is associated with a number of risk factors for falling, besides those gait and balance problems previously discussed. First of all, AD is characterized by a global deterioration of cognitive functioning consisting of memory loss, impaired judgement and decision-making ability, poor reasoning, and impaired attention. These changes may lead to a misperception of environmental dangers, errors in judgement, and a failure by the individual to discriminate between safe and dangerous environmental conditions or activities. As a result, persons may unknowingly place themselves in hazardous situations that cognitively intact persons would normally avoid.

SG is an 81-year-old woman with AD. Although this patient was incapable of independent bathing activities, she attempted to get into the bathtub by herself. Unfortunately, she lost her balance, fell, and fractured her hip. The patient had experienced bathtub falls in the past, and consequently, her access to the tub was restricted by her family, but obviously this effort did not deter the patient.

EH is a 92-year-old woman with AD who exhibited both gait and balance impairments. She attempted to climb a flight of stairs without the assistance of her attendant. The stairs were not equipped with handrails. As a result, she lost her balance, falling backwards, and suffered a subdural hematoma. The home attendant had placed a gate at the bottom of the steps to restrict the patient's activities, but she had inadvertently left the gate unlocked.

The safe utilization of ambulation devices and durable medical equipment may also be problematic in persons with AD. Sometimes health professionals may be responsible for not recognizing the cognitive limitations of AD, and as a result, they may fail to institute appropriate interventions to guard against falls.

GC is a 78-year-old woman with AD and Parkinson's Disease. Due to the patient's gait impairment, she was given a 4-pronged cane to use. Shortly after the patient started to use the cane, she fell while walking. Upon observing the patient's ambulation, it was clear that she repeatedly failed to properly place the cane on the floor, due to poor judgement. She was given a rolling walker to use, and didn't suffer further falls.

LG is an 84-year-old man with AD and degenerative joint disease. The patient exhibited poor toilet transfers and utilized the sink edge and towel bar for balance support while transferring. As a result, his toilet was equipped with grab bars to assist with safe transfers. However, shortly after the toilet grab bars were installed, the patient suffered a fall off the toilet. It was discovered that the patient failed to use the grab bars, but instead, continued to use the sink edge and towel bar.

SO is an 82-year-old woman with AD who was admitted to the hospital for the evaluation of falling. Despite an inability to safely transfer from her bed, the patient occasionally attempted the activity by herself, and each time was caught by the nurses before falling. The patient was repeatedly instructed to use the nurse call system for assistance. However, because of her poor memory and impaired judgement, she failed to comprehend these instructions and continued to leave her bed. On one unfortunate occasion, the patient fell while getting out of bed, and fractured her hip. After her hip was repaired, the patient returned to the unit and her bed was equipped with a bed alarm device, which alerted the staff when the patient was leaving her bed.

Aside from a decline in cognitive abilities, individuals with AD may exhibit a variety of behavioral problems (e.g., delusions, restlessness, aggression, agitation, pacing, and wandering) that can lead to the risk of falling. Marx, Cohen-Mansfield, and Werner (1990), in a nursing home study, found that in comparison to residents who did not fall, residents who fell (many with underlying dementia) manifested significantly more agitated behaviors (i.e., constant pacing, hitting, kicking, grabbing). Moreover, those individuals who fell had significantly greater impairments of mobility and gait that may have contributed to falling. Similarly, Brody et al. (1984) studied a group of institutionalized older women with moderate to severe dementia, and found that falls correlated positively with increased agitation.

SF is an 86-year-old man with AD who resided in the nursing home. The patient engaged in aggressive behavior, which occasionally would lead to falls. In each case, the patient either exhibited aggressive behavior (striking a staff member or other residents) and lost his balance as a result, or else he was knocked over by another resident after an aggressive exchange of behavior.

Conversely, the use of medications such as major tranquilizers, that are often prescribed for the control of agitated behaviors, has been associated with increased falls as well (Granek et al., 1987).

Wandering, defined in general as an impetus to walk without any apparent goal or purpose (Randall et al., 1990), can also pose a serious safety problem. Although several studies have included wandering as part of a spectrum of behavioral problems in dementia sufferers, there has been no research focusing purely on wandering behavior and falling. Hope, Tilling, Gedling, Keene, and Cooper (1994) characterized the types of wandering behavior possible, and coined the term "abnormal walking around" to describe the interrelationship between the different types. These consist of:

1. *checking/trailing:* the person frequently monitors or checks on the whereabouts of their caregiver, or inappropriately follows the caregiver;

2. *increased (hyperactive)/aimless walking:* the person walks around more than normal or without an obvious reason;

3. *pottering:* the person ineffectively tries to accomplish household and other chores; and

4. *inappropriate/"overappropriate" walking:* the person walks around for a reason, but the reason is not apparent to others.

Wandering behavior, as a risk factor, may be especially troublesome in those persons who engage in nighttime excursions, as they can ambulate into unsafe areas and fall.

RN is an 82-year-old woman with AD who lived at home with her family. Frequently the patient would get up at night, wander about without incident, and return to bed. However, on one occasion the patient wandered down the basement steps and fell, suffering multiple rib fractures.

ML is a 79-year-old man with AD who resided in the nursing home. The patient would wander about the unit at night, and eventually he was returned to bed by the nurses. On one night the patient began to wander, turned around a corner, and fell over a wheelchair in the hallway, suffering multiple facial and body bruises.

In addition to behavioral problems, persons with AD have an excess of visual dysfunction that is over and above what would be expected on the basis of other underlying pathologic conditions; this also may increase the risk of falls. Several researchers have described an association between AD and a restriction in visual fields (Levine, Lee, &

Fisher, 1993; Shuren & Heilman, 1993). Steffes and Thralow (1987) studied a group of older males who resided in a veterans' medical center and found that persons with AD had visual field losses significantly greater than in persons with other types of dementing illness. Moreover, the visual field loss became more severe as the AD progressed. Shuren and Heilman (1993) described the case of a 65-year-old woman with AD who developed "blurriness" affecting the right side of her visual field, which progressively worsened until she could not see to her right, a condition consistent with a right homonymous hemianopia. Levine et al. (1993) similarly reported on a patient with AD who developed a non-hemianopic right visual field defect. Individuals with AD and visual field loss are at risk for bumping into door frames, other objects, and persons, or for tripping over hazardous ground surfaces and falling. Other visual problems that have been shown to occur in association with AD include deficits in color discrimination and contrast sensitivity (Cronin-Golomb et al. 1991; Cronin-Golomb, Corkin, & Growden, 1987). These changes are thought to be related to pathologic changes of the disease involving the visual cortex, particularly of the association areas rather than primary visual cortex (Katz & Rimmer, 1989; Lewis, Campbell, Terry, & Morrison, 1987). Some persons with dementing illness may develop a loss of visuospatial function, exhibited as an inaccurate visual perception of the position and movement of objects in the environment in relation to themselves (Cogan, 1985). In this instance, the person's visual function is responding appropriately, but the brain is no longer interpreting visual information correctly. The following case serves as an illustration of visuospatial dysfunction.

> PR is an 81-year-old woman with AD. The patient experienced difficulties with bathtub transfers, and it was felt that the addition of grab bars would improve her mobility. However, she failed to utilize the grab bars correctly and safely, due to an inaccurate visual perception of the bars, and subsequently suffered a fall.

Agnosia—an inability to recognize familiar environmental objects and places—is a common feature of AD (Randall et al., 1990), and can lead to a worsening of visuospatial dysfunction. An example of agnosia is the phenomenon sometimes referred to as "visual cliffing," in which the person with dementia reacts by avoiding or stepping over ground surface objects, such as non-slip adhesive strips, that are contrasting in color, as they perceive these surfaces as a change in depth. Also, persons with AD may experience a loss of spatial orientation (Cummings & Benson, 1986). As a result, the person may not recognize where they are, and can experience difficulty navigating about in the environment. Liu, Gauthier, and Gauthier (1991) compared a group of persons with AD with healthy controls, and examined three types of spatial skills: *perceptual* tasks (the ability to discriminate left from right, and recognition of shapes and sizes); *cognitive* tasks (spatial planning and decision-making, spatial problem-solving, spatial memory, spatial learning); and *functional* tasks (the use of environmental cues and skills of the afore-mentioned in familiar and unfamiliar surroundings). They found that the persons with AD were impaired on half of the perceptual tasks, showing a decreased ability to recognize shapes, and on all of the cognitive tasks. On the functional spatial tasks, however, persons with AD showed impaired skills in new environmental surroundings, but intact skills in familiar environments. This finding tends to support the importance of environmental cues in maintaining safe mobility in demented persons.

MEDICATIONS

Although some studies have failed to demonstrate a relationship between falls and drug use (Bates, Pruess, Sooney, Platt, 1995; Janken, Reynolds, & Swiech, 1986; Morse et al., 1985a; Perry, 1982; Sehested & Severin-Nielsen, 1977), it is generally acknowledged that medications in part contribute to the problem of falls in older people (Campbell, 1991; Ray & Griffin, 1990). Several community and institutional studies, many utilizing a comparative control group, have found a relationship between falls and drugs (Kerman & Mulvihill, 1990; Lipsitz et al., 1991; Lord, 1990). Consequently, the onset of falling in older persons is often ascribed to unfavorable medication effects. However, the findings concerning the relationship between medications and falls has been somewhat conflicting, due to a number of factors. First of all, falls in older persons are often due to multiple etiologies, and drugs may be only one contributing factor. Secondly, it is not entirely clear whether falls are due to medications themselves, to the illness for which they have been prescribed, or to the effects of drugs and medical conditions in combination (Campbell, 1991). For example, Tinetti and colleagues (1988) found that sedatives were associated with an increased risk of falling in a group of older persons living in the community, but after adjusting for the presence of cognitive impairment (i.e., confusion and depression), the relative risk of falling associated with sedative use reduced markedly. Regardless, there are several reasons as to why older persons might be vulnerable for drug-related falls.

First of all, older persons as a group are the primary consumers of medications; they take multiple prescription and over-the-counter medications for the treatment of both acute and chronic diseases. According to several large studies that provide data on the patterns of drug use by community-residing older persons in the United States, up to 93% of persons over 65 years of age take at least one prescription and over-the-counter medication (Hale, May, Marks, & Stewart, 1987). In community-dwelling persons, drug utilization increases with age for both men and women (Helling et al., 1987), with an average of 3.7 drugs per person (Hale et al., 1987). The extent of drug use among older persons residing in acute hospitals and nursing homes is even greater, averaging up to 7 medications per patient (Nolan & O'Malley, 1988). Consequently, older persons are at certain risk for adverse drug reactions and drug-drug interactions simply through their increased exposure to multiple medications. Blake et al. (1988) showed that, compared with individual drugs, polypharmacy significantly increased the risk of falling in a community-dwelling population of older persons.

The drug prescribing patterns of clinicians may further add to fall risk. For instance, Lindley, Tully, Paramsothy, and Tallis (1992), in a study of older people admitted to the hospital, showed a relationship between the inappropriate prescribing of drugs and drug-related adverse effects. While this study didn't specifically focus on falls as an adverse outcome, it is clear that several of the untoward effects found, such as postural hypotension, severe bradycardia, dehydration, hypoglycemia, ataxia, and dizziness, may lead to falls.

Secondly, and perhaps more importantly, with increasing age several physiologic changes in response to medications occur that are independent of disease states (Kelly & O'Malley, 1992). These consist first of *pharmacokinetic* changes, which are those factors having to do with drug disposition (i.e., the movement of medications into, around, and out of the body) and involve the absorption, distribution, metabolism, and excretion of medications. Second, *pharmacodynamic* changes include those factors that influence the specific action of a given drug on the body (i.e., its onset, duration, and intensity), which determines both the degree of therapeutic response and whether or not an adverse reaction will occur.

Pharmacokinetics

With the exception of any meaningful alterations in drug absorption, the remaining pharmacokinetic factors all show a decline with increasing age (Scharf & Christophidis, 1993). The distribution of medications in various body fluids and tissues is substantially altered due to age-related changes in body composition. Lean muscle mass declines and total body fat increases with age. Between the second and eighth decade, it is estimated that body fat increases from about 18% to 36% in men, and 33% to 48% in women (Greenblatt, Sellers, & Shader, 1982). Total body water as a percentage of body weight declines by 10% to 15% between the ages of 20 and 80 years. Together, these changes markedly affect the volume of distribution of fat or lipid- and water-soluble medications. For example, the use of water-soluble drugs (e.g., ethanol, digoxin, lithium, cimetidine), which are mainly distributed in body water or lean body mass, will result in higher blood concentrations and increased pharmacologic activity. On the other hand, lipid-soluble drugs, such as benzodiazepines, have larger volumes of distribution in older persons, as these medications are distributed into adipose tissue. Consequently, a given dose of a benzodiazepine-type medication like diazepam will result in delayed clearance from the body and a prolonged half-life of the drug (i.e., decreased elimination from the body). Finally, serum albumin can be 15% to 25% lower than normal by the time a person reaches age 60. This can lead to increased concentrations of certain medications, such as nonsteroidal anti-inflammatories, oral anticoagulants, and hypoglycemic sulfonylureas, that are highly bound to albumin. A decline in albumin leads to an increased amount of free or unbound drug that is available for action. However, the net effects of age on protein binding may be of greater importance when protein-bound drugs are given together. For instance, aspirin and warfarin are two drugs that typically compete for available protein binding sites when taken together, with one drug winning out over the other. In this case, aspirin prevails (binding to albumin), and warfarin loses out, thus becoming unbound and active. This may result in high levels of warfarin and the possibility of adverse drug complications, such as bleeding. Otherwise, the clinical effect and relevance of protein binding in the aged is uncertain.

Hepatic metabolism declines due to a decrease in liver mass and diminished hepatic blood flow. Liver volume declines on average by 37% between the ages of 24 and 91 years, and hepatic blood flow declines by 35% (Woodhouse & James, 1990). In addition, enzymatic activity decreases and there are alterations in liver microsomal enzyme induction. These changes slow the metabolism of drugs such as psychotropic agents, that are dependent on hepatic metabolism for elimination, and accordingly, can lead to potentially toxic levels.

Renal function declines progressively with age, as a result of a reduction in glomerular filtration rate, blood flow, and tubular secretion. By age 70, there is a 50% decrease in both glomerular filtration rate and renal blood flow. Consequently, the excretion or elimination of drugs through the kidney, such as digoxin, lithium, nonsteroidal anti-inflammatories, and thiazide diuretics is decreased, which can result in prolonged half-lives or duration of action, and toxic drug levels. In general, decreased serum creatinine levels may not accurately represent a decline in glomerular function, as creatinine represents a function of muscle mass, which usually diminishes with age. Instead, creatinine clearance is a better predictor of decreased renal excretion in older persons.

Pharmacodynamics

The effects of aging on pharmacodynamics are in part due to alterations in receptor and target organ responses, and changes in homeostasis. Within the central nervous system, for example, an age-related degeneration in brain matter and neurotransmitters typically results in a reduction of both the number and efficacy of receptor sites. This can lead to a heightened action of psychoactive medications, which may be exhibited in an increase in confusion or body sway and balance loss. In the cardiovascular system, a decline in baroreflex activity can result in an increased sensitivity to antihypertensive medications, and hence, in a greater likelihood of postural stability. As well, changes in homeostatic reserve, such as impaired sodium conservation, volume regulation, electrolyte and glucose control, thermoregulation, and cognitive threshold may increase the sensitivity to a variety of medications, leading to a reduced threshold for adverse drug reactions.

Mechanism of Drug-Related Falls

These pharmacokinetic and pharmacodynamic changes, in combination with an increased utilization of drugs by older persons, heighten the risk of adverse medication effects and falls. For instance, the risk of falling has been shown to be great for drugs with extended half-lives (greater than 24 hours in duration), and increases exponentially with the number of medications a person receives (Blake et al., 1988; Buchner & Larson, 1987; Campbell et al., 1989; Robbins et al., 1989; Tinetti, 1986). In general, those older individuals who take three or more drugs have been found to be at increased fall risk (Granek et al., 1987; Tinetti et al., 1988). A number of medications have been found to be associated with falls, some of which include the use of laxatives (Cumming et al., 1991), sedatives, hypnotics, and anxiolytics (Blake et al., 1988; Campbell et al., 1989; Granek et al., 1987; Janken, Reynolds, & Swiech, 1986; Mayo/ Korner-Bitensky, Becker, & Georges, 1989; Nevitt et al., 1989; Robbins et al., 1989; Sorock & Shimkin, 1988; Tinetti et al., 1988), antidepressants (Blake et al., 1988; Campbell et al., 1989; Mayo et al., 1989; Nevitt et al., 1989; Ray, Griffin, & Malcolm, 1991), cardiovascular medications (Cumming et al., 1991), nonsteroidal anti-inflammatories (Campbell et al., 1989; Granek et al., 1987), and alcohol (Hingson & Howland, 1987).

Medications can lead to falls through a number of direct and/or indirect mechanisms and actions. For example, drugs such as sedatives, hypnotics, anxiolytics, antidepressants, alcohol, and cardiovascular agents (e.g., diuretics, antihypertensives, cardiotonics) may directly lead to a fall by causing postural hypotension, excessive sedation and decreased reaction time, poor balance and gait, arrhythmias, and impaired cognitive awareness. Conversely, other medications, such as nonsteroidal anti-inflammatory agents and laxatives, may not be the direct cause of a fall, but instead, can result in falls through indirect mechanisms. For example, nonsteroidal anti-inflammatory medications are often prescribed for the treatment of arthritic conditions, and as a result, a fall may be the consequence of impaired mobility (i.e., difficulty in rising from a toilet, or getting up from bed). Likewise, laxatives can lead to bowel frequency that generally causes the person to rush to the bathroom. The presence of any mobility dysfunction may cause the individual to exceed their safe level of mobility, and as a result, suffer a fall. Therefore, falls occurring under these conditions may be more of a marker for impaired mobility than for adverse medication effects. However, both nonsteroidal anti-inflammatories and laxatives can directly lead to falling as a result of adverse medication effects (e.g., bleeding, electrolyte disorders, etc.).

Falls may also be due to a combination of direct and indirect actions. For instance, a tricyclic antidepressant medication in the absence of comorbid conditions may not result in adverse effects, such as postural hypotension. However, in the presence of underlying cardiovascular disease, or in certain situations, such as getting up after a period of prolonged recumbency, the antidepressant can exacerbate orthostasis and increase the likelihood of falling. Similarly, taking a psychotropic medication may not lead to confusion in a person who is cognitively intact. However, in an individual with underlying Alzheimer's Disease and a decreased threshold or tolerance for anticholinergic effects, the psychotropic (in even moderately low doses) may result in delirium and falling. Likewise, diuretics may not cause symptomatic postural hypotension, but in a person with hypovolemia (i.e., dehydration, blood loss), or in an individual with a chronic illness such as Parkinson's Disease who is prescribed carbidopa (an anti-Parkinson's agent), the combination is likely to lead to significant hypotension.

Lastly, older persons who are noncompliant with medications may be at fall risk, although this relationship has not been widely explored. For instance, some older persons may fail to take their medications as prescribed, which can result in either a lack of improvement or worsening of the medical problems being treated, and consequently, lead to a fall. Of equal importance and risk is the fact that some persons conversely are hypercompliant with their medications. They may take more than the prescribed dosage, which increases the likelihood of adverse medication effects and falls.

MP is an 83-year-old woman with degenerative joint disease and congestive heart failure who was admitted to the hospital following an exacerbation of her heart failure and falling. The patient's falls were ascribed to her heart condition. Previous to this admission, the patient had been taking both digoxin and furosemide, but took the diuretic sporadically. She complained that the diuretic caused her to have urinary frequency, and nocturia. However, she experienced difficulty and instability walking to the bathroom as often as required, due to her arthritis and a fear of falling. As a consequence, to avoid an accidental loss of urine, she only took the diuretic when the level of lower extremity edema reached her upper thighs.

AB is a relatively healthy 84-year-old woman who was admitted to the hospital with the recent onset of falling. The patient recently had developed a bout of depression and was taking an antidepressant. On physical evaluation she demonstrated poor gait and balance, and the laboratory evaluation revealed a toxic level of the antidepressant. As a result, it was thought that the patient's falls were directly related to adverse side effects. The medication was stopped, and after 2 days the patient's gait and balance returned to normal. Upon questioning, the patient confessed to taking twice the amount of her antidepressant, thinking incorrectly that if "one dose was good, then two and more doses would be even better."

EXTRINSIC FACTORS

In addition to intrinsic factors responsible for falls, there are a number of extrinsic factors that play an important role in fall causation. These consist of the physical environment, such as the design of furnishings and bathroom fixtures, the condition of stairs and ground surfaces, and illumination. As well, several devices used to promote mobility (e.g., ambulation aids, wheelchairs, bathroom equipment) or guard against falls (e.g., mechanical restraints, bedrails) have been implicated in causing falls. Finally, the type and condition of footwear worn by older persons play an important role in fall causation.

Physical Environment

While several community-based studies have reported a high proportion of falls among older persons occurring outside the home (Blake et al., 1988; Lord et al., 1993; Reinsch, MacRae, Lachenbruch, & Tobis, 1992a), most investigations have found that the overwhelming majority of falls experienced by community-dwelling older persons occur in and around the home (Hale et al., 1992; Hornbrook et al., 1991; Nevitt et al., 1989; Shepherd et al., 1992; Tideiksaar, 1995; Tinetti et al., 1988). In one community-based study, Tideiksaar (1995) reported that 80% of falls occurred in the home. Of the remaining 20% of falls that occurred outdoors, most took place within one city block of the patient's home. In a study of fall injuries among older people in Miami Beach, Florida, DeVito et al. (1988) found that 54% of the falls occurred in and around the home. It has been suggested that falls at home may be less likely to cause injury than falls outside if surfaces in the home (for example, carpeted surfaces) are more forgiving than outside surfaces, such as sidewalks (Nevitt et al., 1991). Also, it has been shown that the risk of experiencing a fall at home increases with advancing age (Nevitt et al., 1991). For example, Blake et al. (1988) showed that persons over the age of 75 years experienced more falls at home than they did outdoors. However, this finding is not supported by Lord et al. (1993), who found an increase in falls occurring outdoors, even in the oldest age groups. There are several possible explanations for this disparity. A number of studies have suggested that healthy older adults, due to their active lifestyles, experience more falls outdoors than in their own homes (Hornbrook et al., 1991; Reinsch et al., 1992b). On the other hand, O'Loughlin, Robitaille, Boivin, and Suissa (1994) argued that older persons who are in ill health may not leave their homes as often, and as a result, are at great risk for indoor falls but not for outdoor falls due to the lack of opportunity. Also, there is some recognition that the causes of indoor and outdoor falls among older people may differ (O'Loughlin et al., 1994). For example, Hale and co-workers (1992), in a study of older persons visiting primary care physicians, found that falls occurring in and around the home were usually due to intrinsic factors, whereas falls away from home were more likely to have an extrinsic cause.

Most falls occurring at home take place in the bedroom, bathroom, living room, kitchen, and on stairways (Campbell et al., 1990; DeVito et al., 1988; Downton & Andrews, 1991; Schelp & Svanstrom, 1986). Within the acute hospital and nursing home setting, the majority of falls have been shown to occur within the bedroom and bathroom (Fleming & Pendergast, 1993; Lake & Biro, 1989; Svensson et al., 1992). These findings do not necessarily incriminate environmental locations as being unsafe, or as the cause of falling, as other explanations are also possible. It has been suggested that community-residing older persons, particularly those who are frail and at fall risk, spend more time at home, and as a consequence, have a greater exposure to potential environmental hazards (DeVito et al., 1988). Another likelihood is that older persons may be less cautious or careless around the familiar surroundings of the home, and hence, be at greater likelihood of falling (Nevitt et al., 1989; Sjorgen & Bjornstig, 1991). Similar explanations exist for the institutional setting. Hospital patients and nursing home residents at fall risk may spend more time in the bedroom and bathroom than in other institutional locations, and engage in more balance-displacing activities, such as transferring from beds and toilets. As a result, falls may represent an increased exposure to potential environmental hazards and participating in hazardous activities. In addition, older persons may be unfamiliar with new environmental surroundings in hospitals and nursing homes, especially during the first few days of admission. It may take some time for older persons to adjust to certain environmental features of the institution that are different from their home, such as bed and chair heights, the location of toilets, placement of toilet grab rails, and linoleum floor surfaces. Similar problems may exist when older patients are relocated to new facilities. Friedman et al. (1994) monitored all falls and fall-related injuries occurring in a group of nursing home residents relocated to another facility, and observed a dramatic increase in falls during the first few months following relocation.

Regardless, the environment has been implicated as a factor in one-third to one-half of all falls occurring in the home and institutional setting (Fleming & Pendergast, 1993; Hornbrook et al., 1991; Rodriguez, Sattin, DeVito, Wingo, and the Study to Assess Falls in the Elderly Group, 1991; Sattin, 1992). Several environmental obstacles and design features, in conjunction with host-related activities, have been associated with falling. These consist of transferring from excessively low or elevated bed heights or climbing over side rails; getting up from or sitting down on unstable, low-seated, and armless chairs, and low toilet seats that lack grab bar support; transferring on and off wheelchairs; walking in poorly illuminated areas, or ambulating without assistive devices or wearing proper footwear; tripping over low-lying objects (those objects that rest outside one's field of vision) or floor coverings, such as door thresholds, thick pile carpets, and upended carpet and rug edges, or ground surfaces, such as curbs and uneven sidewalks; slipping on highly polished or wet ground surfaces, such as kitchen, bathroom, and bathtub/shower ground surfaces, sliding rugs, and icy walkways;

climbing and descending steps and stairways, particularly with faulty handrail support, poor illumination, and unsafe coverings on tread surfaces; reaching up (on tiptoes or step stools and chairs) and bending down to place or retrieve objects from excessively high or low kitchen and closet shelves; and reaching for objects such as telephones, nurse call buttons, and urinals (Tideiksaar, 1989, 1993a). This list is by no means exhaustive, but is intended to reflect the variety of environmental factors that have been implicated.

The likelihood of the physical environment contributing to falls is highest for those persons with underlying frailty and mobility dysfunction. Typically, frail persons are physically less competent and have narrower adaptive ranges to cope with environmental demands (Lawton, 1982). As a result, a mismatch between the designed environment and individual tasks can easily occur, as any attempted activity may exceed the person's level of competence and safety (Hogue, 1991). In this scenario, an environmental hazard such as a low toilet seat or elevated bed height, which are both easily negotiated by a healthy person, can become major obstacles for someone with poor mobility, resulting in a fall. Even relatively healthy older persons may suffer falls as a result of environmental hazards. Speechley and Tinetti (1991) studied the extent and circumstances of falls and injuries in a group of frail and vigorous community-dwelling older persons. As expected, the frequency of falling was much higher among the frail than vigorous subjects, often occurring at home, during routine activities, and in the presence of minor environmental hazards. However, compared with frail subjects, vigorous fallers were somewhat more likely to fall away from home, on stairs, during displacing activities, or in the presence of environmental hazards. These results suggest that environmental factors may contribute to falls across a wide spectrum of older persons, both the frail and the healthy and active.

While no one would argue with the assertion that environmental factors contribute to falls, the true extent of this contribution is currently unknown. There are several reasons for the lack of knowledge. First, most fall studies are not designed to allow for the evaluation of environmental hazards as risk factors: they lack standard definitions of "hazards"; validated and reliable instruments to assess environmental hazards are not employed, and comparison control groups that assess the risk of exposure to environmental hazards are not included (Rodriguez et al., 1991; Sattin, 1992). The few available prospective studies which have examined the risk of falls due to environmental hazards have focused on the home setting, and are inconclusive (Nevitt et al., 1989; Tinetti et al., 1988).

Second, the majority of fall episodes in both the home and institutional setting are generally not observed. As a result, the causative role of environmental factors is typically obtained either from self-reports, or from researchers who list what they consider to be "hazardous conditions" present at the time of the fall (Sattin, 1992). This can result in either an over- or under-representation of environmental factors, depending upon the older persons' recall of hazardous conditions present and their willingness to identify features of the environment as being hazardous (Rodriguez et al., 1991) or, when the reporting is done by researchers, a willingness to create a definition of a hazardous condition. Often there is a mistaken tendency for older persons, their family members, and health professionals to blame the environment for falls. On the other hand, the design of institutional incident reports may not be sufficient to record the contribution of environmental factors, leading to an underrepresentation of the problem. Tinetti (1987), in a nursing home study that evaluated the contribution of medical problems and environmental conditions to serious fall injury, did not find an association between environmental factors and injurious falls. The lone exception was the inappropriate use of walking aids and wheelchairs. The author, however, acknowledged that environmental hazards might have been missed because the incident reports did not supply sufficient data in this regard. Lastly, most studies do not categorize falling events as to whether they are due exclusively to an environmental factor or to a combination of extrinsic and host-related factors (Rubenstein et al., 1988).

Devices

In persons who are at fall risk, devices such as bed rails and mechanical restraints are often utilized to protect against falls, and adaptive aids (e.g., grab bars, commodes, toilet risers, bathtub/shower benches and chairs) are provided in an effort to support individual mobility. Ironically, these devices may actually increase fall risk in some instances. Elevated bed rails have been implicated as a cause of bed falls in a number of institutional studies (Heslin, Towers, Lecki, & Thornton-Lawrence, 1992). When a person exits the bed by climbing over elevated bed rails, transferring activity becomes more dangerous (e.g., persons may get their arm and legs caught in the rails) and increases fall risk. Sometimes, when confronted by elevated bed rails, patients may circumvent the rails and exit their bed by climbing over the footboard, an activity that is equally as dangerous. As well, older patients involved in bed rail-related falls may be more susceptible to injury (Innes, 1985;

Morse, Tylko, & Dixon, 1985; Tideiksaar & Osterweil, 1989). First, patients may fall from bed with their extremities still entangled in the bed rails, leading to the risk of a fracture. Second, bed rails increase the height of the fall, and as a result, the distance of falling—from the top of the elevated rail to the floor—and impact against a hard floor surface is great, which increases the likelihood of fractures and head trauma.

The use of mechanical restraints, often employed to protect against falls, may not be an effective intervention (Evans & Strumpf, 1989; Marks, 1992). Mion, Strumpf, and NICHE Faculty (1994) commented that "if restraints were truly beneficial and effective, one would expect that no falls would occur with the use of restraints" (p. 128). This, however, has not been the case. Studies have shown that up to one-half of older people who fall are restrained (Brungardt, 1994; Tinetti, Liu, & Ginter, 1992). Schleenbaker, McDowell, Moore, Costich, and Prater (1994), in a study that examined the extent of restraints in a rehabilitation facility, found that 36% of the patients who used restraints and fell were restrained at the time of the fall. Presumably, the immediate cause of restraint-induced falls is improper application or patient/resident removal. When restraints are improperly applied, persons can slip out of or untie the restraint and can fall from chairs and wheelchairs or out of bed. The contribution of restraints to falls is more plausible, however, by causing deconditioning, muscle wasting, sensory deprivation, and exacerbating underlying gait abnormalities (Marks, 1992), all of which are associated with increased fall risk.

Moreover, the risk of serious injury from falls is greater in facilities that use mechanical restraints (Evans & Strumpf, 1990). During a 1-year nursing home study, Tinetti et al. (1992) found that 17% of restrained residents had a serious fall-related injury, compared to 5% of unre-strained residents. Rubenstein et al. (1983) reported that the hospital fall-fracture rate in the United Kingdom, where restraints are rarely used, is 0.7%–1.7%, compared with 1.8%–3.8% in the United States. Conversely, discontinuing restraints has not been associated with an increase in falls or injury. Powell, Mitchell-Pedersen, Fingerote, and Edmund (1989), in a Canadian hospital study, reported that a reduc-tion in restraint use from 52 per 1000 patient days to 0.3 resulted in a clinically insignificant rise in falls from 7 per 1000 patient days to 8.7, without an increase in fall-related injuries. The role of mechanical restraints as a fall preventive measure is further explored in Chapter 9.

Lastly, adaptive aids such as bathing and toileting equipment that are commonly used to compensate for poor mobility may in some cases contribute to falls as well. Aids that are either defective or broken can result in obvious safety problems. Examples include slippery or loosely mounted toilet/bath rails, and bath chairs/benches that are in ill repair. In response, some persons will avoid using their aid, and instead rely on alternative methods that may be equally as dangerous. For example, rather than relying on a loose toilet grab rail for support, older persons may use the bathroom door handle or towel bar to pull themselves up from the toilet.

In other instances, the particular aid used by the older person may not be safe. Tinker (1979) found that 19% of accidents in one geriatric unit occurred during commode use. The type of commode used had four wheels, with brakes on the two rear wheels. On all but one occasion, the accidents occurred when the commode moved backwards with the brakes applied, as the patient attempted to get up. Likewise, I have had several cases in which older persons were provided with aids that proved to be hazardous.

WL is an obese 79-year-old woman who received a bedside commode to assist with nighttime toileting. However, the commode collapsed underneath her weight when she sat down. The commode was replaced with a similar model; but once again, the device collapsed, causing the patient to fall. Unfortunately, this episode resulted in a fear of falling and curtailment of toileting activities. The patient was provided with an extra-strength commode chair, which supported her seated transfers and diminished her fears.

BS is a 92-year-old woman who, on her own, purchased a bathtub chair with a high backrest. When the patient attempted to sit down in the chair, she held onto the top of the backrest for balance support, an activity that led to both the patient and the chair toppling over backwards. Consequently, she gave up further attempts to bathe in the tub, and instead resorted to sponge baths. I was unable to convince the patient to attempt bathtub transfers with another type of chair that was much more stable.

At other times, the equipment provided may be inappropriate or not suited to meet the mobility needs of the older person, and as a result, may place the individual at further fall risk.

FB is an 83-year-old woman who was observed by a visiting nurse to have poor toilet transfers, the result of a low-seated toilet. To compensate, the nurse ordered a toilet riser for the patient to use. However, the durable equipment company delivered a toilet riser that was too high. As a result, when she was sitting on the riser, her feet dangled in the air, and in order to transfer on and off the toilet, she literally had to jump. This activity, of course, resulted in several falls. The toilet riser was replaced with one thinner in width, which allowed the patient to maintain foot support while transferring.

MN is an 80-year-old female with severe osteoarthritis of her lower extremities. She complained of balance loss while attempting to bathe, and experienced several falls as a result. The patient was provided with a bathtub chair, but this did not solve the problem, and she continued to suffer balance loss. As it turned out, her major difficulty was with the actual tub transfer itself (i.e., in attempting to lift her osteoarthritic legs up and over the tub rim). The bathtub chair was replaced with a bath bench that allowed the patient to safely enter and exit the tub.

Assistive Ambulation Devices

Assistive mobility devices (canes, walkers) are used to support gait and balance, but can have the opposite effect and contribute to unsafe mobility and fall risk. Most device problems are due to design fault and/or improper utilization. For example, Sainsbury and Mulley (1982) surveyed a group of 60 community-dwelling older people who utilized a cane and examined whether each person's cane was appropriate in its size or length, type of handle, and cane tip. They evaluated a total of 62 canes and found that only 15 canes were of the correct length. Of those canes that were of the wrong size, the majority were found to be too long, some up to 10 cm in excess. Seventy-five percent of the patients who reported a fall while using their cane had inappropriate cane heights. A causal relationship between the cane height and fall risk is purely speculative, however, as the lengths of canes in those persons without falls were not reported. In addition, 26 canes had dangerous features, most often consisting of badly worn rubber tips; in some, the cane shafts were splintered. Many of the people had osteoarthritis, which was listed as the primary reason for needing a cane; however, only 3 canes had handles that accommodate people with arthritic and painful hands. As can be imagined, these problems may result in persons being noncompliant with their canes. A British survey that looked at the utilization of assistive aids in a cohort of persons aged 75 and over found that only 66% of the subjects used their canes on a regular basis, and that 47% of the canes were faulty (e.g., had worn or missing rubber tips, damaged shafts, and were either too long or short) (George, Binns, Clayden, & Mulley, 1988).

Aside from design problems, the improper utilization of a cane can contribute to mobility problems as well. Leary (1982) reported that up to 50% of older persons used their cane in the wrong hand (that is, not contralateral to the affected limb). A Swedish study found that 34% of the canes used by community-residing older people were used incorrectly (Parker & Thorsland, 1991). Whether the individuals experienced any adverse effects as a result (e.g., decreased mobility, falls, and injury) was not described. In another study, Imms and Edholm (1981) observed older people both with and without walking aids as they ambulated on a functional obstacle course. They found that subjects using a walking aid, mainly canes, had significantly slower gaits and experienced more "errors" while using their aid. Many errors occurred while walking up and down stairs, but the authors did not elaborate whether the faults were due to design or utilization problems. While they did not find an association between fall incidence and walking aids, others (Campbell et al., 1981; Wild, Nayak, & Isaacs, 1981c) have reported an association between the use of walking aids and fall risk. The circumstances surrounding assistive device-related falls in these studies were not clearly stated, however. While it may be assumed that the risk of falls increases with the use of faulty canes and/or canes that are not utilized properly, other factors need to be considered as well. For example, Dean and Ross (1993), in a Canadian study of community-dwelling cane users aged 61 to 80 years, did not find a relationship between cane length and utilization and fall frequency. However, the results may have been influenced by the makeup of their study population, who were all capable of independently commuting to urban shopping centers and did not report a high frequency of falls. Therefore, persons with poor functional status, as opposed to those "elite" individuals without functional problems, may be at greater fall risk from unsuitable canes or their improper use. The nonuse of canes needs to be considered as well. Perhaps risk of falls is equal to or even greater in those persons who require a cane for mobility, but do not use their device either because of design problems or a failure to receive needed mobility support from the cane. There are topics worthy of further pursuit, as there has been little research in the area.

The faulty design and improper use of ambulatory aids may be due, in part, to the large extent by which ambulatory aids are obtained outside the medical establishment (Hoxie et al., 1994). Canes, more any other ambulation device, tend to be either self-purchased or "handed down" from friends and relatives. Sainsbury and Mulley (1982) found that 56% of older people had obtained their cane from friends, relatives, or had purchased them independently. As a consequence, many older persons may not only fail to have their canes properly fitted, but may never receive instruction on how to use their cane correctly. For instance, in a Swedish study, it was reported that 38% of canes were distributed without any information on correct use (Malmberg, Martin, & Nilsson, 1980). As a result, it was discovered that 39% of the canes were too long or too short, 44% had inadequate grips, and as expected, 30% were not in regular use. Although data on the extent of this problem in the United States is not readily available, little doubt remains that many older people purchase canes without the knowledge or instruction of health professionals. In one community-based study, Tideiksaar (1995) found that three-quarters of the older patients used an assistive device (i.e., a cane or walker). In 70% of these patients, their device was either the wrong size, or was utilized improperly. The majority of patients either self-obtained their device or received the device from others (spouses, neighbors, or family members). However, visiting a doctor on a regular basis may not be protective against having an ill-fitting cane. Many physicians may not be knowledgeable about ambulatory devices, and hence, fail to recommend the use of a cane and/or may not inquire about cane use by older individuals or evaluate the utilization and condition of canes. In a community survey of cane use by older persons receiving frequent medical attention (i.e., visiting their physician at least three times annually), Tideiksaar (1994) found that 60% of the people had a cane that was either unsuited, in poor repair, or was used improperly. The majority of ill-fitting canes were self-obtained without the knowledge of the physician. Moreover, in those persons with faulty canes or canes used improperly, most individuals reported that their doctor never inquired about or evaluated the condition and use of their cane.

Additionally, falls have been identified as a common problem among persons using walkers (Joyce & Kirby, 1991; Mulley, 1990, 1994). Most falls are thought to occur during periods when patients are maximally dependent on their walker for balance support (Pardo, Deathe, & Winter, 1993). Although there is a lack of epidemiological data to support this belief or other causes of walker-related falls, clinical experience suggests a number of possibilities. First, aside from obvious problems caused by devices that are in ill repair (e.g., with loose hardware and wheels, poor braking systems, worn rubber tips), some older persons may use their walkers dangerously, thereby increasing the risk of falls. This problem is especially evident in those individuals with cognitive impairments.

PW is a 78-year-old woman with a balance impairment, mild dementia, and fear of falling. The patient insisted on holding her rolling walker in front of her, up in the air and off the ground, and never placed the device down for support when walking. This pattern of ambulation in part contributed to several of her falls. The device was taken away, but led to a worsening of her balance, and was subsequently returned. It was felt that the patient used her walker both as a visual presence of support (to decrease her fear of falling), and as a countering device in order to maintain stability (avoiding a posterior loss of balance).

MJ is an 82-year-old man with cerebellar ataxia and vascular dementia. When using his rolling walker, he would at times walk faster than the walker travelled, getting his feet caught in the legs and tripping.

EG is an 84-year-old woman with Alzheimer's Disease and balance loss, who uses a wheeled walker to support her ambulation at home. However, rather than using the walker in the conventional manner, she holds onto and pushes the walker in the opposite direction. This activity has led to several falls.

Hazardous environmental conditions, such as persons getting their walker legs caught in thick carpets, upended carpets and tiles, and low-lying objects can lead to balance loss and fall risk. Individuals with visual impairments may be particularly at risk.

Walkers may also not be suited for the user; that is, the device is positioned at the wrong height. Walker frames that are positioned too high can lead to arm and shoulder discomfort and decreased effectiveness (through inadequate weight transmission through the upper extremities). As well, walkers that are set too high can lead to postures with excessive posterior lean, and the risk of balance loss. Conversely, walkers that are set too low can contribute to kyphotic postures, as the individual needs to bend over in order to use the device properly, and as a result, runs the risk of toppling forward over the horizontal bar when walking. Finally, the type of walker used may not be appropriate to adequately support the person's mobility. For example, pickup walkers lead to a decreased base of support when lifted, thereby threatening an individual's stability.

MJ is an 82-year-old man with Parkinson's Disease and poor balance. Despite the use of a pickup walker, the patient continued to complain of balance loss. Upon observing the patient's ambulation, everytime the walker was advanced forward, he experienced a loss of balance. Instead, he was provided with a rolling wheeled walker, which provided a constant base of support, and markedly improved his gait and balance.

In addition, certain features of the walker, such as its weight, wheel or leg tip design, and handgrips may lead to problems. For example, walking frames that are too heavy for the individual to pick up and move forward adequately may interfere with safe mobility.

OW is a 78-year-old woman with arthritis and gait abnormalities. She was dependent upon a pickup walker for ambulation. However, when walking distances, she found the walker a burden to continuously lift up and move forward. As a result, she tended to push the walker along the ground. However, whenever she encountered an uneven ground surface, the walker tipped forward, causing her to fall.

At other times, the walker might be too light in weight, and as a result, may fail to provide adequate balance support. Wheeled walkers can cause problems as well. When encountering obstacles such as thick carpets, door thresholds, and curbs, wheeled walkers may have to be lifted, which can lead to a loss of balance support and fall risk. Two-wheeled walkers equipped with furniture glides or rubber tips on the rear legs may be appropriate for use on smooth linoleum floors, but the rear legs can easily get caught on ground surface irregularities. Similarly, rolling walkers with fixed (nonpivoting) wheels are sometimes difficult to maneuver along thick carpet surfaces, especially when turning. On the other hand, rolling walkers equipped with pivoting wheels, depending on the design of the wheels and composition of ground surface, behave in similar fashion to that of shopping cart wheels; the wheels, rather than the person, control both the direction and safety of travel. Some of the newer three- and four-wheeled walkers on the market are easier to maneuver, particularly over minor ground surface elevations. However, some three-wheeled walkers tend to topple over when turned briskly. Wheeled walkers that are not furnished with brakes or which have braking systems that are difficult for the person to use can easily roll away while walking. Glide walkers equipped with metal tips on the legs tend over time to accumulate a buildup of floor wax, and as a result, can lead to walker hesitation when attempting to advance the device, and thus to the risk of falls. Some patients accommodate to this hesitation by giving their walker an extra push while ambulating. Any correction of the problem, without the person's knowledge, may lead to the walker sliding away unexpectedly and heighten the risk of falls. Also, walker handgrips may interfere with the use of walkers. Reid and Ashby (1982) reported that walkers furnished with hard plastic handgrips may press on the hypothenar eminences, causing ulnar nerve palsies. In other instances, handgrips may not provide sufficient support. In one survey, one in five persons using a walker complained of handgrips that slipped while in use (London Borough of Hillingdon, 1976).

Lastly, there are several other problems that may prohibit the use of walkers and increase fall risk. For example, walkers may not easily fit the person's environmental space (for example, small bathrooms, narrow doorways and hallways), and as a result, the device becomes both difficult and risky to use. In all instances, the walker will generally be abandoned by the older person. As an alternative, persons often attempt to ambulate about by grabbing and holding onto objects in the environment such as walls and furnishings (tables, chairs, etc.) for support. However, this behavior may not always provide the support required to avoid a fall. As well, some older persons and health professionals may perceive certain devices, such as wheeled walkers, to be dangerous. Consequently, older persons may shy away from using rolling walkers, and health professionals may be reluctant to prescribe the devices, even if such use is clinically indicated.

Wheelchairs

Many falls occurring in hospitals and nursing homes involve the use of wheelchairs (Gurwitz et al., 1994; Mion, Frengley, Jakovcic, & Marino, 1989; Vlahov, Myers, & Al-Ibrahim, 1990). It is estimated that three-quarters of wheelchair accidents result from falls (Calder & Kirby, 1990). The incidence of wheelchair-related falls increases with advancing age (Calder & Kirby, 1990; Mion et al., 1989). Wheelchair falls may also be common among community-dwelling persons. Dudley, Cotter, and Mulley (1992), in a community survey of wheelchair users in the United Kingdom, found that 18% had previous accident, with the majority of the accidents due to falls. Kirby, Ackroyd-Stolarz, Brown, Kirkland, and MacLeod (1994), in a survey of noninstitutionalized wheelchair users living in Nova Scotia, found that up to 60% of respondents in the 61–80 year age group reported tips (that is, the chair tipped over partially or fully) or falls from wheelchairs. Very few of the respondents were over 80 years of age. This may represent a decline in wheelchair accidents with advancing age, or else, methodological problems such as poor subject response and recall or inadequate selection of the target population. Aside from these reports, there is a general lack of epidemiologic data on wheelchair-related falls in the community-dwelling older population.

The factors responsible for wheelchair-related falls are for the most part identical in both the institutional and community setting. The design of wheelchairs (i.e., hand brakes, the position of footplates) and certain host characteristics (e.g., cognitive impairment, decreased transfer capacity) contribute to the majority of wheelchair falls. Young, Belfield, Mascie-Taylor, and Mulley (1985) conducted a survey of 123 hospital wheelchairs and found that only 23% were safe and in working order. Nearly two-thirds of the wheelchairs had defective handbrakes, and in a third of the chairs the footrests were faulty. Also, armrests were either dangerous or missing. In many instances, faulty wheelchairs were reported to be responsible for accidents.

Aside from defective wheelchairs, many falls involve host-related activities. Most wheelchair falls take place during transfer activities (Dudley et al., 1992; Vlahov et al., 1990). Some persons may not remember or be able to perform safe transfer (i.e., locking wheel brakes or clearing the footplates with their lower extremities when exiting the chair). As a consequence, the wheelchair may roll away during transfers, or the person may trip over the chair's footplates or can actually stand on the footplates, causing the chair to tip over. Some wheelchair falls are due to a lack of or inappropriate placement of mechanical restraints used to keep persons in their chairs (Dimant, 1985). In addition, wheelchair falls sometimes occur when patients are excessively reaching for objects or leaning too far forward in their chairs (for example, when picking up objects from the ground), leading to loss of stability and balance (Vlahov et al., 1990). As a consequence, individuals either fall out of their wheelchair, or the chair itself can actually tip over. Some agitated individuals confined to wheelchairs may excessively rock their chairs to the point of tipping the wheelchair over. Dudley et al. (1992) found that several falls in community-dwelling persons occurred during either self- or attendant propulsion activities; individuals fell in a forwards direction out of their chair, or else falls occurred while traveling over holes or cracks in the pavement, curbs, steps, and ramps. As well, several studies have found that persons with right-hemispheric stroke are at great risk for multiple wheelchair-related accidents (Webster et al., 1989). Severe attentional deficits such as hemispatial neglect to left space, which are associated with right-sided strokes, may play a role in these wheelchair accidents; the person may not be able to see braking systems or the position of footplates. Perry et al. (1994), in a nursing home study that examined the risk factors for falling in a group of intact older wheelchair-dependent individuals, found that modest decreases in sitting balance were more common in fallers than non-fallers. Moreover, intact sitting balance was found to be significantly protective against wheelchair-related falls.

Footwear

Improper footwear can alter gait and balance and has been cited as a contributory factor in falls (Finlay, 1986; Tinetti & Speechley, 1989). Several mechanisms are likely. First of all, wearing high heels leads to greater instability (Gabell, Simons, & Nayak, 1985). High-heeled shoes narrow both the standing and walking bases of support, displace the body's COG anteriorly beyond the BOS, and as a result, place individuals in a forward leaning posture. These changes by themselves may lead to precarious balance and increase the risk of falls. In addition, high-heeled shoes can prohibit effective gait. Wearing high heels limits ankle plantar flexion, which in turn, alters the angle of the foot with respect to the ground surface throughout the gait cycle. As a consequence, persons wearing these shoes tend to exhibit shorter stride lengths and decreased walking speed. Also, during the swing phase of gait, less hip and knee flexion occurs, which leads to a decrease in ground clearance of the foot. Finally, high heels can easily get caught in thick pile carpets and underneath overhanging step edges while ascending stairs. The likelihood of falls due to wearing high heels may diminish with increasing age. White and Mulley (1989), interviewed a group of persons aged 80 and older, and found that none of the women wore shoes with heels greater than 5 cm in height. It is not clear, however, whether these women had always worn low heels, or had switched from high to low heels for comfort or safety reasons. The latter may not always be a wise choice. Gabell and colleagues (1985) noted that a change to low heels after a lifetime of wearing high heels may increase instability.

Regardless, the appearance of gait and balance problems as a result of wearing high-heeled shoes is highly dependent upon the height of the heel; that is, as the height of the heel increases, the likelihood of any problems increases. However, other factors need to be considered as well. For example, Briggs et al. (1989) examined the effect of footwear (heel height, width, and sole thickness) on static standing balance in a group of noninstitutionalized older women. They found no significant differences in balance with shoes on and shoes off. The subjects in this study were essentially healthy persons. The relationship between high-heeled footwear and fall risk may be greater in those persons with underlying pathological conditions affecting their gait and balance.

Improperly fitting shoes can also negatively affect gait patterns. Shoes that are too narrow in width can compress the forefoot and lead to foot pain when walking. Shoes with a small toe box can constrict the normal triangular shape of the toes and, with time, result in hammer toes and bunions. This becomes more of a problem as the shoe heel height increases (Snow, Williams, & Holmes, 1992). Similarly, loose footwear can be implicated as a cause of gait problems. In an effort to keep large-sized shoes from falling off, persons tend to assume a shuffling type of gait, which can lead to tripping. Similar problems can occur with slippers that are not equipped with adequate heel fastenings (White & Mulley, 1989). Sometimes older individuals with foot problems out of necessity wear larger sized shoes that can result in falls.

EL is a 93-year-old woman who was admitted to the hospital following a
fall. She had poor vision and arthritis that led to decreased manual dex-
terity, and as a result, experienced difficulty cutting her toenails. As a
result, she eventually developed "ram's horn" toenails and started to
wear shoes much larger in size to accommodate her elongated nails. This
change in footwear led to a shuffling gait, and unfortunately caused her to
trip over a telephone cord and fall.

Wearing properly fitting footwear has been found to help achieve
safe stairway ambulation (Simoneau et al., 1991). Excessively loose
footwear may cause the heel to drop off the step while ascending
stairs, and precipitate a fall, especially in those older persons with
decreased foot clearance. Older women in particular may be at risk.
White and Mulley (1989) interviewed 96 community-residing persons
who were over the age of 80, and found that whereas 80% of the men
wore lace-up shoes, half the women preferred to wear slip on footwear.
This variety of footwear can easily slip off, as few may have adequate
heel fastenings. However, there is little data on the extent to which
older persons wear improperly fitting shoes. Tideiksaar (1995), in a
study of older persons referred to a community-based falls clinic, found
that 80% of the individuals wore properly fitting footwear. In the remaining 20% of persons, their footwear was ill-fitting due to foot disorders.
In those persons with leg edema, properly fitting footwear can be an
exceedingly difficult problem. Some older persons with edematous feet
will continue to wear their customary footwear, which are now too
small for their feet, and as a result, they may have gait abnormalities.
Other persons will resort to wearing larger shoes to compensate for the
swelling. In these individuals, however, when their leg edema decreases,
they need to replace their footwear with smaller shoes. Those individuals who continue to wear large-sized footwear, may start to shuffle and
fall, as their shoes become too large for their feet. This, in particular,
can be a common problem following periods of prolonged recumbency.
For instance, older persons with edematous lower extremities are
often told to keep their legs elevated to reduce dependent edema, but
rarely comply with these recommendations. However, when persons
take to bed for several days, and maintain their legs in an elevated
position, the edema quickly subsides. This phenomenon can be seen in
many older persons following a duration of acute hospitalization and
bed rest. Upon discharge back home, several persons develop falls
simply because of improperly fitting footwear; that is, their shoe size is
too large for their feet.

Leather-soled shoes can promote slipping, as do socks worn by themselves. This becomes especially problematic during transfers from beds, chairs, or toilets, etc. Successful transfers, in part, are dependent upon an individual being able to maintain their footing or keeping the pivot foot planted on the ground. Walking upon low slip-resistant flooring (i.e., linoleum, ceramic tiles) with nonresistant soles can lead to slipping. Consequently, wearing rubber or crepe-soled footwear is often recommended. However, slip-resistant soles can sometimes stick to linoleum or carpeted floor surfaces. This becomes problematic in those individuals with decreased steppage height, who tend to exhibit shuffling gaits. Such sticking can halt the gait precipitously, causing forward balance loss and falls, particularly in those persons with decreased foot-ground clearance. Thick-soled footwear (i.e., running shoes, sneakers), while it is comfortable to wear, may be overly absorptive and decrease the proprioceptive feedback derived from striking the foot on the ground when walking, thus increasing the risk of balance loss. Orthopedic footwear (wider and extra-depth shoes) can lead to gait instability, due to its heaviness. And lastly, regardless of the type of footwear and sole surface, the condition of ground surfaces greatly influences fall risk. For example, the presence of certain ground surface contaminants, such as dirt, sand, grease, water, and icy conditions, or unstable surfaces (for example, pebbles, gravel, waxed floors, sliding rugs) can lead to slipping and balance displacements, even when wearing shoes furnished with slip-resistant soles.

SITUATIONAL FACTORS

In addition to these extrinsic factors, there are a number of situational factors such as the length of stay, time of falls, and staff characteristics that may be causally related to falls.

Length of Stay

The majority of falls among older persons in hospitals and nursing homes have been found to occur either during the first week of institutional stay (Mion et al., 1989; Rodgers, 1994), or shortly thereafter (Janken et al., 1986; Mayo et al., 1989; Svensson, Rundgren, Larsson, & Landahl, 1992). For example, one nursing home study reported that up to one-third of falls occurred within the first 45 days of admission (Gray-Micelli, Waxman, Cavalieri, & Lage, 1994). Another study found that 61% of resident falls in the nursing home occurred during the first year of residence (Tinetti, 1987). Vlahov and co-workers (1990) found that 82% of falls occurring in a rehabilitation hospital occurred during the first 60 days of admission. In a hospital-based study, Swartzbeck and Milligan (1982) found that 41% of patients fell during the first week of stay.

In the hospital setting, several researchers have found that the number of first-time falls and total falls occurring decline over the length of stay (Mion et al., 1989). However, Catchen (1983) reported a positive correlation between length of hospital stay and increased falls. Other studies have shown that a large segment of older patients fall near the end of their hospitalization (DeVincenzo & Watkins, 1987). Within the nursing home setting, there is a general lack of information about fall occurrences with respect to prolonged periods of stay.

Several possible explanations exist for an association between falls and length of institutional stay. During the first few days of hospitalization, older patients may be at great risk due to the presence of acute illness (i.e., altered homeostasis). This may be a factor in U.S. long-term care facilities as well. While most older persons discharged from the hospital to the nursing home are considered to be medically stable, this situation may have changed somewhat since the inception of hospital capitation systems (i.e., Diagnostic-Related Groupings). In an effort by hospitals to discharge patients as early as possible, some persons continue to be at high risk for falls, as they are still recovering from their acute illness. As well, both older hospital and nursing home patients may be unfamiliar with their surrounding environment during the early phase of institutionalization, and as a consequence, are at greater fall risk. This may especially be a problem in those individuals exhibiting cognitive and mobility problems. Conversely, the association between falls and increased length of stay is presumably due to a greater chance of iatrogenic factors contributing to fall risk (i.e., complications arising from prolonged bed/chair rest). Additionally, hospital patients nearing the end of their stay may be falsely perceived by staff to be capable of independent mobility, and as a result, be at risk for falls. Sometimes, older patients are likely to test their mobility, against the better judgement of staff, and place themselves at fall risk. In nursing homes, even residents with functional limitations are, after admission, allowed freedom of movement, partly due to a reluctance to restrain individuals, which may account for some falls. A decline in falls over time may reflect that patients are either supervised during their daily activities, or else are restrained. Some other possibilities may be that with increased time patients become medically stable, and as a result, more mobile; or that patients become familiar with their living environment.

Time of Fall

In the community setting, most falls take place during the daylight hours (DeVito et al., 1988; Schelp & Svanstrom, 1986). Campbell, Borrie, et al. (1990) found that 81% of falls occurred during the daytime and early evening hours, with only 19% of the events taking place between the hours of 9 p.m. and 7 a.m. Similarly, Downton and Andrews (1991) found that most falls occurred during the day, between 6 a.m. and 6 p.m. The majority of falls have been found to occur during periods of maximum activity (Campbell, Borrie, et al., 1990; Downton & Andrews, 1991; Nevitt et al., 1989; Tinetti et al., 1988), such as getting up from chairs and beds, walking about, using the bathroom (both toileting and bathing), and climbing stairs. Lucht (1971) found that falls occur more often on weekends as opposed to weekdays. One possible explanation for this finding is that older persons may spend more time at home on weekends, and hence, have an increased exposure to environmental hazards. However, most community-based studies have not examined the relationship between days of the week and falls.

Within the hospital and nursing home, the time of day when most falls take place varies. Studies have reported an increase in falls during the day shift (7 a.m. to 3 p.m.) (Daley & Goldman, 1987; Mayo et al., 1989; Tack, Ulrich, & Kehr, 1987); evening shift (3 p.m. to 11 p.m.) (Colling & Park, 1983; Walshe & Rosen, 1979; Feist, 1978), and night shift (11 p.m. to 7 a.m.) (Heslin, Towers, Leckie, & Thornton-Lawrence, 1992). More than likely, these different time periods reflect when patients are most active, as the overwhelming number of falls have been reported to occur during maximal patient activity (Gurwitz et al., 1994; Mayo et al., 1989). Common activities include bedroom- and bathroom-related tasks such as getting out of beds and chairs, traveling to the bathroom, and toileting. Falls are generally distributed evenly over the days of the week, although Feist (1978) found a greater prevalence of falls occurring during the weekend, due to decreased staff available.

Staff Characteristics

Within the hospital and nursing home setting, staffing patterns—the number of nurses and aides available on any one shift—may also influence fall occurrence. Researchers have found an inverse correlation between falls and the number of staff available; an increase in falls when staff are decreased (Gross, Shimamoto, Rose, & Frank, 1990), presumably because of a lack of nursing supervision (Rubenstein et al., 1994). Some have found a low frequency of falls when staff levels are high (Clark, 1985; Louis, 1983), while others have reported an increase in falls with high staff levels (Tutuarima, deHann, & Limburg, 1993). Finally, some find no relationship between staff levels and falls (Daley & Goldman, 1987; Morse et al., 1987; Puetz, 1988). The reason for these differences between staff levels and falls is not entirely clear. It may not strictly relate to availability (that is, staff:patient ratios), but rather to staff attitudes (Harris, 1989) and competence levels (Tutuarima, deHann, & Limburg, 1993) toward assisting patients at fall risk, and applying safety procedures. That is, positive staff attitudes and increased knowledge with respect to caring for older patients at risk may decrease the frequency of falls, whereas negative attitudes and poor knowledge may lead to acts of omission (e.g., failure to assess for risk and implement preventive strategies), and thus, to increased falls. Another factor related to nursing care includes the distance from the nursing station to patient rooms (Tideiksaar, 1989, 1993b). If patient bedrooms are located a considerable distance from the nursing station, a number of time-consuming trips by the staff may be required to assist patients at fall risk, with sometimes negative outcomes.

> JW is an 82-year-old woman who was admitted to the hospital because of a recent fall. As the patient was at fall risk, she was instructed to call the nurse whenever she needed to leave her bed. Unfortunately, the patient was placed in the furthest bedroom available. As a result, the nurses were not always available to respond to her calls for assistance. Once, the patient couldn't wait any longer to toilet, attempted to exit her bed, and fell to the floor. This problem was solved by switching patient rooms and placing the patient next to the nursing station.

Within the community setting, the availability of caregivers (spouses, family members, and home attendants) may influence the frequency of falls as well. Campbell and co-workers (1981) found that older-aged females who lived alone were at increased risk of falling and sustaining a serious fall-related injury as compared to all others. Several other researchers have observed higher rates of falls among community-dwelling individuals who were socially isolated (that is, divorced, widowed, or single) (Lucht, 1971). Presumably, in these individuals, the lack of caregiver assistance with mobility tasks contributed to falls. In other community-based studies, however, neither marital status nor the individual's living arrangements were related to falling (Perry, 1982; Prudham & Evans, 1981). Whether these individuals received formal caregiver services or assistance from friends and neighbors, thereby decreasing their risk of falls, is not entirely clear. Notwithstanding the availability of support services, the attitudes of caregivers, whether they are positive or negative, may be of equal or greater importance in reducing or increasing fall risk. While remarkably little research has focused on this relationship, the following case examples help to illustrate the problem.

QG is an 80-year-old woman who exhibited poor toilet and bathtub transfers, and as a result, required bathroom aids. However, her husband refused to have the aids installed, because they detracted from the aesthetic appearance of the bathroom. As a consequence, the patient continued to experience difficulty with her bathroom mobility, and eventually fell while entering the tub, suffering a hip fracture.

FB is a 76-year-old woman with poor mobility, who lived alone, and required 12-hour caregiver support. However, her attendant was frequently late in arriving in the morning. On one occasion, the patient needed to go to the bathroom, attempted to toilet independently, and experienced a fall. Subsequently, the patient developed a fear of falling, and wore urinary diapers when the aide was not available. This home attendant was replaced with one who was more attentive to the patient's mobility needs.

JM is a 78-year-old male who lived alone and experienced multiple falls. He requested a falls evaluation, but required the help of his daughter to bring him to the clinic. However, his daughter canceled three scheduled appointments, always finding an excuse why she was unavailable to bring her father to the clinic. As an alternative, a home visit was arranged. Following this visit, a number of relatively simple environmental modifications were recommended that required the help of his daughter to accomplish. However, once again, his daughter procrastinated, and didn't implement the recommended modifications. After several telephone calls and much persuasion, his daughter eventually instituted the recommendations. As a result, the patient's mobility improved and he stopped falling.

CONSIDERING FALL ETIOLOGY

Earlier investigations have attempted to ascribe the etiology of falls to a single recognizable cause, attributing the fall either to an acute or chronic medical episode or "accidental" environmental encounter that may have resulted in a trip or slip. For example, Sheldon (1960), in a community survey of falls, divided the causes of falling into two categories: accidental (on stairs, slipping, falling over objects, etc.), and medical (drop attacks, vertigo, central nervous system disorders, vertebrobasilar insufficiency, postural hypotension, and weakness in the legs).

More recently, Lach and colleagues (1991) developed a comprehensive fall classification system for community-dwelling older persons that was intended to separate out the different causes of falls and identify multiple contributors to falling. The fall classification system is divided into four major categories with operational definitions for each. The first category encompasses extrinsic or environmental falls including slips, trips, or externally induced displacements. The second category includes intrinsic falls, such as mobility or balance disorders, misperceiving the environment, or loss of consciousness. Category three includes falls in which the person was not in a bipedal stance, such as a fall from a bed or chair. The fourth category includes falls that can not be identified or described by either the person or collateral source. Based on an examination of 366 falls occurring in 258 community-dwelling older persons, the authors were able to reliably classify falls: 55% of falls were related to extrinsic factors, 39% ascribed to intrinsic factors, 8% were nonbipedal, and the remaining were unclassified. Luukinen et al. (1994), in a community-based study of Finnish people 70 years and older, compared their results with the classification developed by Lach et al. (1991) and found a similar distribution between intrinsic and extrinsic factors as a cause of falls.

However, to view the etiology of falls as separate or distinct intrinsic and extrinsic events, and to assign cause according to whether intrinsic or environmental factors are involved, is somewhat artificial and potentially dangerous. For instance, attempting to identify a single medical diagnosis or environmental hazard as the culprit may lead to premature abandonment of a broader assessment. The following cases serve as an illustration.

MM is an 83-year-old nursing home resident. One night she was found by the nursing staff sitting on the floor next to her bed, after attempting to get out of bed. The nursing staff ascribed the fall to an elevated bed height and accordingly lowered the bed height. MM, however, continued to experience several more bed falls. When the resident's bed mobility was observed, she repeatedly slipped on the linoleum floor while getting up, even though the floor surface was not slippery. As a result, the resident lost her balance, which caused her to fall back onto the bed. She was wearing ankle stockings at the time—a usual bedtime habit to keep her feet warm—which caused her foot to slip on the floor, and on subsequent examination, MM was found to have Parkinson's Disease that caused her to lose her balance after slipping. Treatment of both conditions, which consisted of providing MM with non-slip socks and anti-Parkinson's medications, resulted in improved bed mobility and no further falling episodes.

CD is an 80-year-old man with Parkinson's Disease and mild left-sided hemiparesis secondary to a cerebrovascular accident. He had recently experienced two falls at home while attempting to get up from his kitchen chair. These events were attributed to the stroke and insufficient treatment of his Parkinson's Disease. As a result, his anti-Parkinson's medications were readjusted, although this was somewhat difficult, as CD experienced a few minor adverse medication effects in the process. Shortly after his medications were regulated, however, he experienced another fall under similar circumstances. Subsequently, a home visit was arranged to evaluate CD's mobility. Several problems were observed with the patient's seated transfers. When getting up from his kitchen chair he required the use of the armrests, but was able only to use his right arm for assistance, due to his residual hemiparesis; hence, the lightweight chair became unstable and both the chair and patient tipped precariously to the right side. Also, in order to rise from the chair, CD would rock back and forth several times to gain the required force to stand; however, as a result, the chair tipped forward, causing him to lose his balance. Thus, it was hypothesized that CD's falls were more due to a problem with his kitchen chairs than to his stroke and Parkinson's Disease. The patient was provided with seating to accommodate his mobility problems, and since his threshold for adverse medication effects was low, the anti-Parkinson's medications were decreased shortly afterwards without incident.

Therefore, the classification of falls into either intrinsic or extrinsic groupings, as presented in this chapter, is probably more useful as an educational model, intended to illustrate the variety of causative factors involved; it may not be very practical clinically, given the complex nature of falls. Moreover, as multiple intrinsic, activity-related, and environmental factors are mentioned as contributing to most falls, several investigators (Rubenstein et al., 1988; Tinetti et al., 1988) have called into question the usefulness of simple categorization, particularly with respect to designing interventions intended to decrease fall frequency.

Clearly, the etiology of falls in older people may be due to intrinsic problems, such as the onset of an acute disease(s) (i.e., syncope, arrhythmias, infections) or a chronic disease(s) affecting gait and balance, or to extrinsic factor(s) (i.e., environmental hazard, unsuitable footwear, inappropriate cane/walker) occurring in isolation. As one advances in age, the causative factors leading to falls differ somewhat between these two sets of interactions. In the "young" old—those persons younger than 75 years of age who are relatively healthy—falls are more likely to be the consequence of "normal" aging changes and their interaction with unfavorable environmental conditions. For instance, a person with poor visual acuity may be walking outdoors in the early evening during twilight, and trip over an uneven walkway surface that was not easily visualized. However, in those persons 75 years and older, the accumulated effects of multiple medical conditions, whether in isolation or in combination with environmental conditions interfering with safe mobility, are likely to be more important as the cause of falling. Perry (1982), in a community-based study, reported that environmental factors, such as stairs and obstacles on the floor, were important causes of falls in younger, healthier older persons, whereas pathological conditions (dizziness, syncope, cardiac and neurologic disease, and functional disability) were more important factors in very old, frail persons. Morfitt (1983), in a study of older persons attending an Accident and Emergency Department, found the cause of falls to vary with age; trips and slips due to environmental hazards were more important in the 65–74 age group, while intrinsic causes (illness and disability) assumed greater importance in those over the age of 75. Campbell et al. (1981) distinguished between "pattern" or recurrent falls (i.e., those caused primarily by disorders in postural stability or balance) and "occasional" falls (i.e., those caused by extrinsic influences). Pattern falls were described as being more common among persons aged 80 and older who had more functional disabilities and impairments in mobility, whereas occasional falls occurred more often in the young old who are generally in better health. Isaacs (1978) described a topological model to catalog falls, which is based on the transaction that is occurring with the fall. The six categories consist of:

1. imposed (falls occurring as a result of contact with a major extrinsic hazard);
2. judgmental error (falls that might occur during hurried activities);
3. perceptual mistakes (falls occurring as a result of contact with an object that could have been avoided);
4. postural shifts (falls occurring as a result of movement from different body positions with no extrinsic hazard);
5. walking (falls occurring during normal, unhurried walking, with no extrinsic hazard); and
6. standing (falls occurring while standing unaided).

Isaacs suggested that as internal body displacements increase, less extrinsic influences are needed for a fall to occur, and that while people of any age may fall as a result of extrinsic factors, older persons of advanced age are more likely to fall as a consequence of intrinsic factors (i.e., in the absence of extrinsic factors). Similar age differences in the causation of falls (intrinsic vs. extrinsic) between the young and old-old have been reported by others (Brockelhurst et al., 1978; Overstall et al., 1977). According to Gibson (1987, p. 6), however, "In essence, such categories are efforts to discriminate between two ends of a continuum in which intrinsic and extrinsic play greater and lesser roles in causing falls by older people" . . . "They clearly are not intended to describe the wide range of falls experienced . . ., in which both intrinsic and extrinsic factors usually interact."

As we are now beginning to understand, most falls are not simply the result of either an intrinsic or extrinsic factor acting alone, regardless of the age of the faller, but are complex events, often due to a combination of both factors. The initiating event may involve an intrinsic factor such as poor vision and lower extremity dysfunction (muscle weakness, unstable joints); host-related activity engaged in at the time, such as transferring or stepping in the bathtub; and an extrinsic factor, such as a wet bathtub floor that is unexpected or unperceived. Under these circumstances the fall is likely to be due to the person's balance-displacing activity (that is, the body is displaced beyond its base of support), combined with the failure to detect the wet ground surface because of poor vision and, because of lower extremity dysfunction, the inability of the body to initiate corrective postural strategies in time to avoid a fall. As a consequence, the etiology of falls in older people should always be viewed as an interaction between the person (intrinsic factors) and environment (extrinsic factors).

With an understanding of the various age-related and pathological causes of falls, and situational factors influencing fall causation, the next step is to explore those factors that place older people at risk for falls and fall-related injury. These are discussed in the following chapter.

CHAPTER 4

Fall and Injury Risk

INTRODUCTION

Numerous factors—both intrinsic and extrinsic—can cause falls in older people and lead to injury. These have been fully detailed in Chapter 3. The exact cause of a fall or the conditions responsible for injury, however, is frequently difficult to determine, particularly in those older individuals who have multiple medical problems and/or are subject to extrinsic factors that may further complicate their conditions. Current research efforts have attempted to identify those factors that occur most often in association with falls and injury or that represent the greatest risk. To determine this, groups of fallers are compared with non-fallers to see what adverse factors (e.g., disease condition, drug exposures) might contribute to the risk of falls or fall injuries. Studies, in fact, have isolated a number of host-related and extrinsic risk factors that are associated with falls and fall-related injury among both the community-dwelling and institutionalized older population.

FALL RISK FACTORS

First of all, numerous researchers have found a past history of falls and recurrent falls to be strongly related to the risk of further falls (Campbell, Borrie, & Spears, 1989; Cwikel, 1992; Janken, Reynolds, & Sweich, 1986; Myers, Baker, VanNatta, Abbey, & Robinson, 1991; Nevitt, Cummings, Kidd, & Black, 1989; O'Loughlin, Robitaille, Boirin, & Suissa, 1993;

Ryynanen, Kivela, Honkanen, & Laippala, 1992a; Tinetti, Speechley, & Ginter, 1988). As well, there is general agreement in the literature that old age (particularly over 80 years) is a risk factor for falling (Blake et al., 1988; Myers et al., 1991; Nevitt et al., 1989; Ryynanen, Kivela, Honkanen, Laippala, & Saano, 1993; Tinetti et al., 1988). This risk may not depend so much on old age in itself as it might on the increasing illness and frailty that accompanies aging. It has also been suggested that older women are at greater fall risk than older men (Campbell, Borrie, et al., 1990; Sorock & Shimkin, 1988). These findings are inconsistent, as others have not reported an association between gender and falls (Svensson, Rundgren, & Landahl, 1992). However, since neither age nor gender are modifiable, identifying those individual intrinsic risk factors that are potentially modifiable may of greater benefit, especially in the design of preventive efforts. Towards this end, studies have begun to distinguish several physical, cognitive, and pharmacologic risk factors.

PHYSICAL RISK FACTORS

Numerous studies have shown that mobility impairment or reduced functional capacity is strongly associated with a greater risk of falling (Cwikel, 1992; Lipsitz, Johsson, Kelley, & Koestner, 1991; Lord , Caplan, & Ward, 1993; Mayo, Korner-Bitensky, Becker, & Georges, 1989; Nevitt et al., 1989; Robbins et al., 1989; Ryynanen, 1994; Tinetti et al., 1988). Harris and Kovar (1991) extracted data from the 1984 National Health Interview Survey Supplement on Aging, and found that those persons aged 75 to 84 years who required help with their activities of daily living were 14 times more likely to report two or more falls than were persons without limitations. Moreover, those persons who had limitations in walking and balance were 10 times more likely to report multiple falling episodes than were similarly aged persons without limitations.

As normal gait and balance are dependent upon the proper function of sensory and neuromuscular systems (including proprioception, visual input, musculoskeletal strength, and flexibility; see Chapter 3), it is reasonable to conclude that any compromised function of these systems would contribute to poor mobility and a greater risk of falls. A number of specific intrinsic risk factors for falls, in fact, have been found. One of the strongest is lower extremity dysfunction. The most commonly reported medical conditions shown to affect lower extremity function and increase fall risk include arthritis (Blake et al., 1988; Buchner & Larson, 1987; Granek et al., 1987; Myers et al., 1991; Robbins et al., 1989; Tinetti et al., 1988), foot impairment (Blake et al., 1988; Nevitt et al., 1989;

Tinetti et al., 1988), stroke or hemiplegia (Campbell et al., 1989; Mayo et al., 1989; Nevitt et al., 1989; Yasumura et al., 1994), peripheral neuropathy (Richardson, Ching, & Hurvitz, 1992), and Parkinson's disease (Campbell et al., 1989; Granek et al., 1987; Koller, Glatt, Vetere-Overfield, & Hassanein, 1989; Nevitt et al., 1989). In addition, several neuromuscular factors relevant to gait and balance have been shown to increase fall risk. These include decreased lower extremity strength (hip, knee, and ankle weakness) and sensory impairment (Campbell et al., 1989; Gehlsen & Whaley, 1990; Nevitt et al., 1989; Robbins et al., 1989; Sorock & Labiner, 1992; Tinetti, 1986; Tinetti et al., 1986; Whipple, Wolfson, & Amerman, 1987), poor back flexibility (Tinetti et al., 1986), impaired knee and plantar reflexes (Nevitt et al., 1989), and poor vision (e.g., decreased visual acuity, depth perception) (Campbell et al., 1989; Jantti, Pyykko, & Hervonen, 1993; Lord et al., 1993; Lord, Clark, & Webster, 1991; Nevitt et al., 1989; Robbins et al., 1989; Tinetti et al., 1988; Yasumura et al., 1994).

Weak leg muscles, unstable or painful joints, and sensory dysfunction can impair ambulation, postural stability, and the ability to maintain safe transfer activities. Moreover, in the event of balance loss, postural recovery becomes more difficult as the speed and reliability of appropriate motor responses to correct balance displacements declines. In fact, several studies have found that compared with non-fallers, fallers exhibit more walking difficulties (Robbins et al., 1989), reduced walking speed (Campbell et al., 1989; McClaran, Forette, Hervy, & Bouchacourt, 1991; Nevitt et al., 1989), increased postural sway (Campbell et al., 1989; Maki, Holliday, & Topper, 1994; Nevitt et al., 1989; Ring, Nayak, & Isaacs, 1988), poor dynamic balance (Nevitt et al., 1989; Ring et al., 1988; Robbins et al., 1989; Tinetti et al., 1988), impaired tandem gait, inability to balance on one leg (Buchner & Larson, 1987; Nevitt et al., 1989; Tinetti et al., 1988), and difficulty arising from seated positions, such as getting up from a chair (Campbell et al., 1989; Campbell, Spears, & Borrie, 1990; Lipsitz et al., 1991; Nevitt et al., 1989; Tinetti, 1986; Tinetti et al., 1988). In comparing older persons with multiple falls (two or more falls) to individuals with either no falls or only one fall, Lord et al. (1991) found that reduced vision, decreased peripheral sensation, slower reaction times, and decreased ankle dorsiflexion and quadriceps strength were associated with a greater risk of falls.

A number of other medical conditions have been associated with a greater risk of falling. These consist of urinary dysfunction (i.e., incontinence, nocturia) (Barker & Mitteness, 1988; Campbell et al., 1989; Janken & Reynolds, 1987; Janken et al., 1986; Mayo et al., 1989; Nevitt et al., 1989; Rapport et al., 1993; Robbins et al., 1989; Stewart, Moore, May, Marks, & Hale, 1992; Tinetti et al., 1988) and sleep disturbances (Janken &

Reynolds, 1987; Vellas & Albarede, 1993). As a risk factor, both urinary dysfunction and sleeplessness are multivariable. Toileting by itself is a complex task. It requires that an individual get up out of a bed or chair, ambulate to the bathroom, adjust clothing (remove pants, lift dresses, pull down underwear, etc.), position his or her body directly over or on the toilet while urinating, maintain balance, stand up afterwards (if sitting), and exit the bathroom. The task is much more complicated if the person has to climb stairs in order to reach the bathroom, access a small bathroom with a walker or wheelchair, or sit on a low-seated toilet. At any point a fall is likely to occur, especially in those individuals with underlying mobility problems. As well, there is always a risk that a person might lose continence and slip in the urine. Diuretics may contribute to the risk of falls, as they increase both urinary frequency and exposure to toileting activity, which may be hazardous. Nocturia may increase the risk of falling by increasing the number of nighttime transfers from bed to toilet (under varying conditions of illumination, and distance to the bathroom). Combined with sleepiness, these factors may be significant, particularly if the person hurries to the bathroom in order to avoid an embarrassing "accident." The use of hypnotic agents can contribute to gait and postural instability and increase fall risk as well. Concurrent use of medications such as antihypertensives predisposes to postural hypotension, particularly when getting up at night from a supine position. Apart from nocturia, Vellas and Albarede (1993) suggested that sleeplessness may lead to lower attention and coordination during the daytime. In a hospitalized population of older people, Janken and Reynolds (1987) found that sleeplessness was significantly related to fall status and that the falls experienced by patients with sleeplessness were evenly distributed throughout the 24-hour period.

Cognitive Risk Factors

Altered cognitive function has been shown to be a significant risk factor for falls. Many studies have reported that older persons who are depressed tend to fall more often than those individuals without depressive symptoms (Downton & Andrews, 1991; Granek et al., 1987; Tinetti et al., 1988; Vetter & Ford, 1989), although these findings are not universal (Myers et al., 1991). The use of antidepressants has been cited as the major factor contributing to falls (Lipsitz et al., 1991; Ray, Griffin, & Schaffner, 1987; Ruthazer & Lipsitz, 1993), leading to the risk of both psychomotor retardation and postural hypotension. Some researchers have failed to find a relationship between antidepressants and falls in older men (Campbell et al., 1989; Ruthazer & Lipsitz, 1993), and have attributed the difference to greater comorbidity in women (i.e., their loss of lower extremity strength).

However, other factors are responsible as well. Some of these may account for the negative association between depression and fall risk. Asada, Kariya, Kitajiwa, Kakuma, and Yoshioka (1993) found that the severity of depression was the most important factor related to falling, whereas antidepressant use was associated with a lower likelihood of falling. In certain cases, antidepressants appear to have a protective benefit, guarding against fall risk.

Dementia has received considerable attention as a risk factor. Several researchers have reported that dementia represents a significant risk factor for falls (Asada et al., 1993; Jantti, Pyykko, & Hervonen, 1993; Spar, LaRue, Hewes, & Fairbanks, 1987). However, the risk of dementia may not be equal between men and women, and the mechanism by which dementia leads to falls is uncertain. Campbell et al. (1981) assessed all persons aged 80 years and older living in the community and found that dementia, as determined by low mental status scores, was significantly associated with falls, although falls were more common in men than women. Brody, Kleban, Moss, and Kleban (1984) studied 60 institutionalized older women with moderate-to-severe Alzheimer's disease (AD) over a 2-year period in an attempt to predict fall risk factors. Those individuals who had been physically "vigorous" but who experienced a decline in vigor were found to have the highest number of falls, whereas persons with less initial vigor who had maintained stable levels of vigor tended to have fewer falls. The fallers also showed declines in their cognitive status, mobility, and ADL status comparable with their decline in vigor. Bucher and Larson (1987) conducted a community-based prospective study of falls in older persons with AD. At the time of initial evaluation 31% of the 157 participants reported falling, and all but one person walked independently. Those persons who experienced toxic or adverse drug reactions were more likely to have fallen prior to study entry. During a 3-year followup on 117 of the persons, 50% either had fallen or lost their ability to walk. They also found that comorbid conditions (e.g., peripheral neuropathy, self-reported musculoskeletal problems, cataracts, and poor tandem gait) were associated with the risk of falls. Of interest, they did not find a significant association between falls and severity of dementia. Conversely, Morris, Rubin, Morris, and Mandel (1987) compared the occurrence of falls in older persons with AD and cognitively healthy controls over a 4-year period. They found no difference between the two groups in neurological deficits or drug use; however, dementia alone, regardless of severity, was a potent risk factor for falls. Males with AD and falls had higher blood pressure and were more likely to be medicated than males with AD who did not fall. These differences were not observed in the women. There was an indirect association between fall occurrence and institutionalization in those with dementia, suggesting again that falls are a marker for increasing functional disability. Over a 2-year period, van Dijk, Meulenberg, van de Sande, and Habbema (1993) analyzed risk factors associated with falls in a nursing home for older persons with dementia. They found that the risk of falling was especially high shortly after admission and after transfer to another ward. Also fall risk increased with the severity of dementia and physical impairment (e.g., gait and equilibrium disturbances), but decreased for those individuals who were very severely demented or functionally dependent. Men had twice the risk of falling compared to women. The type of dementia present in the study subjects was not identified. It appears, then, that the severity of dementia (i.e., amount of confusion) and resulting functional disability, comorbid conditions and medications, and an inability to cope with environmental surroundings all contribute to the risk of falls in persons with dementia.

Pharmacologic Risk Factors

It has been suggested that a number of medications are associated with fall risk. The association between fall risk and psychotropic medications (hypnotic sedatives, tranquilizers, anxiolytics, antidepressants, etc.) is strong (Campbell, 1991; Campbell et al., 1989, 1990; Granek et al., 1987; Kerman & Mulvihill, 1990; Nevitt et al., 1989; Sorock & Shimkin, 1988; Tinetti et al., 1988). This risk appears to be independent of underlying diagnosis and mental impairment (Granek et al., 1987; Tinetti et al., 1988). Most of the pharmacokinetic response to psychotropics in older persons has been studied in relationship to benzodiazepines, the most common type of hypnotic-anxiolytic prescribed. It has been demonstrated that older persons taking a benzodiazepine, such as temazepam or diazepam, develop greater body sway than do younger persons taking the same dose (Swift & Stevenson, 1983; Swift, Ewen, & Stevenson, 1985). The mechanism by which these medications may lead to instability is influenced by age-related changes in the brain's sensitivity to benzodiazepines, and depression of central nervous system function (Swift, 1985). However, other factors may be involved. For example, Overstall et al. (1977) failed to demonstrate a relationship between increased postural sway and hypnotic use. Likewise, Swift et al. (1984) showed no increase in postural sway in older persons who were long-term users of flurazepam and nitrazepam, and suggested that postural instability due to benzodiazepine medication may occur with acute dosing or during the first few days of therapy before pharmacodynamic "tolerance" has begun to develop. This view is partly supported by a study conducted by Aisen, DeLuca, and Lawler (1992), who compared a group of older geropsychiatric patients with falls, and a similar group of patients without falls. While the percentage of patients on benzodiazepines between the two groups was similar, the researchers found that falls were significantly more frequent in those patients who were prescribed PRN benzodiazepines for agitation. This finding suggests that the acute administration of benzodiazepines may be associated with greater fall risk, although agitation as a contributing factor cannot be eliminated.

When assessing the risk introduced by psychotropics, other factors need to be considered as well. For instance, Trewin, Lawrence, and Veitch (1992) examined data from 2,878 hospital admissions to determine the association between hypnotics and benzodiazepines and the incidence of falls. They found no significant link between these drugs and falls, although the percentage of falls in both men and women was higher in persons taking hypnotics and benzodiazepines than in those not taking the medication. On further examination they discovered that only lorazepam in older females and nitrazepam in older men was associated with fall risk. Thus, the risk of psychotropics as a causative factor in falls might be gender-related, a relationship that requires further study. Also, the findings suggest that fall risk may be dependent on the type of drug utilized, as both lorazepam and nitrazepam are long-acting benzodiazepines. Studies have reported that hypnotic and anxiolytic medications with short half-lives (that is, a short duration of action) are less likely to increase the risk of falls (Ray, Griffin, Schaffner, & Melton, 1987; Ray, Griffin, & Downey, 1989).

Another factor to consider in assessing psychotropics is the dosage. Granek et al. (1987) found that depressed patients taking antidepressants were 1.5 times more likely to fall than nondepressed patients taking antidepressants (for urinary incontinence or peripheral neuropathy), and that depressed patients taking antidepressants were 1.8 times more likely to fall as depressed patients not taking antidepressants. They concluded from these findings that both depression and antidepressants were associated with an increased risk of falls. However, the increased risk of falling in the patients with depression may have been due to higher treatment doses of the antidepressant than those used when treating other indicated conditions, such as urinary incontinence, in those patients without depression. Thus, the risk posed by psychotropics might be dose-dependent, with high doses leading to greater risk, and smaller, but effective doses decreasing the risk of falls.

And finally, aside from the psychotropic type and dosage, the risk of falls with psychotropic use may be greater because of additional concurrent psychotropics and other medications. Jones (1992) studied a sample of 253 older persons from two general practices who had been taking psychotropic medications for at least 3 months and a control group of 484 older persons not taking psychotropics. Those persons who were taking a psychotropic experienced a significantly higher frequency of falls. However, in comparison to the control group, those individuals with falls were on average taking more nonpsychotropic medications, and also used one or more additional psychotropic medications. Similarly, in a study of older persons admitted to long-term health care facilities, Tinetti and colleagues (1986) reported an association between the addition of psychotropic drugs to the person's existing drug regimen and risk of falls. Moreover, studies have shown that older persons who take multiple drugs are at increased fall risk (Lord et al., 1993). Robbins et al. (1989) found that nursing home residents taking four or more prescription drugs had a significantly greater risk of falling.

An association between the use of alcohol and fall risk has been found by some (McConnell, 1988) but not by others (Campbell et al., 1989; Nelson, Sattin, Langlois, DeVito, & Stevens, 1992; Nevitt et al., 1989; O'Loughlin et al., 1993; Teno et al., 1990; Tinetti et al., 1988). Adams et al. (1992) reported a low prevalence of alcohol abuse in those older persons who presented to the emergency room with falls. The lack of association between alcohol and falls is surprising, particularly when one considers the high prevalence of alcohol abuse in older people, which has been estimated by some to be between 15% and 50% (Bristow & Clare, 1992; Curtis, Geller, Stokes, Levine, & Moore, 1989), and alcohol's association with several adverse affects such as impaired motor and sensory coordination and altered cognition, any of which could lead to falls. In an attempt to explain this phenomenon, several explanations have been offered. Teno and colleagues (1990) suggested that just as older people may fail to report falls, they also may not report the use of alcohol. Tinetti et al. (1988) postulated that persons who use alcohol and are at fall risk may die as a consequence before reaching old age. Campbell (1991) proposed that persons in poor health who are at risk for falls may either abstain from or decrease their use of alcohol. O'Loughlin et al. (1993), on the other hand, suggested that daily use of alcohol might be a marker of good health. Nevertheless, the risk of alcohol-related falls is great, especially in frail older persons who are taking medications such as chloral hydrate, tricyclic antidepressants, and benzodiazepines that commonly interact adversely with alcohol causing hypotension, sedation, and confusion. As a result, the contribution of alcohol as a factor for falls requires further investigation, and should not be quickly dismissed.

Other classes of medications that have been implicated to increase fall risk include diuretics and antihypertensives (Cumming et al., 1991), cardiac drugs (Granek et al., 1987; Kerman & Mulvihill, 1990; Myers et al., 1991; Ryynanen et al., 1993), nonsteroidal anti-inflammatories (Granek et al., 1987; Myers et al., 1991), and laxatives (Cumming et al., 1991). Nevertheless, the association between these medications and falls is uncertain. For instance, Ray and Griffin (1990), after reviewing the literature on diuretics and antihypertensives, concluded that these drugs do not substantially increase the risk of falls. This is supported by several other studies that have failed to demonstrate a strong relationship between taking diuretics and the occurrence of falls (Blake et al., 1988; Granek et al., 1987; Nevitt et al., 1989; Tinetti et al., 1988). Moreover, the precise mechanism by which diuretics and antihypertensives lead to falls is poorly understood. For instance, postural hypotension is often cited as a contributing factor. However, as discussed in Chapter 3 the prevalence of postural hypotension caused by diuretics is quite low. The risk of postural hypotension may be greatest in those individuals whose homeostatic reserves are already impaired by concurrent medical conditions, such as volume depletion, autonomic neuropathy, or underlying cardiovascular disease. Cumming et al. (1991) suggested that hypokalemia and cardiac arrhythmias, both induced by diuretics, are a potential mechanism for falls. As well, high doses of diuretics and antihypertensives and the concurrent use of other drugs such as psychotropics that can cause hypotension may be particularly hazardous with respect to increasing fall risk.

The relationship between fall risk, cardiac drugs, nonsteroidal anti-inflammatories, and laxatives may not be so much the result of adverse drug effects as of the presence of comorbid conditions. For example, Cumming et al. (1991) found that after controlling for arthritis, the risk of falls due to analgesics and nonsteroidal anti-inflammatories diminished markedly. Similarly, with respect to cardiac drugs, falls may be more the result of poor mobility due to the effects of chronic cardiac disease, such as congestive heart failure. In the case of laxatives, the presence of gait and balance disorders may lead to unsafe mobility while hurrying to the bathroom. On the other hand, these medications can at the same time be protective against falls, especially if they modify the underlying medical condition. For instance, O'Loughlin et al.

(1993) found that cardiac drugs were protective against falls, presumably through the control of heart failure and/ or symptoms of dizziness.

Considering Fall Risk

Several studies have found that the risk of falling increases markedly as the number of intrinsic risk factors or disabilities increases (Granek et al., 1987; Robbins et al., 1989; Tinetti et al., 1986, 1988). Tinetti and co-workers (1986) developed a fall risk index based on nine identified disabilities, some of which included declines in mobility, mental status, distance vision, back flexibility, leg strength, and multiple use of medications. They found that the likelihood of falling increased with the number of disabilities present in a population of ambulatory nursing home residents. No resident with three or fewer disabilities fell more than once, whereas every resident with seven or more disabilities fell two or more times. Nearly all recurrent fallers had poor back flexibility, decreased strength in the lower extremities, and poor distance vision. Similarly, Robbins et al. (1989) showed that the risk of falling increased with the presence of three intrinsic factors (hip weakness, unstable balance, and taking four or more prescribed medications). The authors found that the predicted 1-year risk of falling ranged from 12% for persons with none of the three factors to 100% for persons with all three factors. When these intrinsic risk factors are combined with undesirable environmental or extrinsic factors, the risk of falling is increased further. For example, unsuitable environments such as low-seated furnishings and toilets, reduced illumination, and hazardous ground surfaces may be relatively easy for "healthy" older persons to negotiate safely. Wearing improper footwear may not even present much of a risk. However, for individuals with altered gait and balance, unfavorable environmental conditions and/or faulty footwear can become major obstacles, interfering with safe mobility and significantly increasing the risk of falls.

The relationship between fall risk and falls, however, is more complex than this. For example, there are many older persons who have one or more intrinsic risk factors, such as lower extremity weakness or psychotropic drug use, but who never fall. On the other hand, there are other individuals with similar risk factors who may experience frequent falls. Thus, while intrinsic risk factors are necessary for a fall to occur, they may not be sufficient factors to cause a fall in all older people. In addition, the likelihood of falls is dependent upon a number of interacting psychosocial, environmental, and behavioral risk factors. For instance, some studies have found that older persons living alone, especially women, are at increased fall risk (Campbell et al., 1989, 1990;

Cwikel, 1992). In this context, persons may be required to accomplish their activities of daily living independently. However, because of failing health they may not be equal to the task, thus increasing their risk of falls. Conversely, those individuals in poor health who live with their adult children or have formal help to assist with unsafe activities may be at low fall risk. An association between physical activity and falls has also been found in some studies. Active persons fall more often (presumably due to increased exposure to hazardous environmental conditions or to poor mobility) than do less active persons (O'Loughlin et al., 1993), although not universally (Campbell et al., 1990; Lord et al., 1993). Again, any positive association between increased activity and fall risk may be due to the fact that persons living alone without help to support mobility are, as a result, unable to accomplish tasks in a safe manner, especially in poorly designed or hazardous environments. Conversely, negative findings may be related to people either having help, living in safe environmental surroundings, or using assistive devices such as canes and walkers to support poor mobility. Assistive devices by themselves, however, may increase fall risk if they are inappropriate for the individual. Also, regular physical activity may protect against falls, as it maintains muscular strength and joint flexibility, thereby improving gait and balance.

It has been suggested that previous experience or familiarity with particular environmental obstacles may reduce the risk of increased exposure (Tinetti & Speechley, 1989). As a result, persons living in one place, such as their own home, for an extended period of time may have a lower risk of falls due to extrinsic factors. However, the risk of environmental exposure may increase when individuals find themselves in unfamiliar settings or relocate to other settings (for example, the home of an adult child or institutional facility). Behavioral influences can be involved as well. Some older persons at fall risk will recognize their limitations and curtail potentially unsafe activities accordingly. Others, however, because of their need for autonomy may insist on attempting to accomplish hazardous tasks, thereby increasing their risk of falls. Also, cognitive disturbances can influence how an individual perceives and adapts to their environment and activity demands. For instance, persons with cognitive decline may be less aware of environmental hazards or the need to ask for help with activities that increase fall risk. Some individuals with memory deficits may be less cautious in avoiding certain hazardous activities, such as rising quickly from a seated or supine position and suffering drug-related postural hypotension (when it would be of help to sit at the edge of the chair or bed for several minutes before rising).

Injury Risk Factors

Injurious falls are fall events that lead to physical injury (for example, fracture, dislocation, sprain, laceration, and soft tissue trauma). Fall injuries can result in long lie times (an inability to get up following a fall) and psychological injury (fear of falling), although both conditions may occur without physical injury. The extent and complications of injurious falls, long lie times, and fear of falling are discussed in Chapter 2.

Physical Injury

While the majority of falls among older people do not result in significant injury, the risk factors for injurious falls appear to be similar to those of noninjurious falls. Nevitt et al. (1991) conducted a 1-year prospective study of the consequences of falls in 325 community-dwelling persons 60 years and older (mean age 70.3 years) who were both ambulatory and had a history of at least one fall in the past year. The majority of the participants were white (82%) and mainly women (82%). During followup, 58% of the subjects reported 539 falls; of which 6% resulted in major injury, such as fracture, dislocation, or laceration requiring suture, and 55% resulted in minor soft tissue injury. In essence, the authors found that:

1. the risk of injury was strongly related to the number of falls a person had;
2. the risk of major injury was greater in persons having a previous fall with fracture;
3. the risk of injury was greater in those persons with neuromuscular and cognitive deficits; and
4. the risk of injury was associated with certain fall-related activities (climbing stairs and steps, turning around, or reaching for objects).

Lord, McLean, and Stathers (1992), in a study that compared a group of community-dwelling older persons who were admitted to the hospital with fall injury (excluding lower limb fractures) with a group of individuals without falls, found that the fallers had greater declines in tactile sensation and quadriceps strength, and used more psychoactive medications (sedatives, anxiolytics, antipsychotics, and antidepressants). The fallers also performed poorly in clinical tests of static and dynamic balance, exhibiting greater body sway on both firm and compliant surfaces. Furthermore, on followup 10% of the fallers were found to have experienced three or more additional falls in the following 12 months. O'Loughlin et al. (1993) conducted a prospective study to determine the risk factors for falls and injurious falls among noninstitutionalized persons aged 65 years and older living in Montreal, Quebec, Canada. They found that stroke, frequent physical activity (undertaking 10 or more activities a week), activity-limitation days because of health problems, and having a respiratory disorder were significantly associated with increased risk for injurious falls. Both stroke and respiratory disorders were independently associated with about a twofold risk for injurious falls. Myers et al. (1991) designed a case-control study of patients 65 years of age and older to identify risk factors with falls and injuries in a long-term care facility located in Baltimore, Maryland. They found that dementia, taking a diuretic, or dementia plus taking a diuretic were significantly associated with the risk of injurious falls. Interestingly enough, the risk of both factors combined (dementia plus a diuretic) was no different from having only one factor. Other factors found to be associated with injurious falls in the institutional setting include previous falls, lower extremity weakness, being more independent (having less assistance with ADL activities), poor vision, disorientation, and use of mechanical restraints (Mayo, Korner-Bitensky, & Levy, 1993; Svensson et al., 1991; Tinetti, 1987; Tinetti et al., 1992).

Fracture Risk

Most of the research on fracture risk and falls has focused on two sites: the upper extremity and hip area. Kelsey et al. (1992), using data from the Study of Osteoporotic Fractures, a prospective cohort study, examined the risk factors for distal forearm and proximal humerus fractures, including risk factors associated with low bone density and falls in community-dwelling women 65 years and older. They reported that most fractures at both sites occurred as a result of a fall, and that low bone density was a strong predictor of fracture. Poor visual acuity, number of falls, and frequent walking were associated with the risk of distal forearm fracture, while a recent decline in health status, insulin-dependent diabetes mellitus, infrequent walking, and neuromuscular weakness (inability to stand with feet in a tandem position) were independently associated with an increased risk of proximal humerus fracture. The authors concluded that their findings support the hypotheses:

1. that distal forearm fractures occur most often as a result of a fall in women with low bone density who are both active and in good health (that is, with intact neuromuscular function); and

2. that proximal humerus fractures tend to occur as a result of a fall in women with low bone density who are less active and less healthy (that is, with poor neuromuscular function).

In addition, the direction of falling has been shown to increase the risk of distal forearm fracture. For example, conventional wisdom holds that a fall in the forward direction, such as might occur following a trip or rapid walk, will automatically cause an individual to protectively extend their arms outward in an effort to break the fall. As a result, the theory holds, landing forward with great force on a hyperextended wrist, especially against a hard surface, is likely to increase the risk of fracture. This assumption, however, has been challenged. Nevitt, Cummings, and the Study of Osteoporotic Fractures Research Group (1993) conducted a case-controlled prospective study in which they examined fall type and the risk of osteoporotic fracture in women aged 65 and older living in the community. The researchers found that older women with wrist fractures were more likely to have fallen backward, rather than forward, and to have landed on their hands, than were those individuals who fell without a fracture. Furthermore, among women who landed on the hand, those with wrist fracture were taller in height, presumably due to a greater potential energy or force produced by an increased distance of falling; had a greater decrease in bone density at the site of the fracture; and were less likely to break their fall by grabbing onto an object for support or hitting an object.

Several studies have reported an association between the risk of hip fracture and the number of previous falls (Cumming & Klineberg, 1994b; Lau & Donnan, 1990; Wolinsky & Fitzgerald, 1994). The risk of hip fracture in general is greater in older women than men (Kelsey & Hoffman, 1987; Wolinsky & Fitzgerald, 1994). However, Cumming and Klineberg (1994b), in a population-based study, found that the relationship between the number of reported falls and hip fracture was stronger among men than women. While the researchers did not explain the gender difference, one interpretation is plausible if an assumption can be made that—as is usually the case—the men in this study were taller in height than the women. Several studies of aged fallers have found that individuals with hip fracture are significantly taller than controls (Hayes et al., 1993; Nevitt et al., 1993). The reason for this relationship is similar to the one provided by Nevitt and colleagues (1993) for why tall people are at risk for distal forearm fracture: that because tall people fall from a greater height when standing or walking, they can impact the landing surface at greater velocity (Greenspan, Meyer, Maitland, Resnick, & Hayes, 1994).

While low bone mass is associated with an increased risk of hip fracture (Cummings et al., 1990), many women with osteoporosis who fall do not fracture a bone and some women who sustain a fracture have above-average bone mass. Therefore, while low bone mass or osteoporosis may predispose for hip fracture, it appears to be not the single cause. Several researchers have suggested a variety of other factors that may contribute to the risk of hip fracture (Cummings & Nevitt, 1989; Melton & Riggs, 1985, 1989).

(A) Fall Characteristics. In contrast to fall-related studies that focus on *why* older people fall, several researchers have focused on *how* people fall in order to determine if a particular kind of fall has a high risk of hip fracture. Hayes et al. (1993), in a case-control study of fallers in a nursing home, reported that 59% of falls that resulted in hip fractures involved landing on the hip or side of the leg compared with just 6% of falls that did not lead to a hip fracture. Nevitt and co-workers (1993) compared the fall circumstances in a group of community-dwelling older women who had a hip fracture with a comparable group of women with a recent fall who had not suffered a fracture. They found that those who suffered hip fractures were more likely to have fallen sideways or straight down, and to have landed on or near the hip, than women who fell without a fracture. Greenspan et al. (1994) compared a group of older community-dwelling persons with falls and hip fracture against a group of fallers without hip fracture, and found that for both men and women the direction of falling to the side of the body significantly increased the risk of hip fracture. In addition, the researchers found that thin body habitus and decreased femoral bone density was significantly associated with the risk of hip fracture; more important, perhaps, was the evidence that fall direction as a risk factor was unaffected by the addition or removal of bone mineral density from the paradigm. Cumming and Klineberg (1994b), in a case-control study of older persons residing in the community and nursing home, showed that hip fractures were more likely to occur if a fall occurred during turning maneuvers. The researchers explained that older people who fall while turning are more likely to land on their sides and on their hips than if the fall occurs while walking, while getting up, or sitting down.

(B) Height of the Fall. In order to build up sufficient momentum to produce injury, that is, bone fracture, an individual must fall a considerable distance. For example, an unexpected fall from a standing height resulting from a sudden slip or a loss of consciousness, or falling from an elevated bed height over side rails, is more likely to result in frac-

ture because of the increased force of impact, than is a fall from a relatively low height, such as a chair or toilet, with its decreased force of impact. Tinetti (1987) studied factors associated with serious fall-related injury in ambulatory nursing home residents, and found that no injuries occurred while getting up from a sitting position, such as rising from a chair. Similarly, Nevitt, Cummings, and Hudes (1991) found that falls occurring from relatively low heights, such as while transferring, stooping, and bending, tended to be associated with a decreased risk of injury.

Conversely, Grisso et al. (1991), in a hospital-based case-control study, compared the circumstances of hip-related falls in a group of patients with the circumstances of the most recent fall in a group of controls who had fallen in the previous 6 months. They found that falls from greater than a standing height were more likely to lead to hip fracture than were falls from a lower level. Similarly, Mayo et al. (1993) conducted a matched case-control study in a rehabilitation hospital and found that most hip fractures occurred from falls from the upright position or standing height. Nevitt and colleagues (1991) reported that the risk of major injury such as a hip fracture was greater in falls associated with loss of consciousness, compared to nonsyncopal falls.

(C) Protective Reflexes.   The onset of a fall elicits a number of protective reflexes: extending the arms, grabbing onto walls and furnishings for support, and quick shifting movements of the feet in order to regain balance, (that is, realigning the COG and BOS). Any of these actions may avert a fall or minimize the force of impact on the ground. Conversely, a loss of protective reflexes may increase the risk of hip fracture. For instance, prior to age 60, age-related incidences of both hip and wrist fractures in postmenopausal women increase in parallel. After about age 60, however, the incidence of wrist fractures plateaus and then declines, whereas hip fracture incidence increases exponentially (Nevitt et al., 1993). It has been suggested that the decline in distal forearm fractures may be due to a diminished ability of the older person to exhibit the protective reflex, that is, outstretching the arms (Evans, 1982). This hypothesis, however, has been challenged by Melton and Riggs (1985) who argued that the dissociation between the incidence of distal forearm and hip fractures occurs too early in life for it to be due to an age-specific loss of protective responses.

Regardless, there are a number of conditions that can either blunt or delay the protective response and increase the risk of hip fracture. Certain diseases that affect upper extremity function (e.g., hemiplegia or paresis, Parkinsonism, arthritis), and drugs (e.g., psychotropics, hypnotics) are the most likely. These conditions, as well, may adversely affect lower extremity function and, as a result, interfere with the ability to regain balance. Lower extremity dysfunction, neurological conditions, barbiturate use, and long-acting benzodiazepines have all been associated with an increase in hip fracture (Grisso et al., 1991; Ray et al., 1987). In addition, Lauritzen, Peterson, and Lund (1993) found that older women who suffered an upper extremity fracture (distal forearm or proximal humerus fracture) were at increased risk of hip fracture. The risk of sustaining a hip fracture was highest within the first year following a fracture of the upper extremity. The authors suggested that a greater propensity to fall and/or increased osteoporosis may have been responsible for the increase in hip fracture risk. Moreover, distal forearm fractures may affect one's balance, thereby increasing the risk of hip fracture. Crilly et al. (1987) reported a relationship between Colles' fracture and increased postural sway.

(D) Shock Absorbers.   Increased fat and muscle bulk surrounding vulnerable areas of the hip may be capable of absorbing the impact of a fall, and thus decrease the risk of hip fracture (Cummings & Nevitt, 1989). Malmivaara, Heliovaara, Knekt, Revnanen, and Aromaa (1993), in a study examining the risk factors for injurious falls, found that being overweight was protective against the risk of injury in older people. Lauritzen et al. (1993), in a population of nursing home residents, found that an external hip pad protector (a device that simulates the protective layer of fat padding around the hip) decreased the risk of hip fracture by 50%. Moreover, heavy women have a higher bone mass than do thin women with hip fracture. Increased adipose tissue may in part lead to higher levels of circulating estrogen and, as a result, heavier persons may have more bone mass to lose before the process of osteoporosis leads to critically low levels. Conversely, individuals who are thin in stature or underweight, with decreased bone density and fat padding, may be at increased risk for hip fracture. Several studies have shown that thinner women are substantially at higher risk for hip fracture than heavier controls, a finding consistent for both white and Black women (Grisso et al., 1991, 1994; Kelsey & Hoffman, 1987; Pruzansky, Turano, Lucky, & Senie, 1989).

(E) Impact Surface.   Falls upon hard, nonabsorptive ground surfaces, such as linoleum tile, concrete, and wood, are more likely to result in injury than are falls onto absorptive surfaces like carpets, due to the decreased force of impact. In support, Hayes et al. (1993) examined the relationship between the risk of hip fracture and the mechanics of falling in a group of older nursing home patients, and found that direct

impact of the fall on the hip region increased the risk of hip fracture. Grisso et al. (1991), in a study examining hip fracture risk, suggested that falling on a hard surface was more likely to lead to a hip fracture than was falling on a soft surface. Nevitt and colleagues (1991) found that older persons with falls in the home experienced a decrease in hip fractures, presumably due to the protective, cushioning effect of carpeted floor surfaces. Falling onto a hard surface was associated with major injury, that is, hip fracture.

Medications

Some studies have failed to demonstrate an association between drug use and hip fracture (Jensen et al., 1991; Rashiq & Logan, 1986; Taggart, 1988). However, there is accumulating evidence from a number of studies that psychotropic medications are associated with an increased risk of hip fractures (Cumming & Klineberg, 1993; Ray et al., 1987, 1989, 1991). In particular, the long-acting benzodiazepines (Cumming & Klineberg, 1993; Ray et al., 1987, 1989), cyclic antidepressants (Granek et al., 1987; Lipsitz et al., 1991; Ray et al., 1987, 1991), and antipsychotics (Ray, 1987; Yip & Cumming, 1994) have all been found to be associated with increased risk. As well, Schorr, Griffin, Dougherty, and Ray (1992) found that the risk of hip fracture for older persons concurrently receiving psychotropics and opioid analgesics (codine, propoxyphene) was nearly three times that for nonusers of these drugs. Presumably psychotropics lead to hip fracture through the mechanism of psychomotor impairment leading to balance loss, decreased reaction time, loss of protective righting reflex (outstretched arms), and landing directly on the hip. Ray and colleagues (1989) found that the use of long-acting benzodiazepines (that is, those with an increased half-life) was associated with a 70% increase in the risk of hip fracture, but they found no association between hip fractures and the use of short-acting benzodiazepines. However, other studies have failed to find an association between long-acting benzodiazepines and hip fracture (Grisso et al., 1991; Taggart, 1988).

The relationship of alcohol to fall-related injuries in older people, especially hip fractures has been investigated by several researchers. Nelson et al. (1992) analyzed a group of older persons who received treatment for fall-related injuries and found no association between fall injury events and average weekly alcohol use. Grisso et al. (1991), in a case-control study of hip fractures, found no association between alcohol and hip fracture. Similarly, Cumming and Klineberg (1994a), in a population-based study of older persons in Sydney, Australia, failed to find an association between alcohol intake and risk of hip fracture. Felson et al. (1988), using the Framingham cohort, found that alcohol consumption increased the risk of hip fracture in those under the age of 65 years, although in the older age groups alcohol had no effect on hip fracture risk. In contrast, Malmivaara et al. (1993) analyzed a large population sample of persons aged 20 to 92 years in Finland in order to identify risk factors for fall injuries, and found a relationship between heavy alcohol consumption and the risk for injuries from falls in older persons of both sexes. Thus, exposure to alcohol as a risk factor may be similar to that of fall risk, in that the amount of alcohol intake and some traits closely correlated with alcohol use (for example, acute or chronic gait and balance impairments; cognitive disturbances; lack of protective righting response) strongly contribute to injuries.

As well, the chronic use of steroids to treat such conditions as asthma, arthritis, and inflammatory disease have been shown to be associated with bone loss (up to 10% per year) (Lukert & Raisz, 1990), and the effect persists for as long as this treatment is being given. Steroids affect cortical bone sites such as the neck of the femur, thereby increasing the risk of fracture. Excessive thyroxine replacement therapy, which leads to bone loss, can increase hip fracture risk as well (Franklin & Sheppard, 1990). The use of opioid analgesics such as codeine and propoxyphene for pain relief has also been associated with the risk of hip fracture in older persons (Schorr et al., 1992), although this finding is not universal (Sorock, 1983).

Conversely, several studies have shown that thiazide diuretics decrease the risk of osteoporosis in women (Cauley et al., 1993; Morton, Barrett-Connor, & Edelstern, 1994; Peh, 1993), and hip fracture risk (Felson, Sloutskis, Anderson, Anthony, & Kiel, 1991; LaCroix et al., 1990; Ray et al., 1989). The proposed mechanism for this effect is a reduction in urinary calcium excretion resulting in a reduction in bone loss (LaCroix et al., 1990). However, the relationship between thiazide diuretics and a decrease in osteoporosis or hip fracture has not been a consistent observation. Others have not found an association between either higher bone density levels or lower hip fracture rates among thiazide users (Heidrich, Stergachis, & Gross, 1991; Taggart, 1988). Heidrich and colleagues (1991) found an association between thiazides and increased hip fracture. In contrast, Cauley et al. (1993) showed that older women who used thiazide diuretics had an incidence of fall that was comparable to those individuals who had never used these drugs. Thus, it appears that low-dose thiazide therapy (25 mg/day) may be beneficial in reducing the risk of hip fractures, but that long-term therapy (greater than 10 years) may be needed to produce clinically significant effects

(Cauley et al., 1993). Ray et al. (1989) found that short thiazide therapy (less than 2 years) did not decrease the risk of hip fractures, whereas treatment greater than 6 years of therapy was associated with a halving of the risk of hip fracture. It appears that the longer the duration of thiazide use, the greater the protective effect on risk of hip fractures.

On the other hand, the use of furosemide has been found to be associated with nearly a fourfold increase for hip fracture (Heidrich et al., 1991). Unlike thiazides, furosemide is a diuretic agent that promotes calcium excretion by the kidney. Other possible mechanisms by which furosemide might lead to both falls and fracture include hypokalemia (potassium wasting), postural hypotension and syncope, and nocturia.

A number of studies have shown a significant reduction in bone loss and hip fractures in women taking estrogen (Cauley et al., 1995; Kanis et al., 1992; Kiel, Felson, Anderson, Wilson, & Moskowitz, 1987). A retrospective analysis of a Framingham cohort of 2873 women showed that postmenopausal use of estrogen decreased the risk of hip fracture by 35% after adjustments were made for age and body weight (Keil et al., 1987). Several studies have suggested that estrogen is effective in preventing hip fracture, even among the very old (Marx, Dailey, Cheney, Vint, & Muchmore, 1992; Quigley, Martin, Burnier, & Brooks, 1987). Cauley et al. (1995), in a prospective cohort study of 9704 women 65 years of age and older who were members of the Study of Osteoporotic Fractures, found that the relative risk of hip fracture tended to be lower among users of estrogen (defined as those taking estrogen within 5 years of menopause) than among never-users. Estrogen was found to be most effective in preventing hip fractures among those older than 75 years. Current use of estrogen, however, was not associated with a statistically significant reduction in the risk of hip fracture in women with osteoporosis. Women without a history of osteoporosis had a reduced risk of hip fracture even if they started estrogen therapy late with respect to menopause or if they had taken estrogen for less than 10 years, although these observations were not statistically significant. The authors of this study suggested that for optimal protection against fractures, estrogen should be taken soon after menopause and continued indefinitely. Moreover, several studies have shown that the use of thiazides and estrogen together has an additive affect on bone density (Morton et al., 1994; Wasnich et al., 1986), although it is not certain whether this translates into a lower risk of hip fracture. As well, some studies have found a small protective effect against hip fracture associated with calcium intake (Cooper, Barker, & Wickman, 1988; Lau, Donnan, Baker, & Cooper, 1988; Wickman et al., 1989).

Dementia and Hip Fracture Risk

Several epidemiologic studies have shown an association between Alzheimer's Disease (AD) and the risk of hip fracture. Buchner and Larson (1987), in a prospective study of 157 ambulatory, community-dwelling persons with AD, reported a fracture rate that was more than three times the age- and sex-specific adjusted rate for the general population. A hip fracture was the most common fracture, occurring in 8% of the patients. This represented a sevenfold increase in hip fracture risk relative to expected rates. Self-reported musculoskeletal problems, wandering, cataracts, and arthritis were significantly associated with all fractures. In addition, the subjects exhibited poor tandem gait, although this finding was not statistically significant. Wandering was found to be strongly associated with the risk of hip fracture. Seventy percent of the patients with hip fracture wandered compared with 25% of the patients without fracture. Melton, Beard, Kokmen, Atkinson, and O'Fallon (1994), in a retrospective cohort study that examined the risk of fractures in older persons with AD residing in Rochester, Minnesota, found that the patients with AD were no more likely to have a history of fracture prior to onset of dementia than were matched controls. However, following the year of onset (that is, when dementia first came to clinical attention) there was a twofold excess of fractures compared with controls. They found nearly a threefold excess of hip fractures among those with AD. The authors of this study hypothesized that the reduced gait speed commonly found with advanced AD (Visser, 1983) may have contributed to the risk of hip fracture. For instance, individuals with normal or rapid gait are more likely to fall forward and suffer distal forearm fractures, while those with shuffling gait (decreased stride length) tend to fall backward or to the side and experience a hip fracture.

The Risk of Long Lies

A number of factors have been shown to be associated with long lie times, that is, an inability to get up from the ground following a fall and, subsequently, lying helpless on the ground for 5–15 minutes or more. Cummings and Nevitt (1991), in their prospective study of falls and their consequences in community-dwelling older persons, reported that long lies (defined as those lasting 5 minutes or more) were significantly more common in those older than 80 years, were more likely to occur at home than away, and were about twice as likely to occur after syncopal falls. Similarly, Nevitt et al. (1991) found that syncope was the only identified risk factor for inability to get up after falling. Ryynanen et al. (1992a) compared a group of community-dwelling older people with falls who were able to get up within 5 minutes after a fall against a group of older fallers who reported long lies of 15 minutes or more. They found that long lies were associated with severe injury, an intrinsic cause of falling or an unknown mechanism, falling indoors, poor functional capacity, and use of walking aids (a marker of altered mobility). The authors also found that body temperature of 37.5 degrees Centigrade or higher and serum potassium concentration of under 3.5 mmol/l were both associated with long lie times, although they stated that these changes may represent the effects of long lies, rather than their cause.

Aside from an acute medical condition and/or injury as a cause of long lies, the findings by Ryynanen et al. (1992) suggest that chronic neuromuscular impairment may be associated with an inability to get up from the ground and with long lies. In an earlier study, Hodkinson (1962) examined a group of 100 ambulatory persons aged 70 to 95 years with a history of past falls and observed their ability to get up from the ground. It was found that 47% of the participants were unable to rise independently from the supine position. Severe lower extremity limitations (i.e., hip and knee movements), Parkinsonism with leg rigidity, upper extremity weakness, and obesity were associated with an inability to rise. The 53 individuals who were able to get up independently did so by two methods, both requiring considerable hip and knee flexion. They either rolled to all fours and, while in the kneeling position, stood up, or else they tucked both legs under their buttocks and then rose from a deep squatting position. However, this study did not comment on whether difficulty with rising was associated with long lie times.

Tideiksaar (1995), in a study of a community-dwelling group of older people with falls, found that an inability to get up from the ground was associated with lower extremity dysfunction (i.e., loss of muscle strength and joint impairment) and long lie times. Tinetti, Liu, and Claus (1993) compared a group of community-dwelling persons aged 72 years and older with noninjurious falls against a group of non-fallers and found that an age of at least 80 years, depression, and poor gait and balance were significantly associated with an inability to get up. Previous stroke and sedative use were not found to be significant factors. Other factors that occurred more frequently among fallers who were unable to get up included decreased shoulder and knee strength, arthritis, and dependency on others for help with activities of daily living. Moreover, older people with an inability to get up may be at greater risk for long lies if they live alone. For instance, Tideiksaar (1995) reported that 70% of older people with long lies lived by themselves and, thus, were unable to receive help in getting up. However, several other studies have found that living alone does not seem to be related to the risk of long lies

(Campbell, Borrie, et al., 1990; Ryynanen et al., 1992a; Tinetti et al., 1993); that is, fallers living with a spouse are as likely to experience long lie times as those fallers who live alone. This seems curious in that one would expect to find that having help would lower the risk of long lies, especially in the absence of severe injury or a medical event such as syncope. One explanation for this may relate to the health status of spouses. They may be too incapacitated to offer assistance.

Psychological Injury

A number of factors have been found to be associated with the likelihood of developing a fear of falling. Falls that result in physical injury, functional loss, or long lies are most likely to be associated with significant fear of falling (Tideiksaar, 1995). The fear of falling can also be precipitated by episodes of near-falls (i.e., events in which persons lose balance, but avert coming to rest on the ground by grabbing hold of environmental objects for support). Several comorbid conditions have been shown to be associated with fear of falling, which are similar to those responsible for falls and injury. Cwikel and colleagues (1989/90) found that fallers with poor vision were more likely to restrict their activities and expressed more "caution." In a study of older people with falls admitted to the hospital, Guimaraes and Issacs (1980) reported that the great majority of persons with fear of falling displayed abnormal gaits. Maki et al. (1991) demonstrated that older persons with fear of falling exhibited increased anterior-posterior sway when blindfolded on measures of static balance. Franzoni et al. (1994) compared a group of nursing home residents with and without fear of falling and found that declines in functional status, poor gait and balance, and taking more psychotropic drugs was associated with a greater fear of falling. Fife and Baloh (1993) studied a group of 26 individuals over age 75 who complained of disequilibrium, with no apparent cause on clinical evaluation. Several of the individuals expressed a fear of falling in association with their balance loss, although the relationship between the two was not assessed in this study. Thus, gait and balance disorders appear to play a significant role in the fear of falling. However, whether gait and balance disorders are causes or effects of fear of falling remains speculative.

SUMMARY

As with the etiology of falls, there are a variety of factors that are associated with the risk of falls and injury. Taken in the main, however, those that appear to be the most critical, and necessary for both falls and injury to occur, include a history of falls; visual impairment, gait and balance disorders; lower extremity dysfunction; psychotropic medications; and cognitive impairment. As discussed above, however, these factors may not be sufficient to cause falls and injury, since numerous other factors—and sometimes, depending on the circumstances, more significant ones—including medical, environmental, psychosocial, and behavioral effects influence both falls and injury. Approaches to preventing falls should focus on all of these considerations. Also, the consequences of falls or injury, such as functional limitations, restricted activity or immobility, long lies, and fear of falling) should receive adequate attention.

The goal of fall prevention strategies is to design interventions that minimize fall risk by ameliorating or eliminating contributing factors while, at the same time, maintaining or improving the older person's mobility. Potential preventive strategies must be based on known risk factors and postulated causes of falls, which are classified as medical, psychosocial, rehabilitative, and environmental. In most cases, the management of persons at risk for falls and injury includes components derived from each category. A discussion of these strategies follows in the ensuing chapters.

CHAPTER 5

Medical Strategies to Reduce Fall Risk

INTRODUCTION

The accumulated effects of multiple diseases, medications, and resulting disabilities, combined with extrinsic factors; for example, environmental settings that are hazardous or unsuitable for safe mobility, may predispose or subsequently cause many community-and institutional-residing older persons to falls. However, the degree of individual fall risk and the causes of falls among older people vary considerably. Some of the factors that may account for this variability consist of differences in coexisting medical problems, their number, and their severity; the number, types, and dosages of medications utilized; the level of cognitive function and mobility capacity; design and structure of home and institutional environments; degree of family and formal social supports in the community; and the degree of staff support available in the hospital and nursing home. As a consequence of these factors, some persons are at greater fall risk than others. The etiology of falls will be diverse as well. Consequently, without a comprehensive systematic approach, both the prediction of individual fall risk and the determination of fall etiology are difficult tasks.

This chapter has several goals. The first is to discuss the diagnostic approach to both falls and fall risk. This begins with the history. In those persons with falls, the history helps to identify the causative factors and the risk of further falls; in those persons without falls, it helps recognize fall risk factors. After the history, a clinical evaluation ensues in order to isolate specific causes of falls and modifiable fall risk fac-

168

tors. Uncovering the cause of falls and risk factors for further falls represents an initial and crucial part of the medical strategy. Prescribing medical treatments and designing intervention strategies aimed at reducing fall risk makes up the remainder of the medical strategy.

The second goal of the chapter is to discuss the documentation of falls and fall risk and any interventions that are recommended. Capturing this information in the older person's medical records is as important as identifying and modifying falls and fall risk because it informs all subsequent health professionals who may provide care of the patient's potential for falls. The last goal is to review a number of existing clinical programs and trials specifically designed to prevent falls.

FALL ASSESSMENT

A fall is defined as an event—expected or unexpected—that leads to a person coming to rest on the ground or other lower level, such as a bed, chair, toilet, or step. All falling episodes should be followed by an evaluation and treatment of physical injury and/or life-threatening medical conditions that might have precipitated or followed them. In the institutional setting, where physicians and other medical personnel are readily available, an emergency evaluation does not usually present a problem, although not all nursing homes have medical services available around the clock. However, for those older persons who reside in the community and fall either at home or outside in the street or other public place, acute medical problems and/or injuries sustained may not always receive adequate attention. In these circumstances, either a family member or formal caregiver, if available, will often be the first individual to come to the assistance of the older person who has fallen. Consequently, it is important that these individuals are aware that any time a fall has occurred, the older person should not be moved, or even assisted in getting up from the ground if serious physical injury is apparent. Instead, emergency services should be called. Also, any complaints or signs of acute medical illness should be immediately referred for medical evaluation. Explaining some of the important reportable signs and symptoms to family members and formal caregivers who care for older persons at fall risk will help ensure that emergency treatment is provided. These are listed in Table 5.1. For nursing and other allied health professionals involved in home care practices and nursing home settings, where physicians on site may not always be available, an acute medical and injury assessment protocol

TABLE 5.1   Signs and Symptoms Requiring Medical Evaluation

Difficulty moving arms or legs
Pain/injury in arm, legs, or back
Headache/injury
Confusion/lethargy
Dizziness or lightheadedness
Blackouts
Sudden visual loss
Chest pain/difficulty breathing
Palpitations
Unable to get up from ground without experiencing injury
Increased lie time
Repeat falls occurring over short time period with or without injury

(Table 5.2) will help them evaluate the seriousness of the immediate fall and the need for medical referral.

FALL HISTORY

Once the person is medically stable, a well-directed history of the events surrounding the fall should follow so as to help uncover the specific cause. This procedure is analogous to inquiring about any other medical symptom, such as abdominal or chest pain. To discover the cause, a history of the circumstances, such as the duration, severity, and location of the pain, is obtained so as to establish a differential diagnosis. In the event of abdominal pain, this historical information may suggest, for example, the presence of peptic ulcer disease, appendicitis, gall bladder disease, or diverticulitis, and help guide the investigation to establish the precise cause. Similarly, a thorough history aimed at identifying the circumstances associated with falling represents the foundation of determining fall etiology and, in part, guides all subsequent diagnostic evaluations.

The fall history consists of asking the person about the circumstances surrounding the most recent event. This consists of inquiring about the presence of any symptoms experienced at the time or occurring prior to the fall (e.g., dizziness, heart palpitations, loss of consciousness or balance, legs giving away, tripping or slipping); the location of the fall (whether it occurred outdoors or indoors, and the specific area); a description of the activity the person was engaged in at the time of the fall (e.g., walking, transferring onto or from a bed, chair, or toilet); the time (hour of the day, and day of week) of the fall; and the consequences of the fall (injuries sustained, prolonged post-fall lie

TABLE 5.2   Acute Medical and Injury Assessment Protocol

Vital signs
    Temperature: _____
    Pulse rate: _____ Regular: _____ Irregular: _____
    Respiratory rate: _____
    Blood pressure: Supine _____ / _____ Sitting:_____ / _____

Head trauma
    Injury? Yes: _____ No: _____
    If yes, describe type and location of injury:_____
    _____
    _____

    Ear or nasal discharge (bloody or watery)? Yes: _____ No: _____
    If yes, describe type and location of discharge: _____
    _____
    _____

Visual dysfunction
    Transient blindness?   Yes: _____ No:_____
    Hemianoptic defects?   Yes: _____ No:_____
    Dimness or blurriness?   Yes: _____ No:_____
    Pupils unequal in size?   Yes: _____ No:_____
    Pupils not reactive to light? Yes: _____ No:_____

Speech dysfunction
    Sudden aphasia? Yes: _____ No: _____

Level of consciousness
    Drowsy or lethargic? Yes: _____ No: _____
    Delayed responses? Yes: _____ No: _____
    Confused? Yes: _____ No: _____
    Semi-comatose? Yes: _____ No: _____
    Stuporous? Yes: _____ No: _____
    Comatose? Yes: _____ No: _____

Cardiorespiratory dysfunction
    Abnormal respiration? Yes: _____ No: _____
    Cardiac chest pain? Yes: _____ No: _____
    Sudden irregularity of pulse? Yes: _____ No: _____
    Hemoptysis? Yes: _____ No: _____
    Abnormal or absent arterial pulses? Yes: _____ No: _____

Bleeding
    Gastrointestinal? Yes: _____ No: _____
    Genitourinary? Yes: _____ No: _____
    Ear/nasal? Yes: _____ No: _____

Neurologic dysfunction
    Convulsions? Yes: _____ No: _____
    Extremity weakness? Yes: _____ No: _____
    Headache? Yes: _____ No: _____
    Dizziness? Yes: _____ No: _____
    Vertigo? Yes: _____ No: _____

(continued)

TABLE 5.2   *(Continued)*

Lightheadedness?   Yes: _____   No: _____
Extremity paresis?   Yes: _____   No: _____
Extremity paralysis? Yes: _____   No: _____
If yes, describe for each "yes" response onset, nature, frequency,
description, and duration as applicable: _____

_____

_____

_____

_____

Extremity pain
Pain present when patient is asked to move upper/lower extremities?
Yes: _____   No: _____
If yes, describe type and location of pain: _____

_____

Lower extremities
  Internally/externally rotated?   Yes: _____   No: _____   R/L
  Abducted/adducted?   Yes: _____   No: _____   R/L
  Bone crepitus present?   Yes: _____   No: _____   R/L
  Limb shortening present?   Yes: _____   No: _____   R/L
  Decreased limb range of motion? Yes: _____   No: _____   R/L
Upper extremities
  Bone crepitus present?   Yes: _____   No: _____   R/L
  Decreased limb range of motion? Yes: _____   No: _____   R/L
  Tenderness upon palpation?   Yes: _____   No: _____   R/L

A "yes" response to any question indicates immediate medical referral.

From Tideiksaar, R. (1989). *Falling in old age* (pp. 124–125). New York: Springer Publishing
Co. Reprinted with permission.

time, and mobility restrictions). Also, ask about the type of footwear
worn (slippers, high heels, sneakers) and composition of the soles
(rubber, leather) and whether an assistive device (cane, walker) or
wheelchair was being used at the time of the fall.

In addition, the person should be asked about any falls, and their circumstances, that might have occurred over the previous 3 months.
This information may help to establish a "pattern" of falling, and determine an etiology. Sometimes older people who repeatedly fall over a
relatively short period of time under similar circumstances of symptoms, location, or activity are falling due to a single cause. Within hospitals and nursing homes, this information may be gathered from a
review of available incident reports. A convenient acronym to help

remember the components of the fall history is **SPLATT** (Symptoms, Previous falls, Location of fall, Activity at time of fall, Time of fall, and Trauma both physical and psychological).

It is equally important to also ask about near-falls (sometimes referred to as "almost falling" or "incomplete falls"). These are defined as events in which a person loses balance, but manages to avert a fall by grabbing onto an environmental object, such as the back of a chair, a table edge, wall, or door frame, for support. If the environmental support had not been available, the person would probably have suffered a fall to the ground. One can readily appreciate near-falls by observing frail older persons with gait and balance disorders as they attempt to ambulate about their environment surroundings without the support of assistive devices. Furthermore, the risk of falling appears to increase with the frequency of near-falls experienced. Teno et al. (1990) found that older persons who reported two or more previous "stumbles" were twice as likely to experience a subsequent fall than those individuals who did not report stumbles. In this respect, near-falls should be regarded with an importance equal to actual falling episodes. To elicit information on near-falls, the presentation of a scenario may sometimes be beneficial in helping the older person interpret what is meant by a near-fall, and perhaps, to help individuals recall such events. For example, the person can be asked "Have you ever experienced a loss of balance, but avoided falling to the ground by grabbing hold of an object, such as the edge of a table, or dresser, or wall, for support?" "Has this occurred frequently, occasionally, rarely, or never?"

Asking older persons to recount the circumstances of their falls or near-falls will provide valuable clues to their possible causes. For example, individuals who report symptoms near the time of their episode(s) may point to specific medical problems. Common complaints and their associated medical conditions include dizziness (orthostatic hypotension, arrhythmia, vestibular problem, anemia, dehydration, adverse drug effects), loss of consciousness (syncope, seizure), chest pain or palpitations (myocardial infarction, coronary insufficiency), confusion (adverse drug effect, decreased cerebral perfusion), impaired vision (glaucoma, macular degeneration), and gait abnormalities (myopathies, arthritis, stroke, decreased proprioception, foot disorders, Parkinsonism). Likewise, activities performed at the time of the fall may provide evidence of potential medical problems. Some examples are the flexion of the neck that occurs when looking upwards or obtaining an object from a high shelf or turning one's head to look sideways to view the peripheral environment (basilar artery and carotid sinus compression, respectively); assuming the upright position from a lying or sitting position (orthostatic hypotension, vestibular dysfunction); urination and defecation (reflex hypotension, syncope); and after eating a meal (post-prandial hypotension).

Conversely, nonspecific complaints, such as tripping, slipping, and balance loss, may implicate causative extrinsic factors such as environmental hazards (cluttered, wet, or elevated ground surfaces, sliding rugs, poor lighting); poor design of furnishings (beds and chairs); toilets and bathtubs/showers, and stairs; or inappropriate ambulation devices and footwear. Extrinsic factors as a cause of falls or near-falls may occur either in isolation or in combination with underlying medical conditions. For instance, the complaint of "balance loss" while attempting to sit on a chair or toilet may be due to either poor design by itself (low seats, lack of hand support) or in association with underlying neuromuscular dysfunction (arthritis, muscle weakness). If a person complains of "tripping" or "slipping," a hazardous ground surface camouflaged by poor lighting or a sliding rug may be the precipitating cause, either separately or in combination with associated gait, balance, or visual disorders.

Also, knowing the time and hour of the fall may help establish a possible cause. Falls occurring in the evening or night may be due to a lack of sufficient lighting or poor vision. In persons with congestive heart failure, falls that occur from bed or soon after leaving the bed in the early morning hours may be a sign of nocturia and worsening heart failure. In diabetic individuals, falls occurring after meals may be a manifestation of post-prandial hypotension, while falls experienced in the late morning or early evening hours may be due to insulin-induced hypoglycemia. Similarly, knowing the day of the week that falls occur may provide valuable clues. For instance, repetitive falls that occur on specific days of the week may indicate the performance of certain habitual activities that the person is no longer equal to, such as bathing, descending a steep flight of steps to the basement to do the wash, or shopping for groceries and carrying heavy, cumbersome bags.

Knowing the type of injuries and location on the body may suggest a cause, particularly if the person is a poor oral historian. For example, a report of bruises on the buttocks or side of the hip strongly signifies a fall in the backward or sideways direction, indicating possible lower extremity dysfunction and poor postural response. On the other hand, upper extremity trauma often occurs following falls in the forward direction, while the consequence of tripping suggests gait abnormalities and/or environmental ground hazards as a predisposing factor. The presence of any head trauma may be the result of an inability to exhibit a protective reflex (outstretching the arms) subsequent to a possible syncopal episode. Also, the location and type of injury might suggest possible fall complications. For example, bruises or abrasions on the knees and elbows may indicate that the person was crawling around on the floor after the fall, unable to get up. The presence of pressure sores implies that the person may have experienced a prolonged post-fall lie time on the ground. Any reported loss of self-confidence in performing activities, or restrictions of physical and social mobility, as a consequence of falling or near-falls may indicate a fear of stability and further falls.

If an assistive device, such as a cane or walker, or wheelchair was used at the time of the fall, this might indicate that the device or wheelchair may be at fault, either due to mechanical problems (for example, structural defects, worn cane and walker tips, wheelchair locks not working properly) or improper utilization. On the other hand, if the older person was not using the device, this may in part have contributed to the fall. Likewise, knowing the type of footwear worn at the time can be valuable. For instance, slippers by design often lead to a shuffling gait that can contribute to trip-related falls, particularly in persons with poor steppage height and other gait disorders. Wearing sneakers or running shoes furnished with thick, absorbent rubber soles may contribute to a loss of balance through decreased proprioceptive input through the soles, or gait impairment through soles sticking to carpeted and linoleum floor surfaces.

The following case studies help to illustrate the value of the fall history.

MB is an 82-year-old woman with a history of five recent falls. Her medical history was remarkable for osteoarthritis of the knees, treated with a nonsteroidal anti-inflammatory drug (NSAID). During questioning, MB stated that all her falls occurred in the bedroom while getting out of bed in the morning, and were accompanied by symptoms of "dizziness." She also expressed a fear of falling and sustaining a hip fracture. The circumstances surrounding MB's falls suggested a differential diagnosis of postural hypotension. An evaluation revealed the presence of orthostatic hypotension and an iron-deficiency anemia. Further diagnostic studies uncovered gastrointestinal bleeding secondary to the use of NSAIDs. Her orthostasis, falls, and, eventually, her fear of falls subsided after treatment of the anemia and discontinuation of the NSAID.

HH is an 86-year-old woman who reported three recent falls. Her medical problems included a history of congestive heart failure (digoxin and Lasix), diabetes mellitus (NPH insulin), and depression (trazodone), all of which could have contributed to falling. Upon inquiry, the patient stated that all episodes occurred from bed, in the middle of the night, and were associated with the need to urinate. The patient complained that her urinary problems had become much worse over the past few weeks. A probable diagnosis of nocturia secondary to heart failure was entertained and confirmed on physical examination, and the patient's cardiac drugs were adjusted appropriately. Her bed falls were ascribed in part to her antidepressant (increased sedation) and to carelessness (in the dark), while attempting to hurry to the bathroom. As a consequence, her traz0done dose was decreased. Night-lights were also recommended. In spite of these interventions, however, the falls continued. Finally, I asked her point blank: "What were you doing at the time of each fall?" After hesitating, HH admitted that she was afraid of walking to the bathroom during the night because she was afraid of losing her balance and falling. Instead, she urinated into a plastic quart container while sitting on the edge of her bed. Occasionally, she would lose her sitting balance and slide to the floor. Once she was furnished with a bedside commode, her falls stopped.

Each time the older person falls, a new fall history should be obtained as well. It is erroneous to assume that all falls experienced by the individual are due to similar causes. The following cases serve as illustrations.

CD is a 79-year-old man with Parkinson's Disease who lives alone. He experienced several bed falls, the result of a "saggy" mattress (which led to poor sitting balance) and a low bed height (difficulty with rising). As a consequence, it was recommended to his family that they purchase a new bed of the appropriate height with a supportive mattress for the patient. The family, hoping to stop the falls, purchased a new bed and mattress. However, one month later, he once more began to fall. The family was quite upset, as they assumed that the bed modifications had failed to have the desired effect. They also feared that the patient might either require caregiver assistance to help with mobility tasks, or need to relocate to a nursing home for safety reasons. However, upon investigation, the patient stated that his recent falls did not occur from bed; as a matter of fact, his bed mobility had improved markedly as a result of the modifications. Rather, his falls resulted from a low-seated bedroom chair (and thus from difficulty with rising). Once the chair was equipped with a seating cushion that allowed him to transfer independently, his falls stopped.

PG is an 82-year-old woman who resided in a nursing home. Her medical problems consisted of dementia and psychosis, which was treated with an antipsychotic (risperidone). Soon after the medication was started PG suffered two falls. Both episodes occurred while the resident was ambulating. It was felt that the falls were caused by the medication's adverse effects (somnolence, dizziness) and the dose was decreased. This resulted in a marked improvement of the resident's gait and balance, and she experienced no further falls. However, approximately one month later, she began to fall again. Reviewing the resident's past incident reports, it was concluded that the falls were due once more to the ill effects of risperidone, which was then stopped. But the resident continued to fall and now began to exhibit greater psychosis. As it turned out, all the falls following the initial decrease in medication occurred while getting out of bed. More than likely, the risperidone led to extrapyramidal reactions that resulted in poor bed mobility and falls. The resident's bed was modified to support independent bed transfers and the risperidone was restarted at a lower dose. Her falls stopped and her psychosis diminished to controllable levels.

While some older persons give clear accounts of their fall(s), others, because of memory problems (depression or dementia), may not be able to recall accurately the number or circumstance of their fall(s). As well, the vast majority of falls occurring in both the community and institutional settings are unwitnessed events. As a result, in those persons with cognitive problems, discrepancies may exist between the person's account of the fall and what actually happened. The recollection of falls, however, may be problematic for the mentally intact as well. This may especially be a problem for community-dwelling older persons, as it may be weeks to months before they visit a doctor and are questioned about falling episodes, especially if they haven't suffered any injuries and/or loss of functional abilities. As a result, reports from any significant others (spouses, adult children, neighbors, etc.) and formal caregivers present at the time of the fall who may have witnessed the event can be helpful. Within the hospital and nursing home setting, nurses, other staff members, and family members who may be visiting at the time can also be asked about any falling episodes witnessed.

The use of a fall diary (Figure 5.1) that records the circumstances of each fall may be helpful as an adjunct in community-dwelling persons at fall risk. The diary is given to those individuals with poor recall of their falling episodes, and is reviewed by their doctor at the time of the individual's office visits. Experience has shown that compliance with the diary is good; about 70% of persons complete the fall diary. However, compliance rates begin to decrease inversely to the length of time between receiving the diary and experiencing one or more falls. In other words, those individuals with recent and recurrent falls appear to be both motivated and the most compliant in completing the diary. If available, family members and formal caregivers living with the person should be supplied with a fall diary as well, and asked to complete an entry every time they witness the person's fall. This helps obtain a better accounting of falls and their circumstances. Included on the

FIGURE 5.1   Fall diary.

Falling down is not a normal part of growing old. There are many causes of falls that can be treated. In order to prevent falls, we need to know as much as possible about your falls. This diary will help you remember the circumstances of your fall(s). Each time you fall, write down the date of the fall, time of day when the fall occurred, where the fall occurred (location), what you were doing at the time (activity), and how you felt at the time (symptoms). Below we have listed two examples to guide you.

EXAMPLES:

DATE	TIME	LOCATION	ACTIVITY	SYMPTOMS
10/2	8 AM	Bedroom	Getting out of bed	Dizziness
10/8	3 PM	Outdoors	Walking	Tripping

1.

2.

3.

4.

5.

back pages of the diary are a list of general fall prevention recommendations that can be used as an educational device to instruct older persons about safety in the home. Some community-based research studies have utilized a calendar or postcard system for similar purposes. Calendars with daily dates are distributed to those persons with falls so that they are able to record their falls whenever they occur. The older person is instructed to mail back the completed calendars at the end of each month. Other studies use a postcard system to record fall episodes, addressed and prestamped for easy return. The accuracy of reporting falls through these systems has been estimated to be nearly 100% (Nevitt et al., 1989). This unusually high completion rate, however, may be due to the fact that these older persons were research subjects, and as a result, received constant verbal and written reminders to reinforce their diaries' completion.

As well, some older individuals may be reluctant to provide a history of falls or depict the true extent of their falls or near-falls. This may be due to embarrassment, as they may want to avoid an image of frailty; or they want to preserve their autonomy, fearing that if they report one or more falling or near-fall events their mobility will be restricted or they will be forced to relocate to safer locations, such as sheltered housing or a nursing home. Therefore, it should never be assumed that persons who fail to report falls or near-falls are not doing so. Likewise, those individuals who report only one recent episode may have experienced several previous falls or near-falls that they are not disclosing. In general, a better accounting of both events can be obtained once the older person's anxieties and fears about divulging the information are relieved.

When obtaining a fall history it is important to avoid open-ended questions about the circumstances of the event. Older persons may experience great difficulty in describing precisely what happened, or they may confuse different episodes. As a result, they may instead ascribe the fall to events that they are more familiar with saying "I must have tripped . . . or slipped." However, the individual's fall may not have been due to these events. Since an accurate description of the symptoms and activities at the time of the fall is crucial to help determine the mechanism and cause of the episode(s), direct questions may be more useful. For example, more precise information can be obtained by asking the person "Do you remember falling?" "Did you feel dizzy or lightheaded before falling?" "Did you lose consciousness?" "Did you lose balance?" "Were you using the toilet?" "Were you getting in or out of the bathtub?" or "Were you walking up the stairs at the time?" As well, it is helpful to inquire specifically about the events that occurred after the fall, asking "Did you have trouble getting up from the ground?" "Did you injure yourself in any way?" "Are you afraid of falling again?" or "Have you restricted your activities in any way?"

Although family members and formal caregivers can make valuable contributions to the history, reliance on these individuals or allowing them to dominate the conversation interferes with the older person's view of the problem. Also, their presence can make it embarrassing for the older person to divulge certain information. As a result, it is best to conduct the initial interview with the older person alone, and to speak with family members and others separately to gain further information.

FALL RISK ASSESSMENT

Regardless of whether the older person resides in the community, acute care hospital, or nursing home, the assessment of fall risk begins with the identification of individual risk factors. As was discussed in Chapter 4, there are a number of host-related or intrinsic factors associated with the risk of falls in older persons. Some of the most significant include a history of previous falls, lower extremity weakness and sensory impairment, gait and balance disorders, urinary dysfunction (nocturia, incontinence), visual impairment, altered cognition (depression, dementia), and taking more than four medications or certain medications (psychotropics, antihypertensives). These factors, particularly when they occur simultaneously, have been repeatedly associated with an increased risk of falling. Attempts to ascertain their presence should be included in the medical and nursing assessment of older persons. As a first step, this is accomplished by taking a history from the older person, and reviewing the medical history for disease processes (e.g., glaucoma, arthritis, stroke, Parkinsonism) and medications that place individuals at risk. In the event that the individual is a poor historian or is cognitively impaired, this information may be obtained from additional sources, such as previous health care practitioners, medical records, and input from significant others (spouses, adult children, etc.) and formal caregivers. Additionally, if the person has experienced previous falls, an inquiry into the number of falls and their surrounding circumstances (the fall history) should be attempted.

While the presence of risk factors increases fall susceptibility, their relationship to precipitating falls is highly dependent upon the extent of morbidity and its interaction with other comorbid diseases and medications. For example, a severe degree of Parkinson's Disease will typically represent a greater risk of balance loss and falls than mild expressions of the disease that may be associated with little symptomatology. However, the occurrence of mild Parkinson's Disease in combination with other diseases, such as lower extremity arthritis, may markedly increase the likelihood of experiencing instability and falls. Likewise, utilizing a psychotropic alone may represent only minimal risk, but when the psychotropic is taken with other medications, such as a diuretic, for instance, the combination can lead to orthostatic hypotension and thus to an increased risk of falls. A similar situation arises when a high-risk medication, such as a hypnotic, is prescribed for an individual with Alzheimer's Disease. Each medication in itself may represent only a slight risk, but when combined may increase the risk of falling appreciably. The following case helps to illustrates this point:

> RC is an 83-year-old man who was admitted to the hospital for the evaluation of urinary incontinence and decreased cognition. He had a history of Parkinson's Disease that was treated with a low dose of carbidopa. Upon admission his gait and balance and cognitive state were mildly abnormal, but he was able to function within the unit independently and safely.

However, this changed rapidly. During the first week of admission, he was diagnosed with hypertension and treated with captopril, depression (fluoxetine), angina (isosorbide), and nocturnal agitation (p.r.n. haloperidol). At the end of the week, he attempted to get out of bed, lost his balance, and suffered a fall to the floor. Thus, while on admission this patient had several risk factors for falls, these did not interfere with his mobility. However, the addition of numerous medications, which interfered with the ability to maintain adequate levels of blood pressure and as a result, his balance, significantly increased fall risk to the point where he fell.

A more accurate measure of fall risk is reflected by the effects of disease processes and medications on an individual's mobility (that is, the capacity to walk and transfer safely and independently). In other words, any mobility impairment that occurs as a result of multiple morbidity is a stronger predictor of subsequent falls than is the presence of medical conditions occurring in isolation. Therefore, in addition to ascertaining historical risk factors, it is of equal importance, and arguably of greater relevance, to assess an individual's mobility. This then constitutes the second step in the assessment of fall risk.

MOBILITY ASSESSMENT

To gather information regarding mobility, older persons should be asked directly about their capacity to ambulate; transfer from beds, chairs, toilets; get into and out of bathtubs/showers; and climb and descend stairs, etc. Similar details may be available from family members and formal caregivers if the person is unable to provide answers themselves. However, relying solely on historical information may not always provide an accurate assessment of the person's mobility. Some older persons, to avoid an image of frailty or dependency, will overstate their mobility capacity, particularly with respect to their safety. For example, I questioned one older woman in the clinic about her ability to rise from the toilet in her home. She stated emphatically that she was able to transfer from the toilet independently, requiring no help. On a subsequent home visit, I observed her transfers; indeed, she was able to get up from the toilet by herself, but only by using the sink edge and bathtub rim for assistive hand support. Without the use of these supports, she repeatedly lost her balance and fell back onto the toilet seat. As was mentioned earlier in this chapter, another older woman denied any difficulty with toileting, but as it turned out, during the night she urinated into a plastic cup rather than use the toilet because she was fearful of falling.

On the other hand, some family members and even formal care-givers will underestimate the mobility capacity of the older person and, instead, make them out to appear more dependent than they actually are. For instance, one older woman told me that she was capable of independent toileting, and was observed to be just that. In contrast, the daughter stated that her mother was incapable of autonomous toilet transfers, and as result, was maintained in adult diapers in order to cut down on the need for assisted help with toileting. In actuality, the daughter's perception of her mother's decreased function was clouded by a fear that her mother might fall if allowed to travel to the bathroom by herself. As well, any responses obtained through self-report or observer-report may not always be accurate for reasons of cultural or language differences. Finally, any responses received may not reflect the older person's current level of mobility. What the person was capable of accomplishing one month or one week ago may not always indicate their present mobility level.

A more accurate way to assess mobility is to perform a sensory and neuromuscular examination which measures many components of mobility such as vision, position sense, coordination, and muscle strength of the lower extremities. However, while these evaluations may be useful in establishing a diagnosis and determining the severity of disease, they tend to be a poor predictor of functional capacity or mobility in older persons. Tinetti and Ginter (1988) evaluated the sensitivity of a conventional neuromuscular examination for identifying mobility problems in a group of community-dwelling persons 75 years and older. The researchers compared relevant sensory and neuromuscular findings (vision, frontal reflexes, position sense, knee flexion and extension, and hip flexion, abduction, and adduction) with performance during mobility maneuvers such as rising and sitting in a chair, and turning around while walking. They found that many persons who performed poorly during mobility maneuvers did not have the corresponding neuromuscular abnormalities. For example, of the subjects who exhibited unsteady turning, only 71% had a decrease in either hip or knee strength, 60% had poor vision, 51% had abnormal position sense, and 27% had abnormal coordination test results. Similarly, while hip and knee flexion are needed to sit down safely, only 15% of the subjects who had difficulty sitting down had abnormal hip flexion and only 30% had abnormal knee flexion. Only 44% of subjects with problems in chair rising had decreased knee extension, an essential component required to perform this activity.

As a result, the most accurate way to assess mobility and, in particular, the effects of comorbidity, is to observe the mobility performance of the older person. In response, clinicians have relied upon quantitative tests of gait and balance, the main components of mobility, to supplement the traditional clinical evaluation. These are generally laboratory-based and require the use of balance platforms, treadmills, or computerized gait analysis (Lichtenstein et al., 1988; Sharma & MacLennan, 1988). While these techniques are beneficial, there are several problems associated with their routine application. The equipment is generally expensive to purchase and requires both additional storage space and special training of individuals to both operate and analyze the data. Also, the exposure of older persons to a complicated apparatus and special laboratory conditions may itself affect confidence and adversely affect the test results. For instance, Greig, Butler, Skelton, Mahmud, and Young (1993) examined a group of healthy older people and younger people, comparing treadmill walking and corridor walking. The researchers showed that, even after thorough familiarization with the treadmill, the older people exhibited higher heart rates when walking on a treadmill than when walking along a corridor. The younger subjects did not show a comparable treadmill-corridor difference in heart rate. The authors hypothesized two reasons for this: older people found balancing on the treadmill more demanding, or their anxiety about their ability to walk on the treadmill affected the outcome. Similarly, Maki and colleagues (1991) investigated the association between fear of falling and postural performance in a group of older people, using a balance platform. They found that subjects who expressed a fear of falling exhibited significantly poorer performance on a number of balance tests. The researchers, however, expressed caution in interpreting the results, suggesting that the fear of falling might have affected balance test performance in an artificial manner, rather than signifying a true deterioration in postural control. Thus, using special equipment to analyze gait and balance in older persons may not represent "real-life" situations and, moreover, may not be practical for most clinical settings, at least as an initial assessment. Instead, this technology is more useful as a way to identify more subtle mobility impairments, or else to conduct research where objective measurements are crucial.

Gait and Balance Assessment

In response, researchers have attempted to develop gait and balance tests and assessment instruments that are more pragmatic for clinical use. These tests are based on observing the older person perform one or more specific gait and/ or balance tasks, and evaluating or measuring their performance in an objective, uniform manner, using a predetermined set of criteria.

Balance Tests. In general, these instruments are good predictors of fall risk, as they measure dynamic balance. This, in contrast to static balance (standing quietly), tends to challenge a person's ability to retain postural control by simulating situations that tend to displace the center of gravity; that is, situations that place persons at increased fall risk. Some examples from the literature follow.

Wolfson, Whipple, Amerman, and Kleinberg (1986) designed the postural stress test (PST). In this test, motor responses to postural perturbations of varying degrees are measured during normal standing by using a simple pulley-weight system that displaces the center of gravity behind and beyond the base of support. Specifically, the PST measures an individual's ability to withstand a series of destabilizing forces applied at the level of the person's waist. Scoring is based on a 9-point ordinal scale, with a score of 9 representing the most efficient postural response and a score of 0 symbolizing a complete failure to remain upright.

Wolfson et al. (1986) compared nursing home residents with and without falls, and found that fallers scored significantly lower PST scores than non-fallers. From these results, the researchers concluded that the PST can be used to effectively predict individuals at high risk of falling. In support of these findings, Chandler, Duncan, and Studenski (1990), in a group of community-dwelling older persons with falls, also demonstrated that fallers scored significantly lower on the PST than a group of non-fallers.

Duncan, Weiner, Chandler, and Studenski (1990) developed a clinical measure of balance called "Functional Reach." They defined functional reach as representing the maximum distance an individual can reach forward beyond arm's length while maintaining a fixed base of support in the standing position. The degree of functional reach is measured using a yardstick secured to a wall at the height of the acromion (the shoulder joint), and is measured as follows:

0 = unable to reach
1 = reach less than or equal to 6 inches
2 = reach greater than 6 but less than 10 inches
3 = reach greater than or equal to 10 inches

Duncan, Studenski, Chandler, and Prescott (1992) studied the predictability of functional reach in identifying older people at risk for recurrent falls in a group of community-dwelling male veterans aged 70 to 104 years and found a significant association between functional reach and recurrent falls. That is, the risk of falling increased in proportion to an inability to reach or a limited ability to reach; this was defined as a distance of less than or equal to 6 inches, or reach greater than 6 inches but less than 10 inches, respectively.

Fleming, Wilson, and Pendergast (1991) assembled a portable "Muscle Power Test" (MPT) to screen for the risk of falling in older people who resided in adult care facilities. In performing the MPT, persons are instructed to stand up as fast and forcefully as possible from a chair, without using the armrests, while the chair is mounted on a portable balance platform, and then after a period of 5 seconds to resume sitting as fast as possible. The MPT assesses the ability of individuals to maximally recruit hip, knee, and ankle muscles in a controlled safe movement. The researchers compared a group of older persons with and without falls and found that fallers, as measured by the MPT, got up from the chair more slowly than non-fallers, as a result of low peak power or decreased lower extremity strength. They concluded that the MPT can identify individuals at fall risk, and that this risk may extend to identifying other activities that require dependable neuromuscular function of the lower extremities, such as stair climbing, and maintaining of balance to sudden displacements of stability, such as slipping on a rug.

Gait Tests. Wolfson et al. (1990) devised the "Gait Abnormality Rating Scale" (GARS) that is intended to serve as a simple and easy method of evaluating the gait of older persons in a clinic setting. The GARS consists, first, of videotaping the gait of a person. Then two individuals replay the tapes on a monitor and independently evaluate 16 variables of gait using a four point scale: 0 = normal, 1 = mildly impaired, 2 = moderately impaired, 3 = severely impaired. In a study of nursing home residents, the researchers evaluated the gait of individuals with and without falls, and found that stride length, walking velocity, and gait quality (as measured by the GARS) were significantly reduced in those persons with falls, as compared to non-fallers. The researchers concluded that the GARS correlated with falls, and thus, may serve as a clinical tool that can be used to predict fall risk.

Fried, Cwikel, Ring, and Galinsky (1990) designed the "Extra-Laboratory Gait Assessment Method" (ELGAM) that was designed to assess gait in the home or outpatient setting. In this test, a 5-m length of toweling paper 60 cm in width is unrolled on a bare floor. The older person is asked to walk the length of the paper, and their gait speed is measured with a stop-watch and calculated by the amount of time it takes for the person to travel the distance. The person is asked to walk the length of the paper once more, and instructed to turn the head to the left and right at the same time. During this maneuver, gait initiation and balance are recorded. Then spongy stickers are applied to the heel and toe of the older person's footwear, and dipped into a shallow pan of water. Wearing the footwear, the older person is instructed to walk along the length of the paper one last time and the footprints are outlined in a marker pen. Subsequently a number of gait parameters are measured. In a study of 36 community-residing older persons averaging 73 years of age with and without a history of falls, the researchers found that slow gait, small steps, and impaired balance on head-turning were significantly associated both with reported fall frequency and episodes of near-falls, but only among women. An explanation for the lack of significant findings in older men was not discussed, but may relate to an underreporting of falls and near-falls in this group. Nevertheless, the researchers concluded that the ELGAM is a useful method for collecting data on gait patterns and for identifying fall risk in older persons.

While these tests are extremely useful in detecting gait and balance problems and determining the extent of fall risk, they are still limited to a certain degree, as some equipment is required. Consequently, their use may be restricted to institutional and outpatient environments. These tests may not, in some situations, be appropriate for use in these settings, as well as in other environments, such as the older person's home. However, for some tests, such as the functional reach test, one can easily imagine that a carpenter's measuring tape could be used in place of a yardstick. At any rate, there are a multitude of other mobility instruments that are of equal benefit, which are not restricted by their equipment and may be more "user-friendly" or simpler to use. Collectively, these are referred to as Performance-Oriented Mobility Assessments.

Performance-Oriented Mobility Assessments.   Tinetti (1986) developed the "Performance-Oriented Assessment of Mobility" (Table 5.3). This test consists of asking an older person to perform a number of gait and balance maneuvers and then observing the manner in which each task is accomplished. The maximum achievable score is 28 (balance, 16; gait, 12), and the lowest score is zero. Several community- and institutional-based studies have found that poor execution of the gait and balance maneuvers as described in the performance-oriented assessment of mobility is associated with an increased risk of future falls (Robbins et al., 1989; Tinetti, 1986; Tinetti, Speechley, & Ginter, 1988).

TABLE 5.3 Performance-Oriented Assessment of Mobility

Balance	Gait
Instructions: Seat the subject in a hard armless chair. Test the following maneuvers. Select one number that best describes the subject's performance in each test, and add up the scores at the end.	**Instructions:** The subject stands with the examiner, and then walks down hallway or across room, first at the usual pace and then back at a rapid but safe pace, using a cane or walker if accustomed to one.

Balance

1. Sitting balance
Leans or slides in chair = 0
Steady, safe = 1 ____

2. Arising
Unable without help = 0
Able but uses arms to help = 1
Able without use of arms = 2 ____

3. Attempt to arise
Unable without help = 0
Able but requires more than one attempt = 1
Able to arise with one attempt = 2 ____

4. Immediate standing balance (first 5 seconds)
Unsteady (staggers, moves feet, marked trunk sway) = 0
Steady but uses walker or cane, or grabs other objects for support = 1
Steady without walker, cane, or other support = 2 ____

5. Standing balance
Unsteady = 0
Steady but wide stance (medial heels more than 4 inches apart) or uses cane, walker, or other support = 1
Narrow stance without support = 2 ____

Gait

10. Initiation of gait (immediately after being told to go)
Any hesitancy or several attempts to start = 0
No hesitancy = 1 ____

11. Step length and height
Right swing foot:
Fails to pass left stance foot with step = 0
Passes left stance foot = 1
Fails to clear floor completely with step = 0
Completely clears floor = 1
Left swing foot:
Fails to pass right stance foot with step = 0
Passes right stance foot = 1
Fails to clear floor completely with step = 0
Completely clears floor = 1 ____

12. Step symmetry
Right and left step length unequal = 0
Right and left step equal = 1 ____

13. Step continuity
Stopping or discontinuity between steps = 0
Steps appear continuous = 1 ____

14. Path (Observe excursion of either left or right foot over about 10 feet of the course.)
Marked deviation = 0

(continued)

TABLE 5.3 (*Continued*)

Balance	Gait
6. Nudging (With subject's feet as close together as possible, push lightly on the sternum with palm of hand three times.)	Mild to moderate deviation or uses walking aid = 1
Begins to fall = 0	Walks straight without aid = 2 _____
Staggers and grabs, but catches self = 1	15. Trunk
Steady = 2 _____	Marked sway or uses walking aid = 0
7. Eyes closed (at same position as in No. 6)	No sway but flexion of knees or back, or spreads arms out while walking = 1
Unsteady = 0	No sway, flexion, use of arms, or use of walking aid = 2 _____
Steady = 1 _____	16. Walking stance
8. Turning 360 degrees	Heels apart = 0
Discontinuous steps = 0	Heels almost touch while walking = 1 _____
Continuous steps = 1 _____	
Unsteady (grabs and staggers) = 0	
Steady = 1 _____	
9. Sitting down	
Unsafe (misjudges distance, falls into chair) = 0	
Uses arms or lacks smooth motion = 1	
Safe, smooth motion = 2 _____	

Balance score: _____ /16   **Gait score:** _____ /12

Total score: _____ /28

Note. From "Performance-oriented assessment of mobility in elderly patients," by M. E. Tinetti, 1986, *Journal of the American Geriatrics Society, 34*, 119–126. Copyright 1986 by Patient Care. Adapted with permission.

Berg, Wood-Dauphinee, Williams, and Gayton (1989) developed the "Berg Balance Scale." This instrument is designed to evaluate a person's performance on 14 activities common in everyday life, which are each scored on a 5-point scale (0 to 4) for a total of 56 points. Specific mobility items include:

1. getting in and out of a chair, sitting unsupported, and transferring from bed to chair;
2. maintaining standing balance with feet together, feet apart, and with eyes closed;
3. turning to each side and turning 360 degrees;
4. reaching forward;
5. picking an object up from the floor;
6. tandem and single-leg stance; and
7. dynamic weight shifting.

A balance scale score of 45 appears to be the cut-off point between older persons who are safe in independent mobility and those individuals at increased fall risk. Berg, Wood-Dauphinee, Williams, and Maki (1992) monitored the functional performance and balance of 113 older persons residing in a home for the elderly over a 9-month period, and their fall occurrences for a year. At the end of the 12 months, it was found that in those individuals with an initial balance scale score of less than 45, the relative risk of multiple falls over the next 12 months was nearly threefold.

Mathias, Nayak, and Isaacs (1986) developed a mobility instrument labelled the "Get-Up-and-Go" test. This mobility test simply requires the person to stand up from a chair, walk a short distance, turn around, return, and sit down again. Each task is scored on the following scale: 1 = normal; 2 = very slightly abnormal; 3 = mildly abnormal; 4 = moderately abnormal; 5 = severely abnormal. Podsiadlo and Richardson (1991) developed a modified, timed version of the "Get-Up-and-Go" test. In this test the person is asked to perform similar tasks; however, the score given is the time taken in seconds to complete the test. The authors assessed the clinical usefulness of the timed "Get-Up-and-Go" test as an evaluation of basic mobility skills in a population of frail community-dwelling older persons and found the test to be both reliable and valid for quantifying balance, gait speed, and mobility capacity. Those older persons who were independent in mobility skills completed the test in less than 20 seconds; those individuals who tended to be more dependent took more than 30 seconds to complete the tasks. Of those persons who were dependent, many required help with their mobility tasks (for example, chair and toilet transfers, getting in and out of tubs/showers, and climbing stairs).

Guralnik et al. (1994) generated a short battery of physical performance tests to assess lower extremity function. These tests require the older person to perform three separate timed tasks: an 8-foot walk test, a repeated chair stand test, and a standing balance test. The latter test consists of the person starting with a semi-tandem stand (with the heel of one foot touching the side of the big toe on the other foot). They proceed to a full tandem stance if they can hold the semi-tandem position for at least 10 seconds, or a side-by-side stand (placing the feet together) if they are unable to maintain semi-tandem. Scoring is determined by assigning a score of zero for persons unable to complete the walk and chair stand task. Those who complete each task are assigned scores of 1 to 4, corresponding to the time needed to complete the task, with the fastest times scored as 4. The balance standing tests are assigned a score of 0 to 4, with scores of 0 to 1 denoting impairment.

In a study of more than 5,000 persons aged 71 years and older in original communities (of the Established Populations for Epidemiological Studies of the Elderly [EPESE]), the authors found a strong association between these performance measures of lower extremity dysfunction and self-reported disability, but a discordance for assessments of walking (Coroni-Hantley, Brock, Ostfeld, Taylor, & Wallace, 1986). Of those persons unable to complete the walk test, 13.6% stated that they were able to walk a half mile without help. Aside from participant mistakes in responding to questions regarding self-reported disability, or researcher error in coding the individual's responses, the authors speculated that temporary disability may have constituted one of the reasons for the discordance.

An even simpler test is the "Timed Chair Stands," a functional measure of balance performance that assesses the ability of a person to rise from a chair. In this test, the person is instructed to rise as rapidly as possible from a chair without using the armrests and with arms crossed over the chest. At the same time, a stop-watch is activated, and stopped when the person is fully upright and has attained stable standing balance. This maneuver is repeated 3 times, with a short rest period between each trial. If the person cannot rise after a period of 30 seconds, then the maneuver is repeated by allowing the individual to use the chair's armrests. Poor performance is exhibited if the person cannot rise after 30 seconds. Several community-based studies have found that poor performance in rising from a chair is a strong predictor of fall risk (Campbell, Borrie, & Spears, 1989; Nevitt, Cummings, Kidd, & Black, 1989).

These mobility assessments are extremely useful and relatively easy to perform; they require no extra equipment other than a standard chair or stop-watch), and need relatively little clinical training to master. However, most of these instruments have been developed primarily for research purposes, and may not be practical for clinical purposes in all cases. Specifically, some of these scoring systems may be time-consuming, and the terminology used can sometimes be difficult to understand and interpret correctly. As a result, these performance-oriented mobility assessments may not be user-friendly for every health professional in every clinical setting. In an effort to address this problem, I have designed the "Performance-Oriented Mobility Screen" (POMS), which has been adapted in part from several of the aforementioned mobility instruments (Table 5.4). The POMS is designed to function as a quick clinical screen of mobility, and is based on observing the older person perform 10 specific gait and balance tasks, scoring each performance as either normal or abnormal.

The POMS is performed in the following manner. Ask the individual to sit down in a chair without using the armrests for assistive support and then to rise from the chair, again, without using the armrests, seat edge, or their knees for assistance. Observe the person's ability to accomplish each activity in a smooth and controlled movement without experiencing a loss of balance. To initially avoid using the armrests for transfer support, instruct the individual to keep his or her arms crossed over the chest. If the person cannot accomplish these maneuvers, then ask them to repeat both the sitting and rising maneuver by relying on the chair's armrests for hand support, and again observe their ability to do so independently and safely. Most persons are able to do this without difficulty. However, recognize that this is an abnormal position, and may in itself lead to balance problems, especially in frail older persons. Also, some persons with either language problems or cognitive loss may fail to fully comprehend this task, and the initial avoidance of armrests to accomplish seated transfers as well. In these individuals the use of two different chairs, one with and one without armrests, may be a better choice.

Next, after the person rises from the chair, he or she should be instructed to remain standing in place for approximately 15 seconds. Observe whether the person is able to stand without unsteadiness or support from the chair to maintain balance. Then ask the person to remain standing, with both eyes closed, arms placed by the sides, and feet placed approximately 3 inches apart. This is the Romberg maneuver, and is used to assess proprioceptive function. An inability to maintain balance, as demonstrated by increased postural sway or grabbing

TABLE 5.4 Performance-Oriented Mobility Screen (POMS)

Instructions: Ask the person to perform the following maneuvers. For each, indicate whether the person's performance is normal or abnormal.

Ask Person To:	Observe:	Response:
1. Sit down in chair. Select a chair with armrests that is approximately 16 to 17 inches in seat height	Able to sit down in one smooth, controlled movement without using armrests.	Normal
	Sitting is not a smooth movement; falls into chair or needs armrests to guide self into chair.	Abnormal
2. Rise up from chair.	Able to get up in one smooth, controlled movement without using armrests.	Normal
	Uses armrests and/or moves forward in chair to propel self up; requires several attempts to get up.	Abnormal
3. Stand after rising from chair for approximately 30 seconds in place.	Steady; able to stand without support.	Normal
	Unsteady; loses balance.	Abnormal
4. Stand with eyes closed for approximately 15 seconds in place.	Steady; able to stand without support.	Normal
	Unsteady; loses balance.	Abnormal
5. Stand with feet together, push lightly on sternum 2 to 3 times	Steady; maintains balance.	Normal
	Unsteady; loses balance.	Abnormal
6. Reach up into tiptoes as if attempting to reach an object.	Steady, without loss of balance.	Normal
	Unsteady; loses balance.	Abnormal
7. Bend down as if attempting to obtain object from floor.	Steady, without loss of balance.	Normal
	Unsteady; loses balance.	Abnormal

TABLE 5.4 *(Continued)*

Instructions: If the person uses a walking aid such as a cane or walker, the following walking maneuvers are tested separately with and without the aid. Indicate type of aid used.

8. Walk in a straight line, in your "usual" pace (a distance approximately 15 feet); then walk back.	Gait is continuous without hesitation; walks in a straight line and both feet clear the floor.	Normal (with aid)
	Gait is noncontinuous with hesitation; deviates from straight path; feet scrape or shuffle on floor.	Abnormal (with aid) Abnormal (without aid)
9. Walk a distance of 5 feet and turn around.	Does not stagger; steps are smooth, continuous	Normal (with aid) Normal (without aid)
	Staggers; steps are unsteady, discontinuous	Abnormal (with aid) Abnormal (without aid)
10. Lie down on the floor and get up.	Able to rise, without loss of balance.	Normal
	Unable to rise, or loses balance in the process	Abnormal

From Tideiksaar, R. (1994b). Falls. In B. R. Bonder & M. B. Wagner (Eds.), *Functional Performance in Older Adults* (p. 232). Philadelphia: F. A. Davis. Reprinted with permission.

hold of environmental furnishings or walls for support, indicates an abnormality. To further challenge the individual's balance, a "sharpened" Romberg maneuver—placing the feet in a tandem position—may be performed, but caution is advised, as many older people may not be capable of performing this maneuver without experiencing a loss of balance. To avoid having the person's footwear (for example, thick, spongy soles) influence the results of the Romberg maneuver, the task should initially be performed with the shoes removed. However, to discover whether the person's footwear interferes with proprioceptive input, the Romberg should also be repeated with the shoes on.

Sometimes the person will not cooperate in performing the Romberg maneuver. Those persons with dementia who are either incapable of comprehending directions or paranoid may find it difficult to keep their eyes closed. Also, some persons with a fear of instability or falling will avoid closing their eyes completely and attempt to "look." More than likely, these individuals have learned from previous episodes of instability the value of visual input in helping them to maintain balance. As an alternative to the traditional Romberg maneuver, persons can be asked to stand in a darkened room, and their balance can be observed. The darkened room closely approximates the task of closing one's eyes.

An additional test of balance that may be obtained is the one-leg stance. This maneuver is accomplished by asking the person to stand on one leg without holding onto external supports and to maintain their balance for as long as possible. In general, the ability to support this position for at least 5 to 10 seconds without experiencing a loss of balance is normal. However, this maneuver may be of greater benefit in the evaluation of community-dwelling persons, rather than those individuals residing in institutional settings, as the test helps to assess common everyday tasks that call for momentary one-leg balance support, such as stepping on/off curbs, climbing/descending steps without handrail support, stepping on/off buses, and stepping in/out of bathtubs. For individuals residing in hospital and nursing homes, these tasks are not routinely performed.

Next, perform a sternal push or nudge test. First, have the person stand with both eyes open and ask them to place their feet as close together as possible. Then nudge the person's sternum lightly with the fingers, while applying enough force to induce balance displacement. This maneuver tests postural competence in response to loss of balance. The normal reaction is to stretch the arms forward, away from the body, and take one or two steps backwards. Both movements represent protective responses, indicating the body's ability to compensate for sudden balance shifts. An inability to maintain balance, represented by a fall backwards, signifies an abnormality.

It is advisable to have another person present during this test, positioned behind the individual being examined, in the event of a sudden fall. If another person is not available for assistance, a shoulder-pull test can be used as an alternative. This maneuver is performed by stationing yourself directly behind the person and pulling or tugging lightly on both their shoulders, thus inducing a posterior loss of displacement. Expect a similar response to that in the sternal nudge test, and be prepared to catch the person in the event of severe balance loss. This maneuver may be more acceptable than the sternal nudge in those persons with dementia, especially those with associated paranoia, who may become quite upset and agitated when poked in the chest.

Next, ask the person to bend down from a normal standing position, as if retrieving an object from the floor. Then instruct the person to stand up straight, and ask them to reach up onto tiptoes, as if attempting to obtain an object from a high closet or kitchen shelf. For both maneuvers, observe whether the person is steady, and able to maintain balance without holding onto walls and furnishings for support.

Next, ask the person to walk in a straight line for a distance of about 15 feet, turn around, and walk back. Persons should use their assistive ambulation device (canes, walkers) if these are used to accomplish ambulation. If they use their cane or walker occasionally, such as only when ambulating outdoors, test the individual's gait both with and without the device. This helps to determine the influence of the person's assistive device on their gait patterns. Some persons will utilize both a cane and a walker, but on separate occasions. For instance, a person may use a cane indoors, and a walker outdoors, or vice versa. Canes may be favored for indoor use either because the person feels more secure in familiar surroundings, or because they hold onto furnishings/walls at the same time, thereby requiring less support; or else the walker may be difficult to use in small, cramped living quarters. On the other hand, walkers may be used indoors, but the cane outdoors either for convenience and ease of use with public transportation, while shopping, or to avoid an image of frailty and dependency, particularly if they have a fear of crime, or because the walker is difficult to use on outdoor ground surfaces. In those instances where different types of assistive ambulation devices are employed, the person's gait should be examined separately using each device.

Observe the person's gait and notice whether or not their walking is continuous, without hesitation—particularly upon gait initiation—or excessive path deviation and trunk motion from side to side; whether or not step length is decreased (the swing foot should normally pass the stance foot); whether or not both feet clear the floor surface; and whether or not walking stance is wide (normally, the heels almost touch as they pass each other). Also, observe the individual's turning balance, and notice whether or not their steps are smooth, continuous, and whether or not any staggering or balance loss, or grabbing of environmental surfaces (chair backs, walls) for support occurs. Additionally, note whether the ambulation device is the proper size and utilized correctly, and in a safe manner. At the same time, observe the person's footwear, notice whether their shoes fit properly, and whether the consistency of the soles interferes with gait.

Lastly, instruct the person to lie down on the floor and then rise. This maneuver is used to assess for the risk of prolonged post-fall lie times. Observe their ability to get up without the use of external supports. If they are unable to rise from the floor unassisted, place a chair next to the person and observe whether or not they are able to rise with the assistance of the chair. An inability to rise indicates that the individual is at risk for lie times. This maneuver is of particular benefit in evaluating those community-dwelling persons who live by themselves without social supports and who are at fall risk. For the institutional-dwelling person, this maneuver has little relevance, although it is worthwhile to perform it for those individuals prior to discharge from hospitals back to the community.

If the POMS is normal, that is, the individual is able to perform the above maneuvers independently without experiencing balance loss, then the person is considered to be at low fall risk. However, any impairment in the execution of one or more of these tasks places the person at certain risk for falls and injury. Of course, as the number of abnormalities increases, so does the risk of falling. Furthermore, any abnormality observed may indicate the presence of an underlying intrinsic condition that places the individual at fall risk. Abnormal findings can also suggest contributing or potential environmental problems in the person's living environment that can result in fall risk (Table 5.5). For instance, those persons who are unable to perform chair-rising maneuvers without the assistive support of armrests more than likely will also have difficulties with toilet transfers, especially if the toilet is not equipped with grab bars. Individuals who exhibit a positive Romberg response may be at greater fall risk if their environments are poorly illuminated. Moreover, if the person is unable or refuses to perform the balance maneuvers (Romberg test, sternal nudge, bending and reaching), this may itself signify a fear of falling.

Table 5.5   Differential Diagnoses of Abnormal POMS Maneuvers

Impaired Maneuver	Intrinsic Factor	Extrinsic Factor
Chair transfer (possibly impaired bed, toilet and bathtub transfers)	Parkinsonism Arthritis Deconditioning	Poor chair design (possibly faulty bed, toilet, and bathtub design)
Standing balance	Postural hypotension Vestibular dysfunction Adverse drug effects	
Romberg test	Proprioceptive dysfunction Adverse drug effects	Poor illumination Overly absorptive footwear and/or carpeting
Sternal nudge test	Parkinsonism Normal pressure hydrocephalus Adverse drug effects	
Bending down	Neuromuscular dysfunction Adverse drug effects	
Walking/turning	Gait disorders (Parkinsonism, hemiparesis, or foot problem) Sensory dysfunction Adverse drug effects	Improper footwear Improper size, utilization of ambulation devices Hazardous ground surfaces (slippery, uneven)
Rising up from floor	Neuromuscular dysfunction	

From. "Falls in older persons," by R. Tideiksaar. In B. S. Spivack (Ed.), (1995b), *Evaluation and management of gait disorders,* (p. 256), New York: Marcel Dekker. © 1995 by Marcel Dekker. Reprinted with permission.

The POMS has several other advantages. It is easy to understand and administer by health professionals in both the community (home, outpatient clinic, private office) and institutional settings (hospital, nursing home). It generally takes less than 5 minutes to complete, even with the frailest of persons. In addition to detecting mobility dysfunction and fall risk, the POMS can also be used to monitor clinical changes over time, such as the effects of medical conditions. Any impairment discovered can also help to design environmental interventions. For example, in the case of persons with poor chair transfers, the addition of chairs with armrests in the environment may be beneficial. Equally, these individuals may profit from attaching grab bars that surround the toilet, or the addition of increased illumination may help persons with poor proprioceptive function. Likewise, abnormalities found on the POMS can suggest possible rehabilitative interventions. Persons with poor chair transfers can be provided with lower-extremity strengthening exercises with the aim of improving their seated transfers. Individuals with poor gait and balance may benefit from a trial of exercises directed towards improving their ambulation and stability.

The POMS, however, like the other mobility instruments discussed in this chapter has its limitations. For example, any assessment of mobility that is performed outside the older person's living environment—for example, in the doctor's private office, outpatient clinic setting, or physical therapy department—will typically fail to elicit specific information about the individual's mobility status with respect to conditions in their own specific environment, such as the design of chairs, toilets, bathtubs, stairs, lighting, and ground surfaces. The performance of mobility in the office or clinic setting may also be influenced by several environmental conditions—the type of floor surface, such as carpet versus linoleum; the amount of lighting available; the design of chairs used to evaluate seated transfers—all of which may not reflect the conditions present in the persons' own living environment. As a result, it is not unusual to find some persons who have better mobility in the clinic setting, than at home.

For example, I evaluated the mobility of an older man in our outpatient clinic, and found that his gait and balance were within normal limits. However, during a home visit two days later, his gait and balance were observed to be markedly abnormal. In contrast to the clinic setting, which has narrow hallways—a visual means of support—and good lighting—optimal visual input for balance—this individual's home had wide open spaces and thus no visual presence of support, and poor illumination, which contributed to his poor gait and balance. Conversely, some older persons will perform poorly in the clinic setting, but demonstrate improved mobility in their home. Upon evaluating one older woman in the clinic, I found her gait to be remarkably poor and she expressed a great deal of anxiety about her inadequate performance, no doubt in part due to embarrassment. On a subsequent home visit performed shortly thereafter, her gait was very much improved, and she showed no anxiety. Her home has carpeted flooring; but the clinic has linoleum floor surfaces that emits a great deal of glare produced from overhead fluorescent lighting fixtures. More than likely, the difference in gait patterns between the two settings was the result of the floor glare that interfered with this patient's vision, already compromised by glaucoma, compounded by her anxiety. Her familiar home surroundings were undoubtedly much more comfortable.

Therefore, mobility assessments are best accomplished within the person's living environment; for community-dwelling persons, this is their home, and for institutionalized individuals this is their specific unit and bedroom/bathroom. This allows for the direct evaluation of environmental conditions and hazards that interfere with safe mobility and increase fall risk.

Within the home setting, the POMS, for example, is accomplished by observing the individual's seated transfers from sofas and easy chairs as well from other seating commonly used; bed and toilet transfers; getting in and out of bathtubs/showers; reaching up and bending down to place and retrieve objects from kitchen and closet shelves; climbing and descending stairs; and walking and turning about in different rooms. The person's mobility is also observed with respect to floor and step surfaces, lighting conditions, footwear, utilization of canes and walkers, and durable medical equipment, such as bathroom grab bars and tub chairs that may be in place.

Within the hospital and nursing home setting, the assessment of mobility with respect to the designed environment is of equal importance in determining fall risk. Several instruments have been developed that are moving in this direction. Winograd et al. (1994) developed the "Physical Performance and Mobility Examination" (PPME), a performance-based instrument designed to assess physical functioning and mobility in hospitalized older patients. The PPME assesses six domains of mobility arranged in order of increasing difficulty: bed mobility (sit-up from supine position); transfer skills (seated bed and chair transfers); multiple stands from chair; standing balance (ability to maintain feet apart/together, semi-tandem, and tandem stance); step-up (climb one step with handrail support); and ambulation (walk 5 meters, 2 times). For each task there are two separate scoring systems, suitable for two potential uses: (1) screening for gross level of function, using a pass-fail scale, and (2) detecting clinically relevant changes in mobility, employing a timed 3-level score, where independent performance = high pass, the need for human assistance = low pass, and an inability to complete the task = fail. Thus, for a patient who is able to sit up in bed without physical assistance, a pass score is awarded. If they are able to accomplish the task in under 10 seconds, according to the 3-level score system, they receive a high pass, and a low pass if it takes them more than 10 seconds to sit up in two tries. The summary pass-fail score represents a count of the tasks passed, and for the 3-level scale, a sum is made of scores for the six tasks; 2 = high pass, 1 = low pass, and 0 = fail). Winograd et al. (1994) found the PPME to be a reliable and valid performance-based instrument capable of measuring physical function and mobility in hospitalized and frail older patients. They suggested that the PPME can be administered easily in the hospital, home, or outpatient setting, but only tested the instrument in a hospitalized population.

Schnelle et al. (1994) designed the "Safety Assessment for the Frail Elderly" (SAFE), an instrument that measures behavioral factors related to falls and risk of injury in nursing home residents. The SAFE assesses two major mobility skills: transitioning (tasks related to seated wheelchair transfers) and walking (gait and balance maneuvers). Residents are scored on three different point scales (0–4, 0–3, or 0–2; with the highest number given to those individuals who complete the tasks independently, and the lowest number (zero) assigned to persons demonstrating poor function. The researchers found that the SAFE is a reliable method of assessing seated transfers and walking skills in nursing home residents.

While these mobility instruments assess the relationship between the older person's mobility and certain environmental features, they are somewhat limited in that they do not evaluate the specific role played by the environment in contributing to mobility problems or fall risk. In an attempt to solve this problem I have developed the "Performance-Oriented Environmental Mobility Screen" (POEMS). The POEMS is similar to the POMS in that it assesses several mobility tasks; but in addition, the POEMS is used to evaluate the individual's mobility in relation to their surrounding environment in the hospital and nursing home setting (see Appendix A). The POEMS measures the following performance items: seated transfers from the bedroom chair, bed, and toilet; standing balance; bending down from a standing position; and walking in both the bedroom and bathroom with respect to the designed environment. Transfer and walking maneuvers are tested both with or without ambulation devices, as applicable. Testing the person's capacity to ambulate in both the bedroom and bathroom takes into account that space limitations, ground surfaces, and illumination may be dissimilar in each area, and represent different risks. Persons are scored on each task as being either independent or impaired. An impairment signifies either that the person is unsteady during performance, or that they are unable to accomplish the task.

The POEMS is performed in the following manner. Ask the older person to sit and rise from their bedroom chair, a task similar to that of the POMS. The chair should not tip or slide away and the person's feet should not slide but, rather, rest flat on the ground. Next, after the person has risen from the chair, observe their immediate standing balance and assess their response to the Romberg, sternal push, and bending down maneuvers. Next, the person should be asked to transfer onto and off of the bed. Observe the person's ability to perform this activity in a smooth, controlled movement without balance loss or the use of arm support to maintain sitting balance on the mattress. Also, the bed should remain steady (without movement). Both feet should rest flat on the ground while the person is sitting on the bed. Next, ask the person to walk about and turn around, first in the bedroom and then in the bathroom, and observe their gait and balance. If ambulation devices such as walkers are used, observe whether the person is able to use the device in tight spaces (for example, on both sides of the bed; in the bathroom). Finally, ask the person to transfer onto and off the toilet. Observe whether the person is able to perform this activity in a smooth, controlled movement, without balance loss or the need to hold onto the sink edge or grab bars for support.

If the person is able to perform the above maneuvers independently, then the POEMS is normal and the individual is considered for the moment to be at low fall risk. However, any impairment in the performance of the tasks indicates that the person is at fall risk, because of either intrinsic and/or extrinsic factors. As with the POMS, the greater the number of impairments discovered on the POEMS, the greater the risk of falls. Klein, Taylor, Tsai, and Tdeiksaar (1992) studied an acute hospital population of older patients and found the POEMS to be both reliable and valid in evaluating mobility dysfunction, determining fall risk, and separating out intrinsic and extrinsic risk factors.

Performing Fall Risk Assessments

As an individual's mobility and fall risk factors are constantly changing, a risk assessment should be completed on a regular basis. In an outpatient setting, for individuals who are at low risk of falls, the risk assessment should be performed at least annually as part of the person's physical examination. However, in those persons who are at increased fall risk, or those with unstable medical conditions and changing medication regimens, consideration should be given to performing the risk assessment more often.

In addition to using the fall risk and mobility instruments described in this chapter, Isaacs (1985) reported on a novel approach to monitoring mobility and fall risk in the community. He developed, along with colleagues, a "mobility index" that is based on the concept of "life-space diameter." "Life space" is defined as that area in which a person moves about in a 24-hour period, which is divided into different zones. For example, in the home setting, the center of life space is the bed, typically the place where a person starts the day. From the bed an individual moves through different zones: into the bedroom, the rest of the home (the bathroom, living room, kitchen, etc.), into the yard, then onto the block, and finally, off the block (into streets, shops, churches, etc.). Mobility is measured by asking persons to complete a life-space diary that indicates the number of times they penetrate the different zones on a daily basis, and then by counting the frequency by which they move away from the home.

It was found that persons who stayed at home, as measured by the mobility index were characterized by low gait speed and increased sway path, both risk factors for falling; whereas those individuals who functioned freely away from the home had high gait speed and low sway path. While it appears that the diary is a useful assessment tool, compliance with the life-space diary may be difficult for older persons. Moreover, the utility of this instrument in the community-dwelling population has not been examined by others to any great extent.

I have taken the life-space model and fashioned a Mobility Scale (Table 5.6) for use in a population of community-dwelling and frail older persons. The zones and frequency of mobility were modified from the research of Tinetti and Ginter (1990), which is described subsequently. Rather than having the older person keep a record of their daily mobility, the mobility scale is completed by the health professional during a medical visit. The older person is asked about their mobility within the last 2 weeks. If the individual has experienced a decrease in mobility, they are also asked whether they felt that their mobility restriction was due to a physical condition, emotional problem such as fear of falling, or a fall and injury, if these events occurred. Based on clinical experience, the mobility scale appears to be an effective method of screening for mobility problems and fall risk.

Within the institutional setting, the fall risk assessment should optimally be completed when persons are first admitted to the hospital and nursing home, as the risk of falling is greatest during the first few days of stay. However, this may not always be feasible or practical, particularly in an acute care hospital. Upon admission, hospital patients may be injured (for example, hip fracture) or severely ill, and as a result, are often maintained by bed rest. In these instances, risk assessment is best administered after any acute problem or condition is treated and stabilized, or at a time when the patient is permitted to assume an independent level of function or activity. Furthermore, in both the hos-

TABLE 5.6 Home Mobility Scale

Within the last 2 weeks how often have you moved around . . . ?

Zone
1. Outside your bedroom.
2. Outside the bedroom, within your home.
3. Outside your home, within the building (apartment dwellers).
4. Outside your home, within the yard.
5. Outside your home, within the block.
6. Outside your home, off the block (into community).

Frequency

Would you say . . . (indicate mobility, both with and without human assistance).
5. >3 times a day.
4. 1–3 times a day.
3. >2 times a week.
2. At least weekly.
1. Less than weekly.
0. Never.

If the patient has experienced a decrease in frequency in any zone, ask the patient, "Were you kept from your usual activities because of a fall and injury, a physical condition, or emotional problem (fear of falling, depression, etc.)?" (Indicate response).

pital and nursing home setting, fall risk should be reassessed at every point of change—in medical condition; medication regimen (the addition or subtraction of drugs, dosage modifications); functional status (declining or improving); or whenever patient relocation to another unit occurs (a change in environmental surroundings). Additionally, in the nursing home and certain hospital units, such as psychiatric wards, where patients may reside for prolonged time periods, risk assessments (the POEMS, for example) should be repeated at set intervals, approximately every 1 to 3 months. The aim is to discover persons with altered mobility, since any decline may represent an early sign of deteriorating health condition and/or environmental incompatibility and thus increased fall risk.

A number of institutional-based studies have attempted to develop assessment instruments that identify mobility problems and fall risk. Tinetti and Ginter (1990) adapted the Life-Space Diary to the nursing home setting and developed the "Nursing Home Life-Space Diameter" (NHLSD) as a measure of the extent and frequency of mobility in the nursing home. The extent of mobility was measured by dividing the nursing home into a number of zones: the resident's bedroom, the unit on which the resident resides, the rest of the facility beyond the unit, and any area outside the facility. The frequency of mobility (movement into the different zones) was divided and scored into the following categories: 5 = more than three times a day; 4 = one to three times a day; 3 = more than two times a day; 2 = at least weekly; 1 = less than weekly; and 0 = never. It was found that decreased vision, neurologic disease, and arthritis were all associated with low NHLSD scores. The researchers concluded that the NHLSD represents a simple and reliable assessment of mobility among nursing home residents, and may be beneficial in capturing mobility changes, particularly those that increase the risk of falls.

Over the years, several acute hospital and nursing home studies have developed fall risk profiles and assessment instruments to identify and monitor risk (Berryman, Gaskin, Jones, Tolley, & MacMullen, 1989; Byers, Arrington, & Finstuen, 1990; Brians, Alexander, Grotta, Chen, & Dumas, 1991; Corbett & Pennypacker, 1992; Gross et al., 1990; Hernandez

TABLE 5.7   Fall Risk Assessment Instrument

Directions: To establish a nursing diagnosis of potential for injury, identify the following patient risk categories and place on falls precaution.

High Risk Categories for Falls

To place on precautions, 1 or more checks are necessary:
_____ History of previous falls
_____ Mental status changes (disoriented, confused, unable to make purposeful decisions)
_____ Debilitated or weak

To place on precautions, 2 or more checks are necessary:

_____ Advanced age (65 and above)
_____ Mobility deficit (general debility, hemiparesis/plegia, ataxia, use of cane, etc.)
_____ Communication deficit (dysarthria, aphasia, foreign language)
_____ Sensory deficit (auditory and visual deficits)
_____ Medications (diuretics, barbiturates, tranquilizers, narcotics, post 24-hour anesthesia, hypnotics, eye drops, laxatives)
_____ Urinary alteration (urgency, frequency, use of bathroom at night)
_____ Improperly fitting footwear
_____ Emotional upset
_____ Orthostatic hypotension

From "Improving safety for hospitalized elderly," by A.M. Spellbring, M.E. Gannon, T. Kleckner, and K. Conway 1988. *Journal of Gerontological Nursing, 14*(2), 31–37. Adapted with permission.

& Miller, 1986; Janken, Reynolds, & Swiech, 1986; Tack, Ulrich, & Kehr, 1987; Young, Abedzadeh, & White, 1989; see Table 5.7 for one example of a commonly used fall risk assessment instrument developed by Spellbring, Gannon, Kleckner, & Conway, 1988). Whedon and Shedd (1989) and, more recently, Morse (1993) have reviewed many of these studies, and have identified several potential problems with existing risk profiles. First of all, the source of data used to develop these risk profiles and instruments varies greatly (for example, it includes both incident report data and literature reviews of risk factors) and, consequently, they may not adequately represent the extent of fall risk.

For instance, data from fall incident reports and chart review are often used to determine risk profiles. However, individual staff members may have varying definitions of what constitutes a fall, as well as variations in the type of fall they formally report. Institutional policies may have different definitions for reportable falls, some requiring only those falls with physical injury to be reported. In addition, the design of risk profiles based on retrospective chart review may miss key risk factors or variables that were not identified or not reported. As a result, the risk factor profile may not be truly reflective of all fallers. Fall risk profiles developed from the existing literature are often skewed towards characteristics of a particular institution and may not be comparable to other hospital and nursing home settings. Moreover, specific risk factors derived from specialized units (oncology, orthopedic, surgery, psychiatric, rehabilitation, neurology or stroke, dementia wards, etc.) may not apply to different institutions or settings. Also staffing patterns and environmental designs may affect fall risk, and these are not similar across all institutions.

Secondly, the risk profiles are not always consistent among the factors identified. Some studies have identified major risk factors that are absent in other studies; in some studies the risk factors identified are only rarely present in fallers. Furthermore, not all risk factors have been found to be significant when subjected to controlled research design. Lastly, most of the risk profiles developed have not been adequately tested to establish their interrater reliability, nor have they been examined prospectively with respect to outcomes that is, their usefulness in reducing falls. As a result, both the effectiveness of risk profiles in identifying fall risk and preventing falls is questionable. At any rate, the major risk factors identified by many of the risk profile studies appear to be remarkably consistent with those identified by Spellbring and colleagues (1988).

The best procedure for institutions contemplating the use of an available fall risk assessment instrument is to examine a variety of

instruments and choose a few that seem to reflect the facility's population. Then examine the instruments to see if they work, that is, if they
do indeed identify fall risk. This can be accomplished by assessing a
group of persons who have experienced falls and comparing them with
a group who have not fallen. This should determine whether or not the
instrument is sensitive enough to identify individuals at fall risk.

CLINICAL EVALUATION OF FALLS AND FALL RISK

Once the fall history and fall risk assessment have been completed,
multiple causative and risk factors may be identified. There are two
principal aims of the clinical evaluation: first, in those persons with a
fall, to isolate a specific cause and in persons with identifiable risk factors, to discover the presence of modifiable factors, and second, to
determine in both groups the existence of any new factors that may
not have been detected previously.

The clinical evaluation of the older person with falls begins with a
review of the person's medical records, current medical problems, and
medications. The presence of comorbid conditions affecting gait and
balance (e.g., Parkinson's Disease, previous stroke, arthritis, peripheral neuropathy, or myopathy), cardiovascular homeostasis (e.g., congestive heart failure, hypertension, or arrhythmias, etc.), cognition
(e.g., dementia, depression), and medications, such as those that have
hypotensive, cognitive, and motor/sensory effects may provide important clues to the factors contributing to falling. For example, if a person
has a history of lower extremity arthritis and suffers a fall while transferring from a chair or getting into the bathtub, the former may in part
be responsible. Similarly, if a person experienced dizziness prior to the
fall and records indicate the recent addition of a diuretic or psychotropic medication, the association of the two may indicate that the
fall has been caused by an adverse medication effect.

Once the older person's historical data is compiled, and if the individual is not in acute medical crisis or suffering from injuries, one of
several mobility evaluations previously described (for example, the
POMS or POEMS) should be obtained. As in persons at fall risk, the
value of the mobility assessment in fallers lies in isolating those organ
systems and environmental problems that may provide insight into the
possible etiology of the fall.

The next step, for both those persons with falls and those at fall risk,
is to perform a physical examination. This includes a comprehensive

cognitive, neurological, musculoskeletal, and cardiac evaluation. The important aspects of the physical examination to pay particular attention to are listed in Table 5.8.

In addition to the individual's medical history, information gathered from the fall/fall risk assessment and mobility screen can help guide the physical examination. For example, if the fall history reveals that a fall occurred in association with dizziness and changes in position (for example, when rising from a prone or seated position), and the mobility screen demonstrates a loss of balance, unsteadiness, and/or the complaint of dizziness upon immediate standing, postural changes in blood pressure need to be assessed to rule out or confirm orthostatic hypotension. Similarly, if the person at fall risk exhibits difficulty with seated transfers during the mobility screen, the physical examination should concentrate on evaluating the musculoskeletal system for reduced muscle strength and joint dysfunction. Not only will any abnormality discovered during the physical examination help to identify the cause of falling and risk factors, but other physical findings not directly related but that might increase the risk of subsequent falls may be detected.

Once the physical examination has been completed, the next step is to perform laboratory and diagnostic studies. The extent of this testing is dictated by a large extent to the information gathered from all previous evaluations. For example, if the physical examination confirms the presence of orthostatic hypotension, then blood and stool tests to evaluate for volume-depleted states such as dehydration, blood loss, and anemia need to be ordered. If the person is diabetic and the history suggests falls due to hypoglycemia, then a blood glucose test should be obtained. If the fall is associated with a syncopal episode and the physical examination reveals an irregular pulse rate, an electrocardiogram and possibly a Holter monitor study should be considered. Any

TABLE 5.8 Aspects of the Fall-Related Physical Examination

Postural blood pressure (e.g., orthostatic hypotension)
Mental status evaluation (e.g., delirium, dementia, depression)
Visual assessment (e.g., visual acuity, cataracts, glaucoma, macular
    degeneration)
Cardiac evaluation (e.g., arrhythmias, valvular disorders, bruits)
Neurological evaluation (e.g., focal deficits, peripheral neuropathy, tremor)
Musculoskeletal evaluation (e.g., muscular weakness, arthritis)
Podiatric evaluation (e.g., nail disorders, toe deformities, condition of
    footwear)

fall that results in head trauma and the onset of confusion, or a worsening of mental status in those persons with dementia, calls for skull films and a CT scan to rule out subdural hematoma. In persons at fall risk, a history of bladder dysfunction should call for urine and blood tests and urodynamic studies to examine for underlying causes. Similarly, manifestations of lower extremity weakness on physical examination indicates the need for tests that might explain the etiology. In the absence of specific complaints and findings on the physical and mobility examination, comprehensive laboratory screens will rarely yield any significant discoveries, and are not recommended. After all evaluations are complete, a list of intrinsic and/or extrinsic factors responsible for fall risk or falls can be compiled. From it should follow interventions to reduce the risk of further falls.

Followup is important to ensure that the intervention strategies put in place are effective. Repeat the fall risk assessment on a regular basis to identify new or changing risk factors. If the person continues to fall, repeat the fall assessment and evaluation. Either something may have been missed initially or else has been overlooked in previous evaluations, or the person may have developed an additional condition that is causing falls. It is important to remember that both fall etiology and fall risk factors can change as often as the person's medical conditions and environmental surroundings themselves change. The steps involved in both the fall and fall risk assessment are outlined in Table 5.9.

TABLE 5.9   Fall and Fall Risk Assessment

Step 1:	Person has fallen. If yes, proceed to step 2. If no falls have occurred, proceed to step 3 and assess fall risk.
Step 2:	After evaluating and treating for physical injury, obtain a fall history.
Step 3:	Review medical and medication history.
Step 4:	Obtain performance-oriented mobility screens (POMS).
Step 5:	Perform physical examination.
Step 6:	Obtain laboratory studies and diagnostic tests.
Step 7:	List differential diagnosis of fall(s) or identify fall risk factors.
Step 8:	Implement interventions to reduce fall risk.
Step 9:	Followup to determine success of interventions.
Step 10:	Repeat evaluation if person continues to fall. Repeat fall risk assessment on a regular basis.

FALL AND FALL RISK DOCUMENTATION

The documentation of falls, their circumstances and complications; fall risk factors; the interventions attempted; and recording the information into the older person's medical record is essential. First, such documentation informs all health professionals involved in the care of the patient that the individual is at fall risk, identifying fall etiologies, the risk factors involved, and the interventions taken to reduce that risk. Secondly, documenting falls and fall risk highlights the need for practitioners to take caution when prescribing certain medications or permitting the person to engage in certain activities that place them at fall risk, so as to prevent subsequent falls.

For example, documenting an association between previous adverse medication effects and falls will either prevent or make more conservative the use of the offending medications as treatment options. Individuals with a history of bed falls who are transferred to a hospital or nursing home and vice versa for continued care require proactive preventive steps to guard against bed falls. Omission of this history information in the patient's medical record is likely to lead to increased fall risk. Lastly, a record of all previous falls and circumstances and complications experienced, fall risk factors, and intervention should be readily available for review, both to suggest causative factors, should subsequent falling episodes occur, and to guide in the reevaluation of preventive interventions.

For community health settings such as outpatient clinics, private physician practices, and home care services the recording of fall episodes can be accomplished simply by including a Fall History Form (Table 5.10) as part of the patient's initial medical history or ongoing progress notes, and updating the information whenever new fall episodes occur. If fall diaries or other patient recording devices are employed, these may be kept in the medical record as well, or else the information can be transferred to the Fall History form. Likewise, recording and documenting fall risk can be achieved by including a simple checklist in the older person's medical chart (Table 5.11).

For hospitals and nursing homes, similar rules apply concerning the recording of patient and resident falls and fall risk in the medical chart. A similar Fall Risk Checklist as that outlined in Table 5.11 can be utilized, or else one of the several available risk profiles and instruments previously discussed can be used. Once patients and residents are identified as being at fall risk, all staff need to be alerted to their presence. The nursing literature contains a number of measures that can

TABLE 5.10   Fall History Form

For each fall experience, the circumstances (symptoms, location, etc.) and complications (physical, psychological, etc.) are recorded.

Numbers of falls:

Circumstances:	1	2	3	4	5	6
Symptoms						
Location						
Activities						
Time						
Complications:						
Physical						
Psychological						
Social						
Mobility						
Post-fall lie time						

be used for easy identification of those individuals at fall risk. These include the application of brightly colored stickers on the person's medical and nursing chart, bedroom door, and bedside, and distinctive colored wrist-identification bands or slippers to be worn by the person. However, the effectiveness of these measures has not been adequately evaluated.

The documentation of falls within institutional settings, however, carries the additional responsibility of completing an incident report. The incident report has two purposes. First, it serves as a means of documenting all institutional falling episodes so that changes can be implemented to prevent subsequent incidents. Secondly, it serves as a way of assessing institutional liability in the event of medicolegal claims. Although health professionals are usually not held liable for unforeseen or unpredictable falls, "negligent conduct" is generally based upon whether or not it was known that a particular patient was

TABLE 5.11   Fall Risk Checklist

Previous falls (past 3 months)
Defined as an event where the person unintentionally comes to rest on the ground or other lower level—chair, bed, toilet, bathtub, stairs, etc.

Near falls
Defined as an event where the person almost falls—suffers a loss of balance— but is able to catch themselves by holding on to walls, furnishings, and other environmental features for support

Poor vision
Cataracts
Macular degeneration
Glaucoma
Wears glasses
Other

Lower extremity weakness
Arthritis
Muscle weakness
Impaired sensory function
Foot problems
Other

Gait/balance disorder
Stroke
Parkinsonism
Uses cane/walker
Other

Bladder dysfunction
Nocturia
Urinary incontinence
Frequency
Other

Cognitive dysfunction
Dementia
Depression
Anxiety
Fear of falling
Other

Medications
>4 drugs
Diuretics
Antihypertensives
Sedatives
Psychotropics
Other

at fall risk. Staff failure to take proper preventive steps in patients and residents in whom falls can be anticipated, such as those with previous falls or fall risk, are likely to place the institution at risk for medical malpractice.

One way that institutions and staff can protect themselves against legal claims is to incorporate the components of the Fall History and Fall Risk Checklist into existing incident reports. This has several advantages. Not only are patients at fall risk identified, but the specific risky circumstances, such as leaving the bed, or using the toilet are identified. This also provides a means for analyzing or determining intrinsic and extrinsic causative factors, adopting a care plan focused on modifying fall risk and protecting the individual against harm, and developing educational inservice programs for health personnel on the causes of and effective measures to prevent falls.

MEDICAL STRATEGIES TO REDUCE FALLS AND FALL RISK

There are several medical strategies clinicians can take to reduce the risk of falls. Foremost is to identify those older persons at fall risk and those with falls, and then following through with a clinical evaluation to search for modifiable factors. As a fall or the presence of risk factors may represent a sign of an underlying disease or medication effect, the importance of this strategy cannot be overemphasized.

Once the possible cause(s) of falls are uncovered and/or several risk factors are recognized, the clinician's attention should focus first on ruling out contributing acute and chronic medical conditions and medications, and second, treating each condition accordingly. Of equal importance is to monitor the individual's clinical response to treatment and following up to see whether falls and risk factors in fact diminish; this is done by inquiring about falls and assessing fall risk on a regular basis. Also, in those older women with osteoporosis and fall risk who may thus be at increased fracture risk, consideration should be given to treatment with estrogen and calcium supplements as appropriate.

In addition, all medications, both prescription and over-the-counter drugs, should be reviewed routinely in terms of their risks and benefits to those persons at increased fall risk. This is especially important in those frail older individuals with underlying dementia and/or gait and balance impairments, as they may be at great fall risk because of medication side effects. Dosages should be examined with an eye towards reduction whenever possible. Any combination of drugs should be monitored on a regular basis for potential drug-drug interactions that may increase risk. In particular, those drugs known to affect mobility or increase fall risk, such as sedatives, hypnotics, hypotensives, and psychoactive medications, should receive particular attention. As a general rule, medications in older persons should be initiated at their lowest effective dose, increased slowly while monitoring for side effects and clinical efficacy, maintained at the lowest possible dose, and discontinued when no longer effective.

Furthermore, older people and their family members, as appropriate, need to be informed as to what they can do themselves to avoid falls. It is essential to provide individuals with knowledge about their specific medical conditions and medications that place them at fall risk. This can be of great benefit in helping to prevent subsequent falling episodes.

For example, when individuals are beginning treatment with a diuretic or other antihypertensive medication, it is important to inform them that they may experience momentary dizziness, especially when rising rapidly from either a bed or chair. If any dizziness occurs, the individual should be instructed to remain seated until their dizziness passes, and thereafter get up slowly. However, if the problem of dizziness persists or worsens in intensity, causing a loss of stability or falls, the older person and/or their family member(s) should be instructed to immediately bring the matter to the attention of their primary care provider. Moreover, it is important to instruct older persons in general that all episodes of falling, experiencing near-falls, or mobility problems should be reported right away.

Older persons and their family members will benefit from knowing about the causes of falls in general, and about their prevention, particularly as this relates to identifying and eliminating environmental fall hazards in the home and initiating self-care preventive measures, for example, pursuing visual and podiatric care, wearing proper footwear, participating in regular exercise, and avoiding risk-taking activities. This is of particular importance in community-dwelling persons, since the success of these preventive fall measures to a large extent is dependent upon the actions of the older individuals themselves and of their families. In hospitals and nursing homes, much of the responsibility for initiating similar fall preventive measures has been relegated to the nursing staff. Table 5.12 lists a number of nursing interventions that have been described in the literature.

And lastly, while both falls and fall risk can result from the effects of acute medical problems, it is important to recognize that the majority of falls and many fall risk factors are due to interacting chronic medical

TABLE 5.12   Nursing Interventions Aimed at Reducing Fall Risk

Assessment
> Identify fall risk on admission.
> After admission reassess risk level at regular intervals (for example, daily, every shift, etc.).
> Observe patient/resident mobility.
> Monitor drug patterns; polypharmacy.

Care
> Identify high-risk patients/residents with colored tags (wrist band, slippers, door/bed sticker, etc.).
> Maintain regular toileting schedules.
> Provide proper-fitting, nonslip footwear.
> Place disoriented patients/residents near nursing station for close observation.
> Use family members as "sitters" to stay with high-risk patients/residents.
> Frequent nursing rounds on high-risk patients/residents (i.e., every hour per shift).
> Provide ambulation devices (for example, canes and walkers) for patients/residents with gait/balance disorders.
> Provide assistive ambulation.
> Encourage daily exercise (e.g., muscle strengthening of lower extremities).
> Increase nursing staff.

Environmental
> Keep beds in low position and call lights within easy patient/resident reach.
> Keep bed wheels locked.
> Elevate bedrails when patients/residents are in bed.
> Use bed/chair alarms to monitor unsafe activity.
> Increase bedroom and bathroom illumination.
> Maintain nonslip floor surfaces.
> Provide grab rails and toilet risers in bathroom.

Education
> Orient patients/residents to bedroom, unit, activities, and routines.
> Instruct patient/resident on proper use of equipment (e.g., electric beds, call bells, ambulation devices, wheelchairs).
> Instruct high-risk patients/residents to call for help when getting out of bed, ambulating, and toileting.
> Educate family members on safety measures and fall prevention.
> Provide regular inservice education to staff on fall prevention.

conditions and environmental problems. As a result, in those persons who fail to improve with conventional medical treatments and remain at fall risk, it is important for clinicians to recognize and consider other interventions that might be of benefit in reducing fall risk. These consist of a number of psychosocial, rehabilitative, and environmental strategies, which are discussed more fully in the subsequent chapters. However, before proceeding, existing literature on fall preventive programs and clinical trials will be briefly reviewed.

FALL PREVENTION PROGRAMS AND CLINICAL TRIALS

CLINICAL PROGRAMS

Recently, a number of community-based studies have described the effects of a specialized "falls clinic" on preventing falls. Wolf-Klein et al. (1988) developed an outpatient Falls Clinic at a geriatric center on Long Island, New York which emphasized a multidisciplinary approach towards the assessment and treatment of older persons with falls. The clinic is staffed by a geriatrician, neurologist, cardiologist, and psychiatrist who individually evaluate the intrinsic and extrinsic causes of falls and confer together to develop treatment plans. In addition to intensive medical management, patients receive home visits from occupational and physical therapists, and attend an educational program on fall prevention directed for patients and their families.

The researchers studied a group of 36 older people with one or more falls in whom they identified a total of 120 potential fall-related diagnoses. During a 12-month followup, 28 patients (77.7%) of the patients experienced no additional falls; 6 patients continued to fall, but less frequently; and the remaining two patients continued to fall as often as before. Benefits were attributed to the education of patients and families, including awareness of environmental hazards, and medication adjustment, regulation of blood pressure, correction of sensory impairment, and training in ambulation and transfers.

Edwards, Cere, and Leblond (1993) initiated a "falls clinic" located in an apartment complex for older persons located in Ontario, Canada. The purpose of the clinic is to provide on-site screening for falls risk and home visits. Areas of assessment included history of falls, lower limb disability, balance as assessed using the "Get Up and Go Test" for mobility, postural hypotension, medications, and cognitive impairment. Those older persons identified as being at high risk for falls (defined as having two or more risk factors) were offered an in-home assessment and intervention program conducted by a public health nurse. This program included medication management, environmental safety, use of assistive devices, exercise and strength training, and referrals to community resources. Those individuals at low risk (defined as having less than two risk factors) were provided with a low-intensity educational session on the use of an environmental checklist to assess their home for fall hazards and suggested interventions for specific hazards.

The researchers examined the response rate of older persons to the falls clinic (a single clinic in each apartment building), the older person's fall risk profile, and their feedback regarding the clinic. During a 3-month period, a total of 61 older persons attended the falls clinic, a response rate that ranged from 18% to 60% of all residents in the building. The most frequently identified risk factors were medication use (defined as use of four or more prescription drugs) and a history of falls within the past 12 months. Of the clinic attendees, 45 older persons (73.8%) were identified as at high fall risk. However, only 23.7% of all clinic attendees indicated a desire to make changes to avoid falls as a result of the clinic visit. The authors did not report on the results of the intervention strategy, and are currently studying its impact on reducing falls.

Tideiksaar (1995) reported on the operation of a Falls and Immobility Clinic (FIC) at the Department of Geriatrics, Mount Sinai Medical Center in New York, New York. The purpose of the FIC is to assess and manage community-dwelling persons 65 years and older who are at fall risk. Attendees consist of individuals with a recent history of one or more falls, gait and balance impairment, and/or poor mobility. The FIC is staffed by a core team consisting of a clinical gerontologist/physician assistant and a geriatrician. The core team is supplemented by a peripheral team made up of other health professionals such as neurologists, physiatrists, orthopedists, podiatrists, physical and occupational therapists, social workers, and other medical specialists. These individuals are available on a consultative basis as needed and are specifically requested by the core team after the initial evaluation.

Each patient receives a comprehensive medical, functional, social, and psychological evaluation. The medical history, in addition to a review of the medical problems and medications, consists of a fall history, both their circumstances and complications including physical injury, increased lie times, and fear of falling, and history of near-falls. The functional history includes a review of basic activities of daily living, instrumental activities of daily living, current mobility status, use of assistive devices such as canes and walkers, presence of durable medical equipment in the home such as bathroom grab bars, toilet risers, bathtub chairs and benches, and extent of formal and informal caregiver assistance. The social history gathers information on significant others such as spouse, adult children, friends, and, for each individual named, assesses the level of caregiving involvement, coping, and adaptive patterns, and level of stress or burden experienced. The psychological evaluation consists of assessing mental status, mood, extent of fear of falling, and other emotional disorders, such as depression.

Once the historical data is obtained, patients receive a performance-oriented mobility evaluation of gait and balance and a physical examination focusing on the neuromuscular and cardiovascular systems. Ancillary tests such as laboratory studies, x-rays, and electrocardiograms are ordered based on the results of the mobility and physical evaluations. On a separate visit, if indicated, a visit to the patient's home is made to evaluate for potential fall hazards and to assess the individual's mobility performance in relation to their living environment. After all evaluations are complete a list of factors contributing to falls and fall risk is assembled and intervention strategies are designed. Potential interventions are based on identified fall risk factors and postulated causes of falls and consist of medical, psychosocial, rehabilitative, and environmental strategies. After the inception of interventions, patients are followed up via telephone, office or home visit every 3 months to review their progress. This includes inquiring about any problems or barriers with the implementation of preventive strategies, their mobility status, and whether they have experienced falls. At the same time the efficacy of interventions are assessed, and followup visits are scheduled to design alternative strategies if needed. Patients are encouraged to report all falls, and are seen immediately afterwards for evaluation of the event.

To assess the efficacy of the FIC, a cohort of 250 consecutive older persons referred to the clinic during a 12-month period was followed over a 3-year period. Of these attendees, 220 persons (80%) were referred specifically because of falls, while the remainder of referrals were made because of a combination of fall risk, poor mobility, and fear of falling. As a result of the initial evaluation it was felt that 20% of the patients had an isolated medical cause of their falls and/or poor mobility. These consisted of one or more of the following risk factors: visual (e.g., cataracts, glaucoma, macular degeneration); neurologic (e.g., Parkinson's Disease, dementia, and gait and balance abnormalities); musculoskeletal (e.g., lower extremity weakness, arthritis, and foot abnormalities); cardiovascular problems (e.g., postural hypotension, arrhythmias); and adverse medication effects. In the remaining 80% of patients it was thought that their problems were caused by a combination of chronic diseases, medications, faulty assistive devices, and extrinsic or environmental factors in the home affecting safe mobility. The most frequent interventions consisted of medical strategies (e.g., medication change, chronic disease treatment); psychosocial strategies (e.g., treatment of fear of falling, providing caregiving services); rehabilitative strategies (e.g., providing assistive devices, modifying existing canes and walkers, muscle-strengthening exercises, gait and balance training, personal emergency alarms, and instruction in how to get up from the floor). During a 3-year follow up, of the 220 initial patients who reported falls, 190 remained alive. Of these individuals 50% reported no further falls, without experiencing a decline in mobility, and the remaining patients reported nearly a fourfold decrease in fall frequency. Because a combination of interventions were employed, it was difficult to determine with any certainty which strategies were most effective.

Similar fall preventive efforts in the institutional setting have been reported. Neufeld et al. (1991) described the effects of a multidisciplinary Falls Consultation Service on fall reduction in a nursing home. The consultation service, which consisted of members from the medical, nursing, rehabilitative, administration, and activities departments, evaluated 24 residents with one or more falls and identified acute, subacute, or chronic illnesses or drugs that contributed to the falling episodes. Based on their findings they recommended a number of interventions including further clinical evaluation and treatment (referral to neurology, ophthalmic, orthopedic, and urodynamic clinics), gait, balance, and transfer training, environmental modifications (maintaining beds at lowest position, using bed alarm devices, eliminating hazardous conditions), and reducing, eliminating, or changing medication regimens. The authors presented several case studies attesting to the effectiveness of their approach in preventing falls, but did not discuss the results for the entire study population.

Lawrence and Maher (1992), using the multidisciplinary approach to patient falls established by Neufeld and colleagues (1991), developed a collaborative approach to patient falls in an acute hospital. Members of the consulting team included two nurse practitioners, a clinical pharmacist, a physical therapist, and a physician. The team identified and evaluated 14 older patients with falls. The evaluation consisted of a description of the fall, a cognitive and sensory assessment, elimination (bladder and bowel function) assessment, environmental and mobility evaluation, and medication review. After the individual assessments, the team met together to design preventive interventions. The majority of the subjects (57%) fell from bed, and of these, all had their bed side rails elevated. The researchers reported that implementation of the recommendations contributed to improved mentation and function in 7 of the 14 patients. However, the specific interventions, and whether any falls occurred in the subjects, was not discussed.

While these programs have met with varying degrees of success in reducing falls, the results are difficult to evaluate. For the most part, the studies are based on examining one group of subjects—fallers receiving interventions—using a pretest-posttest design, the results of which have not been verified by controlled trials. Without a control group—fallers not receiving interventions—the interventions' contribution to fall reduction cannot be easily determined. Moreover, neither the number of subjects or sample size has been of sufficient magnitude or statistical power to determine the effectiveness of the interventions. And lastly, a reduction of falls as an outcome measure has not been rigorously monitored. As a result, prospective clinical trials using a controlled study design are needed to better understand whether designed interventions can prevent falls. The results of several published preventive clinical trials follow.

PREVENTIVE TRIALS

Fife, Solomon, and Stanton (1984) evaluated nursing interventions to prevent falls in a community hospital in Cleveland, Ohio. Patients on admission on two experimental hospital units were identified at high risk for falling and compared against controls, which consisted of patients on two other hospital units that were comparable in census and age. A total of 538 patients were assessed upon admission to the experimental units; of these, 437 patients (82%) were identified as being at fall risk. The subjects on the experimental units received interventions consisting of patient and family education, environmental modifications (for example, placing beds in low positions, locating call bells within easy reach), and staff education through inservice training. At the end of a 12-week study period there were 12 falls on the experimental units and 16 falls on the control units, but the difference was statistically insignificant. Most of the reported falls occurred at the bedside, usually during the night shift. The authors, however, cited a reduction of falls on the experimental units compared with historical controls as evidence of effectiveness.

Rubenstein et al. (1990) conducted a 2-year randomized clinical trial to measure the effects of a specialized post-fall assessment in a long-term care residential facility. All residents with falls were assessed and then divided into intervention and control groups. Residents who were nonambulatory or suffering from dementia severe enough to preclude cooperation were excluded from the study. Subjects in the intervention group ($n = 79$) were treated for identified risk factors (for example, weakness, orthostatic hypotension, drug side effects, gait abnormalities, and environmental hazards); the control group (*n* = 81) received usual care. A number of interventions were designed and provided to the residents' primary care physician for implementation. At the end of the followup period, residents in the intervention group had 9% fewer falls and 17% fewer deaths than controls, but these trends were not found to be statistically significant. However, treated patients did have significantly fewer hospitalizations (26%) and hospital days (52%) than controls. As the proportion of recommended interventions completed by the primary care physician was not reported, it is uncertain as to whether poor adherence or ineffective recommendations led to the negative results.

Reinsch, MacRae, Lachenbruch, and Tobis (1992a) studied the effects of exercise and cognitive-behavioral intervention strategies on reducing falls among 230 persons 60 years of age and older who were members of 16 senior centers located in Orange and Los Angeles Counties, California. The senior centers were randomly assigned to one of four groups: exercise intervention (improving lower-extremity muscular strength and balance); cognitive-behavioral intervention (improving awareness of environmental hazards and medically related risk factors, as well as improving confidence and lowering anxiety); exercise and cognitive-behavioral intervention combined; and a discussion program that served as a control. After one year of the programs, the researchers observed no significant differences in fall rates or reports of fear of falling between the intervention groups and controls. The authors of this study offered several explanations as to why the interventions were not effective. Perhaps the exercise regimen tested was not of sufficient intensity to produce desired effects (for example, improving strength and balance); the cognitive-behavioral intervention may not have been frequent enough to have an effect; or else, both interventions were actually effective in making subjects more confident in their abilities, so much so that they increased their activities away from home and exposed themselves to more fall risk activities.

In a British study, Vetter, Lewis, and Ford (1992) examined the effectiveness of various interventions in reducing the number of fractures in a community-dwelling population of persons aged 70 and older. The researchers obtained a history of falls and fractures from 674 older persons who were part of a general group and randomly assigned each person to either an intervention or control group. The intervention group (*n* = 350) received an assessment of fall and fracture risk conducted by a health visitor, and treatments were provided to those individuals at high risk. Included were nutritional counseling, evaluation of medical conditions and medications, environmental assessments for hazards, and exercises to improve muscle strength. However, after a 4-year period, Vetter et al. failed to show a significant effect on the incidence of falls and fractures between the intervention and control group. The authors hypothesized that fall reporting bias by the subjects, due to poor memory, or improved activity, resulting in increased exposure to fall or fracture risk, may have led to the negative results.

Hornbrook, Stevens, Wingfield, Hollis, Greenlick, and Ory (1994) examined the effects of a multiple fall risk factor intervention program on a community-dwelling population of persons 65 years of age and older who were members of a large health maintenance organization located in the Northwestern United States. The participants (n = 3,182) were randomly assigned by household (n = 2,509) to either an intervention or control group. Both groups were provided with the results of an initial home inspection for safety hazards, given a home safety booklet that identified common hazards, and were assessed for fall risk factors, including measures of strength and balance. The intervention group received assistance in completing repairs and environmental modifications in the home, and attended a series of falls prevention classes that consisted of exercises to improve strength, balance, and posture; falls risk awareness and risk control; development of social support skills; and group reinforcement. After a 23-month period, 39% of the intervention group reported at least one fall, compared to 44% of the control group. This represented a marginal decrease in falls by the intervention group, but reduced the average number of falls among those who fell by only 7%. Moreover, the prospect of avoiding falls requiring medical attention was not significantly affected by the interventions. The authors concluded that the duration of intervention may not have been of sufficient intensity to have a protective effect on reducing falls.

Wagner et al. (1994) studied the effectiveness of a disability and fall prevention intervention among a random sample of health maintenance organization enrollees 65 years and older. The researchers assigned 1559 older subjects to one of three groups: Group 1, a nurse assessment visit and follow-up interventions targeting risk factors for disability and falls (for example, physical inactivity, excessive alcohol intake, environmental fall hazards in the home, prescription drugs increasing risk, mental impairment, and uncorrected visual and hearing impairment); group 2, a general health promotion nurse visit (assessments and counseling of chronic disease conditions); and group 3, usual care or no preventive interventions. After 1 year, the subjects assigned to group 1, the intervention group, reported a significantly lower incidence of declining functional status and falls than the subjects in group 3. Individuals assigned to group 2 had an intermediate level of new disability and an incidence of falls which was similar to that of the intervention group. The frequency of home safety inspections focused on eliminating hazardous conditions, and exercises aimed at modifying physical inactivity, which favored the intervention group, were the only intervention found to be clinically important in reducing disability and falls. However, after 2 years of followup, with no active interventions occurring during the second year, the differences between group 1 and group 2 with respect to disability and fall incidence diminished. These authors suggested that any beneficial effects produced by interventions will disappear if the interventions are not continued over time.

Tinetti, Mendes de Leon, Doucette, and Baker (1994) conducted a randomized trial comparing the effectiveness of usual care and social visits and a multifactorial, targeted risk abatement strategy in reducing falls among at-risk community-dwelling older persons. The subjects included members of a participating health maintenance organization who were 70 years of age and older and had at least one fall risk factor. The targeted risk factors included postural hypotension, sedatives, use of four or more medications, poor upper and lower extremity strength, decreased range of motion, gait and balance impairments, and transfer dysfunction. The researchers randomly divided the subjects into an intervention and control group. The individuals assigned to the intervention group (n = 153) received risk factor modifications including home physical therapy (a program of gait and balance training and muscle strengthening), education (about use of medication), environmental modifications by visiting nurses and physical therapists, and physician contact to reduce or change medications. The control group (n = 148) only received home visits by social work students, and the risk factors were not addressed.

During 1 year of followup, 35% of the intervention group fell, compared with 47% of the control group. The intervention group experienced a 30% reduction in fall rate and had a decline in total risk factors, mostly consisting of decrease in the number of medications and improvements in gait and transfer abilities. The researchers estimated the cost of preventing each fall at about $12,400, while the typical cost of hospital treatment of falls for older people is $11,800. However, they argued that hospital-related costs for falls do not include other expenses associated with extended disability and reduced independence. When these fall-related health costs are examined, the interventions may indeed be economically beneficial. This showed that falls can actually be reduced in a community-dwelling population at risk and suggest that a targeted multiple risk factor abatement strategy is a feasible, safe, and effective approach to reducing fall risk.

CONCLUSION

Clearly, the problem of falls and their prevention is complex. Intrinsic or medical strategies alone have not been found to be particularly effective in reducing falls. Rather, multiple interventions are often required, and even then they need to be targeted specifically to the person. These intervention strategies will be discussed in the following pages, beginning with psychosocial strategies, the topic of Chapter 6.

APPENDIX A Performance-Oriented Environmental Mobility Screen (POEMS)

INSTRUCTIONS:

Ask the patient or resident to perform the indicated maneuvers. If the individual uses an ambulation device (e.g., cane, walker), each maneuver is tested with device as appropriate. For each maneuver indicate whenever the person's performance is independent or impaired.

Maneuver	Observation	
	✓ Independent	✓ Impaired
Sit down and rise up from chair(s).	☐ Chair transfer is smooth, controlled movement (sits down and rises from chair in one attempt: does not use armrests; chair does not tip or slide away).	☐ Chair transfer is not smooth movement (requires several attempts to sit or rise; falls on to seat; uses armrest or seat edge to guide transfers: chair tips or slides away).
	☐ Sitting balance is stable (does not use armrest support to maintain balance).	☐ Sitting balance is unstable (slides down from seat or uses armrest support to maintain balance).
	☐ Seated, both feet rest flat on ground.	☐ Seated, feet don't rest on ground.
		☐ Unable to perform maneuver.
Device used to perform maneuver: Yes ☐ No ☐	☐ Device appropriate for space (able to transfer with device). ☐ Device used correctly for transfers.	☐ Device not appropriate for space (unable to transfer with device). ☐ Device used incorrectly for transfers.
Stand in place (for approximately	☐ Steady, able to stand without balance loss.	☐ Unsteady, unable to maintain standing balance

Maneuver	Observation	
	✓ Independent	✓ Impaired
15 seconds) with arms by side and eyes open.	☐ Does not use chair or other furnishing to maintain balance. ☐ Does not use device to maintain balance.	☐ Uses chair or other furnishings to maintain balance. ☐ Uses device to maintain balance. ☐ Unable to perform maneuver.
Stand in place with both eyes closed (for approximately 15 seconds).	☐ Steady, able to stand without balance loss. ☐ Does not use chair or other furnishing to maintain balance.	☐ Unsteady, unable to maintain standing balance. ☐ Uses chair or other furnishing to maintain balance. ☐ Unable to perform maneuver.
Stand in place (both eyes open). Nudge person's sternum lightly 3 times.	☐ Steady, able to withstand pressure without balance loss. ☐ Does not use chair or other furnishings to maintain balance.	☐ Unsteady, unable to withstand pressure and maintain balance. ☐ Uses chair or other furnishing to maintain balance. ☐ Unable to perform maneuver.
From standing position bend down and pick up object from ground.	☐ Steady, able to bend down and rise up without balance loss. ☐ Does not use furnishings to maintain balance. ☐ Does not use device to maintain balance.	☐ Unsteady, unable to bend down and rise up and maintain balance. ☐ Uses furnishings to maintain balance. ☐ Uses device to maintain balance. ☐ Unable to perform maneuver.
Transfer on to and off of bed.	☐ Bed transfer is smooth, controlled movement (sits on and rises from bed in one attempt). ☐ Feet do not slide away on ground during transfers. ☐ Bed does not slide away during transfers. ☐ Sitting balance is stable (does not use arm	☐ Bed transfer is not smooth (requires several attempts to sit or rise; falls on to mattress; uses mattress edge to guide transfers). ☐ Feet slide away on ground during transfers. ☐ Bed slides away during transfers. ☐ Sitting balance is unstable (uses arm

Maneuver	Observation	
	✓ Independent	✓ Impaired
	support to maintain balance).	support to maintain balance).
	☐ Able to lie down (in supine position) and rise in one smooth, controlled movement.	☐ Unable to lie down (in supine position) and rise in one smooth, controlled movement.
		☐ Unable to perform unassisted transfers.
Device used to perform maneuver;	☐ Device appropriate for space (able to transfer with device).	☐ Device not appropriate for space (unable to transfer with device).
Yes ☐ No ☐	☐ Device used correctly for transfers.	☐ Device used incorrectly for transfers.
Walk and turn in bedroom and bathroom.	☐ Gait is continuous without hesitation.	☐ Gait is non-continuous, with hesitation.
	☐ Gait is straight, without deviation from path.	☐ Gait deviates from straight path.
	☐ Both feet clear ground surface.	☐ One or both feet scrape ground surface.
	☐ Turns are smooth, continuous without balance loss.	☐ Turns are discontinuous, with balance loss.
	☐ Does not use wall, furnishings, sink, or towel bar for balance support.	☐ Uses wall, furnishings, sink, or towel bar for balance support.
		☐ Unable to perform maneuver.
Device used to perform maneuver;	☐ Device appropriate for space (able to walk with environmental interference).	☐ Device not appropriate for space (unable to walk due to environmental interference).
Yes ☐ No ☐	☐ Device used correctly for walking and turning.	☐ Device used incorrectly for walking and turning.
Sit down and rise up from toilet.	☐ Toilet transfer is smooth, controlled movement (sits down and rise from toilet in one attempt; does not use grab bars, seat or sink edge for support; feet do not slide away on ground).	☐ Toilet transfer is not smooth movement (requires several attempts to sit or rise; falls on to toilet seat; uses grab bars, seat, or sink edge for support; feet slide away on ground).
	☐ Seated, both feet rest flat on ground.	☐ Seated, feet do not rest flat on ground.

CHAPTER 6

Psychosocial Strategies to Reduce Fall Risk

INTRODUCTION

Recall, as was discussed in Chapter 2, that the problem of falls in older people is associated with a number of psychosocial consequences. Foremost are the complications that accompany the fear of falling, and other psychological reactions, such as depression, anxiety, and poor coping strategies that may affect both the older person with falls or those who are at fall risk. Family members and other caregivers may be equally affected by the older person at fall risk. As a result, a psychosocial evaluation should always accompany both the falls and fall risk assessment. The purpose of this chapter is to first address the fear of falling and psychosocial reactions, as they relate to both older persons and their caregivers, and secondly, to present an approach for identifying the problems and practical interventions for reducing their occurrence.

FEAR OF FALLING

The spectrum and clinical course of fear of falling in older people is varied. A fear of falling may start simply as an unpleasant feeling, the aftermath of one or more recent falls or near-fall episodes. At this stage, individuals may feel that the next fall may end in either psychological or physical damage—embarrassment, injury, or functional dependency.

As a result, these persons are more alert to potential hazards in their surrounding environment and perform their ADL activities cautiously. Within this context, the fear of falling represents a sensible reaction to possible danger and is generally of little consequence as long as the physical and social mobility of the person remains unaffected. However, the fear of falling can progress beyond this point, or it may initially present, as a debilitating condition.

Some persons develop a situational fear of falling. The onset of fear is directly linked to a specific activity, for example, bathing, toileting, climbing stairs, walking outdoors, or crossing the street. Attempting the feared activity typically results in severe anxiety, expressed in heart palpitations, shortness of breath, or a sense of faintness, as the person becomes uncertain as to whether they can perform the activity safely, and without falling. In an effort to reduce their anxiety and fear, persons commonly resort to avoidance behaviors. They circumvent those situations or activities associated with previous falls and injury or with fall risk. For example, if a fall or near-fall occurred in the bathtub, the person may curtail baths or abstain from bathing altogether. Likewise, a fall that occurred outside the home may lead to a decrease in going outdoors. Within institutional settings, similar behaviors are observed. Older persons may avoid walking to the dining room, but instead, insist on the use of a wheelchair for transportation. Or else, instead of travelling to the bathroom to urinate, some individuals, because of their fear of falling, will opt to use a bedpan in the safe surroundings of their bed.

Some older persons can progress, or initially present, with a nonsituational fear of falling. At this degree of fear, some individuals become so preoccupied with fall avoidance that, in addition to limiting fall risk activities, they generalize their fear to other ADL activities as well. The person may decide against performing a task, even if they believe themselves capable of accomplishing it, because of the possible risk of falling. Conversely, a failure by the person to adopt a safe behavior, or a continuance of falls and near-fall episodes, may result in further fear of falling, anxiety, and restrictions of activity.

Consequently, a determination of the presence and extent of fear of falling should accompany the evaluation of falls and fall risk, regardless as to whether the person resides in the community or institution. One method of accomplishing this is to simply ask the person "Are you afraid of falling?" or "Are you afraid of falling during any usual daily activity, and if so, which ones?" A positive response should be followed up by asking the person to explain the duration and magnitude of their fear. Specifically inquire as to whether the individual has limited their functional and social activities as a result, and what effect this has had on them. However, some older persons may deny the presence of fear or dismiss its significance in an effort to preserve their autonomy and prevent an image of frailty. Also, persons with cognitive impairment may not be able to adequately express a fear of falling.

An alternative method is to ask the person, "Have you recently avoided any activities?" Inquiring about whether the person has experienced a restriction of activities in association with recent falls and near-falls may yield a better indication of a clinically significant fear of falling than directly asking individuals if they are fearful of falling. Most persons who may have an aversion towards admitting that they are fearful will discuss their reluctance to perform or engage in certain activities with surprising openness, and even after a period of time will confess to their fear. As well, family members, home attendants and institutional staff, can be asked whether the person has begun to avoid certain activities that were previously performed. This line of questioning will also help to ascertain whether persons with dementia have restricted their activities, a possible indication of a fear of falling.

Several instruments have been specifically developed to ascertain the fear of falling. Tinetti, Richman, and Powell (1990) designed the "Falls Efficacy Scale" (FES) (Table 6.1), an instrument that can be used

TABLE 6.1   Falls Efficacy Scale (FES)

Items

1. Take a bath or shower
2. Reach into cabinets or closets
3. Prepare meals not requiring heavy or hot objects
4. Walk around the house
5. Get in and out of bed
6. Answer the door or telephone
7. Get in and out of a chair
8. Get dressed and undressed
9. Light housekeeping
10. Simple shopping

Note. Word each question with "How confident are you that you can . . . without falling?"

1	2	3	4	5	6	7	8	9	10
extreme confidence								no confidence at all	

From "Falls efficacy as a measure of fear of falling," by M. E. Tinetti, D. Richman, & L. Powell, 1990, *Journal of Gerontology, 45,* p. 241. Reprinted with permission.

to measure the fear of falling. Efficacy refers to an individual's perception or self-confidence in performing an activity. This scale is based on the operational definition of fear as "low perceived self-confidence at avoiding falls" (Tinetti, Richman, & Powell, 1990, p. 239). More recently, Tinetti and Powell (1993, p. 6) modified their definition of fear to read "low perceived self-confidence at avoiding falls during essential, relatively nonhazardous activities." Persons are asked to identify how confident they feel at performing each of the activities listed in the scale without falling. The total efficacy score represents the sum of scores on the individual activity items, a high score represents higher efficacy or confidence and a low score reflects lower confidence, or fear.

Powell and Myers (1995) developed the "Activities-Specific Balance Confidence Scale" (ABC) (Table 6.2). This instrument is similar in design to the FES, but includes a wider continuum of activity difficulty and

TABLE 6.2   Activities-Specific Balance Confidence Scale (ABC)

1. "How confident are you that you will not lose your balance or become unsteady when you walk around the house?"

   0%   10   20   30   40   50   60   70   80   90   100%
   No   Completely
   Confidence   Confident

2. . . . walk up and down stairs inside your home.
3. . . . bend over and pick up a slipper from the front of a closet floor.
4. . . . reach for a small can off a shelf at eye level.
5. . . . stand on your tip toes and reach for something above your head.
6. . . . stand on a chair and reach for something.
7. . . . sweep the floor.
8. . . . walk outside the house to a car parked in the driveway.
9. . . . get into or out of a car.
10. . . . walk across a parking lot to the mall.
11. . . . walk up or down a ramp.
12. . . . walk in a crowded mall where people rapidly walk towards you and pass you by.
13. . . . when people bump into you as you walk through the mall.
14. . . . step onto or off of an escalator while holding onto a railing.
15. . . . step onto or off an escalator while holding onto parcels such that you cannot hold onto the railing.
16. . . . walk outside on icy sidewalks.

Note. From "The activities-specific balance confidence (ABC) scale," by L. E. Powell and A. M. Myers, 1995, *Journal of Gerontology, 50A,* p. M30. Reprinted with permission.

more detailed activity descriptions. Tideiksaar developed the "Fear of Falling Questionnaire" (FOFQ, 1994, unpublished) (Table 6.3). This instrument is based on asking the person to indicate whether and to what extent they avoid certain activities and situations. The greater the number of activities and situations avoided, the greater the fear of falling as a clinical problem. Any one of these instruments is extremely helpful in determining which activities or situations lead to either low confidence or fear of falling, and is of great benefit in developing treatment plans. Although these instruments mainly deal with community-related activities, some creative reorganization of the items included would no doubt make them applicable to the acute hospital and nursing home setting as well.

Once the fear of falling is identified, a number of treatment strategies may be attempted in an effort to reduce the fear. Pharmacotherapy may be effective in treating anxiety or depression provoked by the

TABLE 6.3   Fear of Falling Questionnaire (FOFQ)

Indicate the degree to which you avoid the following activities or situations because of fear or other unpleasant feelings (i.e., embarrassment, anxiety).

1. Never avoid
2. Rarely avoid
3. Avoid most of the time
4. Always avoid

ACTIVITIES:

☐ Walking alone outdoors
☐ Walking alone indoors
☐ Getting on/off the toilet
☐ Getting in/out of the bathtub/ shower
☐ Taking a bath/shower
☐ Getting in/out of chairs
☐ Getting on/off the bed
☐ Reaching up into closets/cabinets
☐ Bending down (cabinets, ground) to place/retrieve objects
☐ Climbing stairs/curbs
☐ Descending stairs/curbs
☐ Other activities (describe) _____

_____

_____

_____

SITUATIONS:

☐ Living alone
☐ Housekeeping
☐ Shopping
☐ Using public transportation
☐ Visiting friends/family
☐ Visiting restaurants
☐ Attending movies, theater, concerts
☐ Other situations (describe) _____

_____

_____

_____

fear. However, any use of benzodiazepines and tricyclic medications that may be tried should be used cautiously and only for a short time period, since they can impair balance and increase the risk of falls. Some forms of habituation therapy have been used with success in phobic patients (Bhala, 1982; Discipio & Feldman, 1971; Feldman & Discipio, 1972; Watson, 1971). They consist of asking the person to participate in the feared activity or situation for increasing periods of time until their discomfort or fear is reduced or extinguished. For example, persons who avoid bathing because of a fear of falling in the bathtub can be started out with a program of assisted tub transfers. Once they feel comfortable with this activity, they can progress to supervised tub transfers, and eventually to independent transfers. It is remarkable how quickly some older people, even those with significant fear of falling, respond to habituation therapy. I knew one older woman who literally was almost chairbound, sitting at home because of a fear of falling. She had not left her apartment in over a year. However, with the help of a home attendant who walked with the patient daily, at first providing maximum assistance, then progressing to supervised assistance, the patient was able to circle her block after 3 weeks.

Balance and muscle-strengthening exercises (see Chapter 7) may be of benefit in improving mobility and, at the same time, reducing the fear of falling. Some persons with fear of falling benefit from the short-term use of a walker, as the device provides both a sense of visual and physical support. For those persons with increased fall lie times who are fearful, providing personal emergency alarm devices (see Chapter 8), and teaching persons how to get up from the floor by themselves (see Chapter 7) is also beneficial. Lastly, employing environmental modifications (see Chapter 8) aimed at supporting individual mobility can help to ensure a feeling of confidence and alleviate the fear of falling. For example, a situational fear of falling, such as when ambulating on the stairway, may be eliminated by increasing the surrounding illumination of steps to ensure proper and safe foot support and balance. Likewise, the addition of bathroom grab bars can help to reduce any fear associated with toileting and bathing activities. In general, a mixture of interventions such as habituation therapy, exercises, and environmental modifications is likely to be more effective than attempting solitary interventions.

PSYCHOSOCIAL REACTIONS

Aside from a fear of falling, there are a number of other psychosocial effects that the older person may experience as a result of suffering falls.

Each new fall experienced may represent to the person a further decline in the competency and capacity to maintain independent mobility. This may elicit feelings of frailty and loss of control or autonomy. Similar emotions may be expressed by individuals at fall risk, especially if they experience progressive declines in mobility. For those older persons who live by themselves and lack the availability of family members to provide support, these feelings tend to be aggravated. As a result, these individuals often express considerable anxiety about the management of their daily lives and activities, and, if they require home assistance, the financial burden this may represent. Moreover, individuals may become apprehensive about the future, worrying in particular that they may have to relocate to assisted housing or a nursing home if they continue to fall or experience further functional losses. On the other hand, some persons may welcome this intervention, especially if they are homebound, lack social activity, and become socially isolated.

Even if the older person has a spouse or family member available to provide support, it may be difficult emotionally to accept becoming dependent upon others to accomplish daily tasks. Some persons cherish their autonomy and hate being reliant on others for anything, a habit that they have maintained throughout their lives, which continues to persist even with frailty. Some individuals fail to accept a reversal of the "parent–child" relationship that results from adult children providing caregiving services. In response, older persons may openly rebel and reject any help or assistance from their children. This may occur for institutional-dwelling persons as well; even in the hospital and nursing home, older individuals may not accept assistance from nurses.

Still others may not wish to place a burden of care on their spouse or adult children, or may feel embarrassed by their helplessness, and may not ask for assistance, even though it is required. Some of these persons are more relaxed about accepting help from home attendants and other formal caregivers. At other times, sheltered housing may be the only option, or a certain amount of risk must be accepted in allowing them to accomplish mobility by themselves. A set of questions aimed at discerning the presence of psychosocial symptoms in the older person is included in Table 6.4.

For the involved spouse or family member the responsibilities of caring or providing support for the older person at fall risk can be equally troubling. They may perceive the person to be constantly vulnerable, and at risk for further falls and injury. As a consequence they may become overly protective of the individual, restricting their activities, particularly going outdoors alone. Sometimes the unpredictability

TABLE 6.4   Psychosocial Interview Questions (Patient)

1. Have you experienced a previous fall(s)? If yes, did you report the episodes to your doctor or other health care provider? If not, why not? Why have you decided to report this fall? (Explore reasons.)
2. Are you concerned about your gait/balance and/or falling again? If yes, why? (Any positive response should trigger an evaluation for fear of falling.)
3. Has your gait/balance and/or fall(s) worried your spouse? Children? Caregiver? If yes, in what way? How do you feel about this?
4. Since your fall(s) has your spouse/children spent more time with you? How do you feel about this?
5. Has your gait/balance and/or fall(s) affected your activities of daily living (ADL, e.g., dressing, ambulating, toileting, bathing) or instrumental activities of daily living (IADL, e.g., shopping, housekeeping, transportation)? If yes, specify how. Who helps you accomplish your daily tasks? Who provides the majority of care? How do you feel about this? (Explore issues.)
6. Has your gait/balance and/or fall(s) affected your social life? Friendships? Family relationships? If yes, how? How do you feel about this? (Explore reasons.)
7. Are you concerned that your gait/balance will become worse? Or that you will experience greater problems with your mobility?
8. Are you worried that you might have to give up your home and need to move to an assisted living residence or a nursing home in the near future? If yes, why? (Explore reasons.)

of the older person's condition and the caregiving requirements involved can lead to considerable anxiety. Moreover, because spouses may not be physically capable of providing mobility support, such as assistance with bathing and toileting, they may feel guilty and anxious as a result. In some cases, the spouse may be as incapacitated or even more disabled than the older person, and become physically exhausted from the caregiving tasks required. In these instances, the children (if available) may fear that the situation is unsafe. Conflict with their parent(s) over continuing to live alone, and conflict within their own family about having the parent(s) move in with them, is likely to arise. Family members may feel guilty if they are not able to provide an adequate amount of care because of work and their own family commitments. Sometimes family members can be emotionally stretched between both responsibilities. In some cases, caregivers may become so angered at the additional responsibilities of having to do everything for the older person that they detach and isolate themselves from the older person and opt for sheltered housing. At other times, families may not be able to provide the required assistance, even if they want to, because they themselves are physically incapacitated or live too far away to provide regular help. Sometimes, family members may not be overly delighted at the prospect of caring for a parent, because of unresolved conflicts in their relationships. At other times, the burdened family member or spouse may be overly vigilant in caring for the older person without taking the consequences into consideration. A list of questions to ask family members and other caregivers with respect to their relationship with the older person and any problems experienced is included in Table 6.5.

Based on clinical experience, certain psychosocial interventions appear to be of equal benefit for both older people and their family members or other caregivers. First of all, discuss in clear language the reasons for falling and/or why the older person is at fall risk. In those frail older individuals with multiple chronic illnesses, attempt to address the prognosis or anticipated course of the problem; whether you expect it to be of short or long duration; and the various social and financial consequences that might arise. At the same time, allow all concerned parties to express their fears and concerns, and attempt to allay their apprehension. One method for accomplishing this is to discuss the plan for reducing the risk of further falls. This may consist of

TABLE 6.5   Psychosocial Interview Questions (Family/Caregiver)

1. What are the major problems you (the family member/caregiver) have faced in taking care of (the patient)? (Explore costs of care, providing daily ADL/IADL assistance, etc.)
2. Are you worried about the safety of (the patient)? Are you concerned about (the patient) living alone? Are you worried that (the patient) will fall when you are not there? Are you concerned that (the patient's) condition will get worse? (Explore issues.)
3. Have you experienced any physical or emotional problems as a result of caregiving? If yes, are you receiving any medical treatment or medications? Have the burdens of caregiving affected your own family? Social life? Employment? (If yes, have the caregiver explain in what way.)
4. Has the relationship between you (the family member/caregiver) and (the patient) remained the same, improved, or declined as a result of caregiving? (Ask the family member/caregiver to explain in what way.)
5. If the patient is living alone, have you (the family member) considered having (the patient) move in with you? Have you (the family member) thought of long-term nursing home placement for (the patient)? (Explore issues.)
6. Do you (the family member/caregiver) require additional help in caring for (the patient)? (Explore issues.)

treating disease processes and/or modifying medications that may be responsible, and attempting rehabilitative and environmental interventions aimed at reducing the risk of falls. These topics are discussed in Chapters 7 and 8.

Educating older people and family members as to what they can do to reduce the risk of falls is beneficial as well. In those older persons who live alone, and who may not have family members to help with daily mobility tasks, providing formal caregiver assistance either on a temporary or more permanent basis may help to alleviate any fears that arise. Similarly, for those older persons and family members who have maladaptive relationships, or when the responsibilities of caregiving are burdensome for families—both situations that may prohibit the older person from receiving assistive support—providing caregiving assistance might help to reduce problems. However, any prolonged conflict that arises between older persons and family members should be referred to a social worker for ongoing care, as the resolution of these problems will greatly facilitate efforts to prevent falls. And lastly, older persons and family members need to be counseled about nursing home placement when required. Often older persons are reluctant to accept nursing home care, and family members may experience guilt over "abandoning" a parent. Under these circumstances, discuss the benefits and risks involved in remaining at home, as opposed to entering a nursing home.

CHAPTER 7

Rehabilitative Strategies to Reduce Fall Risk

INTRODUCTION

Those older persons who fail to respond to or improve with medical treatment and continue to remain at fall risk may respond to a number of rehabilitative strategies, which will be discussed in this chapter. These include engaging in exercise therapy, wearing proper footwear, and utilizing appropriate ambulation devices to assist with mobility. Teaching older people to get up from the floor to reduce long lies, and modifying the risk of wheelchair falls, is also discussed.

EXERCISE

Persons with impaired mobility resulting from underlying medical conditions and/or deconditioning may benefit from a trial of exercises. Research has shown that older persons who exercise perform better on neuromuscular tests of function (reaction time, strength, flexibility, walking, and balance maneuvers) than older persons who do not participate in exercises on a regular basis (Baylor, 1988; Lord, Caplan, & Word, 1993; Spirduso, 1988). Subsequently, exercises that focus on enhancing muscular strength, joint flexibility, and sensory interaction may be of great benefit in improving the gait and balance of older persons. Weight-bearing exercises may be of equal benefit, and at the same time can help to reduce the rate of bone loss and guard against the risk of fractures.

236

MUSCULAR STRENGTHENING AND FLEXIBILITY

As previously discussed (see Chapter 3) there is a strong relationship between muscular weakness, particularly of the lower extremities, and the risk of falls. In particular, poor quadriceps strength has been shown to be closely correlated with impaired gait function (slow velocity and small steps) (Imms & Edholm, 1981) and poor balance (Judge, Underwood, & Gennosa, 1993). Furthermore, several studies have shown that decreased strength and flexibility of the muscles surrounding the ankle joint is associated with both balance impairment and the risk of falling (Studenski, Duncan, & Chandler, 1991; Whipple, Wolfson, & Amerman, 1987). Adequate coordination of the ankle dorsiflexors and plantarflexors is required for maintaining gait and balance and recovering from any displacements or disruptions of stability. Subsequently, research efforts have focused on improving muscular strength and joint flexibility, which in turn might benefit gait and balance.

A number of studies have demonstrated that older people, even up to 90 years of age, maintain their ability to increase muscle strength (Charette et al., 1991; Stamford, 1988). Frontera et al. (1988) studied the effects of a progressive resistance strength conditioning program of the thigh muscles in healthy men aged 60 to 72 years. After a 12-week period of weight-lifting, both knee extensor and flexor strength increased 107.4%, along with evidence of considerable muscle hypertrophy. Similarly, Pyka, Lindenberger, Charette, and Marcus (1994) studied the effects of resistance training on muscle strength and size in healthy older people, mean age 68.2 years. Subjects participated in a progressive strength training protocol, 1 year in duration, that consisted of 12 different resistance exercises aimed at improving muscle groups of the major back (erector spinae, gluteus maximus); lower extremity (quadriceps, hamstrings, hip abductors and adductors, hip flexors and extensors); and upper extremity (pectoralis major, deltoids, triceps, trapezius). The training program led to an improvement in muscle strength, with average increases ranging from 30% for hip extensors to 97% for hip flexors. The greatest increase in muscle strength occurred over the first 3 months of exercising, and plateaued thereafter for the duration of the training program.

Aside from benefitting healthy groups of older people, the effects of muscle strengthening extend to frail older populations as well. Fiatarone et al. (1989) examined the effects of strength training in 10 nursing home residents ranging in age from 87 to 96 years. The researchers designed an 8-week program of weight training that consisted of leg-lifting exercises, utilizing a standard weight-and-pulley system, and performed three times per week. The training protocol consisted of three sets of repetitions, each lasting 6 to 9 seconds, with a 1–2 minute rest period between sets. During followup, the average strength gain was 174%, and even among the oldest-old group, the capacity for increasing muscle strength and size was preserved. Furthermore, changes in functional capacity, such as tandem gait speed and time taken to rise from a chair, correlated with improvements in muscle strength. More recently, Fiatarone, O'Neill, Ryan, and colleagues (1994) extended their research in the area of muscular strength training. They compared the effects of progressive resistance training, multinutrient supplementation, both interventions, and neither in a group of 100 frail nursing home residents, mean age was 87, and about one-third of the subjects were in their 90s. Subjects were randomly assigned either to participate in ordinary nursing home activities (aerobic or flexibility exercises) or an exercise program consisting of high-intensity resistance training of the hip and knee extensors for 45 minutes, 3 days per week for 10 weeks. Each subject received either a nutritional supplement to minimize the effect of exercise training on habitual food intake, or a placebo supplement.

The researchers found that muscle strength increased by 113% in the residents who underwent resistance training. Moreover, these individuals increased their walking speed by 12% and their ability to climb stairs by 28%. As a result, some of the individuals who required a walker for ambulation were now able to use a cane instead. It is of interest that the use of nutritional supplements without concomitant strengthening exercise did not reduce muscle weakness.

In another nursing home study, Fisher, Pendergast, and Calkins (1991) examined the effects of resistance training in a group of 18 residents, ranging in age from 60 to 90 years. After participating in a 6-week program of muscle strengthening aimed at improving knee extension (a combination of isometric training and weight lifting), the researchers found that in those persons engaging in the exercise program, muscle strength increased by 15%. While these results in muscular strength were not as dramatic or impressive as those cited by others, the improvements in strength were still evident 4 months after training, and many of the residents were felt to have achieved greater independence in their mobility.

In support of this research, a number of other community- and institutional-based studies have found a significant relationship between strength training and increased lower extremity muscle strength (Agre, Pierce, Raab, McAdams, & Smith, 1998; Buchner et al., 1993; Heislein, Harris, & Jette, 1994; Lord & Castell, 1994; Mulrow et al., 1994; Sauvage et al., 1992). Even light resistance and stretching exercises of the legs (hamstrings, quadriceps) has been shown to be effective in increasing lower extremity flexibility and strength (Agre et al., 1988; Brown & Holloszy, 1991; Raab, Agre, McAdam, & Smith 1988). Other researchers have found that regular, low-intensity exercises in institutionalized older persons, such as participating in a regular program of seated exercises aimed at strengthening quadriceps muscles and improving joint flexibility, may be effective as well in improving functional capacity (McMurdo & Rennie, 1993, 1994).

EFFECTS OF EXERCISE ON GAIT AND BALANCE

Researchers have also begun to examine the effects of muscle strengthening and other forms of training specifically on improving gait and balance. Judge, Underwood, and Gennosa (1993), for instance, studied a group of older persons aged 71 to 97 years in order to show the effects of a vigorous exercise program on muscular strength in the lower extremities and walking speed. The program consisted of flexibility exercises (body-stretching movements), resistance exercises (hip abduction, knee extension, ankle dorsiflexion), and balance exercises (lateral and anterior-posterior weight shifts from one leg to the other, and tai chi movements), performed three times a week for 12 weeks, in sessions lasting 60 to 70 minutes. The subjects who completed the exercise program showed a significant increase in muscular strength, up to 30%, and an increase in walking speed. Similarly, Sauvage et al. (1992) examined the effects of a moderate- to high-intensity strengthening and aerobic exercise program on gait and balance in a group of deconditioned nursing home men (mean age 73). After completion of a 12-week program consisting of lower extremity weight training and stationary training, the individuals demonstrated significant improvements in stride length and gait velocity, although their balance was not affected.

Blanpied and Smidt (1993) studied the effects of a strengthening exercise program in decreasing ankle plantar flexor stiffness. After a 6-week program consisting of plantar flexor strengthening using a resistant elastic band, the subjects exhibited a decrease in ankle stiffness. While this study did not examine the functional outcome or effects of improved ankle flexibility, the possibility of improved gait and balance remains.

Judge, Lindsey, Underwood, and Winsemius (1993) examined the effect of specific types of physical exercise on improving balance in a group of older women. A treatment group exercised three times weekly for 6 months using a leg press, including standing hip extensions, hip abductions using muscle weights, and walking around an indoor track for 20 minutes. This was combined with flexibility and balance training consisting of hip muscle stretches, hip muscle abduction exercises, and simplified tai chi exercises: slow controlled body movements, anterior-posterior weight shifts, and turning and pivoting on the foot. A control or comparison group did not begin to exercise until week 13 and, thereafter, did exercises similar to the treatment group, except that they did not use ankle weights for hip abduction and exercised only 30 minutes once weekly. The combined treatment group improved their balance by 18%, while the control group experienced no improvement. Combined treatment group members also experienced a 26% increase in muscle force on knee extension. The control group also had a significant increase in force in leg press maneuvers, but not in knee extension. This study demonstrates that specific muscle-strengthening exercises may have a significant effect on improving balance.

Hu and Woollacott (1994a) studied the effects of standing balance training on the ability of older persons to maintain balance. Participants completed a 10-hour (1 hour daily) multisensory training program consisting of exercises that manipulated sensory inputs from the visual, vestibular, and somatosensory systems. The program included standing with bare feet on a platform system while sensory inputs relevant to postural stability were systematically manipulated. The training subjects showed significant improvements in their stability, and when tested 1 month later, fell less frequently when the ankle and foot somatosensory inputs were minimized; they were able to stand on one leg for prolonged periods. In a followup study, Hu and Woollacott (1994b) examined the effects of a multisensory balance training program on the postural responses in older persons. After a 15-day training period, subjects exhibited significantly shortened onset latencies of the neck flexor muscle and decreased response frequency of antagonist muscles. As well, the individuals showed a trend towards an increased response frequency of the trunk flexor muscles, and decreased excursion of ankle joint rotation. From the results of these studies, the authors concluded that balance training designed to improve sensory interaction can effectively enhance the balance performance of older people.

Exercise regimens that are less complicated or vigorous may be effective in improving gait and balance as well. For example, Conright et al. (1990) showed that a simple walking program consisting of frail, chairbound nursing home residents walking at least once a week to their tolerance could improve gait and balance. Roberts (1989) found that participation in a 6-week program of aerobic walking improved balance, attributing this to improved lower extremity strength, coordination, and flexibility. Lord, Caplan, and Ward (1993) found that older women, aged 57 to 75 years, who participated in a program of aerobic exercises emphasizing balance and flexibility for periods of 12 months or greater, demonstrated better quadriceps strength, reaction time, and sway than nonexercising women. Hopkins, Murich, Hoeger, and Rhodes (1990) showed that a low-impact aerobic dancing program was effective in improving balance performance in older women. Fansler, Pott, and Shepard (1985) found that older women increased their balance performance on one-leg stance tests after 5 days of practicing this position. One-leg standing draws on several components of balance, including the vestibular system, strength, flexibility, proprioception, and vision. Also, the movements of tai chi, a traditional Chinese exercise, may be effective in improving neuromuscular function (quadriceps strength, joint flexibility). Tai chi consists of a series of individual dancelike movements, stressing slow graceful movement and awareness of body weight and alignment. Several researchers investigating the value of tai chi in healthy older persons have shown that these persons exhibit significantly better postural control (Province et al., 1995; Tse & Bailey, 1992).

Despite an abundance of research demonstrating a positive association between participating in exercise programs and improvements of muscle strength, gait, and balance, not all research has been equally optimistic. Several researchers have failed to demonstrate an effect of exercises on joint flexibility or muscle strength (Hanson, Agostinucci, Dasler, & Creel, 1992; Morey et al., 1991), measures of balance (Crilly et al., 1989; Lichtenstein, Shields, Shiavi, & Burger, 1989; Topp, Mikesky, Wigglesworth, Holt, & Edwards, 1993) or gait (Brown & Holloszy, 1991), or even at reducing the occurrence of falls (Mulrow et al., 1994). There are a number of possible reasons for these negative findings. Strengthening exercises selected may have lacked sufficient magnitude or were too low in intensity or resistance to affect muscle strength. In general, resistance exercises need to be performed to fatigue with resistance, for example, using sandbag leg weights, elastic bands to achieve a beneficial response. Also, the exercise programs may have not been of sufficient duration or time to influence muscle strength, joint flexibility, and measures of gait and balance. Another possibility is that exercises designed to improve a single component of balance, such as the vestibular system or lower extremity strength, are more effective in the improvement of balance than are exercise programs that are more generalized. For instance, some investigators (Crilly et al., 1989; Lichtenstein et al., 1989) have failed to demonstrate balance improvement in response to a generalized total body exercise program that consists of one leg standing, flexibility, stretching, strengthening, and walking trials, whereas other training protocols with identified aims toward specific deficiencies related to balance or postural control have reported positive effects (Fiatarone, 1990, 1994; Hu & Woollacott, 1994a, 1994b). Poor compliance with exercise regimens, and effects of concurrent morbidity not amenable to intervention, may be additional factors. And lastly, the selection of research subjects may have had an effect. For instance, the selection of healthy persons may have a ceiling effect, in that is there is little or no room left for additional improvement.

EXERCISES AIMED AT COMBATING OSTEOPOROSIS

Exercise also plays an important role in preventing osteoporosis and possibly, the risk of distal forearm and hip fractures. Most studies show that participating in regular, moderate weight-bearing exercises can either maintain or increase bone mass (Ayalon, Simkin, Leichter, & Raitman, 1987; Chow, Harrison, & Notarius, 1987; Dalsky et al., 1988; Smith, Gilligan, Shea, Ensign, & Smith, 1989), and that a failure to engage in similar exercises may lead to a decline in bone mass (Smith, 1995). Also, there appears to be no upper age limit to the capacity of bone to respond effectively to physical activity (Talmage, Stinett, Landwehr, Vincent, & McCartney, 1986).

Perhaps the most common form of weight-bearing exercise prescribed is that of walking. A daily program of walking is often incorporated into an exercise regimen directed at combating osteoporosis (Smith et al., 1989), and appears to be effective in slowing the rate of bone loss. Krall and Dawson-Huges (1994) evaluated 239 healthy, white, postmenopausal women aged 43 to 72 years. They found that women who walked 7.5 miles per week, reflecting lifelong walking habits, had significantly higher mean whole-body, leg, and trunk bone densities than did women who walked less than 1 mile per week. In order to be effective in increasing bone density, it is suggested that walking should be accomplished at a brisk pace, for 45 to 60 minutes a day, three days a week or 20 minutes daily (Breslau, 1992). For those individuals with gait and balance impairments, exercising on a stationary bicycle may be recommended as an effective alternative (Steinberg & Roettger, 1993).

In addition, participating in strength training may have a positive effect on osteoporosis as well. Nelson et al. (1994) evaluated the effects of a 1-year, high-intensity strength training program on bone, muscle strength, and balance. Study subjects consisted of 40 postmenopausal white women, 50 to 70 years of age, who were all sedentary (that is, did not engage in a regular program of exercise) and were estrogen-deplete. Twenty-one women were randomized to an exercise-training or intervention group and 19 women to a control group. Subjects assigned to the intervention group participated in high-intensity strength training (hip and knee extension, lateral pull-down, back extension, and abdominal flexion using a pneumatic resistance machine) 2 days per week, 45 minutes per session, for 52 weeks. Subjects in the control group did not participate in the exercise-training program, and were asked to simply maintain their current level of physical activity during the study period. With the exception of one woman in the exercise group who suffered a heart attack during the first month of the study, all of the subjects completed the 1-year intervention program. Seven women in the intervention group experienced transient musculoskeletal pain that required minor modifications in the training program, but all completed the exercise program without further problems. In the control group, one woman suffered an ankle sprain, and two other women experienced falls that resulted in wrist fractures, but all were able to finish the study. During followup, femoral neck and lumbar bone mineral density increased significantly in the intervention group and decreased in the control group. Moreover, muscle mass and strength, and dynamic balance (timed backward tandem walk test) increased in the strength-training group and decreased in the control group. It was concluded that high-intensity strength training had a protective effect on the femoral neck and lumbar spine, and increased muscle strength and dynamic balance.

While these programs are of benefit in improving lower-extremity muscle and bone strength and guarding against hip fracture, their effects on upper-extremity bone strength and the prevention of distal forearm fractures are negligible. Recommending weight-bearing exercises of the upper extremity (concentrating on the shoulders and arms) may help to improve both muscle strength and bone density. In particular, these exercises may be beneficial in helping older persons with poor balance to both protectively stretch out their arms, in the event of a fall, and to avoid the likelihood of distal forearm fractures. As well, a program of back extension exercises may be beneficial for the improvement of back strength (upper spine extensors) (Steinberg & Roettger, 1993). While this type of exercise may not improve bone density, as it is non-weight-bearing, it can help to counteract kyphotic posture which, in turn, may improve balance. In those older persons with suspected osteoporosis, flexion exercises that involve bending at the waist should be avoided, as they may cause undue vertebral stress that can result in a fracture.

SELECTING EXERCISES

As demonstrated, a growing and convincing body of evidence suggests that older people, even those who are very old and frail, respond to exercise therapy. These observations raise the possibility that the decline in muscle strength and mass in old age and accompanying loss of mobility can be reduced by appropriate exercise regimens, although the long-term effects of this intervention on the frequency of falls remain to be studied. At any rate, some form of habitual exercise is better than not exercising at all, as it may prevent further deterioration of mobility, and should be attempted. By increasing the strength of the muscles used in walking and stair ambulation, transferring from a chair, toilet, and bed, getting in and out of bathtubs, and stooping, it may be possible to improve the older person's mobility, which in turn, may reduce the risk of falls. Furthermore, exercise can enhance the functioning of other organ systems involved in mobility endurance, such as cardiovascular and pulmonary performance. Also, by building self-confidence in performing activities to reduce the fear of falling or instability, improvements in psychological functioning may be realized as well.

All individuals with poor mobility or who may be at fall risk should be encouraged to participate in a program of exercises. Even modest improvements are possible at low levels of exercise, regardless of an individual's life history of engaging in exercise. For most individuals, a general remedial program of strength training and joint flexibility aimed at improving gait and balance, as profiled in Figure 7.1, can be safe and effective. Family members, home attendants, and nursing home staff can be taught to supervise older individuals with balance disorders so that the exercises can be performed safely.

Older hospital patients can benefit from participating in exercise programs as well. Hirsch et al. (1990) described the "natural history of functional morbidity" in a group of older persons, mean age 84, who were hospitalized. They found a striking decline in mobility from the time of hospital admission to discharge; 70% of patients who were dependent in mobility on discharge had been completely independent at baseline, 2 weeks prior to admission. Hospital exercise programs, consisting of early daily ambulation and bedside strengthening exercises, may therefore be beneficial in limiting the risk of falls while in the hospital. One geriatric unit of an acute hospital located in Cleveland, Ohio, developed a program to help combat the problems associated with immobility (Palmer, Landefeld, Kresevic, & Kowal, 1994). Patients were expected to ambulate and/or stand at least three times daily, and to ambulate to the activity room for group exercises and meals daily. The patients and their caregivers were instructed on active and passive range-of-motion exercises, weight-bearing exercises, and resistive and aerobic exercises. Recommending a similar home-based exercise

FIGURE 7.1 Flexibility and balance exercises. Strength-building (in figures 1, 2, 3, 8, and 10) can be intensified by using weights (about 2 lbs to start with and progressing to higher weights as tolerated).

program at discharge may help to further improve mobility, and decrease the risk of falls and re-admission back to the hospital.

However, for other individuals, the selection of exercises needs to be more specific, tailored towards modifying specific impairments. For example, for those persons with impaired transfer function, strengthening the muscle groups involved in getting up from a seated position (shoulder depressors, elbow extensors, hip extensors, and quadriceps) is beneficial. Likewise, persons with gait and balance problems should be provided with strengthening exercises aimed at improving major lower-extremity muscle groups (quadriceps, hamstrings, hip adductors and abductors, hip flexors and extensors, ankle plantars and dorsiflexors). For those older individuals with lower-extremity muscle weakness sufficient to impair mobility and increase the risk of falls and fractures, a more vigorous strengthening program as described by Fiatarone et al. (1990, 1994) may be beneficial. Likewise, individuals with balance problems due to sensory losses may benefit from a multisensory balance training program as described by Hu and Woollacott (1994a).

For most older persons, these exercise programs are suitable, with minimal risk of adverse effects such as injury. However, as older persons at fall risk may obviously be susceptible to falls and injury, certain caution is advised. Sometimes a renewed sense of confidence and ability to execute mobility tasks may lead older individuals to attempt activities that exceed their capabilities. However, this should not discourage health professionals and caregivers from encouraging independent mobility. Instead, persons should receive assistance at the beginning of any exercise program, which should continue until the individual can perform the exercise routinely. For persons who fall, mobility should be encouraged. Exercise should be resumed as soon as possible to avoid the potential consequences of immobility and fear of falling. This is similar to falling off a horse; it is best to get back on as soon as one is able.

TEACHING OLDER PERSONS TO GET UP FROM THE FLOOR

Community-dwelling older persons at fall risk who live alone and either demonstrate difficulty rising from the floor unassisted and/or have a past history of increased lie times should be instructed on how to get up from the floor. Most persons can be taught to move along the floor to a chair or sofa, and with its support, move into a side-sitting position. They can then kneel with the support of the chair, and with the stronger knee push themselves onto the chair. However, some older persons may be reluctant to learn how to get up from the floor, due to fear or anxiety or because they feel physically unable to accomplish this activity (Simpson & Mandelstam, 1993; Simpson & Salkin, 1993). In these individuals, a personal emergency response or alarm system, a device designed to provide persons at risk for increased lie times with a means to summon help (see Chapter 8), may be recommended.

FOOTWEAR

Paying attention to the type and fit of footwear worn by older people is important, as it can either interfere with or support safe gait and balance. Common problems associated with footwear that can lead to fall risk are reviewed in Chapter 3. All shoes and slippers worn by older persons should fit properly (should not be too tight or loose) and their soles should be slip-resistant. If foot problems (hammer toes, bunions, calluses, or nail disorders) prohibit wearing properly sized footwear, individuals should be referred for podiatric care.

Shoes and slippers with rubber or crepe soles provide adequate slip resistance on slippery ground surfaces, such as linoleum. Robbins, Gouw, and McClaran (1992) suggest that shoes with thin, hard soles are preferred to soft-soled "walking shoes," since they increase the proprioceptive input that comes from striking the ground and help to maintain balance. Socks with non-skid tread designs on the soles are a good choice for persons who are accustomed to walking about without shoes or slippers. In the institutional setting, socks with non-skid treads are particularly useful for those patients and residents with nocturia who get up out of bed and travel to the bathroom, sometimes across slippery floor surfaces. Moreover, these non-slip socks are superior to the traditional rubber crepe sole "hospital slippers" that are often worn by older hospital patients, and which can sometimes lead to hesitant gait. When compared to bare feet or "hospital slippers," preliminary data shows that walking with non-skid tread-soled socks improves a variety of gait parameters (for example, steppage height, stride length, and single support time), and may help to reduce the risk of falls (Tideiksaar, 1993e).

For some individuals with shuffling gait or poor steppage height (that is, an inability to pick up the feet adequately from the floor), such as those with Parkinsonism and poor ankle dorsiflexion, footwear with leather-type soles that promote gliding on linoleum and carpeted floor surfaces may be a better choice. The best way to evaluate the adequacy of the sole surface of footwear is to observe older persons as they walk on different floor surfaces in their environment, and notice whether their footwear interferes with gait.

High-heeled shoes should be avoided. Rather, footwear with low broad heels should be encouraged. These are better suited for safe walking and balance. However, if high heels are insisted upon, either out of vanity or because of a real need (high heels worn over a long period of time cause a shortening of the Achilles tendon, which then necessitates their use), shoes with wedge heels are preferable and should be encouraged. They provide a better base of support than do spike-heeled shoes; also, the wedge heel is less likely to catch on elevated floor surfaces, (such as upended carpet or a linoleum tile edge or door threshold). The selection of exercise footwear, such as walking or running shoes, is dependent upon the type of activity desired. Running sneakers or shoes may be used for both activities, as they provide good stability and cushioning for the foot. However, recall that running shoes may have overly absorbent padding and can rob persons from receiving proprioceptive input needed for balance. Also, some styles of running shoes have thick "waffle-style" soles that can interfere with gait, especially in those persons with decreased steppage height. Table 7.1 provides a set of guidelines for purchasing footwear and can be used by older persons to help them select appropriate shoes.

AMBULATION DEVICES

For those persons with gait and balance disorders, assistive ambulation devices such as canes and walkers can be used to maintain or improve mobility. These devices function by increasing the person's standing and walking base of support and stability. Ambulation devices furnish proprioceptive feedback through the handle, and reduce or shift the load on weight-bearing joints (such as the hips, knees, ankle, or foot). Furthermore, both canes and walkers provide the person with a visual presence of support that can instill confidence in the person during ambulation, and may help to reduce the fear of instability and falls.

CANES

A cane is the simplest device for ambulation, capable of shifting and supporting up to 25% of body weight away from the lower extremities.

TABLE 7.1   Guidelines for Purchasing Footwear

1. Buy shoes in the late afternoon, as your feet swell during the day.
2. Never buy shoes without trying them both on, as your feet may be of different sizes. Buy the pair that fits the longer, wider foot. Shoe inserts can be used to make the larger shoe fit the smaller foot.
3. Select shoes that are equipped with slip-resistant soles to prevent slipping on wet surfaces.
4. Select shoes with low heels. The shoe heel should be no more than 3.5 cm in height and at least 5.5 cm in width. These dimensions provide maximum balance support.
5. Select shoes with ample room in the toe box (the space between the tip of the longest toe and front of the shoe). This space should be at least 1/4 of an inch in length, about the size of your thumbnail, and wide enough to avoid rubbing your large and small toe against the sides of the shoe. These dimensions will allow free movement of your toes when walking and prevent injury.
6. Select shoes with inner soles that cushion the feet. A cushioned sole absorbs pressure on the feet and protects your feet from impact injuries that may occur when walking on hard surfaces.
7. Select shoes that have firm heel support. When walking, the heel of the shoe should remain stable on your foot, not sway from side to side, and fit the foot snugly, not ride up and down.

Canes are generally indicated for people whose ability to walk is limited by unilateral extremity dysfunction (pain, weakness, etc.) and/or who may require minimal balance support. A variety of cane designs are available. However, most older persons can be adequately managed by either a single or multitipped base cane. A single-tip or standard cane is the most commonly used. The shaft is normally constructed of either wood, fiberglass, or aluminum. Wooden canes are the least expensive, the most cosmetically appealing, and socially acceptable ambulation device. However, wood or fiberglass canes are nonadjustable in length, and as a result, the cane when purchased must be of the appropriate height for the user or else cut to fit the individual. Also, wood canes may splinter or fatigue with prolonged use or excessive weight bearing. Aluminum canes are lightweight, more sturdy than those constructed with wood or fiberglass, and are adjustable in length via a pushbutton pin mechanism, so that the cane can be quickly adjusted to the user's height. However, aluminum canes, particularly those that are "steel" in color, have less cosmetic appeal than wooden and fiberglass canes. Some aluminum canes are available in different colors such as black or bronze, which may be more acceptable for older persons. Moreover, the health care professional can have an aluminum cane available in the office to measure proper cane height for those persons who prefer to use a wooden cane. Once the proper cane height is determined the person can purchase a properly sized cane on their own, and choose one that they find stylish.

Some cane shafts are offset or "swan-necked" in shape (Figure 7.2). This design provides extra balance support, as the user's body support is directly positioned over the cane shaft. Folding metal canes are also available. Their shaft is constructed in sections joined together by elastic cable. This design allows the cane to be broken down to fit into a purse or other carry-all when not in use. Both nonadjustable and adjustable folding canes are available. However, folding canes tend to offer less weight-bearing support than do cane stems that are rigid in construction. Some single-tipped canes come equipped with a seat attachment. This design allows the person to sit and rest, and may be helpful for persons with cardiopulmonary problems. However, canes with seats are heavy, weighing about 2 to 4 pounds and are cumbersome to use, and can thus lead to unsafe gaits. Individuals with poor sitting balance may be at fall risk when using these devices.

Figure 7.2 Offset cane. Photograph courtesy of Lumex, Inc.

The second type of cane is the pedestal-based or "quad" cane, which offers more support than single-tip canes (Figure 7.3), but has less cosmetic appeal. The quad cane has four prongs or tips and is constructed with an aluminum shaft, which is both offset and height-adjustable in design. The quad cane is available in both a narrow and wide base of ground support. The wider base offers greater stability, but is difficult to use on stairs; several of the prongs may hang over the steps when ambulating and lead to balance instability; and problematic to maneuver in small areas. Also, quad canes are less stable on uneven terrains such as sidewalks and streets. Moreover, quad canes may produce a halting, almost "crab-like" gait. When walking quickly, the "rocking" back-and-forth motion between the legs of the quad cane can also lead to instability. In general, persons utilizing a quad cane need to have good judgement. If the quad cane is held improperly, and the legs project laterally toward the body rather than away, the device becomes extremely unsteady and increases the risk of falling. Furthermore, in this position an individual can easily get their feet caught up in the legs of the quad cane, which may lead to tripping.

WALKERS

Walkers are designed to provide more support than canes, and are indicated for people whose ability to ambulate is limited by bilateral lower-extremity dysfunction and/or poor balance. However, as opposed to single-stem canes, walkers have two major drawbacks; they are difficult to use in space-limited areas (such as bathrooms or narrow hallways), and cannot be used on stairways. A variety of walker designs are available.

A hemiwalker (Figure 7.4) helps reduce lateral instability, and is particularly effective for persons with hemiplegia. The bilevel handgrips add extra hand support to help with seated transfers. However, the hemiwalker is limited, in that it requires the user to walk slowly for safe ambulation. Also, holding the device incorrectly may lead to instability and can result in the person getting their feet caught up in the legs of the walker. Both situations can increase the risk of falls.

The traditional standard walking frame or "pick-up walker" provides a wide base of support, and good anterior and lateral stability. The legs are equipped with rubber tips to prevent the walker from sliding away. For individuals who are obese, a sturdy wide-based design walker is available. Pickup walkers, though, may not be useful for people with poor balance, as the user must "pick up and place down" the walker when ambulating. As a result, the walker is actually providing ground

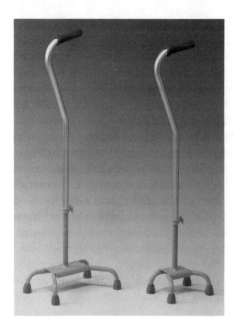

Figure 7.3   Quad cane. Photograph courtesy of Lumex, Inc.

support only half the time, that is, when the walker's four legs of support are in contact with the floor, requiring the user to maintain balance on one or both feet while moving the walker along. Moreover, this
"pick up and place down" movement leads to halting patterns of gait.
Persons with poor upper-extremity strength or pain due to arthritis of
the shoulders are not good candidates for this type of device, as they
may find it burdensome to repeatedly pick up and move the walker forward. Sometimes, rather than picking the walker up, individuals will
push the walker along the floor, which can increase the risk of falls, as
the walker may suddenly come to a screeching halt or tip over if uneven
floor surfaces are encountered. Lifting a pickup walker can also be difficult if saddlebags are attached to the front horizontal bar in order to
carry objects.

Persons with cognitive dysfunction such as Alzheimer's Disease may
have difficulty ambulating in sequence with a pickup walker. One alternative to the pickup walker in this situation is to try a "gliding" walker,
which has metal tips or plastic glides rather than rubber tips attached
to the bottom of the legs. This design allows the person to ambulate by
pushing the walker forward, rather than by picking it up. This action
provides a smoother pattern of gait than that achieved with the pickup

Figure 7.4   Hemi walker. Photograph
courtesy of Lumex, Inc.

walker, and more closely resembles a "natural" pattern of gait. Pickup
walkers can easily be converted into gliding walkers by simply fasten-
ing furniture glides to the rubber tips. However, gliding walkers have a
few disadvantages. They generally are not equipped with braking systems; hence, persons with rapid propulsion, such as those with Parkinson's Disease, may be at risk for balance loss. Also, in order to use a
gliding walker the floor surface must be flat and smooth, as any uneven
surfaces such as carpet/rug edges or door thresholds will cause the
walker to come to an immediate stop and tip over. As a result, gliding
walkers are generally limited to institutional settings that have smooth
linoleum floor surfaces.

Stair-climbing walkers are also available. These are similar to pickup
walkers, but have dual handgrips that are used to assist either with
stair ascent or descent. However, stair-climbing walkers are usually
limited to stairs with one or two steps, as they may be difficult and
even dangerous for older people to use on long flights of stairs. Furthermore, most older people find stair-climbing walkers difficult to master.
Generally, in cases where people require the support of a walker and

have long stairways in their homes, it is preferable to provide the individual with two walkers; one that they keep and use downstairs, and the other walker they maintain upstairs.

A wheeled or "rolling" walker is similar to a gliding walker, in that it allows the user to ambulate by pushing or rolling the walker forward. Rolling walkers are easier for older persons to use and maintain better balance control than pickup walkers. In addition, rolling walkers have an additional advantage; they are easier to maneuver on carpeted and uneven ground surfaces than are gliding walkers. On the other hand, rolling walkers tend to be less sturdy and have less stability than pickup walkers. For added balance in those individuals with retropulsive balance loss, a saddle bag with 5 lb weights attached to the front horizontal bar of the walker can effectively act as a counterweight. In addition, rolling walkers can be equipped with automatic braking systems that slow down the walker's forward movement, and these are especially beneficial in those individuals with propulsive balance loss.

Both pickup and two-wheeled walkers may be either fixed (rigid) or foldable in design. The choice between the two should be based on the user's lifestyle. For instance, community-dwelling individuals who need to occasionally transport their walkers via a car or other vehicle are better off with a folding walker. However, for those persons who are housebound or reside in a hospital and nursing home, and don't require the advantages offered by a folding walker, a non-foldable walker may be preferable, as it tends to be sturdier in construction and provides better support. Conversely, some institutional settings with limited storage space may find folding walkers easier to store than non-folding walkers.

Rolling walkers are equipped with either two, three, or four wheels. Two-wheeled walkers can either be outfitted with nonswivel or swivel wheels. In general, swivel wheels that pivot are easier to use, particularly when turning on carpeted surfaces. The size of the wheels can also influence the performance of the walker; the larger the wheel radius, the easier it becomes to travel over uneven floor surfaces and thick carpets. In those persons who require a walker for outdoor ambulation, using a two-wheeled walker, even with large wheels, can be difficult on uneven ground surfaces (such as sidewalks, small curbs, grass, or gravel) if not actually impossible, as the walker's rear legs tend to interfere with smooth ambulation. As a result, some older people will use supermarket shopping carts and wheeled shopping baskets instead of their two-wheeled walkers. Many older people find these alternative devices more acceptable than walkers for several reasons. First of all, shopping baskets are universally used, and older persons don't feel stigmatized when using the shopping basket, as they do when using walkers. Secondly, older persons find these devices convenient to use, as they are able to transport groceries and other items. Sometimes wheelchairs are used for similar purposes; individuals place objects onto the seat and push the chair along. However, these alternative choices may not be ideal for maintaining balance support.

A more sensible option, particularly for outdoor ambulation, is the use of a four-wheeled walker (Figure 7.5). These devices have been shown to have a greater positive impact on gait and balance than have two-wheeled walkers (Eblen & Koeneman, 1993; Tideiksaar, 1993d). Moreover, they offer greater stability and maneuverability on thick carpets and uneven ground surfaces (such as door thresholds and sidewalks) than do standard rolling walkers. Some models are available with carrying baskets for groceries, a tray attachment, and padded seat bars. The seat attachment is especially beneficial for those older persons with osteoarthritis whose legs give way after walking a distance, and in those individuals with underlying pulmonary disease and heart failure who need to frequently stop and rest while ambulating outdoors. However, the seating bar may be difficult for people with poor seated transfers and sitting balance to use, resulting in the risk of falls.

The tray attachment is extremely useful; it allows the user to keep both hands on the walking frame while transporting meals and objects like books, newspapers, and eyeglasses from room to room. The addition of a tray may be recommended for those persons who are observed attempting to ambulate with one hand pushing or picking up the walker, and with the other hand, carrying objects; or else, for those individuals who sometimes will carry objects with both hands, risking a loss of balance, and retrieve the walker later. Both tasks can be extremely hazardous to perform. Sometimes, a trolley with wheels can serve as a viable alternative to both transport objects and act as a walker in the home, although a trolley can sometimes roll away from the user leaving them without support.

Three-wheeled walkers have been found to improve mobility when compared to two-wheeled walkers (Mahoney, Euhardy, & Carnes, 1992). However, some models are more likely than either two- or four-wheeled walkers to lose stability, as they tend to tip over when turned quickly or sharply, or when traveling over low curb heights. Therefore, extra caution should be taken when recommending these devices to persons with balance impairment. Three- and four-wheeled walkers are equipped with hand braking systems to prevent the walker from rolling away from the user. However, some persons with severe arthritis or cognitive dysfunction may find hand brakes difficult to use, and as a

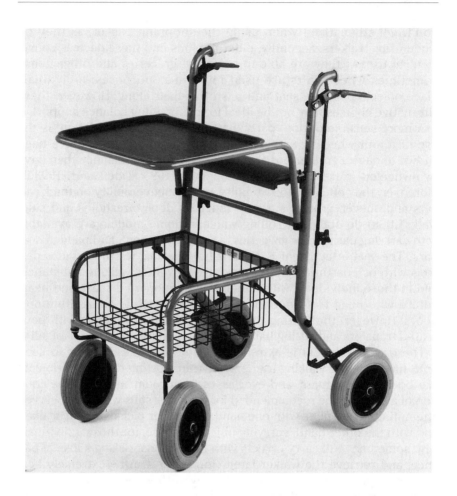

FIGURE 7.5 Four-wheel rolling walker. Displayed with optional tray attachment for meal service. Photograph courtesy of Noble Motion, Inc.

result, the walker may roll away and increase the risk of falls. For the most part, however, clinical experience has not shown this to be a problem, as persons who are reliant on a walker tend to display reduced gait speed, and rarely ever build up enough speed to cause the walker to roll away unexpectedly. Some individuals may be better off with two-wheeled walkers equipped with automatic weight-activated brakes that engage when the user leans too far forward on the walker.

Perhaps most important, both three- and four-wheeled walkers are aesthetically more appealing than conventional rolling walkers, thereby improving both patient acceptance and compliance. Their only drawback is their cost, which may not be covered completely by third-party payers. Both these walkers are priced from about $200 to $350, compared to about $85 for a standard two-wheeled walker, and as a result, they may not be easily affordable by older people. As a result, before offering either of these devices, it is best to determine the patient's and/or family's financial status, so as to avoid disappointing the patient. This may particularly be the case in those individuals who find that their mobility is greatly improved after a trial run with these devices.

MEASUREMENT OF AMBULATION DEVICES

To ensure that ambulation devices are properly used, they need to be tailored to fit the older person. The measurement of cane height is the same, regardless of cane type. Have the person wear their everyday footwear and stand erect, with arms hanging loosely by their sides. Place the cane tip, or center of multistem cane, about 6 inches in front and 6 inches lateral to the person's forefoot. With the cane in this position, two landmarks are used to determine proper height: (1) the greater trochanter of the hip or ulnar styloid process (wrist crease), and (2) the angle of the elbow. The top of the cane should be aligned with the person's ulnar styloid process (wrist crease) or greater trochanter, and when the cane is held, the person's elbow should be flexed to about 20 to 30 degrees. This degree of elbow flexion allows the arm to shorten or lengthen during the different phases of gait, and provides adequate support. The degree of elbow flexion is the most useful indicator of correct cane height.

At the same time, the cane should be equipped with an appropriate handle. The selection of a cane handle is based on two criteria: their ability to provide comfort, and to provide support. A curved handle allows a person to retain the cane over their arm while opening doors and performing other activities, and is good for short walks. But this type of handle may produce discomfort with extended use and/or excessive weight-bearing, because the person's weight is centered and pressed down on the small part of the palm (the hypothenar prominence). With age, fat padding surrounding the hypothenar process tends to atrophy, and further contributes to the discomfort. Also, a curved handle may lead to balance instability, as the point of weight support on the handle is anterior to the hand and not directly underneath it. The "T" design cane handle provides better support than a curved handle, as the distribution of support is centered directly over the cane shaft. Straight cane handles provide better grip support and comfort than curved handles. These are indicated for persons with arthritis and those with extended cane use and/or excessive weight-bearing.

The cane handle should fit the shape of the person's hand. If the diameter of the handle is too small, producing close contact between the fingers and palm, discomfort may result. The addition of contoured foam or an enlarged molded hand grip may provide adequate handle fit. As well, make certain that the cane is equipped with a non-slip rubber tip. The best type of tips for single stem canes that provide optimum slip resistance has flared sides and a flat base with concentric rings 3 cm in diameter. Avoid rounded rubber tips; these tips do not grip the ground as well, and may slide away during weight-bearing, especially on slippery ground surfaces.

The measurement of walker height is similar to the measurement of a cane. Place the walker 10 to 12 inches in front of the person's feet so that the walker partially surrounds the individual. In this position, the walker handles should align with the greater trochanter of the hip, and the elbows should be flexed at 20 to 30 degrees. The walker handles or hand grips should fit the shape of the person's hand, be comfortable to grip, and slip-resistant. Hard plastic handles that press on the hypothenar eminences may cause ulnar nerve palsies. Consider padding the handles with foam or using enlarged molded hand grips, particularly in those persons who place excessive weight on the frame during ambulation.

UTILIZING AMBULATION DEVICES

Assistive devices should never be dispensed unless full directions on their use are provided and persons are observed using their device. When ambulating on level surfaces, the cane is held on the side opposite the affected limb. This provides the greatest base of support and simulates normal gait. When the cane is held on the same side as the affected limb, the person's center of gravity tends to shift from side to side and produces instability. For balance stability (no affected limb) or when there is bilateral limb involvement, the cane is held in the hand which offers the most grip strength, comfort, and safe ambulation. Also, when walking the cane should not be placed too far to the side of the body or ahead of the affected limb. Placing the cane too far to the side or forward of the body will result in a loss of stability. Likewise, persons should receive instruction on the proper use of walkers on level surfaces and during seated transfers.

SELECTION AND EVALUATION OF AMBULATION DEVICES

The choice of a cane, whether it is single or multi-stemmed, or a walker, whether a pickup or wheeled type, should be determined by the needs of the individual person. In some ways, devices should be treated as medications and taken as seriously. For example, drugs are given to treat a specific condition and their dosages are adjusted to compensate for individual pharmacokinetic differences. Of equal importance, the patient is instructed in how to take their medication, which ensures both a beneficial therapeutic outcome and the avoidance of adverse effects. Medications are also periodically examined to ensure their effectiveness and that their benefits outweigh any risks. Similarly, the "prescription" of a cane or walker is not generic, but is dependent upon the patient's condition—their physical and cognitive state—and the type of environment in which they live. Therefore, when prescribing an ambulation device, the interaction of the user, cane or walker, and environment are fundamental concerns that need to be addressed. As an individual's mobility status and device requirements are likely to change over time, canes and walkers, like medications, should be routinely evaluated. This includes asking individuals about the utilization of their device and checking for structural defects, the proper size and fit, and correct use of the ambulation device. The steps involved in this process are represented by the acronym RATE (Table 7.2).

WHEELCHAIRS

Similar to ambulation devices, wheelchairs should be tailored to meet the specific needs of the individual, and evaluated routinely to ensure that they are being utilized safely. Recall that some of the common problems leading to wheelchair falls include a failure by persons to properly lock the wheels prior to transferring; getting the feet caught behind the foot rests and tripping; or stepping on the footrests, causing the chair to tip over while transferring. These problems are reviewed completely in Chapter 3.

Subsequently, several measures can be taken to decrease the risk of wheelchair falls. First, evaluate the person's wheelchair mobility. Ask the individual to get up from their wheelchair, and observe whether they accomplish the task in a safe manner. Most importantly, did they remember to engage the wheel brakes and move the foot rests away? Seated wheelchair transfers in the bedroom and bathroom should also

TABLE 7.2   Prescribing and Assessing Ambulation Devices—The RATE Procedure

R-ecognition
1. Recognize that the patient's gait/balance may be improved with the use of a cane or walker.
2. Recognize indications for ambulation device. Consider type of cane or walker that is appropriate for the patient (i.e., one that provides balance support and/or one that reduces weight-bearing on the joints of the lower extremities).
3. Recognize that the patient's condition may improve or deteriorate over time, requiring either an upgrade to a walker or downgrade to a cane.

A-ssessment
1. Assess patient's physical status and determine the type and extent of gait/balance impairment. This will help determine the appropriate ambulation device.
2. Assess patient's psychological status. Will impaired mental status interfere with proper, safe use of ambulation device? Will patient accept an ambulation device or because of the stigma attached to ambulation devices (particularly walkers) be noncompliant?
3. Assess patient's living environment. Will patient be able to use ambulation device on stairs? Narrow hallway passages? Space-limited bathrooms? Carpeted floor surfaces? Will patient be able to transport the ambulation device in a car, buses, taxis, etc.?
4. Assess proper ambulation device for the patient and measure size of cane or walker to fit individual. Assess proper cane handle.

T-rain
1. Provide the patient with instruction on how to properly use their ambulation device (e.g., on level ground, stairs, and seated transfers).
2. Observe the patient using their ambulation device to be certain that they are doing so properly and safely.
3. Instruct the patient to be cautious when encountering environmental ground hazards, such as wet/icy surfaces, with canes, and elevated surfaces (e.g., curbs, door thresholds, thick carpet surfaces, etc.) with walkers.

E-valuate
1. On a regular basis, inquire of the patient: Are you using your ambulation device? Does the ambulation device improve your gait/balance? Are you experiencing any problems with your ambulation device? (Any negative response requires a reassessment of the patient's ambulation device.)
2. On a regular basis inspect the patient's ambulation device. Examine the cane or walker for presence of cracks, splintering, warping, loose hardware and wheels, and worn rubber tips. Replace as indicated.
3. On a regular basis observe the patient using their ambulation device. Ask the patient to perform walking, transferring and step climbing/descending maneuvers with their ambulation device, and observe whether they are accomplishing the tasks properly and safely.

be observed, with respect to whether bed and toilet transfers are performed safely. In addition, observe whether individuals can safely utilize their wheelchair in small spaces, such as the bathroom and the area between the person's bedside and wall or dresser.

Once this is accomplished and potential problems leading to fall risk are identified, a number of strategies aimed at reducing risk can be recommended. Persons exhibiting poor wheelchair transfers should be referred to physical therapy for training. To prevent the individual's feet from becoming entangled in the footplates, the use of heel loops attached to footplates or an H-shaped strap connected from footplate hanger bracket to hanger bracket are effective. Attaching specially designed anti-tip devices to the wheelchair can guard against the chair from tipping, which may occur if an individual bends forward excessively, or else steps on the footplate during transfers. In those persons with cognitive impairment who are noncompliant with braking the chair wheels when transferring, consideration should be given to prohibiting independent transfers. A variety of devices, such as wedge cushions and chair alarm systems, are available for this purpose. These devices are discussed in Chapter 9.

In addition to these rehabilitative efforts aimed at reducing fall risk, attempts to modify the environmental conditions that contribute to fall risk should be investigated as well (see Chapter 8). This is of particular importance in those older individuals with chronic neuromuscular diseases and poor mobility.

CHAPTER 8

Environmental Strategies
to Reduce Fall Risk

INTRODUCTION

Whenever older persons are exposed to a new or changed physical environment, such as a hospital or nursing home, or during community relocation (i.e., to sheltered housing, the homes of family members or others), they are exposed to unfamiliar environmental conditions, for example, in the design of furnishings, illumination, and ground surfaces. Any condition that interferes with the individual's mobility places them at certain fall risk. Those older persons with diminished functional capacity are especially at risk. Due to multiple chronic diseases this population begins with a narrower adaptive range. As they are required to cope with certain environmental demands, such as elevated bed heights, low-seated furnishings, and poor illumination, the increased demands of the environment may exceed their capacity to function safely, contributing to hazardous mobility and increased fall risk. This principle holds true for both the home and institutional setting. Despite the fact that, at least in theory, hospital and nursing home environments have been designed to accommodate the safety of older persons, numerous environmental hazards and obstacles still exist.

The surrounding physical environment within the institutional and home settings should be modified to compensate for individual mobility problems and thereby reduce the risk of falls. For example, poor lighting increases the degree of functional visual loss and adversely affects ambulation; but the illumination can be increased to provide a level

262

that provides for safe walking. Low-seated chairs without arm support can result in unsafe transfers for persons with diminished muscular strength; but with the addition of seat cushions and armrests, these chairs can be made more supportive. Low-seated toilets can result in similar problems; but by adding grab rails, transfers can be made safer. Bathtub rims can inhibit safe transfers for persons with lower extremity dysfunction; but the use of bathtub seats/benches can make getting in and out of the tub easier. As a consequence, environmental modifications can potentially serve as a powerful adaptive strategy to promote mobility and reduce the likelihood of falling, especially for those older persons with decreased mobility.

While there are no definitive studies that clearly demonstrate the advantages of environmental modifications in reducing the risk of falls, recent studies have shown promising results. Tideiksaar (1990) studied a group of community-dwelling elders with multiple slip and trip falls to determine the underlying intrinsic and extrinsic factors, and to discern whether medical and environmental interventions would reduce falls. Environmental factors that included foot-ground conditions such as low-frictional resistant or irregular ground surfaces in the home were a leading contributor to falls. Elimination of these hazards decreased the number of falls after a 1-year period. However, the precise contribution of environmental modifications in fall reduction was difficult to assess, since these persons also received medical interventions. Gray-Vickrey (1984) developed a 1-hour home safety program, including a checklist on how to "fall-proof" the home, that aimed to increase awareness of potential fall hazards in the home. However, the actual effectiveness of the safety program in reducing falls was not examined. Wolf-Klein et al. (1988) developed a multidisciplinary approach towards the prevention of falls in community-dwelling older people. In addition to intensive medical management, patients were visited at home by occupational and physical therapists and, along with their families, partook in an educational program on fall prevention. During a 12-month followup, the study authors found a substantial decline in falls. They concluded that one of the most important factors in preventing falls was educating patients and caregivers, which increased their awareness of environmental hazards. Tideiksaar (1992) designed a community-based fall prevention program in a rural county, which consisted of medical interventions, educational programs for older persons at senior centers on "fall hazards found in the home," educational programs for home care nurses on environmental modifications, and a "device bank" to supply assistive walking aids and durable medical equipment to older people at fall risk. After a 1-year period, the nurses who participated in the program perceived that the frequency of falls decreased substantially. Most of the decline was attributed to the educational programs directed at the older persons and nurses themselves, and to the device bank. Hornbrook and colleagues (1991) conducted a large-scale study of fall prevention and showed that modification of home environment risks and participation in group education sessions both increased appropriate health practices and reduced the risk of falling. While these studies are far from definitive, they suggest that identification and correction of environmental fall hazards and correcting them may be of benefit in reducing fall risk, and should be attempted.

Environmental strategies aimed at supporting safe mobility and reducing fall risk consist of three general approaches. One must first identify and eliminate hazardous environmental conditions that increase the risk of falls. Second, simplify or maximize mobility tasks by modifying the environment and existing furnishings and using durable medical equipment. Third, reduce the risk of injurious falls, such as hip fractures and prolonged post-fall lie times, by providing devices such as hip pads and emergency alarm systems. And lastly, ensure individual compliance with the recommended interventions.

ENVIRONMENTAL "HAZARD" ASSESSMENT

SAFETY CHECKLISTS

Safety checklists are the most popular method used both to identify and correct fall hazards in the home and institutional environment. There are several published safety checklists available (Dalziel, Kelly, & Cherkin, 1985; Gibson, 1987; Tideiksaar, 1986). The most common environmental hazards and modifications cited by these checklists are listed in Table 8.1.

There are several ways in which safety checklists are used by health professionals. In the community setting, safety checklists are frequently distributed at senior centers, health fairs, and by organizations that serve older populations with home safety awareness programs. In the physician's office or outpatient clinic setting, safety checklists are frequently given to older persons who have experienced falls or those at fall risk, and, if available, to family members or other formal caregivers. Sometimes these checklists are used when a home visit is not possible. Patient education teaches individuals or their caregivers how to recognize and eliminate environmental hazards found in the home.

TABLE 8.1   Environmental Hazards and Modifications Obtained from Safety Checklists

Illumination
   Eliminate low lighting; provide sufficient lighting, especially in high-risk areas (e.g., bedroom, bathroom, stairways, etc.). Place illuminated light switches in similar locations for easy visibility.
   Place nightlights along the pathway from the bedroom to bathroom to permit safe nighttime travel.
   Avoid lighting glare; use glare-free lightbulbs or shields.

Floor Surfaces
   Maintain nonskid floors; especially avoid waxing kitchen floors.
   Cover slippery surfaces with nonskid carpeting.
   Remove throw rugs; replace with nonskid rugs.
   Wipe up floor spills immediately.
   Avoid floor clutter, low-lying objects, and thick pile carpets to minimize tripping.
   Secure loose lamp and telephone cords that are in walkway.
   Tape upended carpet edges.

Furnishings
   Provide chairs and sofas of proper height to permit safe sitting and standing.
   Remove furniture that is too low and difficult to get up from.
   Provide beds that are low in height to permit safe movement.
   Arrange furniture to allow for wide walkways.

Stairways
   Equip stairways with secure handrails for support.
   Clearly mark step edges with bright nonskid tape to indicate where steps begin and end.
   Check that step surfaces are in good repair and nonskid.

Bathroom
   Install grab bars and toilet risers if toilet seat is too low.
   Place nonskid strips or mats in the bathtub to avoid slipping.
   Install grab bars in the bathtub/shower to support balance.

During subsequent office or clinic visits, any hazards discovered and modifications made are then reviewed. Safety checklists are often used during home visits by nurses and physical or occupational therapists to help identify and correct environmental hazards. Within the acute hospital and nursing home, health professionals frequently use safety checklists in a similar manner. Home safety checklists are often provided to patients and family members prior to discharge home.

The use of safety checklists for these purposes can be valuable; however, there are a number of problems associated with their use. First, definitions of what constitutes a "hazard" are rarely included in checklists, and if stated, are not always clear. For example, identified hazards such as "low illumination" and "thick carpets" may interfere with an older person's safe ambulation, but how "low" must lighting be or how "thick" must a carpet be before they become hazards? Such ambiguity can lead to a number of problems with suggested modifications. For instance, how much additional lighting should be provided? How thin should replacement carpeting be? To add to the confusion, some checklists include suggestions to provide "chairs and beds of proper height," "sufficient lights," and "secure handrails," suggestions that are much too vague and inexplicit to be of any real use.

Another problem with safety checklists is that an "unsafe condition" such as a "low toilet seat" may be unsafe for some older persons, but appropriate for others. Modification or elimination of the hazard may be beneficial for some persons, but unnecessary for others. The real problem is that any subsequent modification, such as raising the toilet seat, may become hazardous and lead to falls.

BA is an 86-year-old woman with Parkinson's Disease and poor balance. As a result, she has had several falls. Her daughter, who was very concerned about providing her mother with a safe environment, diligently followed the advice found in a safety checklist concerning "low toilet seats," and installed a toilet riser. Unfortunately, this device raised the toilet seat to an unsafe height and caused difficulties with toilet transfers for the patient, a problem not encountered with the previous toilet seat. Shortly afterwards, the patient was sent to the emergency room with a fractured shoulder, following a fall from the toilet.

SG and EM were two 80-year-old women who resided in a nursing home and shared a common bathroom. SG had several falls off the toilet, while EM experienced no difficulty with toileting. To decrease SG's falls, the toilet was fitted with a toilet riser. As a result, SG stopped falling, but EM started to fall, as the toilet was now too high for her to transfer off safely.

Similarly, modifications such as maintaining clear pathways, for example, removing furnishings from passageways, may work well for most older persons. But for some individuals, particularly those persons with balance problems, placing stable furnishings along pathways that can be used to support balance when walking may be helpful. For this group, eliminating them may increase fall risk.

MH is an 80-year-old male who lived by himself in a small one-bedroom apartment. Although he had gait and balance problems, he ambulated without incident by grabbing hold of furnishing which he had strategically placed along the pathways. His well-meaning children went to a lecture on safety prevention for older people, and read the safety literature that was distributed. One of the suggested recommendations was to maintain clear circulation pathways in the home to guard against falls. As a result, the children went to MH's home, removed the furnishings from all pathways, and purchased a walker for him to use instead. Unfortunately, he got up one night to go to the bathroom, attempted to grab hold onto the back of an easy chair which had been removed, lost his balance, fell, and broke his hip.

In addition, the suggested modifications included in some safety checklists to maximize poor mobility are often limited, and do not always include the whole variety of options available. For example:

KL is an 82-year-old woman with severe osteoarthritis of the knees, which resulted in poor and painful toilet transfers. As suggested by a safety checklist that her doctor provided, she purchased a toilet riser. She had the option of purchasing a wall-attached grab rail as well. However, she decided against it, as she lived by herself and had no one she could ask to install it. Unfortunately, the toilet riser made the situation worse. Her feet now "dangled" in the air, causing her to "jump" off the toilet when transferring. She quickly abandoned the device, as she was afraid of falling, and returned to her usual state of difficult toilet transfers. When I evaluated her problem, I advised her to use a toilet grab rail with armrests that surrounds each side of the toilet, which solved the problem. Unfortunately, nobody had told the patient about the availability of such a device.

Ironically, strict adherence to recommended modifications of environmental hazards included in safety checklists, without considering individual mobility patterns or the need for specific environmental modifications, can be potentially dangerous and actually increase the risk of falls. Also, expensive modifications are often suggested, such as replacing expensive heirlooms such as chairs and rugs. This becomes especially unsettling if the modification is unsuccessful in its purpose (i.e., to decrease falls or improve mobility). Moreover, certain adaptations, such as bathroom equipment, may not be covered by insurance. As a result, older persons and their families must pay for it themselves. Again, if the equipment fails to solve the problem, not only are individuals left with unusable items, but they may have to pay more to buy appropriate equipment.

JK is an 88-year-old woman with lower extremity dysfunction due to hypothyroidism and osteoarthritis. As a result, she experienced difficulty with bathing in the tub. Her well-meaning daughter, desiring to improve her mother's safety, purchased a bathtub chair recommended by a safety brochure. Unfortunately, the patient did not like the chair as it was too high, and she was afraid of falling. Upon evaluation the patient was provided with an appropriate tub chair. However, the daughter was annoyed that she was unable to return the other chair and had to spend extra money for one that functioned properly.

In summary, relying solely on safety checklists to identify and correct environmental hazards may not work, or be appropriate, for all older persons.

Performance-Oriented Environmental Assessments

Given the limitations and potential dangers associated with safety checklists, the identification and correction or modification of environmental hazards in all clinical settings, such as the home, hospital, and nursing home, is best achieved when based on the person's mobility capacity. Older persons should be asked directly about their mobility (their ability to transfer from beds, chairs, toilets, and get into and out of bathtubs/showers; climb and descend stairways). The information can also be obtained from caregivers (spouses, adult children, or attendants), if available. Persons who have experienced recent falling episodes can be questioned about the surrounding circumstances, such as the specific location or area in which the fall(s) occurred, the activity performed at the time (walking, getting up from a chair, transferring from the bathtub, etc.), and the immediate condition of the surrounding environment (poor lighting, unstable or low-seated chair, wet tub/floor surfaces, etc.). This is helpful in detecting environmental problems or hazards that may be contributing to dysmobility and further fall risk.

However, taken by itself, the information may fail to clarify the specific contribution of environmental factors. Often, any conclusions formed about the role of environmental conditions in causing mobility problems or falls are left to individual or proxy interpretation, which may not always reflect the situation accurately. For example:

DM is an 86-year-old woman who visited the Falls and Immobility Clinic for an evaluation. Upon questioning, the patient stated that she was able to accomplish toilet transfers without difficulties. However, when her toilet transfers were observed at home, it was noted that she also required the use of the sink edge and bathtub rim (for hand support) to get up from the toilet. Clearly, the activity was associated with fall risk. The patient was provided with toilet grab rails.

HW is an 80-year-old woman who also attended the clinic. Similarly, she claimed that she had no difficulty going up and down the stairway in her home. Upon observation at home, however, it was found that due to a lack of handrails she descended the stairs by sitting on her buttocks and ascended on her knees and hands. A stairway handrail was installed.

In both these cases, relying solely on the information—highly literal responses to questions by the older individual—was insufficient to detect fall risk or environmental problems. The best way to identify the true extent and role of environmental factors, and the risk of further falls, is to observe the older person's mobility within their living environment. Visit the home and have the person perform the following maneuvers: walk through every room and area; climb and descend stairs, if applicable; transfer on and off the bed, chairs, and toilet; get in and out of the bathtub or shower; reach up to obtain objects from kitchen and closet shelves; and bend down to retrieve objects from cabinets. The person's mobility with respect to the type and conditions of floor surfaces (carpets, linoleum and ceramic tiles, door thresholds, etc.), lighting, footwear, and the use of any assistive devices and durable medical equipment (toilet and bathtub grab rails, bathtub benches and chairs, etc.) can be examined simultaneously. The use of an environmental hazard checklist (Table 8.2) can simplify this process. At the same time, the individual's motivation to perform tasks, such as bathtub transfers, and cognitive ability (i.e., judgement and comprehension) to perform each task in a safe manner can be assessed. Note which environmental features interfere with safe mobility so that modifications can be arranged.

The mobility assessment is quite similar in the hospital and nursing home setting. However, the extent of the assessment is limited to those activities and environmental locations and furnishings available for patients and residents. That is, activities that are not routinely performed, such as stair ambulation and independent bathtub transfers, are excluded. The POEMS (described in Chapter 5) can be used to evaluate the institutional environment.

It is important to remember that mobility is not a static process but a dynamic one, subject to change—declining or improving—dependent upon the stability or instability of an individual's medical and cognitive status. Likewise, environmental conditions are subject to changes. Largely dependent upon the person's mobility status, safe environmental conditions may become hazardous, and vice versa. For instance, an individual may have little difficulty with bed transfers, even in the face of elevated bed heights. However, with a worsening of osteoarthritis in

TABLE 8.2   Home Environmental Checklist

Exterior

Are sidewalks even?
Are steps in good repair?
Are step edges marked to permit visibility?
Are step handrails present?
Are handrails securely fastened?
Are outdoor lights bright enough to compensate for poor vision?

Interior

Are indoor lights bright enough to compensate for poor vision?
Are lights glare-free?
Are light switches/lamps accessible?
Are nightlights sufficient to compensate for poor vision?
Are throw rugs equipped with secure rubber backings?
Are carpet edges smooth and straight?
Are carpet surfaces wrinkle-free?
Are rooms/hallways free of clutter to permit safe mobility?
Are raised door thresholds present?
Are door thresholds low enough to permit safe mobility?
Are linoleum/wooden floors non-skid?
Are chairs/sofas of sufficient height for safe transfers?
Are chairs equipped with supportive armrests?
Are canes, walkers, and wheelchairs (if used) in good repair?

Stairs

Are stairways adequately illuminated?
Are stairway handrails present?
Are handrails securely fastened?
Are stairway steps in good repair?
Are step edges marked to permit visibility?

Bathroom

Are non-skid strips or mats present in the tub or shower?
Are non-skid strips or mats in good repair?
Are tub/toilet grab bars present and in good repair?
Are elevated toilet seats available and in good repair?
Are bath chairs/benches available and in good repair?
Are tiled floors non-skid?
Are bathroom rugs/carpets present?
Are bathroom rugs/carpets equipped with non-skid rubber backings?
Are lights bright enough to compensate for poor vision?
Are lights glare-free?
Are light switches easily accessible?

Bedroom

Are bed heights adequate to allow for safe transfers?
Are rugs/carpets non-skid or well anchored to the floor?
Are wooden floors non-skid?
Are nightlights present marking route from bedroom to bathroom?
Are lights bright enough to compensate for poor vision?

270

TABLE 8.2   *(Continued)*

Are light switches illuminated?
Are light switches accessible?
Are storage areas (closet shelves, nightstand) accessible?

Kitchen
Are kitchen chairs of sufficient height for safe transfers?
Are chairs equipped with supportive armrests?
Are storage areas/cabinets accessible?
Are lights bright enough to compensate for poor vision?
Are light switches/pull cords accessible?
Are non-skid rugs/mats present by sink area?

the knees, previously safe bed transfers may now become hazardous. Obviously, mobility and environmental assessments should be made on a regular basis, at least annually for those older persons residing in the community, but more frequently for individuals at fall risk. For residents of a nursing home, review every 30 days should be sufficient; this time period corresponds to the period for completion of medical and nursing notes. In the acute care hospital, assessment should be made at the time of admission or whenever patients are considered to be ready for independent functioning. Furthermore, whenever the person experiences an acute change in any health and/or environmental conditions, regardless of clinical setting, an observed assessment of mobility should be performed to reassess fall risk.

Research efforts specific to this area are currently focusing on developing home-based environmental risk instruments that either observe the person's mobility performance in the home setting (Chandler & Duncan, 1993), or else are performed by a combination of direct observation of environmental fall hazards and patient interviews regarding hazardous conditions (Rodriquez et al., 1991). For instance, I am currently adapting the POEMS to include an environmental risk assessment of the home that examines the individual's mobility with respect to lighting levels, floor surfaces, hallways, bathtubs/shower stalls, stairways/steps, and storage areas (such as kitchen cabinets and closet shelves).

PHYSICAL ENVIRONMENT

Environmental modifications in the home and institutional setting should be based on three general principles. First, any modification that is attempted should support mobility without compromising the individual's autonomy. Second, any subsequent environmental adjustments made must be founded on activity-based standards: function must take precedence over aesthetics. Plainly put, floor surfaces and coverings, lighting, and furnishings (beds, chairs, tables, night stands, etc.), in both structure and design should first maximize or support the ambulation and transferring function of persons and only second be aesthetically pleasing. Lastly, it is important to consider others in the environment. For example, in the home setting, adapting the environment to meet the mobility needs of an older person living alone is relatively simple. However, this task becomes somewhat more difficult when other family members or formal caregivers are in residence. For instance, the addition of a toilet riser may help the older person with transfers, but annoy or inconvenience family members who must remove and replace the device. Similarly, within institutional settings, older persons residing together in the same bedroom and utilizing the identical bathroom, each with different mobility requirements, will require adaptations that are functionally suitable for both. Like everyone else, older persons residing in hospitals and nursing homes differ in their functional capacity; some have no limitations, while others have partial to severe loss of function.

The following discussion focuses on those aspects of the home, hospital, and nursing home environment most likely to contribute to unsafe mobility, and suggests a number of corrective actions.

CIRCULATION PATHWAYS

Indoors, the paths of hallways, doorways, and floor space should be unobstructed, free of clutter and furnishings, and spacious enough to permit safe ambulation. In general, this may be more of a problem in hospitals and nursing homes than in the older person's home. Once clear pathways are established in the home, they are usually maintained. However, this is harder to achieve within institutional settings. Bedrooms and hallways can become major obstacle courses, cluttered at various times with medication carts, over-the-bed tables, laundry carts, unused devices (such as walkers, wheelchairs, and stretchers), and can be congested with patients sitting in chairs and wheelchairs. As these conditions can interfere with safe ambulation, attempts should be made to provide patients with clear and unobstructed walkways at all times. This becomes even more important in a setting with a large number of demented patients, as they may not have the awareness necessary to avoid objects.

HT is an 80-year-old man with Parkinsonism and dementia, dependent on a walker for ambulation. On one occasion he was ambulating in the hallway of the nursing home and walked directly into a discarded wheelchair. Rather than trying to circumvent the chair, he "bulldozed" straight into the chair with his walker in an attempt to move the chair away. However, his walker legs became entangled in the wheelchair, causing him to lose his balance and fall.

In the home, there are several types of products, for example, accessible shelving, cupboard systems, and wall hooks, that can be used to organize floor clutter and avoid the risk of tripping (Watzke & Kemp, 1992). In general, the arrangement of furnishings such as chairs, tables, and beds should allow an individual sufficient space to walk and turn around in without bumping into objects. Doorways should be kept clear and, in particular, doors should open wide against walls without furnishings behind them that obstruct their opening. Clear walking space is especially important for those persons dependent on assistive ambulation devices such as canes and walkers.

MK is an 89-year-old woman with neurologic impairment, dependent upon a walker for ambulation. The hallways of her home were strewn with clutter—cardboard boxes filled with cans of food, books, discarded walkers and canes, and old clothing. In the living room and bedroom, furnishings like chairs, footstools, and tables obstructed the pathways. As a result, the patient was unable to use her walker, as there was limited space to maneuver the walker safely, and subsequently, she suffered several falls. Organization of the clutter into storage systems and rearrangement of furnishings allowed her to ambulate with the walker, and she experienced no further falls.

Furnishings should be positioned so that they do not protrude into natural walkways. In particular, low-lying furniture that may lie outside one's field of vision, such as coffee tables, small step stools, and chair legs, and that can lead to tripping, should be relocated. As well, the path from the bed to the bathroom should be clear, as many falls in the home and institutional setting originate from the bed during the night, when illumination levels are low.

There are some populations of older persons in which these modifications can be problematic. Some older persons with balance loss and fear of falling won't use ambulation devices; they feel safer walking if they are able to grasp hold of furnishings every few feet for guidance and balance support. In most cases, if a stumble and loss of balance were to occur, grabbing onto furnishings for support will lead to quick recovery. Here, in contrast to wide-open spaces, the placement of sturdy furnishings such as high-backed chairs, tables, and dressers can be used to accommodate persons who prefer to ambulate by holding onto one object for support as they move to the next.

> BS is a 76-year-old man with gait impairment, the result of extrapyramidal effects caused by lithium and haloperidol. He clearly required a walker for ambulation in his home, but steadfastly refused the device. Instead, he walked about the bedroom, bathroom, and hallways by holding onto furnishings and walls for support, without problems. However, when he approached the living room, he immediately "froze" and refused to enter, and instead returned to his bedroom. The living room, as opposed to other locations in the home, was devoid of any furnishings that could be used for balance support. Not being able to walk into the living room interfered with his quality of life, as he was unable to watch television or engage in social activities with family members and friends. Several sturdy chairs were placed a few feet apart in the pathway of the living room. This modification permitted the patient to walk in the living room.

This type of strategy is also useful if furniture can not be relocated or where there is insufficient space to use a walker.

> WK is an 82-year-old woman who required a walker in her home. She lived in a small one-bedroom apartment and with all her furnishings had barely enough space to walk around. As she refused to relinquish any of her furnishings, they were rearranged so as to allow her safe ambulation by holding on for balance support.

Within the institutional setting, handrails should be installed in hallways to provide ambulation support; they are especially helpful in areas that have floor surfaces that promote poor footing, such as polished or slick surfaces. As opposed to the home environment, where individuals have the option of using furnishings for mobility support, institutional hallways are usually wide-open spaces, and handrails serve as substitutes. Handrails are most effective if they are rounded for solid hand grasp, color-contrasted to the walls for easy visibility, located approximately 2 inches from the wall, and 26 to 36 inches in height above the floor.

LIGHTING

The proper amount of illumination in the environment is dependent upon the older person's visual needs. As a rule of thumb, older people require two to three times more light than younger persons to facilitate vision because of a decline in visual function that accompanies aging. This is, however, a generalization. There are instances when lower levels of lighting may be more appropriate. For instance, persons with cataracts or glaucoma tend to be sensitive to bright lights. Any increase in lighting may impair vision and increase fall risk in these individuals.

> MW is an 86-year-old diabetic woman with peripheral neuropathy (proprioceptive loss) and visual dysfunction (glaucoma, cataracts, and macular degeneration). In her home, she preferred to leave the lights off during the day, relying on outside ambient light in order to see. She complained that "The lights are too bright and hurt my eyes, making it difficult to see" and that "Several times I almost tripped and fell." However, when she kept the lights off, she had to be extremely careful to avoid floor hazards while walking. Because of the loss of visual input, she had poor balance, which placed her at increased fall risk. The bright lighting in her home was replaced with low-wattage bulbs that improved both her vision and balance.

Under ideal circumstances, control of lighting levels should rest in the hands of the individual so that each person is able to regulate and maintain a level of illumination that is both visually comfortable and safe for mobility. The use of rheostatic light switches or three-way switches allows a person to increase or decrease illumination levels as desired. The problem with standard toggle light switches is that the light is either on or off, and does not allow for different levels of illumination.

However, individual control of lighting may not always be feasible, especially for persons who are cognitively impaired. Also, sometimes the individual lighting control in hospitals and nursing homes is not easily accessible. In these circumstances, the best way to help determine the lighting needs of an individual is to observe the person ambulating in their environmental surroundings, ask about or note any difficulties encountered, and adjust lighting levels accordingly. Correction may call for either an increase, a decrease, or redistribution in lighting levels.

Low Lighting

Proper illumination is essential to compensate for poor visual function. In one survey, over 90% of older people showed improvements in near or distant vision when the illumination of their homes was improved (Silver, 1978). There are several methods to increase low lighting levels. The easiest and often most effective is to replace current bulbs with ones that are stronger in intensity, such as 100-watt bulbs, and open up or replace window coverings, such as opaque drapes, that reduce available light. Other measures that can be used to increase lighting levels include replacing incandescent lights with fluorescent lighting, which provides greater illumination. In addition, fluorescent lighting is more cost-effective than incandescent lighting, as less electricity is needed to produce the same amount of illumination. Fluorescent bulbs that screw into lamp sockets are available for home use. However, some older people may complain of visual distractions with fluorecent lights, as they sometimes produce a mild flicker. This problem usually indicates that the bulb is ready to burn out or that the ballasts need to be replaced, and can be corrected by routinely replacing bulbs. Incandescent lighting provides better illumination in areas that call for specific tasks, such as above kitchen counters and medicine cabinets, and by easy chairs. Lastly, employing light-colored wall coverings can increase the reflective quality of available light, even with low-wattage bulbs.

In addition to modifying lighting levels in the home, it is important to discover the reasons for low lighting, and especially for failing to turn lights on. It is not uncommon to find that older persons with limited economic resources rarely turn on their lights in an effort to save money on electricity, even if this entails ambulating precariously in darkness. Other persons may not turn on ceiling lights for safety reasons.

> GP is an 88-year-old woman with extremely poor balance. She never turned on the ceiling lights in her home because she was afraid of having to climb onto a chair (to change the bulb) and falling. Instead, she used the light available from a few small table lamps scattered about, which was inadequate to support her balance. The patient was provided with a relatively inexpensive reacher device used for changing ceiling bulbs.

Effective Lighting Sources

In addition to maintaining an adequate quantity of illumination, the quality of available lighting is important to consider as well. Full-spectrum fluorescent lighting is much more effective than incandescent lighting for overall illumination in the environment. "Blue" fluorescent lighting simulates natural sunlight, providing a supply of lighting that is evenly spread, continuous, and free of shadows. However, the best effects are produced by a bulb in the yellow spectrum. Conversely, halogen lamps produce a light that is more like natural sunlight and freer from glare than either fluorescent or incandescent fixtures. Halogen lamps are particularly effective for task lighting.

Strategic Lighting

Extra lighting may be needed in particular locations that represent high fall risk locations, such as the bedroom, bathroom, and stairways. In the bedroom, the path from the bedside to the bathroom may be difficult to visualize, especially at night as many older persons commonly get up during the night to urinate. Recall that nocturia is a fall-risk factor. Some older persons will use one or two flashlights kept by their night table to get to the bathroom, although the amount of light provided may not be enough. A better solution is to provide a bedside lamp with a secure base that will not tip over, or a light attached to the headboard and within easy reach. Nightlights can be used to provide extra illumination in the bedroom and bathroom. A red bulb is suggested for nightlights, since it reduces the time required for dark adaptation, the ability of the eye to become visually sensitive in darkness. A nightlight can be placed on the stairway at least one riser depth below the top landing and above the bottom landing in order to visually communicate the sense of depth to the person. For compliance, photosensitive nightlights that turn on and off automatically, depending on existing lighting levels, are a better choice than are lights requiring manual operation. In those persons with dementia, such as Alzheimer's Disease, nightlights may be hazardous, as they may cast shadows and images that lead to hallucinations and paranoia.

MC is a 72-year-old man with dementia and paranoia who lived at home with his wife. He would on occasion get up at night, either to toilet or just wander about, usually without incident. His wife installed several nightlights in order to provide the patient with safe pathways. She was awakened shortly afterwards by her husband who was screaming, claiming that there were small animals running about the floor—visual creations from the shadows emitted by the nightlights. The nightlights were removed and the patient returned to his usual state.

Lighting Changes

The ability of the eyes to adapt to changes in illumination decreases with age. Any sudden change in lighting intensity, that which occurs when a person moves from a dark to a bright area and vice versa, should be avoided, as it can lead to a momentary loss of vision and the risk of falling. Perhaps the most frequent example of this, at home and within the institutional setting, involves the older person getting out of bed at night, travelling from a darkened bedroom into the bathroom, and turning on a bright bathroom light. Or the opposite may occur when walking from a bright bedroom or bathroom into a darkened area. To avoid this situation, some older people in response will keep a light on at night in either the bedroom or bathroom, or sometimes in both areas. However, this may not be particularly effective, as the person, their spouse, or other roommates often complains of the light interfering with sleep. As an alternative, rheostatic or three-way light switches that vary the amount of light available can ensure an even distribution of light between rooms, and prevent such sudden and pronounced shifts in illumination that may occur, as with toggle light switches. Nightlights can be used as well, but may be less effective. Other common situations involving transient changes in illumination include walking into a dark house or travelling upstairs during the evening. Automatic lighting timers can be used to prevent older individuals from entering a dark house or floor landing.

Lighting Access

All lighting sources such as switchplates, lamps, etc., should be easily accessible, particularly in high-fall risk locations, like the top and bottom of stairways, bedrooms, and bathrooms. Light switches should be positioned approximately 32 inches in height from the floor, and located directly on the outside or inside of doorways, to help persons avoid walking across a darkened room to turn on a light. Switchplates should contrast in color with the wall to allow for greater visibility. If the wall and switchplate colors are identical, the switchplate can be painted in a contrasting color, or a contrasting colored adhesive tape can be placed around the borders of the switchplate to enhance its visibility.

A small light located within the switch or illuminated switchplates will allow for visibility and access at night. In general, pressure-plate controls are easier to use than standard toggle switches. Any bedside or bathroom lighting controlled by a pull cord should have a cord long enough to avoid over-reaching and risk of balance loss.

MA is an 82-year-old woman with poor balance. Her bathroom light at home was controlled by a ceiling pull cord that was too short. When turning on the light she would stand on her tip toes and stretch high above her head in order to reach the pull cord. Frequently, she would not bother to turn on the light because she was afraid of falling. On the other hand, leaving the light off led to precarious balance. A pull cord was attached to the existing cord at the level of her eyes, which allowed MA to turn on the bathroom light without excessive reaching.

If lighting is unavailable, a "clapper light"—a sound-activated device that turns lights on and off by clapping the hands—is a viable and relatively inexpensive alternative.

RS is an 82-year-old woman who lived by herself in a small studio apartment. She experienced balance loss and occasional falls due to a lack of proprioception. These episodes all occurred during the night when she was attempting to walk to the bathroom. The only light available was ambient illumination from street lights shining into her apartment. The patient had ceiling lights, but none of the light switches were near her bed. She had no table lamps, nor could she afford to purchase any. She recognized the need for visual input in order to maintain her balance, so she attempted to sleep with the ceiling lights on. However, this interfered with her sleep. As a alternative, a sound-activated light switch was recommended at a cost of under $5 that solved her problems.

Glare Reduction

Glare from sunlight shining through windows or other light sources may impair vision. Examples include unshielded light bulbs and bright lights reflecting directly on polished waxed floors, furnishings such as laminated tabletops, and plastic chair seats. Window glare can be eliminated by simply blocking sunlight through the use of draperies or venetian blinds, although this also reduces the amount of light available. Instead, polarized window glass or tinted Mylar shades can be used to eliminate glare without loss of light. The use of sheer or transparent draperies will have the same effect.

Glare from unshielded light bulbs can be eliminated by the use of translucent shades or coverings or "frosted" light bulbs that are glare-free. Floor glare can be controlled by using carpets or floor waxes and finishes that diffuse rather than reflect light. As well, wall-mounted valances or cove lighting that conceal the source of light and spread it indirectly upon the ceiling and floor serve the same purpose. Matte or dull finishes on tabletops and nonreflective material on chair seats, or positioning light sources to avoid reflection on furnishing surfaces, can also help to reduce glare.

FLOOR SURFACES

Ceramic, Linoleum, and Wooden Surfaces

Highly polished or wet floor surfaces can contribute to slip-related falls. Two modifications are helpful in eliminating these hazards. First, ceramic tiles and linoleum floors need to be slip-resistant, particularly when wet. For kitchen and bathroom floors, unglazed tiles are particularly effective, as they are non-slip. However, this type of modification is more feasible for institutional settings than for the home setting, especially when involving frail older persons living alone. As an alternative, slip-resistant adhesive strips or decals can be applied to the floor in those areas prone to get wet, such as those next to the sink in the kitchen and bathroom and near the toilet. The color selection of adhesive strips should match the floor surface, that is, be noncontrasting, to prevent easy visualization. Persons, especially those with altered depth perception and dementia, may misinterpret color-contrasted strips, perceiving them as ground elevations or depressions and, as a result, attempt to avoid them. They may try to "step over" the strips, and thereby actually increase their risk of falls because of an alteration of gait. Conversely, some cognitively impaired individuals may perceive floor strips to be barriers and avoid them entirely. The purpose of adhesive strips is to help render the floor slip-resistant; thus, it doesn't matter whether they can be seen by the person. Clear or transparent non-slip strips have been developed that will serve the purpose. Linoleum and wooden floors can be treated with anti-skid acrylic coatings. Minimal buffing of the floors also reduces the likelihood of slipping. As an alternative, bare slippery floors can be covered with textured runners or carpet.

Door thresholds, particularly those that are visually indistinguishable from background ground surfaces, can be hazardous and may lead to tripping. Thresholds may be more of a problem for older persons in institutional settings than for individuals residing in their home who are familiar with the hazard. Within hospitals and nursing homes, the threshold surface between the bedroom and bathroom in many instances may be slightly uneven. For those older persons who are reliant on gliding walkers for support, this can be especially hazardous. Some persons may trip when hitting the threshold with the legs of their walker, while others may lift the walker in order to clear the obstruction, but experience a loss of balance due to a diminished base of support as a result. If door thresholds can not be eliminated, which is the usual case expect for some institutional settings, the placement of a color-contrasted non-skid adhesive strip (for visibility) along the length of the threshold may serve as a visual cue. As some persons with dementia or individuals with decreased depth perception may be confused by this modification, be sure always to observe their ambulation (with assistive devices if used) afterwards to ensure that it functions as a safety measure.

Carpets and Rugs

Carpets offer several advantages. In addition to providing a slip-resistant surface, they may also improve the gait of older persons. One study reported that gait speed and step length were significantly greater on carpeted than on vinyl surfaces (Willmott, 1986). Carpets also supply a cushioned surface that may reduce the risk of injury such as fracture following a fall. In particular, the use of indoor-outdoor carpeting on bathroom floors can be helpful. Carpets also trap water and dry quickly, thus protecting the individual against slipping.

However, carpets also have their disadvantages. Persons who use rolling walkers and wheelchairs may experience difficulties moving the device on carpeted surfaces, especially over thick coverings. Also, canes and walker tips can get caught in deep pile carpets and lead to fall risk. Individuals who walk with a shuffling gait, such as those with Parkinson's Disease, may find that carpets can impede safe mobility, leading to hesitancy of gait and tripping.

The best type of carpet to install is one of uncut low pile with an underlying pad to prevent slippage. Low pile carpets decrease the risk of slips, since friction between footwear and the carpet surface is increased, even if the person is wearing non-slip resistant footwear. Moreover, low pile carpeting does not appear to hamper the mobility of wheeled walkers and wheelchairs, or impede the gait of persons with shuffling gait. Choosing carpets that contrast in color helps persons with visual deficits to define the boundary between the floor and wall. Patterned designs, such as floral or checkered configurations, should be avoided, since they may lead to misjudgment of spatial distances. They are particularly dangerous on stairs and steps. Misperception is heightened in those persons with visual dysfunction such as cataracts or poor depth perception and dementia. Plain unpatterned carpets are less confusing, both visually and intellectually.

Hospitals and nursing homes can benefit as well with carpeting. In the past, carpeting in the institutional setting may not have been a sensible option, as they were easily ruined by various body fluids, such as urine and blood. As a result, vinyl or linoleum is used in most institutional settings since it is easy to clean. However, carpet cleaning and replacement technology has advanced markedly, to the point where these reasons are no longer valid.

All carpets should be checked periodically for wrinkles, curled edges, and excessive wear, and replaced if necessary. Common methods used to repair curled-up carpet edges consist of tacking or taping down the edges to avoid tripping. While effective, these methods can ruin expensive carpets and flooring, and usually do not have very attractive results. As a consequence, the older person may not agree to the modification, and the fall risk remains. A more acceptable solution is to place double-sided adhesive tape underneath curled carpet edges.

> LJ is an 84-year-old woman with impaired gait, that is, decreased steppage height, who experienced several falls in her home. All episodes occurred as a result of tripping over a living room carpet edge. Her nurse recommended that the carpet edges be either tacked or taped down. Because the carpet was an heirloom, the patient rejected this advice and, as a result, continued to trip over the carpet. On a subsequent visit, a physical therapist suggested the use of double-sided adhesive, which the patient found aesthetically acceptable. She suffered no further falls.

Sliding rugs can be slippery and dangerous, as there is no friction between the rug and floor surface. This can be especially hazardous in the bathroom. A sliding rug prevents adequate transfer support for the feet when getting up from the toilet, and into and out of the bathtub. Sliding rugs also tend to bunch up, and can become a tripping hazard. The best solution for this problem is to replace the rug with one that has non-skid backing. Some older persons may prefer not to remove their area rugs. Prevent slipping by applying double-sided adhesive tape or non-skid underlays to the rugs' back side.

STAIRWAYS

Negotiating stairs requires both visual feedback, to detect and judge the position of steps, and kinesthetic input, to ensure proper foot placement. First of all, making the successful transition from level ground to walking on stairs requires that the person look at the stairs as they step onto them. This visual feedback or guidance is used to detect and judge the position of the steps and placement of the feet. At the same time, the individual can observe the stairs for hazardous conditions, such as irregular riser heights and torn step surfaces. During subsequent steps, persons rely on kinesthetic feedback to ensure proper foot placement. As a result, any visual distraction created by the design of step surfaces or decreased illumination may lead to inaccurate placement of the feet on the step. The loss of kinesthetic feedback (i.e., altered proprioception) may lead to faulty perceptual placement of the feet when ascending or descending steps. Dependable lower extremity muscle strength and hip and knee motion also becomes necessary to ensure proper clearance of the steps and foot placement. A loss of strength and joint flexibility may lead to the foot encroaching upon or meeting the step improperly. As a result, the foot may land on the edge of the step, rather than on the top surface, possibly leading to a fall.

There are several modifications that can ensure safe stairway ambulation. First, provide sufficient lighting. Light sources should be located at the top and bottom landings of all stairways so that the individual is not required to ascend and descend steps in the dark. Placing nightlights by the first and last steps provides additional visual cueing. It is important that light sources are positioned so as to eliminate shadows and glare, which may obstruct the view of steps. This is critical for those persons with poor vision. Shadows can sometimes be misread as an additional step, and glare can mask the precise location of step edges.

Second, provide step contrasts to help the individual detect each step. This can be achieved by applying a 1-inch wide white or brightly colored contrasting non-slip adhesive strip along the edge of each step. Step contrasts are particularly helpful for those persons with reduced visual acuity, in those circumstances when adequate levels of illumination are difficult to obtain, or when the step heights are not uniform. Also, make certain that step surfaces are in good repair. In particular, carpeted steps should be firmly affixed to prevent movement during foot placement. As was discussed previously, avoid geometric or floral tread designs, as these patterns tend to disguise step edges and lead to foot misplacements.

In addition, all stairways should be equipped with handrail support. Whereas most older people can climb one or two steps using the power of their leg muscles, individuals with less strength often use handrails to pull themselves up from one step to the next (Archea, 1985), especially when ascending long and steep flights of stairs. Ideally, handrails should be located on both sides of the stairs, approximately 30 inches above the steps. They should be round in shape, and slip-resistant for secure hand grasp. Adequate hand grasp is assured if the person's thumb and forefingers meet when holding on to the hand rail. The ends of the handrail should be shaped, that is, turned inward toward the wall or downward toward the floor, to let a person know they have reached the top or bottom landing of the stairway. Better yet are handrails that extend approximately 10 to 12 inches beyond the top and bottom steps, that ensure that when the end of the handrail has been reached, both feet have come to rest on a flat surface. The handrail should be of contrasted color from the wall to enhance visibility. To protect persons with dementia and sundowning from independent stair ambulation, which might lead to inadvertent falls, a folding "ferry" gate, similar to that used to protect small children, can be installed at both the top and bottom steps.

For those older individuals who continue to experience difficulty despite stairway modifications, there are a number of other technologies, such as stair and chairlifts, that are available (Stowe, 1990). However, these devices are extremely costly and may be difficult to install depending on the amount of stairway space available. As an alternative, it may be acceptable to move the individual's sleeping accomodations to the ground floor, and avoid the use of stairways entirely.

STORAGE AREAS

Closet or kitchen shelves that are too high or low may contribute to balance loss and falls, particularly if persons reach up or bend down beyond their safe capacity to retrieve or replace objects. To remove the hazard, frequently used items should be placed on shelves or counter tops that lie between the individual's eye and hip level; this position does not require excessive bending or reaching. A hand-held reacher device can be employed as an alternative to obtain objects, although experience suggests that compliance with these devices is somewhat problematic. Sometimes, reacher devices either are not readily available or are lost. Reacher devices may also not be affordable for persons with restricted budgets.

Older persons should be discouraged from standing on chairs, ladders, or unsteady stepstools. If the person insists on using a foot stool for reasons of autonomy, recommend one that does not have wheels, or select a stool whose wheels recede when standing weight is applied. Also, it is a good idea to obtain stepstools equipped with hand support, to maintain balance.

BEDS

For those older persons with diminished bed mobility skills, modification of the bed and its surrounding area can be used to support safe mobility.

Bed Height

Bed height is defined as the distance from the floor to the top of the mattress. The height is appropriate when the person is able to sit on the edge of the mattress with the knees flexed at 90 degrees and plant both feet firmly on the floor (Figure 8.1). In the home setting, excessively high and low bed heights can obviously be eliminated by purchasing a bed that is appropriate in height for the person. However, for financial reasons, this solution is often not feasible. As an alterna-

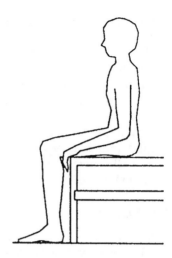

FIGURE 8.1   Proper bed height. Reprinted
with permission of Tactilitics, Inc.

tive, it is sometimes recommended that the bed legs be cut in size in
order to lower the bed height, or that bed leg extenders be used in an
effort to elevate the bed height. In the author's experience, these modifications are awkward and are often viewed unfavorably by older persons or their family members. Some health professionals recommend
instead that the person's mattress be placed on the floor to avoid falling
a great distance. This strategy is also frequently unacceptable, as individuals may experience great difficulty in getting up from the mattress.
Moreover, locating the mattress on the floor will limit ambulation space
and can easily create a tripping hazard. Some family members find this
solution to be unsuitable as well.

> IK is a 79-year-old woman who experienced multiple bed falls at home.
> Upon observing the patient's bed transfers, it was determined that her
> bed was too high. As a result, it was suggested to the patient's daughter
> that the mattress be placed on the floor. This was almost more than the
> daughter could bear. She stated that "If this is what life has become for
> my mother [an indignity], perhaps it is time for a nursing home."

Generally, beds that are either too low or too high can be effectively
altered by changing the mattress. For instance, replacing a thick mattress
with one thinner in width can help to reduce bed height; conversely, low
bed heights can be elevated with mattresses that are thick in width. As a
postscript to the case of IK, replacing her mattress with a thinner model
solved her transfer problems and falls, to the delight of her daughter.

Within institutional settings, a bed height safe enough to support transfer activity can easily be obtained with the use of height adjustable "hi-low" beds. If the bed is still too high or low despite the use of this mechanism, a change in mattress width may be used to achieve the desired height. Since bed heights may be altered routinely to change linens or perform nursing care, it is a good practice to check the height periodically to see that it is maintained at a level appropriate for the older patient. If the adjustable height beds are controlled manually with crank handles, check that these handles are recessed underneath the bed at all times, so that they don't stick out and constitute a low-lying tripping hazard.

Bed Supports

Sometimes, older persons with poor bed mobility and gait impairments use the footboard as an aid in transferring in and out of bed, or ambulating about the bedroom. To provide adequate support, the footboard should be easy to grasp and slip-resistant. Footboards that are low in height can lead to a kyphotic position—reaching downward—contributing to balance loss as the individual's center of gravity exceeds a stable base of support. Non-slip adhesive strips placed along the top length of the footboard will prevent hand slipping. A color-contrasted strip on the footboard can also help a person see the board more easily, and help prevent bumping into the bed. Providing bedspreads that contrast in color with floor surfaces will help visually impaired persons participate in safe bed transfers.

There should also be adequate space between the bed and other furnishings to allow for safe ambulation and transferring, particularly if walkers are used. A circulation space of at least 3 feet provides enough room for patient or resident movement with or without ambulation devices. This can be achieved either by moving furnishings that surround the bed or by relocating the bed itself.

Mattresses

Persons with poor sitting balance may be at risk for bed falls if the mattress sags at the edges. An oversoft mattress will not provide the necessary support needed for safe bed transfers. All mattresses should be firm enough to support the person securely when seated in an upright position. In the home setting, if the mattress can not be replaced, a plywood board placed underneath the length of the mattress is often a viable alternative. Also, mattress edges that are rolled or knurled will offer the person a good grasping surface when transferring.

Bedrails

Side rails on the bed have both disadvantages and advantages. As discussed previously, bedrails in the raised position can contribute to falls and physical injury (see Chapter 3). However, when used properly, bedrails offer real benefits, providing safety and assistance in bed transfers. Full-length bedrails can be helpful in preventing persons under sedation from unexpectedly rolling out of bed. But these rails should not be used for individuals who are able to get out of bed. They encourage patients and residents to climb over the side rail or footboard, unquestionably constituting a hazardous alternative. A better choice is to use bedrails that extend one-half to three quarters the length of the bed, which will not interfere with exiting but will help prevent the person from inadvertently rolling. Appropriately placed half-rails can function as assistive devices, sometimes referred to as "enablers," supporting persons with poor sitting and transfer balance such as patients with Parkinsonism or stroke (Figure 8.2). Similar bed assistive

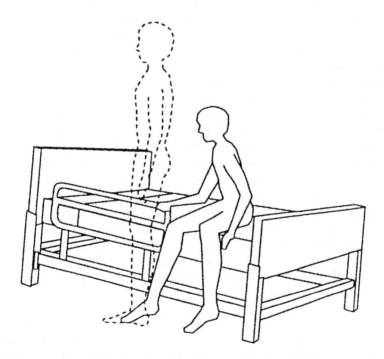

FIGURE 8.2 Bed side rail as "enabler" device. Reprinted with permission of Tactilitics, Inc.

devices have been developed for home use, consisting of a pole that fits securely between the floor and ceiling, or a transfer bar that attaches to the bed itself. When bedrails are not in use and are in the down position, they should recess completely underneath the bed to provide adequate "kick" space for out-of-bed transfers. Also, side rails that rest beneath the bed will prevent persons from climbing on the rails to enter the bed. The issue of bedrails as restraining devices is discussed in Chapter 9.

Bed Wheels

Bed wheels constitute a special hazard, as they may cause the bed to roll or slide away during transfers. Although all beds, even those with adequate wheel-locking systems, are unsteady to some degree, a combination swivel and wheel brake provides the most stability. Even when bed wheels lock properly, the bed may still slide, especially if the wheels are resting on a slippery linoleum floor. In addition, sometimes institutional custodial staff may fail to engage the wheel locks after cleaning underneath beds. In the home setting, bed wheels can easily be removed, generally without incident. As an alternative to removing bed wheels, to prevent the bed from sliding away during transfers it can be placed against the wall for support, if feasible. However, within institutional settings, removing bed wheels or placing beds against the wall is not an alternative because of safety regulations. There are a number of other ways to prevent the bed from sliding. The floor surface can be rendered slip-resistant by placing non-slip adhesive strips or decals on the floor directly underneath the wheels. Placing a carpet underneath the wheels achieves the same goal. Hospital and nursing home beds equipped with immobilizer legs are acceptable alternatives to sliding bed wheels or malfunctioning locking systems; when the legs are down on the floor, the wheels recess. When purchasing a height-adjustable bed with immobilizer legs, make certain that the model is user-friendly. Some designs can actually increase the risk of falls, as the immobilizer legs are only effective when the bed is in the lowest position. This type of design flaw results from bed manufacturers' mistaken belief that all older persons require the bed to be in the lowest possible position, which is far from the truth.

AR is a 79-year-old man with Parkinson's Disease who resided in the nursing home and experienced multiple bed falls. Upon observing his bed mobility, it was determined that the bed was too low for him to achieve safe transfers, partly because he also had proximal muscle weakness. The bed was elevated to a height that allowed him to transfer on and off the bed safely. However, with the bed in this position, the immobilizer legs were ineffective since they did not touch the floor. As a result, when rising from the bed, it would slide away, as the bed wheels did not lock properly; this placed the patient at fall risk.

In addition to rendering the bed immovable, attend to the floor surrounding the bed. A slippery floor surface can cause a person's feet to slide during bed transfers. There are several ways to prevent this. Placing non-slip adhesive strips on the floor along the length of the bed will provide the feet with a slip-resistant surface. The color selection of non-slip strips should blend with the color of the floor or be clear in color so that persons with altered depth perception don't misinterpret the strips as hazards and attempt to step over or avoid the strips. The use of carpeting along the length of the bed offers similar advantages. Older persons should also wear slip-resistant footwear when transferring in and out of bed. A good suggestion is to have the person wear traction-soled socks while in bed. These socks are particularly beneficial for those persons with underlying cognitive problems who may not have the judgement to utilize non-slip footwear when leaving the bed.

SEATING

Seating Criteria

Whether older persons reside in the community or institutional setting, the criteria for proper seating is governed by one simple rule: it should meet the seating needs of the person. The ideal chair should, first, support self-initiated transfers, that is, allow the person to get in and out of the seat with ease, and second, provide the user with comfort while seated.

There are several ways to achieve this objective. Perhaps the most common method employed is to select chairs by their seat height, depth, and width to match the anthropometric dimensions of the older person. Correct seat height is obtained by measuring a person's lower leg length: the distance from the foot on the floor to the knee or popliteal area (generally 15–17 inches). Weiner et al. (1993), in a study that examined chair heights in a group of nursing home and community-dwelling older persons, developed a rough estimate of optimal seat height. They found that 120% of the lower leg length (knee-to-ankle distance) on average, equalled the minimal height required for successful chair rising in impaired individuals. For instance, they determined that a seat height of 19 inches was required for a person with a 16 inch lower leg length, and an 18 inch seat height for individuals with a 15 inche lower leg length. Proper seat depth is obtained by measuring upper leg length: the distance from the plane of the back to the popliteal area, generally 16–20 inches. Appropriate seat width is obtained by measuring the distance across the widest point of the person's hips or thighs, generally 14–16 inches, and adding another 2 inches (1 inch on each side of the hip); this space allowance prevents the body from rubbing or resting against the side of the chair. Choosing chairs based on these anthropometric dimensions will accommodate the seating requirements of most healthy older persons. Consequently, these criteria are often used by hospitals, nursing homes, and community settings such as senior centers, outpatient clinics, and physician offices to select chairs, particularly when purchasing chairs in quantity because of the economic advantages offered.

However, appropriate seating for frail older persons requires more than simply selecting a chair that is anthropometrically correct. Even if these criteria are met, certain older persons, especially those with neuromuscular impairments such as Parkinsonism, stroke, and arthritis may still encounter problems with their seating mobility (in moving from the sitting to standing posture and vice versa). Therefore, the best method of assessing optimal seating is to observe the person sitting down and getting up from chairs in the living environment, and then ascertain whether the task can be performed both independently and safely. This procedure takes into account the effects of different disease conditions as they affect seating mobility. When the person is seated, inquire about the comfort of the chair. Whether a seat is comfortable or not is purely a subjective assessment by the user, dependent upon a number of intrinsic conditions such as the amount of adipose tissue surrounding the ischial tuberosities and the ability to frequently shift seating positions as well as design factors, such as seat height, width, and depth; the angle of seat slope and backrest; the positioning of the armrests; and the resilience of the seating cushion (Ellis, 1988). Any difficulty experienced by the person with seating mobility or discomfort is an indication that the chair is unsuitable for the individual, and suggests the need for modifications.

Seat Height

Seat height, measured as the distance between the floor and the front edge of a chair, is critical to mobility. If the seat height is too low or high, it can interfere with transfers. Seats that are too low require that the body move a great distance between the seated and standing position. As a result, greater knee flexion and leg muscle strength is necessary to initiate the upward thrust required to rise. An equal amount of joint flexion and strength is also required to support the downward motion needed to sit from the standing position. Subsequently, persons whose range of motion in the knees and hips is limited and whose muscle strength is reduced may experience great difficulty in completing on and off transfers from low-seated chairs. Typically, when these individuals attempt to rise they may lose their balance and fall back into the seat, and when attempting to sit down they similarly experience a loss of balance and collapse into the seat. Both situations can increase the risk of falls, especially if the chair slides away or tips over.

Conversely, it is much easier to transfer on and off seats that are high in height. The higher the seat height, the shorter the distance that the person must move between the sitting to standing position and vice versa. As a result, high seating requires less joint flexion and muscle strength to accomplish both transfer functions.

To compensate for low seats, people usually attempt to raise their chair height by themselves. They may either add a cushion or a pillow to the seat, or select a higher chair to sit upon. However, this can cause problems as well. If the person's feet do not rest flat on the floor, the individual may be forced to slouch down and slide from the seat to reach the floor when attempting to stand, and to "climb" onto the seat when attempting to sit. Both these movements can compromise safety. If balance loss occurs, the person risks a fall.

In general, seat height is appropriate when it allows the older person to sit comfortably with both feet firmly planted on the floor and the knees flexed at 90 degrees (Figure 8.3). The front of the seat should be

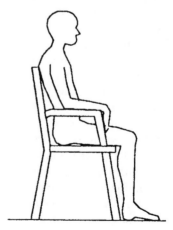

FIGURE 8.3 Appropriate seat height. Reprinted with permission of Tactilitics, Inc.

low enough to allow for a small space between the thighs and the seat. The ability to pass the flat of the hand freely underneath the seated person's thigh and edge of the seat provides a good index of the space required between the seat and the body.

Seating that is too low in height can be corrected by several methods. The best solution is to replace low-seated chairs with ones that are functionally suited for the individual. This approach may be more practical for institutional settings than for older persons residing in the community who may not be able to afford a new chair. In this case, other options for elevating chair heights are available. The simplest consists of adding a seating cushion to the existing chair. Its width, or thickness, should be determined by how much height is needed to achieve independent seating mobility. Leg extenders, available either as metal brackets or drop-in cones, can also be used to elevate the height of chair seats by several inches. Leg extenders fit most chairs designed with rounded or square legs, and are equipped with non slip rubber tips to prevent the chair from sliding away during transfers. Finally, a pneumatic lifter seat may be used to help with transfers from low-seated chairs. This device rests on the seat of an ordinary chair, and when activated the lifter seat gently assists the person to the standing position. Similarly, the lifter seat can assist with sitting-down transfers as well. As an alternative, seat-lift chairs in the form of easy chairs are available.

The choice of any of these should be determined by pragmatic considerations. If the person uses several chairs that are low-seated, a portable seating cushion allows the person to move the cushion from chair to chair. Also, seat cushions are light enough to transport, should the person leave home to visit friends and family; some are even equipped with shoulder straps. If the individual principally uses only one chair, chair leg extenders may be a more appropriate choice. Extenders are also more suitable for persons who find their existing seat cushions comfortable, and prefer not to add anything that will affect this comfort. Other people find the design of the existing seat aesthetically pleasing and may not wish to detract from the chair's appearance with a cushion. A pneumatic seat lifter is rarely a first choice, as the cost of these devices may be prohibitive for the older person. Some persons also complain that the device exerts excessive upward thrust upon rising, or that they slide off the seat, leading to instability. Lastly, some persons state that sitting on these devices is uncomfortable. Easy chair lifters are safer to use and more comfortable to sit in, although exceedingly more expensive than seat lifters. Experience suggests that seat and chair lifters are best reserved for older persons with significant physical limitations of the upper extremities that prohibit the use of armrests to assist with rising.

Likewise, seating that is too high for the older person should be replaced by lower-seated chairs that are functionally appropriate. Alternatives to reduce the height of a seat are somewhat problematic, as there are no good adaptations available. Nonetheless, older people are often given advice about how to adapt elevated chair heights. Sometimes it is suggested that they place a footstool in front of the chair that is used to step on and off when transferring from a high seat height. Unfortunately, footstools can be extremely hazardous. Stepping on and off the stool can lead to balance loss. Also, if the footstool does not remain in sight, it can easily become a tripping hazard. At other times, cutting the chair legs to an appropriate length is recommended, but this option is unacceptable for most older persons.

Leg Space

To facilitate rising from a chair, a space below a seat, sometimes called the leg or "kick" space, is essential. It allows a person to slide their legs underneath the chair to get the leverage necessary for the lower extremities to exert maximum thrust upward. Crossbars or rails on chair legs, used to provide structural support, may interfere with rising if they are positioned too low or too far forward. Sofas and easy chairs with no recessed space underneath their seats can interfere with rising for the same reasons. Sometimes adding a cushion to chairs and sofas to make the seat somewhat higher may compensate for diminished kick space or poorly positioned crossrails. As crossbars add to the chair's stability, their removal is not advisable. The preferred solution is to replace the chair. Select chairs with crossrails that are either positioned high enough or set back far enough to ensure that they don't interfere with the mechanics of rising. Easy chairs with a recessed space will accomplish the same results.

ARMRESTS

All chairs and sofas used by older people should be equipped with armrests. Older persons much more than younger persons depend upon armrests for assistance with seated transfers. When rising, armrests are used to support upward thrust, propel body weight forward, and immediate standing balance. The support offered by armrests while rising has the added advantage of helping to reduce pressure to the knee joints; this is beneficial for persons with arthritis (Hanger, Ball, &

Mulley, 1991). Finlay et al. (1983) examined the use of armrests in a group of older persons residing in a residential home and found that only 48% of residents were able to rise from an armless dining chair independently, compared to 87% of the same group being able to rise using a chair with armrests. Conversely, armrests also play a support-ive role in helping a person sit (Tideiksaar, 1993b). In those older per-sons with decreased strength or joint motion, a point is reached when their leg muscles and knee joints no longer function effectively to sup-port sitting. As a result, they may "kerplotz" or drop their body weight into a seat, risking a fall. Armrests help arrest this quick downward thrust of the body by assisting in its gradual descent. Armrests can also compensate for low seat heights and a loss of kick space by decreasing reliance on the legs for rising.

To support seated transfers, the position of armrests on chairs is cru-cial. Armrests that are too low or high or set back too far may inhibit both rising and sitting. Low armrests force a person to lean too far for-ward when getting up, thereby threatening their balance. Armrests that are too high or set back too far cannot provide a sufficient angle of leverage for the upper extremities when a person attempts to get up out of a seat. To function optimally in providing assistance, armrests should be of the correct height, positioned horizontally approximately 7–7 1/2 inches above the seat (Figure 8.4). They should extend at least to the seat's edge or, ideally, 1–2 inches beyond the front edge. This position allows for maximum leverage when rising, and continues to provide support until stability in standing is achieved. In addition, armrests should be non-slip, easy to grasp, and slightly sloped, more to the back than at the front, for maximum comfort.

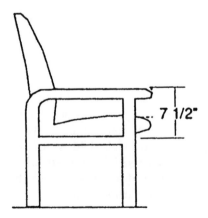

FIGURE 8.4   Proper chair armrest height. Reprinted with permission of Tactilitics, Inc.

A lack of armrests may be a particular problem with sofas. For example, with three-seated sofas, the person sitting in the middle seat will not have access to armrests, and may experience difficulty in getting up. Older persons who experience difficulty with sofa rising should be encouraged to sit next to armrests for transfer support. Two-seated sofas, although not ideal, offer the advantage of providing at least one armrest to assist with rising.

Seat Depth and Backrest Angle

Generally, the deeper the seat, i.e., the distance measured from the back of a person's knee to the buttocks, the greater the effort required of the person to move the body forward to the edge of the seat to rise. Seat depth is also affected by the angle of the backrest. The greater the angle or slant, the deeper the seat depth, and the greater the distance a person must negotiate to pull him or herself up.

The backrest or slope should always be considered in relation to the ability of the person to rise independently and, additionally, support the lower back. If the seat is too deep or the angle of the backrest too great, a seating cushion placed along the length of the backrest can usually rectify the deficiency (Figure 8.5). This will not only correct the seat depth and backrest angle to fit the person, but will also provide two vital elements for proper seating—a firm underseating and back support.

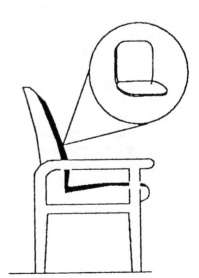

FIGURE 8.5 Correction of seat depth and backrest angle. Reprinted with permission of Tactilitics, Inc.

To facilitate rising out of a chair, the seat, should ideally slope gently backwards at an angle of no more than 1 inch from the front edge of the seat to its back edge. Seating that angles too far backwards may present problems with rising, as the person's knees will be positioned at a higher level than the buttocks. On the other hand, a seating angle tilted too far forward places the person's knees at a lower level than the buttocks and contributes to a slouched sitting position, which encourages sliding out of the chair.

A wedge cushion can correct both these problems. Position the wider part of the cushion to the front of the seat to prevent sliding out, or to the back to help those who experience difficulty rising. Sometimes leg extenders can be used to achieve similar results. In addition to elevating low seat heights, leg extenders can adjust the seat tilt either forward or backward from 1 to 45 degrees, the angle being controlled by a simple finger button. Also, the front edge of the seat should curve gently to avoid pressure on the back of the person's knees to prevent restriction of blood flow and the development of leg swelling or phlebitis.

Seating Cushions

Cushions on chairs should, first, provide comfort and second, be able to absorb the impact of the person sitting down in the seat. If seats are overly soft, people tend to sink into them, making it difficult to get up. Moreover, overly soft cushions reduce effective seat height because the cushion is compressed by the seated person, thus lowering the seat; it is then difficult to get up in one fluid motion. Finally, overly soft cushions prevent persons from shifting their buttocks, a natural, protective motion that helps individuals avoid developing pressure sores.

The best type of seating cushion for chairs is one that is relatively flat and firm, has some resilience, and does not "bottom out" when a person sits on it. A suitable cushion should give way when a fist is pressed firmly into it, yet resist if further pressure is applied. A cushion consisting of latex material provides sufficient pliancy for comfort and firmness without excessive compression. Foam cushions are best avoided, as they lose resilience over time and tend to bottom out. In the home setting, easy chair and sofa cushions that bottom out may be corrected by placing a plywood board underneath the existing seating cushion.

The seat cushion should contrast in color to the chair so that it can be visualized during seating. To prevent sliding, the seat covering should consist of a non-slip material; avoid coverings such as plastic and vinyl. Sometimes these coverings are used for persons with urinary incontinence to preserve the seat. In these situations, the addition of a slip-resistant covering, or the placement of non-slip adhesive strips on the seat, will prevent sliding off the chair.

Seating Stability

The stability of chairs is crucial for safety. During the act of transferring, if the chair tips forward, sideways, or backwards, the risk of balance loss and falls is greatly increased. For example, a common problem in persons with upper extremity hemiplegia or paresis is the application of excess weight on the chair's armrest with their functional arm, so that the chair tips sideways. Avoid chairs whose seat edge overhangs the position of the legs. This design can cause the chair to tip forward when someone moves to its front edge to rise, or sits down on the edge and not directly in the middle of the seat. Casters or metal tips attached to the bottom ends of legs can also be dangerous. The weight of the body can cause chairs equipped with these devices to slide when the person sits, rises, or leans on the chair for balance support.

Chairs are most stable when the legs are straight, positioned well forward of the seat's leading edge but not so splayed so as to invite tripping, and when the seat's edge does not extend too far forward beyond the chair legs. A good test of chair stability is to grasp and lean into a chair, slide and tilt it forward, backwards, and sideways as you sit and rise. It is also good practice to check chairs on a regular basis to make certain they are structurally sound. It is not unusual in both home and institutional settings to discover chairs which are broken to the point that any further use would have greatly increased older persons' risk of falling. Some individuals with balance problems often use chair backrests for mobility support. Backrests should be high enough to provide adequate support. Generally, a height of at least 32 inches, the distance from the floor to the topside of the backrest, is sufficient for this purpose. A non-slip adhesive strip placed along the top length of the chair back will prevent the person's hands from slipping when grasped.

BATHROOM

Doors and Doorways

Bathroom doors and doorways may prohibit safe entry and exit. Doorways can be difficult for older persons who are dependent on walkers to negotiate, as the walker may not easily fit through doorways, especially if the doorway is narrow. Doors that open inward into the bathroom tend to limit the space available for ambulation with a walker. As a result, walkers are often not taken into the bathroom, or else, persons may make an awkward attempt to drag their walker into the bathroom. Both situations inhibit safe ambulation and place the person at fall risk due to a lack of balance support. Bathroom doors that swing inward against the side of the bathtub or toilet can sometimes make it difficult for individuals to use the bathtub or toilet safely. Moreover, bathroom doors may not open fully when certain adaptive equipment is in place, for example, bathtub benches may protrude into the door's swing space. Finally, inward-opening doors may prevent the older person who has fallen and can't get up from receiving help.

Narrow bathroom doorways are more of a problem in the home than in hospitals and nursing homes where doorways are usually constructed with wide openings. Bathroom doorways can be made more accessible by eliminating the door entirely and hanging a curtain in the doorway for privacy. If this approach is unacceptable, doorway space can be enlarged by 1 1/2–1 3/4 inches with the use of double or foldback hinges that allow the door to swing entirely away from the doorway. Inward-swinging bathroom doors that obstruct ambulation, prohibit the use of bathtub equipment, or restrict access to the fallen person can be removed as well. Within the institutional setting, "accordion," "bifold," or "pocket" doors can be used for this purpose. Finally, bathroom doors should be equipped with locks that can be unlocked from both sides, in order to make it easier to enter in the event of a fall.

Fixture Support

Older persons with balance dysfunction, and those who are unable to use their walkers in the bathroom because of space limitations, often resort to the use of sink tops, towel bars, and wall surfaces for support. These structures constitute poor alternatives and may actually contribute to falls, particularly if the individual's hand slips. Several modifications to eliminate this hazard are available.

A grab bar placed horizontally in place of the towel bar or—better yet—a grab rail that runs around the perimeter of the bathroom wall can be used to provide balance support.

Grab bars should contrast in color to the wall for visibility, be slip-resistant, and should be positioned no more than 1 1/2 inches from the wall. This is to guard the person's arm from slipping between the bar and wall. It is important that grab bars are securely attached to wall studs so that they will not give way easily. Non-slip adhesive strips along the top of sink surfaces will prevent hands from sliding if grasped. The strips should be of similar color to the sink top to avoid visual confusion.

Toilets

Toilets that are low in height often lead to transfer problems. Corrective modifications include raised toilet seats and grab bars. Raised toilet seats are available in two types: fixed and adjustable heights. The latter are preferable as they can easily be adjusted to provide the proper toilet sitting height. Toilet seats of fixed heights require the availability of several sizes to accommodate individual needs, and may thus be more useful for institutional settings.

It is advised that raised toilet seats be constructed of materials sturdy enough to provide adequate seating support. The seats themselves should be made of a soft vinyl plastic to provide an absorptive cushion. This is to reduce the risk of pelvic or hip fracture in those persons who tend to drop or "kerplotz" onto the toilet seat. Toilet seats and raised seats should be of a contrasting color to the toilet and surrounding area to facilitate proper sitting placement on the toilet, particularly in those persons dependent upon visual cueing.

The installation of grab bars on the wall next to and behind the toilet, or a double armrest grab bar system that attaches to the toilet, can be used to maintain balance during toilet transfers. The type and height placement of wall grab bars is dependent upon the individual patient or resident, their disability, and the surrounding environment. For example, persons with hemiplegia will find it difficult to use grab bars placed on the dysfunctional side. Persons of short stature or limited reach will find grab bars at heights convenient for the typical person unsatisfactory for their use, because they are beyond their reach. As well, wall-mounted bars installed for the convenience of one person may not be appropriate for all individuals using the toilet. An alternative to wall-mounted grab bars is the double armrest type system (Figure 8.6). Many older people find this type easier to use, since the maximum amount of force exerted during transfers is a straight downward movement of the arms. This provides optimal transferring support. Conversely, wall-mounted grab bars provide less support since, when transferring, the person has to reach to the side and bend forward in order to grab the bar. As a result, the direct benefit of a downward thrust offered by the double armrest system is lost. The double armrest system is convenient for staff, as it is easy to attach and can be readily adjusted for an individual patient or resident. The placement of non-slip adhesive strips on the floor in front of the toilet helps to prevent the person's feet from slipping during transfers. And lastly, the toilet paper holder or receptacle may have to be moved to a location that is easier to reach, especially for persons with balance loss. This modification is often overlooked when redesigning the bathroom.

FIGURE 8.6   Toilet safety frame. Reprinted with permission of Tactilitics, Inc.

In some older individuals, particularly those who get up often to toilet at night and who may be unsafe or fearful of ambulating to the bathroom, the use of a bedside commode can be a reasonable alternative. Commodes should have armrests for hand support when transferring, so that they can be adequately grasped and leaned on without tipping over. Commode backrests provide an additional source of balance support while toileting. Their seat height should be consistent with the person's seating requirements, generally 15–20 inches in height. Some types of bedside commodes also fit over the bathroom toilet, acting as both a toilet riser and grab rail. This design is advantageous for those older persons who prefer the convenience and safety of a bedside commode at night, but who may choose to use their bathroom toilet during the day.

> BG is an 83-year-old woman with congestive heart failure and nocturia. As she also had poor balance, she was fearful of walking to the bathroom, and instead urinated in a plastic container while balancing herself on the edge of the bed. Unfortunately, this resulted in several falling episodes. The patient was offered a standard bedside commode to use as an alternative, but she rejected the device because it would be visible during the day when friends visited and embarrass her. However, after a few more falling episodes, she agreed to using a bedside commode at night, which could be moved to her toilet during the day and thus kept out of sight.

Bathtubs/Showers

Bathtubs present numerous challenges and obstacles inherent in their very design that place older persons at fall risk. First, bathtub rims can be difficult for individuals with lower extremity joint dysfunction or weakness to transfer over. As a result, some older persons will not attempt to get into the tub, but instead ask for help from family members, neighbors, or home attendants. If this assistance is unavailable, for safety reasons stemming from a general fear of falling and/or inability to get out of the tub, these persons will generally not attempt tub transfers and instead resort to sponge baths—typically an unpleasant alternative. Others will attempt to get into the tub, and choose a variety of methods to reduce their risk of falls. Some may sit on the edge of the bathtub and swing their legs into the tub; others will grab hold of tub walls and fixtures for support. Unfortunately, both these methods jeopardize balance. Another method is to use a footstool placed directly outside the bathtub to help transfer in and out, another hazardous activity. Second, once in the bathtub, sitting down to bathe can be a difficult task for these individuals, and may lead to balance loss. Often persons will compromise by opting to shower instead. This may not really be to their liking, as many older persons, especially those with joint complaints, prefer to bathe and become depressed when limited to showering. Lastly, once in the tub, the person may experience similar problems getting out, placing them at risk for certain complications.

Gooptu and Mulley (1994) surveyed a group of community-dwelling older people who experienced difficulty getting out of their tub at home and found that one in seven had been stuck in the bath at least once. These individuals either had difficulty getting out of the tub after bathing, slipped and fell in the tub, or were unable to rise after bathing. As a result, several persons experienced one or more complications consisting of prolonged lie times, pressure sores, burns, and fear of using the tub. Older persons may find shower stalls are somewhat safer to use. However, even taking a shower can be dangerous for persons with balance problems, particularly if they don't have grab bars to hold onto, but use soap dishes and towel bars for support. Several persons with severe balance problems may in the extreme place their head into the corner of the tub/shower wall for additional support, thus allowing their arms to be free while showering. Finally, both bathtub and shower ground surfaces can be extremely slippery, leading to further displacements of balance.

Several modifications can be made to ensure safe bathing. A portable bathtub grab rail can be mounted on the tub rim to provide an extra handhold and assist with safe entrance and exit (Figure 8.7). They have the added benefit of being transportable, which is advantageous for those older persons who on occasion may stay in the homes of family members.

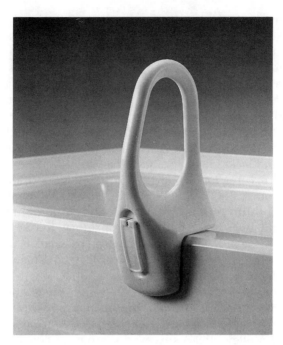

FIGURE 8.7   Bathtub-attached grab rail. Reprinted with permission of Lumex, Inc.

JR is an 82-year-old woman with mild osteoarthritis of both knees; as a result, she had difficulty with bathtub transfers. Her bathtub was furnished with wall-mounted grab rails, which allowed her to get in and out of the tub without incident. The patient visited her daughter for a week over the Christmas holidays. She attempted to take a bath without her usual grab support and fell while stepping into the tub, fracturing her ribs. In retrospect, this patient might have benefitted from a portable bathtub grab rail that she could have attached to her daughter's tub.

There are a variety of bathtub-mounted grab rails available; thus, the proper selection is important. Choose one that is easy to grasp and slip-resistant when wet. The height of the mounted rail should be high enough that the individual does not have to bend down to grasp the rail, thus risking balance loss, when transferring.

For those persons with moderate to severe lower extremity dysfunction, the use of a bathtub bench may be more beneficial than a tub mounted rail. These devices straddle the bathtub rim, resting on both the outside and inside floor of the tub. The person sits on the bench and then slides along the seat, placing their feet into the tub. Bathtub benches equipped with backrests for hand support are recommended. Some bathtub benches are cumbersome, however, and may not easily fit into small-spaced bathrooms. As an alternative, a combination bathboard that simply slides open from 20–31 inches across the top of the tub, secured with safety mechanisms and tub-mounted grab rail, may be used. Bathboards, however, are not as safe as bathtub benches. Even when mounted grab rails and benches are in place, since some individuals will insist on either holding onto or sitting down on the bathtub edge—a slippery porcelain surface—non-slip adhesive strips placed along the length of the tub will provide a slip-resistant surface. In this case, the adhesive strips should be clear in color, rather than color-contrasted, as some persons may perceive these as obstacles.

In the bathtub or shower, grab bars can be placed along the walls to provide hand support. Grab bars should be slip-resistant, especially when wet, and color-contrasted for visual detection. The placement of grab bars in bathtubs and showers should not be random. Rather, observe individuals entering and exiting their tub and shower and watch where they place their hands for support. Then install either a horizontal or vertical grab bar at the point where the person places their hands on the wall for support. This has direct benefits. Arbitrary placement of grab bars may call for the person to change their behavior when entering and exiting the tub or shower stall; locating grab bars at specific points will ensure that their customary behavior is safe. A bath chair or seat in the tub/shower stall allows the person to sit while bathing, and benefits those persons with balance loss. Handheld shower hoses are often used in combination with both bath seats and benches. Bathtub benches and seats should be equipped with rubber-tipped legs for stability, and their heights should be adjusted to allow approximately a 90 degree angle at the hips, knees, and ankles with the feet positioned firmly on the bathtub/shower floor.

Bathtub and shower floors should be slip-resistant. This can be accomplished with the use of rubberized bath mats or the application of clear non-slip adhesive strips placed on the ground surface. Color-contrasted strips can alter depth perception of the tub surface. Non-slip clear strips are preferable to rubber mats, as mats need to be removed and replaced after bathing to ensure their grip. This task may not be easily remembered by individuals with cognitive impairment. In addition, clear non-slip strips applied to tile flooring directly outside the tub or shower will ensure a safe pivot surface for transfers. Lastly, retrieving a dropped bar of soap can lead to the risk of balance loss and falls. To avoid this dangerous activity, recommend the use of soap-on-a-rope or liquid soap dispensers that can be affixed to the wall. A "poor man's soap-on-a-rope" can be constructed by placing the bar of soap into an old pair of women's stockings or pantyhose and tying it to the tub-shower fixtures.

TABLES

Many older persons with balance disorders sometimes hold onto the edges of tabletops when walking for support in lieu of canes and walk-ers. Over-the-bed tables equipped with wheels are another common culprit in falls, and are commonly found in hospital and many nursing home bedrooms. Bedside nightstands are also frequently used by older people for balance support when getting up from beds. Sometimes table edges are either held onto or used to pull individuals up from low-seated chairs in lieu of armrests or inadequate armrest support. If these fur-nishings are unstable or their tops are slippery when grasped, they may fail to provide the required support and lead to balance loss and falls. For instance, tables that are used to support chair transfers can easily give way.

> PB is an 86-year-old woman with Parkinson's Disease and poor seated transfers. She had low-seated chairs without armrest support in her home and, as a result, used the table edge to facilitate rising. She found this method of transferring quite satisfactory. However, on one occasion she suddenly lost her balance when getting up from the chair and grabbed hold of the table for support. Unfortunately, gravity had its way and the table tipped towards her, causing her to fall.

Drop-leaf, pedestal-type, and over-the-bed tables tend to tip over or move away easily when a person's weight is applied to the edge.

> MD is an 80-year-old woman with gait and balance impairments who resided in a nursing home. She preferred to walk about by holding onto furnishings for support rather than using her walker. On one occasion she got up from a chair, walked a few feet, and grabbed hold of a pedestal din-ing table for support. The table tipped over, causing her to lose balance and fall.

> JS is a 74-year-old man with Parkinson's Disease and required a walker while in the hospital. He was able to ambulate about the unit and his bed-room without incident. On one occasion his bed was not replaced in its original position after custodial cleaning, and thereby prohibited access while using a walker. When attempting to walk to the side of his bed, the

patient abandoned the walker because it would not fit between the bed and wall and grabbed hold of his over-the-bed table for balance support; he fell.

Nightstands that are used by older persons to assist with bed transfers may easily tip over or slide away, particularly if they are equipped with wheels or metal casters, both designs commonly found within institutional settings. For example, hospital and nursing home beds are frequently too high for older persons to transfer off safely. As a result, individuals often grab hold of the nearest object they feel to be secure, which in many instances is the nightstand. This can sometimes lead to dire consequences.

RC is a 79-year-old woman who was admitted to the hospital. During the night she attempted to get out of the bed in order to toilet and held on to the bedside nightstand for hand support. Unfortunately, the nightstand was equipped with wheels and slid away, causing her to lose balance and fall. As a result, the patient suffered head trauma—a laceration requiring 14 stitches to close—and a fear of further falls and injury. Subsequently, she became bedbound while in the hospital, requiring a bedpan for toileting.

Lastly, low-lying tables such as coffee tables and other small stands can represent tripping hazards if they are not visually detectable. On the other hand, nightstands or lamp tables that are too low in height may result in balance loss when used for balance support.

An attempt should be made to provide older persons with assistive walking devices and functionally suitable beds and chairs to avoid the use of tables for balance support when walking and transferring. However, under the best of conditions, many older people rely on furnishings for mobility support, and even for psychological reassurance. Therefore, make certain that all tables and nightstands in the older person's environment are stable when grasped or leaned upon, and that their surfaces are non-slip. This can be achieved by selecting tables with four legs and slip-resistant matte surfaces that promote hand grasping. Also, the heights of tables used for balance support should be waist-high to avoid excessive bending. Tables and nightstands with wheels or casters should be avoided if possible. Pedestal tables, often used in institutional settings to accommodate wheelchairs, should be carefully employed, and consideration should be given to avoiding their use entirely around demented populations. The same holds for institutional over-the-bed tables. Low-lying tables should also be removed, and replaced with furnishings that are both sturdy and easily visualized. As a general rule, the minimum height necessary for tables to be visualized by older persons is about 21–24 inches. This recommendation takes into account the reduction in visual fields, both peripheral fields and upward/downward gaze, experienced by older people. If replacing a low-lying or other table is not feasible, which may typically be the case in the home setting, attempt to relocate the table from the person's customary pathway to nonambulatory areas of the home. Color-contrasted adhesive strips can be placed on low-lying tables that may be difficult to visualize from surrounding areas—for example, glass-topped tables—particularly if they remain along pathways. Also, all table edges and corners should be round in shape or equipped with self-adhesive cushions to prevent bumping injuries that may occur as a result of falling or near-falling episodes.

COMPLIANCE

Any attempt to reduce falls and/or improve mobility through environmental modifications and adaptive devices is highly dependent on the compliance of the older person, regardless of whether the individual resides in the community or institution. In this context, compliance may be described as a twofold process, defined first as the extent to which the person's behavior agrees with the initial recommended changes, and second, as the extent to which the person adheres to the changes after their implementation. For community-dwelling persons, compliance carries the additional responsibility of accomplishing the suggested modification or obtaining the required device. Studies reveal that the acceptance and use of modifications and/or adaptive devices is primarily influenced by the older person's perceived need for such changes (Gosselin, Robitaille, Trickey, & Maltais, 1993; Pynoos, Cohen, Davis, & Bernhart, 1987). In other words, those individuals who perceive that environmental modifications and/or adaptive devices will improve their mobility and reduce their risk of falls are more likely to be compliant. Those individuals who are noncompliant or resistant towards the environmental modifications and/or adaptive devices recommended are likely to experience continued mobility problems and fall risk.

KB is an 82-year-old woman living at home alone. She experienced difficulty with her bathtub transfers, which placed her at fall risk. However, she rejected a recommendation to install bathtub grab bars for balance support on the grounds of "autonomy," despite the best efforts of her daughter and health professionals to convince her otherwise. Subsequently, she fell while in the bathtub and fractured her shoulder.

BF is an 87-year-old woman who experienced several falls in her home. All the episodes involved a loss of balance occurring at night when she was walking to the bathroom in darkness. To improve her balance, it was recommended that she either exit her bed on the side where a table lamp was located, or else move the table lamp to the side of the bed she customarily exited from. She rejected both solutions and continued to fall, fortunately without incident.

CA is a 74-year-old man with Parkinson's Disease who experienced balance loss while reaching overhead for canned foods located high in a kitchen cabinet. It was recommended that he move these cans to the countertop to avoid excessive reaching and balance loss. The patient rejected the advice, claiming it was "too much of a bother," and subsequently experienced a fall while reaching in the kitchen cabinet. He experienced a lie time of 2 days, and might have died if it were not for his daughter, who stopped by to check on him because she was unable to reach him by telephone.

HW is a 84-year-old woman living at home who experienced difficulty with her bathtub transfers. She was initially agreeable to a bath seat. However, after using the device for 1 week, she stored the seat in her closet, claiming that the device was "unsafe." Soon after, the patient fell while getting into the tub, and as a result, was fearful of using the tub thereafter. Instead, she now feels safer sponge bathing, although she would prefer to use her bathtub.

LB is an 88-year-old woman living in the nursing home. She experienced several falls while transferring off a low-seated toilet. The nurses provided her with a toilet riser, but she rejected the device, stating it was "uncomfortable." Instead, she used other toilets that were located on the unit, and subsequently fell while transferring off the toilet and fractured her pelvis.

EP is a 72-year-old man who experienced a bed fall while in the hospital. In response, the nurses kept his bed rail elevated to provide transfer support. However, he chose not to use the rail, declaring his "independence," and experienced another fall while transferring from bed.

Noncompliance with environmental modifications and/or adaptive equipment can have other detrimental consequences as well. To compensate for the absence of these modifications, persons are often prescribed home attendants to assist with mobility tasks and reduce fall risk. While beneficial in the short term, human resources are costly, and they may ultimately exacerbate mobility problems, since the older person can become functionally dependent on the attendant for all their tasks. This not only can place the person at increased fall risk, but may lead to premature nursing home placement, especially if the individual requires more mobility support than the attendant can provide. Environmental modifications and adaptive devices, in contrast, can provide the older person with a greater opportunity to engage in independent activity, which may help to forestall mobility dysfunction. It is estimated that about 80% of older persons are able to reduce their dependence on others through the use of assistive technology, and about half of these individuals are able to avoid entering a nursing home prematurely (O'Day & Corcoran, 1994). In addition, home attendants are an expensive health care resource. Environmental modification and durable medical equipment costs are nonrecurrent; personal assistant costs, of course, are recurrent.

It is difficult to know with any exactitude the extent of noncompliance by older persons with environmental modifications and adaptive devices. According to research, the consistent use of prescribed adaptive devices in the home may be as low as 50%–80% (Gitlin, Levine, & Geiger, 1993; Parker & Thorsland, 1991). In a study of 500 older and disabled people in receipt of aids and appliances, Mulley (1988) reported that one-fifth of bath and toilet aids had never been used. In another study cited by Mulley (1992), one-third of older people provided with toilet risers were unhappy with the device. A Canadian study that examined the implementation of home modifications among a group of older people found that almost one in five older persons known to have some activity restriction refused to accept any modification proposed by a occupational therapist, even when the constraint of expense was eliminated (Gosselin et al., 1993). The results of several housing surveys have consistently shown that older people with mobility problems are more likely to live in homes without environmental modifications or adaptations to meet their functional needs (Struyk, 1987; Wister, 1989). Moreover, Reschovsky and Newman (1990) suggested that up to 40% of households with one or more persons with a mobility problem could benefit from at least one modification.

The research literature indicates a wide variety of factors that can contribute to the noncompliance of environmental modifications and adaptive devices (Table 8.3) (Axtell & Yasuda, 1993; Chamberlain, Thornley, & Wright, 1987; George et al., 1988; Gitlin, Levine, & Geiger, 1993; Gosselin et al., 1993; Mulley, 1988; O'Day & Corcoran, 1994; Parker & Thorsland, 1991; Struyk & Katsura, 1987; Wister, 1989). Moreover, family members can also influence compliance; they can encourage

TABLE 8.3   Factors for the Noncompliance of Environmental Modifications (EM) and Adaptive Devices (AD)

System Factors

Increased costs of EM and AD

Lack of health insurance and third-party reimbursement for EM and AD

Long wait for AD or decreased availability of AD

Landlord restrictions (e.g., owner vs. rental dwelling) on permanent EM/AD changes (e.g., wall-mounted grab bars)

Supplies for EM not readily found or difficult to obtain

Lack of knowledge by health professionals and public about types of EM/AD available

Host Factors

Feelings of embarrassment about using AD

EM/AD is socially and/or aesthetically unacceptable

Denial of need for EM/AD

Denial of mobility restrictions/fall risk

Denial of hazardous environmental conditions

Acceptance of mobility limitations

Abandonment of certain activities such as bathing, thereby not requiring grab rails and bath chairs

Decreased cognition to understand proper use of AD

Decreased finances to implement EM/AD

Living alone; lack of assistance to undertake EM and install AD

Lack of family as resource to help pay for and implement EM/AD

Individual does not wish to alter appearance of environment (e.g., moving furniture, throwing out rugs, installing AD)

Individual preference; some individuals choose personal help to EM/AD because of increased social contact

Individual is already receiving personal assistance for mobility tasks and is satisfied with this arrangement

Fear of "technology" or AD

Lack of motivation to accomplish EM or obtain AD

Environmental/Adaptive Device Factors

Poor design of EM/AD; does not improve mobility/decrease fall risk

EM/AD is hazardous and unsafe

AD too complicated to use

AD uncomfortable to use

AD malfunction (broken, in ill repair)

Inappropriate AD prescription (device not suited for person's mobility needs)

AD does not fit environmental surroundings

environmental modifications and the use of adaptive devices, and help with the finances and installation. On the other hand, families can also be detrimental to compliance, especially if the changes interfere with their own activities or lifestyle.

EG is a 78-year-old woman who lived with her daughter. The patient had arthritis and muscle weakness and, as a result, experienced difficulty with her toilet and bathtub transfers. She was provided with a toilet riser and bathtub bench, which improved her mobility. However, on a subsequent home visit, the devices were not visible. The daughter had removed the devices because they interfered with her own toileting and bathing, leaving the patient to struggle with her bathroom activities. As an alternative, the patient was provided with toilet grab bars, a portable bathtub rim grab bar, and a foldable bath seat. These devices were just as effective in supporting the patient's mobility and were acceptable for her daughter as well.

RJ is an 82-year-old woman with Parkinson's Disease who lived with her single daughter. The patient experienced poor gait and balance, and as a result, required a walker for safe ambulation. However, a coffee table in the living room prevented her access to the sofa while using the walker. It was suggested to the daughter that the coffee table be moved several feet away from the front of the sofa to allow the patient safe passage. However, the daughter was adamant against having the coffee table moved, as she felt that this modification would interfere with her entertaining male companions. Unfortunately, this conflict was never resolved, and as a consequence, the patient was unable to use the sofa, but instead sat in a living room chair.

Health professionals can also contribute to the problem of noncompliance, particularly if they are not fully aware of the older person's mobility status and home environmental conditions when prescribing adaptive equipment. Providing inappropriate devices not only increases the likelihood of patient noncompliance, but can also heighten the risk of falls.

GP is an 84-year-old woman with lower-extremity weakness, the result of disuse atrophy. She stated difficulty with her bathtub transfers, and was prescribed a bath seat by the visiting nurse. However, soon after receiving her bath seat, she experienced a fall while attempting to get into the tub. When the patient was asked about the episode, she stated that while attempting to lift her legs over the bathtub rim she held onto the sink edge for support, but lost her balance and fell. In retrospect, the patient would have been better off with a bathtub bench, which would have helped her avoid using the sink top for support.

JW is a 92- year-old woman who was prescribed a bathtub bench for assistance with tub transfers. On a subsequent home visit, the bathtub bench was in the corner of the living room. The patient stated that her bathroom was too small and there wasn't enough room to ambulate in the bathroom with the bench in place. As an alternative, the patient was prescribed a bathboard that easily fit into the bathroom, allowing her ample ambulation space and improving her bathtub transfers.

Sometimes, for the length of time it takes health professionals to carry out environmental modifications, and for durable equipment companies to provide adaptive devices, can also be problematic.

LN is an 88-year-old nursing home resident who experienced several bed falls. It was determined that these falls were in part due to a slippery floor surface. It was suggested that non-slip adhesive strips be placed on the floor along the length of her bed to provide adequate foot support during transfers. However, that very night, the patient again fell while getting out of bed and fractured her wrist. The nurse whose responsibility it was to apply the strips stated that she had it on her "list of things to do" the next day.

CG is a 79-year-old man who was being discharged back home after spending 2 weeks in the hospital for the control of congestive heart failure. While in the hospital the patient suffered muscle atrophy and a decline in mobility as a result of bed rest. Arrangements were made with a local durable equipment company to install a number of bathroom devices in his home by the time he arrived. However, this was not done and the patient fell off his toilet, necessitating rehospitalization. The equipment company stated that they had overbooked their deliveries for that day, and had to reschedule their visit to the patient's home. Unfortunately, they failed to communicate this information to the hospital staff.

Several steps can be taken to ensure compliance when recommending environmental modifications and/or adaptive devices. First, any attempted change must be based on the functional needs of the person. That is, will the modification or device improve the individual's mobility or increase their safety? The person's cognitive ability to accommodate to the planned changes needs to be considered as well. In particular, consider whether the individual will be able to understand the environmental change, and in the case of adaptive devices, whether they will be able to learn and use the equipment safely. Unforeseen problems can usually be detected by giving the person a trial with the equipment prior to its being prescribed. In addition, the presence of other family members or caregivers and their personal lifestyles need to be taken into account when considering environmental modifications and/or adaptive devices. Any change made has to be acceptable for these individuals as well.

Secondly, any change attempted must be aesthetically pleasing for all parties involved. Before accepting environmental modifications and adaptive devices, the older person and resident family members must be satisfied with the appearance of these alterations. For example, when taping down an upended carpet edge, persons are more agreeable to having the carpet remedied by doublesided adhesive tape underneath the edges—which is out of view—than to having the carpet taped down directly and visibly. Also, many persons dislike the "cold" appearance of stainless steel adaptive bathroom equipment, but are more amenable to equipment fashioned with "designer" type colors.

Third, environmental modifications and adaptive equipment must be readily available from stores and durable equipment companies, easy to apply or install by the older person, and simple for the individual to use. The adaptive equipment recommended must also fit into or be compatible with the person's environmental surroundings. For instance, recall the case of JW. Based on her functional needs she was prescribe the appropriate bathtub equipment; however, with respect to the small size of her bathroom, the equipment was inappropriate, as it limited her access to the bathroom and thus was unusable. These type of problems can be avoided by observing the person's mobility after the equipment is installed to ensure its compatibility.

Fourth, always consider the amount of change that will be required. In general, individuals will be more compliant with the least number of changes made and disruptions of the person's environment. One need not eliminate every conceivable environmental hazard discovered, but only those that interfere with mobility or place the person at fall risk. Also, consider the type of environmental modification. Typically, older persons are more likely to be more compliant with passive interventions that don't require an individual's involvement than with active interventions requiring individual involvement. For example, it may be better to apply nonslip adhesive strips on bathtub ground surfaces (an example of passive intervention) to use rubber mats that require continuous removal and placement (an active intervention). On the other hand, some persons may be more compliant with active interventions, as these modifications may remind them of their "risk," whereas passive interventions can fail to warn the person.

Fifth, for those older persons at fall risk, environmental modification and/or adaptive devices should be viewed very similar to medications, which are needed immediately to treat an acute medical condition. Some older persons, for example CG and LN (see page 311), require immediate attention. Therefore, all parties involved—health professionals and durable medical equipment companies—in helping to implement environmental modifications and/or adaptive devices should attend to this task immediately in order to avoid falls.

Finally, once environmental modifications and/or adaptive devices are in place, followup is essential to ensure continued compliance. This can be achieved by either telephone calls, individual and/or family inquiry during routine medical appointment, or by arranging a home visit. The latter method, although not always the most practical, is the most ideal, as the person's mobility and compliance in relation to the environmental changes and adaptive equipment can be directly observed. The use of physical and occupational therapists or visiting nurse services in this regard can be very beneficial. Any noncompliance requires a reevaluation of both the patient's physical and cognitive state and environmental conditions, as well as a consideration of alternative strategies.

Despite these approaches, the older person may still be resistant to any change in their environment or to the use of adaptive equipment, either initially or after the changes are implemented. In this event it is important to identify the reasons for noncompliance (see Table 8.3), and attempt to modify those factors that are discovered. Gosselin et al. (1993) demonstrated that when barriers related to information, availability, expense, and installation are removed, modifications are well received by older people. If the person remains resistant to any changes, don't abandon your attempts at modification. Instead, periodically continue to discuss with the older person the benefits of the proposed changes. The use of visual aids can be extremely helpful in helping the person to understand the suggested modifications and devices. Also, try to point out the consequences of not changing the environment; but avoid creating fear and anxiety, for example, by telling the individual that they are "going to fall and break their hip" if the modifications are not made. Changing environmental conditions that interfere with mobility or place persons at fall risk is not easy, particularly if the individual has not yet suffered any falls as a result; but persistence is advised. Some older persons who are initially resistant may later become compliant on their own, especially if they have suffered further declines in mobility or falls. Recall the case of KB (page 306) who rejected bathtub devices and went on to fracture her shoulder. After coming home from the hospital, this patient was very agreeable to the bathtub modifications, partly due to fear of injury. Zimmer and Chappell (1994), in a study that examined the use of assistive devices in older people with mobility problems, found that as the number of mobility problems increased, the compliance with devices increased as well.

One strategy that can be employed to overcome some barriers to compliance is to develop a community-based "device bank." The function of a device bank is to collect, store, and dispense unused or discarded ambulation devices such as canes, walkers, and wheelchairs and adaptive equipment such as grab bars, toilet risers, bath seats/benches, extended shower hoses, and reacher devices to community-dwelling older persons with mobility problems (Tideiksaar, 1992). There are several recognizable benefits of such a device bank. Equipment is thus readily available for those older persons who are unable to afford devices, either because of personal finances or lack of third-party reimbursement resources. This is especially crucial for bathroom equipment such as grab bars, toilet risers, and bath/shower chairs/benches, as these devices are the most frequent modifications installed in the homes of older people (Struyk, 1987; Trickey, Mallais, Gosselin, & Robitaille, 1993; Wister, 1989), and typically are not paid for by third-party reimbursement sources, at least in the U.S. (O'Day & Corcoran, 1994).

> GC is an 82-year-old woman with poor mobility who was at fall risk. She required several toilet and bathtub devices in her home, but didn't have the finances to pay for the equipment. During her 3-month wait for Medicaid approval she borrowed the equipment from the device bank, and returned the devices after gaining reimbursement coverage.

> RY is a 74-year-old woman who developed an acute attack of arthritis in both knees. Her physician prescribed a nonsteroidal anti-inflammatory drug (NSAID) and advised her to use a walker for weight relief on her knees. However, her Medicaid insurance had expired and she couldn't afford the walker. She was provided a walker from the device bank while waiting for her Medicaid renewal.

The device bank can also be of benefit for those persons who would like to try out equipment prior to purchase, to determine if the device is safe and comfortable to use and improves mobility.

> RL is a 70-year-old woman who wanted to purchase a toilet-attached grab bar, but was unsure if the device would improve her transfer function. She borrowed the toilet device from the bank on a trial basis, and eventually purchased a similar device after finding that she was satisfied with its effectiveness.

The device bank can also be helpful for those older persons recovering from an acute illness and who may require devices for only a short period of time while undergoing rehabilitation, and who may be noncompliant if required to purchase the equipment themselves. Other individuals in this category are those whose disease process is undergoing treatment and whose mobility requirements have not yet stabilized.

SJ is an 82-year-old woman who required a toilet riser and walker at home following repair of a hip fracture. As she only required these devices for a week at most, she was unwilling to purchase them, even though her insurance covered the cost. She complained that it was "a waste of good money" and that she could probably "do without the devices." Her reluctance to obtain the devices placed her at fall risk, so the patient was provided with the devices she needed from the bank during her rehabilitation. She found this to be wonderful.

FT is a 89-year-old man with Parkinson's Disease. He had used a cane for many years, and was independent in his toilet and bathtub transfers. However, of late, his Parkinson's Disease had become much worse, causing him to experience several falls in the bathroom. As a result, he required bathroom equipment. Yet he hesitated to buy the equipment for two reasons. First, he was receiving medication treatment for his Parkinson's Disease and hoped that he would get better and not require the equipment. Second, he stated that the equipment made his home "look like a nursing home." As the patient was at fall risk, he was persuaded to try the bathroom equipment on a temporary basis, and was provided equipment from the device bank. After a 3-week period (with an increase in antiparkinson medication) his Parkinson's Disease improved and he no longer needed the bathroom equipment.

A device bank can be easily set up or housed and operated from one of several community locations, for example, senior centers, home care services, hospital outpatient clinics, and staffed by volunteers. The device bank can be responsible for collecting equipment donated by the community, keeping an inventory, and dispensing devices to older persons in need on a loan basis. The latter is accomplished and controlled through home care professionals and groups to indicate the type of device or equipment required. There are a variety of community sources for obtaining equipment. These include individual donations from older people who no longer need or use their equipment, and are more than happy to rid themselves of the devices. Families of older individuals with discarded devices, or whose relatives may have either entered a nursing home or passed away, may be similarly charitable. Health care institutions such as hospitals, nursing homes, and even durable medical equipment companies will frequently donate unused equipment. Finally, a home repair service provided by volunteer community organizations to help frail older people with any necessary environmental modifications for (example, installation of grab rails and elimination of hazardous conditions) can be utilized to improve compliance.

Compliance with environmental modification and adaptive equipment is most effective if older persons and their family members have access to information about the wide variety of modifications and existing technologies available. Many durable equipment companies and aging organizations publish brochures that can be provided to older persons and families for this purpose. These may be distributed in physician's offices, outpatient clinics, and senior centers. Ideally, community resource centers can be established. These centers would be very similar in function to furniture stores, places where older people and their families can readily obtain information and ask questions about environmental modifications and adaptive devices; view the different modifications in operation; and try out adaptive equipment. On a smaller scale, this can be easily achieved by an "adaptive equipment health fair," conducted by durable medical equipment companies and held at senior centers and other locations frequented by older persons. Similarly, health professionals, particularly those working in home care services, should receive ongoing inservice instruction on environmental modifications and adaptive devices, both to increase their knowledge base and ensure proper utilization.

INJURY PREVENTION DEVICES

HIP PADS

Recall that several factors are associated with the risk of hip fracture following a fall (see Chapter 4). Aside from a loss of bone strength (osteoporosis), one of the principal determinants of injury is a reduction of soft tissue or fat covering the hip area (Lauritzen & Askrgaard, 1992). As a result, the hip's ability to withstand impact on a hard ground surface, and thus protect against a hip fracture, is diminished. Conversely, an increase in fat and muscle surrounding the hip absorbs a greater extent of fall impact. As a result, several researchers have advocated the use of external hip pads as a device to guard against hip fractures (Cummings & Nevitt, 1989; Greenspan et al., 1994; Hayes et al., 1993; Lauritzen & Askrgaard, 1992). Hip pads, in essence, are designed to replace the loss of fat around the hip. They act as shock absorbers, diverting the direct impact of a fall away from the bone. One commercially available model consists of two shock-absorbent pads inserted in a lightweight wrap-around pelvic garment that is worn under outer clothing and over underwear. Once in place the hip pads afford protection to the hip. Velcro closures are used to allow for easy application and removal of hip pads.

The efficacy of hip pads in protecting against hip fractures has been limited. In laboratory simulations of a fall against the hip, a covering of full-thickness human tissue reduced the peak impact force by only 16%, while external hip pads performed slightly better in absorbing impact. For all commercially available hip pads tested, peak hip force remained twice the amount sufficient to fracture the hip (Kiel, 1994). While these results are somewhat disappointing, one clinical trial demonstrated greater success with hip pads. Lauritzen, Peterson, and Lund (1993) studied the efficacy of an external hip protector in preventing against fractures in a group of older residents of a Danish nursing home. Compared against a control group not wearing hip pads, they calculated a 53% reduction in fracture risk for those individuals wearing the hip protector.

Regardless as to whether hip pads are effective or not in preventing hip fractures, if persons fail to wear the device, the question is moot. In their study Lauritzen and colleagues (1993) reported that only 24% of the study subjects who received a hip pad wore them regularly. This study did not explore the reasons for noncompliance, but several are possible. Hip protectors may take time and be somewhat cumbersome to put on, and may not always be fully comfortable. Some persons with dementia have been reported to become agitated while wearing hip protectors (Ross et al., 1992). Also, noncompliance may be complicated by the design of hip pads. Some are crude by design, made either of polyurethane foam (Kiel, 1994) or energy-absorbing plastic material (Wallace, Ross, Huston, Kundel, & Woodworth, 1993), and placed in pockets of specially designed cotton and Spandex garments. As these designs offer active protection, that is, persons have to put them on, passive devices may be more accepted. Some investigators are attempting to develop airbag devices that can be inserted into garments worn by older persons to protect the hip upon ground impact (Rothman, 1990). These devices are not yet commercially available, nor has their efficacy and compliance been tested. Other factors influencing compliance relate to the older individuals themselves. Ross et al. (1992) examined the compliance or wearability of hip pads in a nursing home population. They found that compliance was higher in those individuals who were cognitively intact, and particularly in those persons who had suffered significant injuries or significant fall events. Expanding on these findings, Tideiksaar (1994) found that hip pads were well accepted by a group of community-dwelling older females with recent hip fractures, who were at increased risk for further injurious falls and had significant fear of falling and injury. He concluded that the use of hip pads may be more acceptable as a secondary method of prevention, for example, in older persons at risk for hip fracture and fear of injury, rather than as primary prevention for the general older population. Therefore, hip pads may be tried as a preventive strategy in conjunction with other measures to guard against hip fractures, such as the modification of injurious fall risk factors.

EMERGENCY ALARM SYSTEMS

For community-dwelling older persons, the use of emergency alarms may be useful in decreasing long lies and their complications. These devices are designed to provide frail older persons with a means to summon assistance in the event of a fall in the home. In general, there are two types of alarm systems: fixed and portable. Fixed alarms are "hardwired" systems much like those in place in most hospitals and nursing homes. The basic system consists of wall-mounted "pushbutton" or "pull cord" stations, usually located in high fall-risk areas such as the bathtub/shower and the bedroom. When activated or triggered, the alarm sends a signal to a response center. Fixed alarm systems are typically found in public or sheltered housing for the elderly, and are generally installed during construction. Portable alarms or personal emergency response systems (PERS) consist of a small radio transmitter or portable help button carried by the user usually as a neck pendant; and a console, or receiving unit connected to the person's telephone, which contacts a response center to respond with assistance. Pressing the help button on the radio transmitter activates the system. A remote signal is sent to the receiving unit which, in turn, automatically dials a 24-hour response center. The response center can either call the subscriber back over the telephone, or send help immediately; a neighbor or relative can be sent to check on the person or, if necessary, an ambulance is summoned to take the person to the hospital. Some alarm systems are equipped with two-way speakers, which allow individuals to communicate directly with the response center. Currently, it is estimated that more than 250,000 older people in the United States and Canada have a PERS (Dibner, 1990). The worldwide use of PERS ranges from below 1% to 12% of the older population (Dibner, 1991). While fixed alarm systems are readily available in elderly housing facilities, estimates of the actual extent by which older people use these alarms is not presently known.

Fixed alarm systems are less satisfactory than portable alarms in guarding against long lies, as they are usually located on the wall too far above the ground to be reached after a fall if the person is unable to get up. British studies of older persons in sheltered housing have shown that up to 17% of individuals are unable to activate an alarm after sustaining a fall (Davies, 1990). Tinker (1991) reported that half of all pull-cord type alarms tend to be tied up, thus contributing to a lack of access. Consequently, PERS are more practical for the prevention of long lies; although research examining this relationship is lacking, common sense dictates that PERS should be helpful in this regard. But the potential advantages of PERS can only be recognized first, if the older person accepts the system and, secondly, if they are compliant with the system. Both acceptance and compliance have been found to be problematic. Dibner, Lowy, and Morris (1982) found that only 65% of older persons residing in public assisted housing accepted a PERS when offered. Common reasons for rejection included fear of mechanical devices, fear of their cost, and confusion about how the system operates. Levine and Tideiksaar (1993) surveyed a group of community-dwelling older persons subscribing to a PERS and found that 54% of individuals were noncompliant with the device; either they did not wear the "pendant" around the neck or wrist when alone, and/or they did not activate the system in the case of emergency. Compliance was decreased in those persons who had either obtained the PERS at the insistence of family members, due perhaps to the loss of autonomy, or had negative responses to alarm activations, due to poor response times and/or impolite responders. Those individuals who had self-obtained the PERS, had a history of falls and timely responses to alarm activations, and received instruction on the PERS were found to be significantly more compliant with the alarm system. Additionally, older persons who used an assistive mobility device such as a cane, walker, or wheelchair were more likely to be compliant with the PERS. Assuming that persons requiring mobility devices are more functionally impaired than those individuals not needing a device, this finding supports the findings of others that PERS acceptance is associated with increasing levels of disability (Dibner, 1990). Of interest, in the group studied by Levine and Tideiksaar (1993), several of the patients' primary care physicians were unaware of their noncompliance with the system. Subsequently, it must be ensured that potential PERS users are compliant with the system to avoid exposure to long lies and their untoward complications.

In addition, PERS can have other benefits. These apply to the older person or subscriber, the family or caregiver, and the health care system.

For the older person there are a number of psychological benefits, including a heightened feeling of security, reduced fear of falling, and increased sense of autonomy and independence (Cameron, 1991; Davies, 1990; Dibner, 1990, 1992). For family members, the benefits include reduced anxiety about the safety of their parent, and financial savings (Dibner, 1992), as the cost of the PERS is about $1 per day, much less than paying for home attendants to provide sentry duty. Finally, for the health care system, PERS has been found to reduce the cost of health care resources. Several investigators have demonstrated that community-dwelling older persons subscribing to PERS use less medical resources, spending fewer days in acute care hospitals and nursing homes, and social support services, because of decreased home attendant hours (Dibner, 1990; Hyer & Rudick, 1994; Watzke & Kemp, 1991).

Up to this point, a wide range of strategies to prevent falls has been examined. Mechanical restraints to guard against further falls are often employed when these measures fail. Moreover, restraints sometimes serve as a strategy to avert falls in the first place. While the need for restraints to prevent falls may be evident, concern about their use and widespread practice has emerged during the past several years, particularly at the institutional level. At issue is whether mechanical restraints are effective and safe, and whether their benefits in preventing falls outweigh their risks. The use of mechanical restraints, and their role in preventing falls, is the topic of the next and final chapter.

CHAPTER 9

Mechanical Restraints

INTRODUCTION

Mechanical restraints are defined as any mechanical device, material, or equipment attached or adjacent to the individual's body which the person cannot remove easily and is used to inhibit free, independent movement. These devices include vest and chest jackets or harnesses; waist belts and sheets; leg ties; full length side rails; wheelchair safety bars; and geriatric chairs with fixed tray tables.[1] Until recently, anywhere from 25%–85% of nursing home residents were restrained on a daily basis (Evans & Strumpf, 1989). In acute care and rehabilitation hospitals it is estimated that from 7%–34% of older patients are restrained during their stay (Frengley & Mion, 1986; Mion, Frengley, Jakovcic, & Marino, 1989; Robbins, Boyko, Lane, Cooper, & Jahnigen, 1987; Schleenbaker, McDowell, Moore, Costich, & Prater, 1994). The most frequent reason given for mechanical restraint use is to prevent injury that might result from falls or conditions that place individuals at fall risk: dysmobility, unsafe wandering, and confusion or agitated behavior (Frengley & Mion, 1986; Magee et al., 1993; Strampf & Evans, 1988; Tinetti, Liu, Marottoli, & Ginter, 1991). While the magnitude of mechanical restraint use in the community-dwelling population is essentially unknown,

---

[1]The use of mechanical restraints has been a long-standing practice in nursing homes and acute care hospitals throughout the U.S.

older people living at home are restrained for similar reasons. In particular, some family members, especially those who care for older demented persons at fall risk, may resort to restraining devices when all other measures fail.

> AS is an 83-year-old woman with dementia and multiple falls. Out of extreme frustration, in an effort to prevent her falls, the family kept AS seated in a deep-seated living room easy chair during the day, which she could not get out of without assistance. At night they used a hospital bed with full side rails elevated, and bedsheets tied around the patient's waist as a preventive measure.

> MB is a 79-year-old woman with dementia and multiple bed falls. Her son, although well-meaning, was exasperated over the situation and kept his mother tied down with rope while in bed. This was discovered when the patient was admitted to the hospital for the treatment of severe rope burns of the lower extremities that nearly cut through to the bone.

> RA is an 82-year-old woman with dementia and nocturnal wandering. On several occasions the family found her on the bathroom floor after an apparent attempt to use the toilet. In an effort to prevent wandering and the risk of falls, the family tied one end of a 10-foot rope around her waist and the other end to her bedpost. However, this approach proved unsatisfactory, as the patient was often found on her bedroom floor tangled up in the rope as a result of attempting to free herself.

Aside from protecting older persons against falls and injury, a number of other reasons have been cited for the increased use of mechanical restraints in hospitals and nursing homes. Frequently, family members expect that restraints should be used and that their absence reflects bad care (Johnson, 1990). One recent study surveyed the perception of families towards the use of mechanical restraint in the nursing home. Researchers found that most family members thought their relatives were appropriately restrained (Werner, Cohen-Mansfield, Green, Pasis, & Gerber, 1993). Families may often request and demand "risk-free" care that includes the use of restraints. Nurses may also prefer to over-rather than underutilize restraints and err on the side of "safety," fearing both family and administrative retaliation in the event of a fall (Hardin et al., 1994). Often this approach is supported by a belief that "It doesn't really bother older people to be restrained" (Evans & Strumpf, 1990). Sometimes restraints substitute for nursing supervision and care, especially when staffing levels are inadequate (Evans & Strumpf, 1989; Robbins, 1986; Rose, 1987). Under these circumstances, nurses feel that restraints allow them to provide timely and efficient custodial care, particularly when their patients wander or are confused. Also, restraints are frequently applied to protect the institution and its employees from the legal liability that may occur subsequent to a fall (Johnson, 1990; Kapp, 1992). Many institutional staff believe that a failure to restrain puts them and the facility at risk for legal sanctions. Similarly, nursing home operators use restraints because they fear litigation if the residents injure themselves (Francis, 1989). Finally, health professionals may feel that they have a "moral duty" to protect patients and residents with restraints, especially since few alternatives to their use exist. Yarmesch and Sheafor (1984) presented a group of 23 nurses with a set of clinical cases describing problematic patient behaviors (such as wandering, agitation, and confusion) and asked each of them to respond as to whether they would or would not restrain the patient. They found that 89% of the responses were to restrain, and only 11% said that they would withhold restraints and use alternatives. Neary, Kanski, Janelli, Scherer, & North (1991) found that 51% of nursing aides agreed with the statement "Good alternatives to mechanical restraints don't exist." In another study, Strumpf and Evans (1988) reported that up to 40% of hospital nurses were unable to offer any alternatives to restraint at all. More recently, Hardin et al. (1994) found that nursing staff on extended and nursing home units in a Veterans Administration facility had moderately positive, unambivalent attitudes toward using restraints. Collaborating with another professional, especially a physician, was associated with more positive attitudes toward restraints. Sixty-five percent of the staff were unable to offer any alternatives to restraints; among those who were able to suggest an alternative, increasing staff was cited most frequently.

MECHANICAL RESTRAINT EFFECTS

Many of the firmly entrenched beliefs that support the continued use of mechanical restraints are based largely on myth, as little documented evidence exists arguing that restraints are effective in accomplishing the purposes for which they are used. For instance, restraints may not necessarily represent the best way to protect older persons from falls and injury. The conclusion from the studies cited in Chapter 3 (page 124) is that restraints seldom eliminate the risk of falls and injury. In fact, restrained persons are subject to the same or added fall risks as are individuals without restraints. Werner, Cohen-Mansfield, Braun, and Marx (1989) found that regardless of the frequency of restraint use,

62% of nursing home residents fell at least once. Moreover, facilities that restrain tend to have a higher incidence of serious injury following a fall (Tinetti, Liu, & Ginter, 1992). Cape (1983), in a comparison of two Canadian long-term hospitals, found that the fall-related fracture rate was 50% lower in the hospital which used the fewest restraints. When restraints are removed, there may be an increase in the number of falls, but not in the number that result in significant injury (Ejaz et al., 1994; Ejaz, Jones, & Rose, 1994; Meyer, Kraenzle, Gettman, & Morley, 1994).

Aside from concerns about effectiveness, the use of restraints to "protect and safeguard" patients and residents is questionable. While in some instances restraints may be protective, for example, to prevent falls in confused and wandering persons when an immediate and clear threat of injury exists, it is not certain that these benefits outweigh the risks, particularly with prolonged use.

Rather than protecting persons from harm, restraints may instead inflict harm, placing these persons at risk for numerous detrimental physical consequences. For example, restrained persons can quickly develop immobility and its adverse effects, including pressure sores, bladder and bowel incontinence, and muscle wasting. Warshaw et al. (1982) reported that mechanical restraints reduce functional capacity, as a patient quickly loses steadiness and balance when restricted in a bed or chair.

Also, restraints that are too restrictive or applied too tightly can cause circulatory obstruction of the lower extremities and edema, skin abrasions, respiratory difficulties, and unintentional death by strangulation. Studies examining the cause of restraint-related mortality have found that most deaths are due to asphyxiation, occurring in chairs and beds, with the victims discovered suspended in their vest and strap restraints (Miles & Irvine, 1992; Rubin, Dube, & Mitchell, 1993). Hospital patients who are restrained have twice the length of institutional stay (Lofgren, MacPherson, Granieri, Myllenbeck, & Sprafka, 1989), are more likely to be transferred to nursing homes for care, and are at higher risk of early death than are nonrestrained persons (Frengley & Mion, 1986; Mion et al., 1989; Robbins et al., 1987). Much of the resulting mortality is due to the consequences of immobility.

Mechanical restraints are also associated with numerous psychological consequences, which refutes any notion that older people are not bothered by their use. Restraints frequently precipitate one of several emotional reactions. Persons either feel fear and a sense of panic, which can result in belligerent behavior, or, at the other extreme, a sense of humiliation and abandonment, which can result in aggressive behavior, a loss of self-image, depression, withdrawal, or low social functioning

(Evans & Strumpf, 1989; Folmar & Wilson, 1989; Tinetti, Liu, Marottali, & Ginter, 1991; Werner et al., 1989). Burton, German, Rovner, and Brant (1992) investigated the association between restraint use and decline in cognition in a population of nursing home residents. They found a strong association between restraint use and poor cognitive function, but only in those residents with moderate or no mental impairment. Restraints appeared to have little or no effect on cognitive decline in those residents with greater mental impairment. Additionally, the person's self-esteem may become decreased when restraints are applied, as others typically view restrained individuals as disturbed, dangerous, or mentally incompetent. This can be severely demoralizing for the older person. Moreover, when persons are not informed about the decision to apply restraints, or are not allowed to either accept or refuse their use, the right of self-determination is denied. This constitutes a restriction of an individual's autonomy: the freedom to make choices about engaging in activities. When a person is restrained and denied the ability to get up, sit down, or walk about with undue interference, their quality of life, as well as their psychological well-being is severely impaired.

Health professionals are not immune from the effects of restraints. Nurses are often responsible for initiating restraint orders in hospitals and nursing homes; they struggle with the conflict between patient and resident benefit and the burden brought on by the decision (Hardin et al., 1994; McHutchion & Morse, 1989). On the one hand, they feel a professional duty to protect and safeguard persons who are at fall risk. This obligation is often heightened when nursing allocations are scarce and monitoring of problematic persons is difficult. To avoid the risk of negligence and legal sanctions that may occur in the event of injury, many nurses feel that they have little alternative but to apply restraints. On the other hand, nurses find the act of restraining older persons highly stressful and emotional, often provoking anxiety, dissatisfaction, and guilt. They recognize that restraints deprive persons of their autonomy and dignity, and they empathize with the older person's plight, conceding that they themselves would not want to be placed in a similar position. Furthermore, nurses who believe that providing daily care to persons with mobility problems is accomplished more quickly when they are restrained and accessible can find that in the long run this strategy becomes ineffective. Restrained persons rapidly develop immobility and associated morbidity, which ultimately creates a situation of greater dependency and fall risk and the need for more custodial care from nurses. After controlling for impairment and care needs, Phillips, Hawes, and Fries (1993) found that physically restrained nursing home residents actually required more nursing care than those who were not restrained.

While nurses perceive themselves as less vulnerable to legal sanctions if restraints are used, particularly in the event of injury, the fear of legal liability is ill-founded. Although injury litigation brought against nursing homes is common (Kapp, 1992), lawsuits for damages resulting from falls are relatively uncommon. Johnson (1990) reviewed 247 cases filed against nursing homes in 52 cities over a 4-year period. Sixty of these claims involved residents who had been injured by falls; of these, only 8 claims were solely for the failure to restrain. Kapp (1992) reported that no lawsuit has been successful against a long-term facility solely for failure to restrain a resident, and in the acute care hospital setting, where liability was predicated squarely on the failure to restrain, only one case was successful. In cases involving injury to nonrestrained persons, a preponderance of other factors usually constitutes negligence, including improper assessment and documentation of the person's condition, failure to assess and monitor the person at risk for falls, and failure to respond to falls and injury in a timely manner (Johnson, 1990; Kapp, 1992). Collopy, Boyle, and Jennings (1991, p. 13), commenting upon the risk of litigation involving restraints, stated that "liability is based on whether due care was exercised under the circumstances, not simply on whether the resident was injured."

In reality, the use of restraints may increase the risk of litigation. Lawsuits involving the improper application of restraints that result in injury, for example, falling out of a bed or chair either with restraints intact or after removal by the person themselves, have been successful. Facilities and staff may also be held liable when restraints are used for convenience during staff shortages rather than for an emergency condition, such as the risk of immediate injury.

Family members are also affected by restraint decisions and react in various ways to restraints used on their relatives. Some express dismay at the sight of a relative in restraints and demand their removal, even if it increases the patient's fall risk. Brennan, Gordon, and Zimmerman (1991), in a study of family attitudes toward restraints, reported that prior to restraint removal, most families thought that restraints were overutilized in their older relatives. Others, while not accepting of the practice, come to reluctantly accept restraints as a necessary evil, believing that they will keep the relative from being injured in a fall. This notion is reinforced when family members are informed by staff that they have little recourse, as no alternatives exist.

Much of the justification for using mechanical restraints is based on the belief that there are no alternatives. In reality, this is untrue. Several acute hospitals (Mion & Strumpf, 1994) and nursing homes (Ejaz et al., 1994; Kramer, 1994; Werner, Koroknay, Braun, & Cohen-Mansfield, 1994) have reduced falls without resorting to restraints. Such facilities have adopted a policy of nonrestraint use that is commonly seen in several European countries, among them, the United Kingdom and the Scandinavian nations, where the use of restraints is virtually nonexistent (Evans & Strumpf, 1989; Strumpf & Tomes, 1993; Williams, 1989). Greater emphasis is placed instead on responding to the needs of individuals, such as assisting with toileting and ambulation, structuring and modifying the physical environment to support independent and safe functioning, providing rehabilitative care and activities that promote mobility, and developing trusting relationships between residents/patients, caregivers, and family members (Evans, Strumpf, & Williams, 1991).

CLINICAL IMPLICATIONS

Given the detrimental effects associated with the use of mechanical restraints and their relative ineffectiveness in preventing falls, there is an ongoing movement in the United States to re-examine their use. The major impetus stems from consumer advocates, health providers, and government regulators who are concerned that mechanical restraints have become routine and acceptable forms of treatment. They argue that in many institutions restraints represent the standard approach to common geriatric problems, such as falls and conditions associated with fall risk, for example, mobility dysfunction, and confusion. Furthermore, criteria governing the use of restraints are often lacking and decisions to restrain are seldom either documented or challenged; for the most part, restraints are sanctioned administratively to comply with institutional directives to maintain "safe" practice. As well, proponents of restraint reduction point out that efforts to remove restraints are infrequent, and alternatives to their use are rarely explored; once applied to an individual, restraint use is generally permanent.

As a result, policies aimed at the elimination of mechanical restraints have evolved in the U.S. The most prominent is the Omnibus Budget Reconciliation Act (OBRA) enacted by the federal government in 1987 and in effect since 1990. OBRA represents a legislative concern about the quality of care in nursing homes in general and, specifically, the wide-scale use of restraints. One of OBRA's strongest mandates declared that nursing home residents have the right to be free from mechanical restraints and that nursing homes need to find alternative solutions to their use. Under the new regulations, a physician's order for a mechanical restraint is no longer sufficient justification for use within the nursing home. The guidelines state that the facility is obligated to demonstrate that less restrictive measures to guard against falls were attempted. In those cases in which restraints are used, consent of both the resident and available family member must be obtained and documented. Also, the restraining device selected must enable the resident to attain and maintain their optimal level of physical and psychosocial function (Elon & Pawlson, 1992). As a consequence of OBRA, nursing home restraint use in the U.S. has declined dramatically, from a reported prevalence rate of 41% in 1988 to 22% in 1992, or nearly a 47% drop. The reduction of restraints has been even more dramatic in individual nursing home facilities. Werner et al. (1994) reported a decrease in mechanical restraints from 31.2% to 1.6% over a 2-year period, and that rate has remained below 3%. Kramer (1994) described a decrease in restraints from 57% to 10% occurring over a 1-year period. Meyer and colleagues (1994) reported a reduction in restraints from 35.6% to 8% over a 9-month period in a Veterans Administration nursing home. Researchers at the Jewish Home and Hospital for the Aged in New York City reported on the results of a 2-year restraint minimization project, which included 16 nursing homes from four states. These nursing homes had restraint rates of 30% or more and were in the top quarter of their state for restraint use. The group's restraint rate at the beginning of the project was 41% (851 residents in restraints); 2 years later, only 4.05% (84 residents) were restrained (American Medical Directors Association, 1994).

Despite the decrease in mechanical restraint use in nursing homes, skeptics question the success of the reduction. They argue that the elimination of restraints, while well-intentioned, may lead to an increase in falls and physical injury such as hip fractures. For instance, seat belts are a common type of restraint; by removing these devices it can be argued that it may only "free" individuals to fall out of their chairs (Schnelle et al., 1994). Some have tried to avoid using restraints but ultimately returned to using them to control problematic behaviors because nonrestraint efforts failed (Read, Bagheri, & Strickland, 1991). Further, they maintain that restraint alternatives, which call for environmental modifications and additional resident activities, entail extra staff and furnishings that are costly and may not work in preventing falls. Nursing home operators have estimated that a reduction or elimination of mechanical restraints would increase national nursing home costs by as much as $1 billion per year (Phillips et al., 1993). In many cases, however, these assumptions are ill-founded.

The aforementioned restraint reduction efforts were achieved without an increase in either falls or injurious falls, the use of psychotropic drugs in lieu of mechanical restraints, additional nursing staff, or costs to the nursing home. Meyer et al. (1994), after completing their restraint reduction program, felt that mechanical restraint use in the nursing home can be reduced to a level of 10% without resulting in a major increase in fall-related injuries. Moreover, they showed that the majority of falls were experienced by a relatively small group of patients, and felt that alternative approaches, such as close staff observation and exercise programs to improve gait and balance, were reasonable methods to prevent further falls. Werner et al. (1994) found that the use of psychotropic medications in nursing home residents decreased significantly from 34.5% to 19.5% after removal of restraints. Janelli, Kanski, and Neary (1994) recently surveyed 159 skilled nursing facilities in New York State; of these, 142 reported a decrease in restraint use that was accomplished largely without an increase in staff. Phillips and co-workers (1993) surveyed 11,932 nursing home residents in 276 facilities in seven states and found that residents free of restraints were less costly to care for than restrained residents. Thus, curtailing the use of mechanical restraints could actually reduce costs for facilities. Furthermore, studies have reported better cognitive functioning in the resident (Werner et al., 1994) and more positive, supportive employee attitudes towards restraint reduction (Sundel, Garrett, & Horn, 1994) following the elimination of mechanical restraints.

The movement to reduce mechanical restraints has affected acute care hospitals as well. Increased concern about the safety and use of restraints in hospitals by the U.S. government and the Joint Commission on Accreditation of Healthcare Organizations (JCAHO) has resulted in rigorous standards on the use of restraints (Joint Commission on Accreditation of Healthcare Organizations, 1992; Weick, 1992). Modeled after the OBRA guidelines, the JCAHO standards requires a physician's order for restraints, time limits on the application of restraints, documentation of alternative approaches to mechanical restraints, and documentation of ongoing observation and assessment of the restrained patient. While restraint reduction in acute hospitals has not been equal to that in nursing homes in the U.S., efforts in this direction are being made. For instance, Mion (1994), reporting from the results of the Hospital Outcomes Project for the Elderly (HOPE), a program aimed at addressing the needs of older hospitalized patients, found that by increasing nurses' knowledge and expertise in care of older patients, the use of physical restraints can be reduced in half. Although the prevalence of falls and injuries following this effort was not elaborated upon, researchers in the United States and other countries have demonstrated positive outcomes of restraint reduction in the acute care setting (Evans & Strumpf, 1989; Mitchell-Pedersen et al., 1985).

MANAGEMENT

Falls should not be viewed as end-stage processes, but as signs of underlying medical or environmental conditions that may be modifiable. Ordering a mechanical restraint as initial treatment in prevention is inappropriate. Thus, the onset of falling or confirmation of fall risk should first trigger an investigation to determine the cause, and, secondly, be followed by treatment aimed at modifying the underlying factors responsible. A comparable approach should be taken for behaviors such as wandering and delirium that are associated with both increased fall risk and mechanical restraint use. Exceptions to these principles may arise at times, but they are rare. Under emergency conditions, for example, when a person is at an immediate risk for falls, restraints may be considered to ensure "patient safety," but *only* for a short period of time and *never* as a substitute for surveillance. Avoiding restraints in some urgent situations may, ironically, cause the same problems that stem from their use: falls, injury, immobility, and their untoward consequences. But using restraints for an indefinite period may prove detrimental to patient care. Any decision to restrain should be a collaborative undertaking between all interested parties, such as the nurse, physician, competent patients/residents, and available family members.

If an investigation into the causes of falls or efforts to modify fall risk factors proves unsuccessful and the older person remains at risk for falls, alternative approaches to restraints should be explored. A list of potential alternatives that others have employed to guard against the risk of falls is presented in Table 9.1. (Evans & Strumpf, 1989; Evans et al., 1991; Sloane, Papougenis, & Blakeslee, 1992; Strumpf, Wagner, Evans, & Patterson, 1992; Werner et al., 1994). Several of these alternatives, such as bedrails, alarm systems, "slanting" chair seats, and other seating devices, merit further discussion to clarify their role.

BEDRAILS

Under certain conditions, a bedrail can be classified as being a mechanical restraint. According to interpretive guidelines established for long-term care facilities by the U.S. Health Care Financing Administration (Health Care Financing Administration [HCFA], 1992), bedrails are viewed

TABLE 9.1   Restraint Alternatives

Care
1. Additional nursing supervision and observation
2. Seek assistance of family members and volunteers to provide companionship
3. Daily ambulation, structured activities
4. Gait/balance training
5. Locate patient/resident near nurses' station
6. Regular toileting schedule
7. Attend to physiological needs; for example, thirst, hunger, pain, sleep, rest, exercise
8. Evaluate drugs
9. Correct sensory deficits (eyeglasses, hearing aids)

Environmental
1. Alternative seating
2. Wedge cushions, slanting seats to inhibit unsafe activity
3. Body props/cushions to support seating
4. Bed and chair alarm devices
5. Lower bed height, mattress on floor
6. Remove wheels from bed
7. Accessible call light
8. Bedrails down
9. Bedside commode
10. Safe wandering area

as restraints when they restrict an individual's freedom of movement or ability to leave the bed when desired, regardless of whether they are able to do so in a safe manner. In such cases, bedrail use cannot be justified (Donius & Rader, 1994), and alternatives to their use should be explored. If bedrails are not part of the patient care plan, they should probably be removed, since one nursing home study suggested that the inappropriate use of bedrails had much to do with the fact that they were an integral part of the bed (Sundel, Garrett, & Horn, 1994).

On the other hand, there are instances when bedrails do not qualify as restraints. Recall from earlier discussions that half bedrails can be helpful when used by patients and residents as "enablers" or devices to provide support for safe bed transfers. If the older individual prefers the use of bedrails for better bed mobility, or elects to have the bedrails elevated to prevent falls out of bed, without any intent of leaving their bed, then bedrails should not be regarded as restraints (Donius & Rader, 1994). Regardless of whether bedrails are used as "safety" or "restraining" devices, it is important to obtain consent from competent patients and residents and available family members, and to document the use of bedrails in the person's medical chart. Also, if bedrails are being used as "enablers," it is a good idea to observe the patient or resident getting out of bed periodically to ensure that bedrails are functioning safely and not as a restraint.

BED ALARM SYSTEMS

Even after instituting comprehensive bed modifications (see Chapter 8) and bedrails as enablers, a certain number of older patients and residents with poor mobility and altered cognition may still remain at fall risk. One way to resolve this problem without resorting to mechanical restraints is to use nurse call systems. These systems allow the older person to call and/or communicate directly with staff when they want to leave their bed. However, these devices are notoriously underutilized by older people. One study showed that 93% of hospitalized patients did not use a call light, even though it was within easy reach (Rodgers, 1994). Moreover, older persons with cognitive problems may not understand how and when to use the call system. As an alternative, the use of bed alarm systems may prove beneficial.

Bed alarm systems (BAS) are designed to warn nursing staff that patients who should not be attempting to leave their bed unassisted are doing so. They function by allowing the older person to maintain a free-movement zone or area for normal activity in bed, including turning around or rolling over. However, when the person leaves their bed and thus exceeds the free-movement zone, an alarm sounds, in the person's bedroom and/or the nursing station, indicating that the person is about to transfer unsafely from bed (Figure 9.1). As a result, the nurse or other staff member comes to the assistance of the person.

In addition to guarding against bed falls, BAS can be used to prevent falls in other situations, even when the person is not at risk for bed falls. In those instances, for example, when persons with poor ambulation and impaired toilet mobility leave their bed—conditions that often call for nursing assistance to prevent falls—BAS allow for early intervention by provision of assistance with ambulation and/or toileting.

A variety of BAS designs are available. Some alarms attach to both the bed and the patient. These consist of a sensor unit mounted on the headboard of the bed and a garment clip attached to the person's night garment. When the person leaves the bed, the garment clip disengages from the sensor unit and activates an alarm. Other BAS attach to the individuals themselves, and consist of a small plastic-enclosed unit that attaches to the wearer's upper leg via a fabric band. When the person's leg shifts from the horizontal to vertical position, for

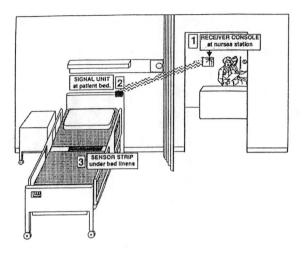

FIGURE 9.1   Bed alarm system. Courtesy of RN + Fall Prevention Systems, Inc.

example, while getting out of bed, the alarm is activated. Lastly, a few alarm systems attach to the bed. These consist of pressure-sensitive pads that are placed underneath either the bed linens or bed mattress. When the person sits up in bed, the pressure on the sensor pad is relieved, activating either a local alarm or one that sounds at the nursing station via a separate console or the existing nurse monitoring system.

For those community-dwelling older persons who are at risk for bed falls, a leg alarm can be used to alert family and other caregivers. Manufacturers of pressure-sensitive pad alarms have adapted their devices for home use as well. In addition, a pressure-sensitive mat is available for use in the home setting (Figure 9.2). This device resembles a rug and is placed on the floor along the older person's bed. When the individual leaves the bed and steps onto the mat, pressure on the mat triggers a warning alarm, via a wireless transmitter, that sounds in the caregiver's room. The mat rests securely on the floor and does not pose a tripping hazard. However, this alarm device may not function adequately in institutional settings, since floor surfaces are frequently cleaned and polished, requiring that the device be removed and replaced frequently.

A number of studies have found the BAS to be an effective strategy in preventing bed falls (Morton, 1989; Tideiksaar, Feiner, & Maby, 1993; Tideiksaar & Osterweil, 1989). Heslin et al. (1992) reported an 85% reduction in institutional bed falls while using a BAS. Furthermore, all

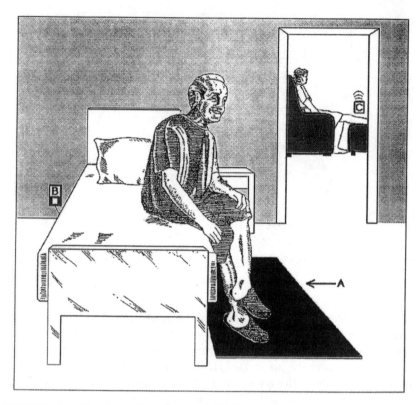

FIGURE 9.2 The SoundMat System. (A) Pressure-sensitive carpet mat. (B) Transmitter unit. (C) Receiver or alarm unit. Reprinted with permission of Tactilitics, Inc.

systems appear to be safe for patients and residents, as there are no published reports indicating that these devices have caused harm or adverse effects. Nurses in both the hospital and nursing home setting perceive bed alarms as able to reduce both the risk of falling and the need for mechanical restraints (Tideiksaar et al., 1993). Without exception, concerned family members of patients and residents prefer alarm systems over the use of restraints, citing the dignity and autonomy they offer.

Once a decision has been reached to use a BAS, individual patient characteristics should determine which type is most appropriate. There are a number of factors that may determine this choice. For example, persons suffering from dementia may become more confused and agitated by systems that attach to their bodies, such as the garment clip and leg-attached devices. Sometimes, demented individuals will remove these systems and thus negate their successful operation. Pressure-sensitive pad systems placed underneath the bed linens or mattress, completely out of view of the patient, can be used instead. Pressure-sensitive systems that have a built-in alarm time delay of several seconds are useful for persons who shift positions frequently during sleep. This type will avoid false alarms that may occur if persons simply move repeatedly off and on the pressure sensor pads while sleeping. The weight of the person can be a factor. People who weigh under 100 pounds may not be able to apply sufficient weight to keep the alarm from sounding in certain pressure-sensitive systems, especially those that fit underneath mattresses. Anti-decubiti (pressure sores) pads added to the mattress may compound the problem. Under these circumstances, pressure-sensitive pads that rest underneath the bed linens, person-attached systems, or pressure-sensitive floor mats may be more appropriate choices. However, a certain amount of caution is advised when using leg-attached and floormat systems. As opposed to bed/person and bed-attached systems that signal risk immediately when the individual sits up in bed, these systems detect unsafe activity at a later stage; the older person is already out of bed and standing when the alarm is activated.

If bed alarm systems fail to achieve their intended purpose, or create excessive numbers of false alarms, nurses may quickly abandon the use of these devices and resort once again, often in frustration, to the use of mechanical restraints. As a result, BAS need to be effective in detecting unplanned bed exits by patients and residents, user-friendly, and easy to install, operate, and maintain for nurses.

All BAS, even when appropriately selected, raise some common concerns. The efficacy of any alarm system is dependent on the response time of the nursing staff (their ability to hear the alarm and respond to offer assistance). One of the leading concerns of nurses and others is that by the time the alarm sounds, the staff member may not be able to respond quickly enough to prevent a fall, particularly if the person's bedroom is located a considerable distance from the nursing station. One solution is to make it difficult for the patient to get out of bed. A decubiti-preventive water mattress filled to one-half capacity and placed on the bed, in combination with full-length bedrails, is very effective in limiting quick bed exits even in the most agile person, thus providing nurses with sufficient response time. Skeptics contend that these systems are expensive both in terms of actual cost and manpower; that is, an increased nursing staff is needed to assist patients and residents. However, if bed alarms prevent falls and injury and avoid restraints, they may well be worth the cost. Also, BAS may actually save money on staff expenditures, especially by reducing the frequency of nurse monitoring every hour to prevent bed falls (Tideiksaar et al., 1993). When measured against the costs of injuries sustained from bed falls and nursing time spent in caring for persons suffering from the complications of falls and restraints, anecdotal evidence indicates that bed alarms are likely to be cost-effective, although studies are needed to document this. Most devices can be billed to DRGs (Diagnostic Related Groupings) and to other third-party payers by charging a daily monitoring fee or by budgeting the expense under capital equipment.

In addition, questions on legal liability and bed alarm use need to be considered. Despite the use of these systems, the risk of bed falls and injuries still exist. Although this has not yet been challenged by the courts, hospitals and nursing homes would do well to assume a defensive position, if only to protect themselves. First, as many as 75% of institutional falls take place during transfers out of bed (Rubenstein et al., 1983). Secondly, while lawsuits involving falls are infrequent, most that are filed involve falls out of bed (Johnson, 1990). Documentation would entail charting the use of bed alarm devices in the patient's chart as well as recording the rationale for their use. This procedure provides the legal system, lawyers, judge, and jury, with evidence of an attempt to prevent injury by using a BAS or at least seems to indicate that the facility and its employees are aware of the potential problems presented by eliminating restraints. Also, the risks and benefits of BAS should be explained to patients, residents (if competent), and family members, and written consent should be obtained from these parties as well.

SEATING ALTERNATIVES TO RESTRAINTS

Those older persons who remain at fall risk because of poor chair transfers and inadequately modified seating (see Chapter 8) may benefit from one of several different types of seating designs that can serve as "restraint-free" alternatives. A deep-seated, soft-cushioned chair or recliner, or a wedge cushion placed on an existing chair seat, with its widest part placed toward the front of the seat, can be used. Also, a beanbag chair filled with styrofoam pellets may be safer than a conventional chair (Johnson, 1991). Similar types of seating alternatives can be used in the home setting, although for most persons a deep-seated easy chair or sofa will be sufficient. These furnishings work by keeping an individual's buttocks at a level lower than the knees, making it exceedingly difficult for the person to rise. Their purpose is to keep the person with unsafe mobility from getting up independently.

Also, they keep the individual from sliding down and falling off the seat. However, caution is advised, as this sitting position puts increased pressure on the buttocks, particularly in the case of thin persons with decreased fat padding, thus placing them at risk for pressure sores. Furthermore, whenever these seating alternatives are used, make certain that they achieve their purpose. Observe on a routine basis if the individual's transfer ability is inhibited. For instance, some types of wedge cushions tend to wear out over time, and will no longer serve to prevent the person from leaving their chair.

While these seating alternatives are still considered "restraints" as they inhibit autonomy—the individual's ability to get up from a chair if the desire is there—they may not be the ideal solution for all individuals. For some, however, these alternatives may avoid the detrimental effects associated with the use of restraints. First of all, they may be more acceptable "psychologically" for both older individuals and their family members than are waist or vest restraints, and even some restraint alternatives, such as self-release waist belts, as these alternatives might remove the stigma that occurs with the visualization of being "tied down." Moreover, Newbern and Lindsey (1994) reported that family members may not be upset with the use of mechanical restraints per se, but more with what these devices symbolize: for example, frailty and dependency. Therefore, "out of sight, out of mind" (as they say) is a good rule to follow. Secondly, these seating alternatives may produce less agitation, combativeness, and thrusting about than mechanical restraints, thus decreasing cognitive distress and other adverse effects such as skin abrasions and asphyxiation. These devices also allow individuals to shift their seating positions more easily than with restraints in place, and thereby decrease the risk of pressure sores.

If these seating choices are unsuitable, a chair alarm system is an additional option. These are battery-powered portable devices that attach to either a chair or wheelchair, and are similar both in design and function to BAS. They consist either of a cord that attaches to the person's garment or a pressure-sensitive pad that rests on the seat or against the backrest. Chair alarms allow the individual to shift about in their seat, thus avoiding pressure sores, and to maintain adequate limits of reach, such as when obtaining an object from a tabletop. However, when the person bends too far forward such as when picking an object off the floor, slides down in their seat, or moves to the edge of the chair prior to standing, they exceed their "safe zone" of movement, which triggers the alarm and alerts the nursing staff. Caution is advised when using chair alarms since they may not be able prevent a fall in progress; the time period between the alarm sounding and the ability of the nurse to arrive in a timely fashion to offer assistance is rather short. However, similar to the bed alarm, the chair alarm can be employed to detect other fall-risk activities requiring nursing assistance (i.e., poor ambulation and toileting). The issues surrounding their efficacy, cost, and risk of legal liability are similar to those of bed alarm systems.

IMPLEMENTATION

There are a number of health professionals and facilities that have developed restraint reduction programs (Blakeslee, Goldman, & Papougenis, 1990; Braun & Lipson, 1993; Ejaz et al., 1994; Evans & Strumpf, 1992; Kramer, 1994; Mion & Mercurio, 1992; Werner et al., 1994). According to this literature, there are several basic operational steps that facilities can take to ensure a successful restraint reduction program.

The first and perhaps most important step is to recognize that mechanical restraints may be overutilized, or that they are not achieving their purpose—preventing falls—or that they may be causing patients and residents undue harm. Review the current restraint practices, attitudes of employees toward their use, and institutional policies that govern the use of mechanical restraints. A checklist of questions is articulated in Table 9.2. The intent of this exercise is to determine the prevalence of restraint use; to determine whether or not restraints are employed for the patients' and residents' own good or self-interest (i.e., they are effective and free of adverse effects); to examine the availability, utilization, and effectiveness of restraint alternatives; and whether policies are viable and provide staff with appropriate direction on the practice of restraints.

This process is best accomplished by the formation of a task force or management group of interested individuals. This group is accountable for rewriting restraint policies, developing staff education, planning restraint alternative approaches, and initiating and following through with a program of restraint reduction. Consequently, this group should ideally consist of individuals in leadership positions, for example, administrator, directors of medicine and nursing, and head of quality assurance, in order to enact policy changes and purchase any furnishings and adaptive equipment that may be required. In addition, the presence of "front line" professionals (nurses, nursing aides, physical and occupational therapists) who actually have the day-to-day responsibility of implementing policy changes and alternative approaches is

TABLE 9.2   Determining the Prevalence, Practice, and Adverse Effects of Mechanical Restraints

Inquire about the following:

1. To what extent are mechanical restraints used?
2. Under what circumstances or conditions are mechanical restraints ordered? Why?
3. Are mechanical restraints the first or last choice of treatment?
4. What types of restraining devices are most often used?
5. Are mechanical restraints used continuously or intermittently? Under what conditions?
6. Are mechanical restraints effective in controlling the indicated behavior? If not, why?
7. Are patients/residents (if competent) and family members consulted on the need for mechanical restraints? Are they given the right of refusal?
8. If patients/residents and/or family members refuse the use of mechanical restraints, what procedures are in place to ensure "safety"?
9. Are restrained individuals monitored for physiological needs (for example, toileting, fluids, nutrition, regular activity)? Are they observed for adverse effects? How often and by whom?
10. What forms of restraint alternatives are available? How often are they employed? Under what circumstances? Are they effective? If not, why?
11. Are institutional mechanical restraint policies clear as to:
    (a) The types of conditions or situations in which restraints can and cannot be used
    (b) The assessment procedure for ordering and discontinuing restraints
    (c) The responsibility of ordering, monitoring, and documenting restraint use
    (d) The responsibility for ordering, monitoring, and documenting restraint alternatives
    (e) Periodic updating of restraint policies
    (f) Responsibility of medical/nursing staff members to be aware of the content in restraint policy statements

Note: From *Falls in older persons. Prevention and management in hospitals and nursing homes,* pp. 110–111, by R. Tideiksaar, 1993, Boulder, CO: Tactilitics. Adapted with permission.

required. Lay individuals to represent the views of family members are also of help in the group.

The process of restraint reduction is, in essence, a three-stage process. First, the staff's awareness must be increased, both of the problem and knowledge of alternative approaches to the use of restraints. This is accomplished by holding an educational inservice program (see Table 9.3) for all employees, including physicians, as they have the responsibility of either ordering or not ordering restraints. The second

TABLE 9.3   Content for Educational Inservice on Mechanical Restraints

Reasons for Restraint Use
  Prevalence
  Prevention of falls
  Prevention of wandering
  Seating/positioning
  Treatment interference (e.g., with intravenous lines, feeding tubes, urinary
    catheters)

Adverse Effects
  Loss of autonomy
  Loss of dignity
  Agitation/depression
  Physiological effects (immobility, pressure sores, joint contractures, muscle
    weakness, etc.)
  Family/staff discomfort

Legal
  Current OBRA and JCAHO regulations concerning mechanical restraint use
  Institutional policies regarding mechanical restraint use
  Staff liability

Restraint Alternatives
  Assess fall risk and modify risk factors
  Devices to support seating (wedge cushions, props, slanting chairs, etc.)
  Bed and chair alarm systems
  Bedrails as "enablers"
  Bathroom equipment (grab bars, toilet risers, etc.)
  Staff/family observation of patients/residents

stage consists of rewriting restraint policies to coincide with restraint reduction efforts. The policy statement should be clear and simple and provide staff with step-by-step guidelines to follow. A set of suggested criteria to follow in developing a policy statement is listed in Table 9.4. These documents can serve as a defense against potential legal liability, as they help to illustrate attempts by the institution and their staff to practice reasonable standards of practice. The final stage of the process consists of actually starting to eliminate mechanical restraints. Although this process may encounter several setbacks, there appear to be a number of key elements that can ensure success (Table 9.5). Maintaining a zero tolerance of mechanical restraints may be difficult to achieve in all instances; however, it is important to recognize that "good" geriatric care consists of helping older people to achieve maximum independence, and that any sustained use of restraints is in direct opposition to this goal.

TABLE 9.4 Criteria for Developing Mechanical Restraint Policy

Institutional restraint policy should be clear and simple to understand and address the following:

1. Define what a mechanical restraint is and describe the types of restraining devices available in the institution.
2. Define and categorize the types of situations in which restraints may be used and not used.
3. Define the assessment procedure for restraint application and discontinuation.
4. Define who has the responsibility for ordering and discontinuing restraints.
5. Define the procedure and staff responsibilities for documenting restraint use and monitoring.
6. Define the types of circumstances when restraint alternatives should be considered.
7. Define the types of restraint alternatives available.
8. Define the procedure to follow when patients/residents and/or family members refuse restraints.
9. Define a procedure for ensuring that all medical/nursing staff are aware of restraint policy and that its contents are updated periodically.

Note: From *Falls in older persons. Prevention and management in hospitals and nursing homes*, p. 113, by R. Tideiksaar, 1993. Boulder, CO: Tactilitics. Adapted with permission.

TABLE 9.5 Key Elements in Attempting to Reduce Mechanical Restraints

1. Administrative support for nonuse of mechanical restraints and consideration of restraint alternatives
2. Adequate staffing and financial resources for restraint-free efforts
3. Involvement of all staff in restraint-free program (for example, physicians, nurses, physical and occupational therapists, social workers)
4. Administrative support to decrease staff fear of legal liability or other repercussions in the event of falls
5. Ongoing staff education regarding types of restraint alternatives
6. Education and involvement of family members in restraint-free efforts
7. Fall prevention and rehabilitative program
8. Adequate time for implementation of restraint-free program; start with the easy cases and move on to the more difficult situations

CONCLUSION

Falling is a complex, debilitating problem that takes a tremendous toll on older individuals, their families, and the health care system. While it is unrealistic and unreasonable to assume that all falls are preventable, clearly the problem can be significantly reduced from its current levels. Even such simple and relatively cost-free measures such as eliminating offending medications and environmental hazards and providing easy-to-perform exercises, modest environmental modification, and adaptive equipment can make a huge difference in reducing falls and their complications. While many other opportunities for intervention are evident, it is obvious that there is still much work to be done in the prevention and control of falls at both the community and institutional level. However, acquiring a base of knowledge is an important start. An awareness of falls (e.g., their extent, complications, causes, and risk factors), and strategies and approaches aimed toward their prevention can in turn, hopefully, lead to greater clinical attention toward the problem of falls in older people.

References

Adams, W. L., Magruder-Habib, K., Trued, S., & Broome, H. L. (1992). Alcohol abuse in elderly emergency department patients. *Journal of the American Geriatrics Society, 40,* 1236–1240.

Agarwal, N., Reyes, J. D., Westerman, D. A., & Cayten, C. G. (1986). Factors influencing DRG 210 (hip fracture) reimbursement. *Journal of Trauma, 26,* 426–431.

Agate, J. (1966). Accidents to old people in their homes. *British Medical Journal, 2,* 785–788.

Agre, J. C., Pierce, L. E., Raab, D. M., McAdams, M., & Smith, E. (1988). Light resistance and stretching exercise in elderly women: Effect upon strength. *Archives of Physical Medicine and Rehabilitation, 69,* 273–276.

Aisen, P. S., Deluca, T., & Lawlor, B. A. (1992). Falls among geropsychiatry inpatients are associated with prn medications for agitation. *International Journal of Geriatric Psychiatry, 7,* 709–712.

Albarede, J. L., Lemieux, A., Vellas, B., & Grouix, B. (1989). Psychological factors in falls in elderly patients. *Canadian Journal of Psychiatry, 34,* 94–96.

Alexander, B. H., Rivara, F. P., & Wolf, M. E. (1992). The cost and frequency of hospitalization for fall-related injuries in older adults. *American Journal of Public Health, 82,* 1020–1023.

Allman, R. M. (1989). Pressure ulcers among the elderly. *New England Journal of Medicine, 320,* 850–853.

American Medical Directors Association. (1994). Minimizing use of restraints. *Nursing Home Medicine, 2,* 4–7.

Andrews, C., & Steinberg, E. (1984). Hospital readmissions in the Medicare population. *New England Journal of Medicine, 311,* 1349–1353.

Andrews, K. (1986). Relevance of readmission of elderly patients discharged from a geriatric unit. *Journal of the American Geriatrics Society, 34,* 5–11.

Aniansson, A., Rundgren, A., & Sperling, L. (1980). Evaluation in functional capacity in activities of daily living in 70-year-old men and women. *Scandinavian Journal of Rehabilitation Medicine, 12,* 145–154.

Archea, J., Collins, B., & Stahl, F. (1979). *Guidelines for stair safety, BSS 120.* Washington DC: National Bureau of Standards.

Archea, J. C. (1985). Environmental factors associated with stair ascending by the elderly. *Clinics in Geriatric Medicine, 1,* 555–569.

Arfken, C. L., Lach, H. W., Birge, S. J., & Miller, J. P. (1994). The prevalence and correlates of fear of falling in elderly persons living in the community. *American Journal of Public Health, 84,* 565–570.

Aronow, W. S., & Ahn, C. (1994). Postprandial hypotension in 499 elderly persons in a long-term health facility. *Journal of the American Geriatrics Society, 42,* 930–932.

Asada, T., Kariya, T., Kitajiwa, E., Kakumar, T., & Yoshioka, M. (1993). Falls among community-dwelling psychogeriatric patients. *International Journal of Geriatric Psychiatry, 9,* 17–23.

Asher, R. A. J. (1947). The dangers of going to bed. *British Medical Journal, 2,* 967–968.

Ashley, M. J., Gryfe, C. I., & Amies, A. (1977). A longitudinal study of falls in an elderly population II. Some circumstances of falling. *Age and Ageing, 6,* 211–220.

Askham, J., Glucksman, E., Owens, P., Swift, C., Tinker, A., & Yu, G. (1990). *Home and leisure accident research: A review of research on falls among elderly people.* London: Institute of Gerontology, King's College.

Axtell, L. A., & Yasuda, Y. L. (1993). Assistive devices and home modification. *Clinics in Geriatric Medicine, 9,* 803–821.

Ayalon, J., Simkin, A., Leichter, I., & Raitman, S. (1987). Dynamic bone loading exercises for postmenopausal females: Effects on the density of the distal radius. *Archives of Physical Medicine and Rehabilitation, 68,* 280–283.

Azar, G. J., & Lawton, A. H. (1964). Gait and stepping as factors in the frequent falls of elderly women. *Gerontologist, 4,* 83–84.

Baker, S. P., & Harvey, A. H. (1985). Fall injuries in the elderly. *Clinics in Geriatric Medicine, 1,* 501–512.

Baker, S. P., O'Neill, B., Ginsburg, M. J., & Guohua, L. (1992). *The injury fact book* (2d ed.) New York: Oxford University Press.

Baloh, R. W. (1992). Dizziness in older people. *Journal of the American Geriatrics Society, 40,* 713–721.

Baloh, R. W., Fife, T. D., Zwerling, L., Socotch, T., Jacobson, K., Bell, T., & Beykirch, K. (1994). Comparison of static and dynamic posturography in young and older normal people. *Journal of the American Geriatrics Society, 42,* 405–412.

Baloh, R. W., Spain, S., Socotch, T. M., Jacobson, K. M., & Bell, T. (1995). Posturography and balance problems in older people. *Journal of the American Geriatrics Society, 43,* 638–644.

Baraff, L. J., Bernstein, E., Bradley, K., Franken, C., Gerson, L. W., Hannegan, S. R., Lee, S., Marotta, M., & Wolfson, A. B. (1992). Perceptions of emergency care by the elderly: Results of multicenter focus group interviews. *Annals of Emergency Medicine, 21,* 814–818.

Barker, J. C., & Mitteness, L. S. (1988). Nocturia in the elderly. *The Gerontologist, 28,* 99–104.

Bassey, E. J., Fiatarone, M. A., O'Neil, E. F., Kelly, M., Evans, W. J., & Lipsitz, L. A. (1992). Leg extensor power and functional performance in very old men and women. *Clinical Science, 82,* 321–327.

Bates, D. W., Pruess, K., Sourey, P., & Platt, R. (1995). Serious falls in hospitalized patients: Correlates and resource utilization. *American Journal of Medicine, 99,* 137–143.

Baum, C., Edward, D., Leavitt, K., Grant, E., & Devel, R. (1988). Performance components in senile dementia of the Alzheimer type: Motor planning, language, and memory. *Occupational Therapy Journal of Research, 8,* 356–368.

Baylor, A. M., & Spirduso, W. W. (1988). Systemic aerobic exercise and components of reaction time in older women. *Journal of Gerontology, 43,* 121–126.

Belfield, P. W., Young, J. B., Bagnall, W. E., & Mulley, G. P. (1987). Deliberate falls in the elderly. *Age and Ageing, 16,* 123–124.

Bellomo, G., Santucci, S., & Parnetti, A. L. (1988). Meal-induced arterial blood pressure variation in the elderly. *Gerontology, 34,* 311–314.

Berfenstam, R., Lagerberg, D., & Smedby, B. (1969). Victim characteristics in fatal home accidents. *Acta Socio-Medica Scandinavica, 1,* 145–164.

Berg, K., Wood-Dauphinee, S. L., Williams, J. I., & Gayton, D. (1989). Measuring balance in the elderly: Preliminary development of an instrument. *Physiotherapy Canada, 41,* 304–311.

Berg, K. O., Wood-Dauphinee, S. L., Williams, J. I., & Maki, B. (1992). Measuring balance in the elderly: Validation of an instrument. *Canadian Journal of Public Health, 2,* S7–S11.

Bergman, B., & Sjostrand, J. (1992). Vision and visual disability in the daily life of a representative population sample aged 82 years. *Acta Ophthalmologica, 70,* 33–43.

Bergman, H., & Clarfield, A. M. (1991). Appropriateness of patient transfers from a nursing home to an acute-care hospital: A study of emergency room visits and hospital admissions. *Journal of the American Geriatrics Society, 39,* 1164–1168.

Bergstrom, G., Bjelle, A., Sorensen, L. B., Sundh, V., & Svanborg, A. (1985). Prevalence of symptoms and signs of joint impairment at age 79. *Scandinavian Journal of Rehabilitation Medicine, 17,* 173–182.

Bernstein, A. B., & Schur, C. L. (1990). Expenditures for unintentional injuries among the elderly. *Journal of Aging and Health, 2,* 157–178.

Berry, G., Fisher, R. H., & Lang, S. (1981). Detrimental incidents, including falls, in an elderly institutional population. *Journal of the American Geriatrics Society, 29,* 322–324.

Berryman, E., Gaskin, D., Jones, A., Tolley, F., & MacMullen, J. (1989). Point by point: Predicting elders' falls. *Geriatric Nursing, 10,* 199–201.

Bhala, R. P., O'Donnell, J., & Thoppil, E. (1982). Phobic fear of falling and its clinical management. *Physical Therapy, 62,* 187–190.

Black, F. O., Wall, C., & Nashner, L. M. (1983). Effects of visual and support surface orientation references upon postural control in vestibular deficient subjects. *Acta Otolaryngologica, 95,* 199–201.

Blake, A. J., Morgan, K., Bendall, M. J., Dallosso, H., Ebrahim, S. B. J., Arie, T. H. D., Tentem, P. H., & Bassey, E. J. (1988). Falls by elderly people at home: prevalence and associated factors. *Age and Ageing, 17,* 365–372.

Blake, C., & Morfitt, J. M. (1986). Falls and staffing in a residential home for elderly people. *Public Health, 100,* 385–391.

Blakeslee, J., Goldman, B., Papougenis, D., & Torrell, C. A. (1991). Making the transition to restraint-free care. *Journal of Gerontological Nursing, 17,* 4–8.

Blanke, D. J., & Hageman, P. A. (1989). Comparison of gait of young men and elderly men. *Physical Therapy, 69,* 144–148.

Blanpied, P., & Smidt, G. L. (1993). The difference in stiffness of the active plantar flexors between young and elderly human females. *Journal of Gerontology, 48,* M58–M63.

Bohannon, R. W., Larkin, P. A., Cook, A. C., Gear, J., & Singer, J. (1984). Decrease in timed balance test scores with aging. *Physical Therapy, 64,* 1067–1070.

Bonar, S. K., Tinetti, M. E., Speechley, M., & Conney, L. M. (1990). Factors associated with short versus long-term skilled nursing facility placement among community-living hip fracture patients. *Journal of the American Geriatrics Society, 38,* 1139–1144.

Borkhan, J. M., & Quirk, M. (1992). Expectations and outcomes after hip fracture among the elderly. *International Journal of Aging and Human Development, 34,* 339–350.

Boucher, C. A. (1959). Accidents among old persons. *Geriatrics, 14,* 293–300.

Brady, R., Chester, F. R., Pierce, L. L., Salter, J. P., Schreck, S., & Radziewicz, R. (1993). Geriatric falls: Prevention strategies for the staff. *Journal of Gerontological Nursing, 19,* 26–32.

Braun, J. V., & Lipson, S. (Eds.) (1993). *Toward a restraint-free environment: Reducing the use of physical and chemical restraints in long-term care and acute care settings.* Baltimore: Health Professions Press.

Brennan, F., Gordon, N., & Zimmerman, S. (1991). Family attitudes on restraint removal. *The Gerontologist, 31* (Special Issue II), 32.

Breslau, N. A. (1992). Osteoporosis management. *Seminars in Nephrology, 12,* 116–126.

Brians, L. K., Alexander, K., Grotta, P., Chen, R. W. H., & Dumas, V. (1991). The development of the RISK tool for fall prevention. *Rehabilitation Nursing, 16,* 67–69.

Briggs, R. C., Gossman, M. R., Birch, R., Drews, J. E., & Shaddeau, S. A. (1989). Balance performance among noninstitutionalized elderly women. *Physical Therapy, 69,* 748–756.

Brinkman, J. R., & Perry, J. (1985). Rate and range of knee motion during ambulation in health and arthritic subjects. *Physical Therapy, 65,* 1055–1060.

Bristow, M. F., & Clare, A. W. (1992). Prevalence and characteristics of at-risk drinkers among elderly acute medical inpatients. *British Journal of Addiction, 87,* 291–294.

Brocklehurst, J. C., Exton-Smith, A. N., Lempert-Barber, S. M., Hunt, L. P., & Palmer, M. K. (1978). Fracture of the femur in old age: A two centre study of associated clinical factors and the cause of the fall. *Age and Ageing, 7,* 7–15.

Brocklehurst, J. C., Robertson, D., & James-Groom, P. (1982). Clinical correlates of sway in old age-sensory modalities. *Age and Ageing, 11,* 1–10.

Brody, E. M. (1981). "Women in the middle" and family help to older people. *Gerontologist, 21,* 471–480.

Brody, E. M., Kleban, M. H., Moss, M. S., & Kleban, E. (1984). Predictors of falls among institutionalized women with Alzheimer's disease. *Journal of the American Geriatrics Society, 32,* 877–882.

Brody, J. A., Brock, D. B., & Williams, T. F. (1987). Trends in the health of the elderly population. *Annual Review of Public Health, 8,* 211–234.

Brown, M. & Holloszy, J. O. (1991). Effects of a low-intensity exercise program on selected physical performance characteristic of 60- to 70-year-olds. *Aging, 3,* 129–139.

Brownlee, M. G., Banks, M. A., Crosbie, W. J., Crosbie, J., Meldrum, F., & Nimmo, M. A. (1989). Consideration of spatial orientation mechanisms as related to elderly fallers. *Gerontology, 35,* 323–331.

Brungardt, G. S. (1994). Patient restraints: New guidelines for a less restrictive approach. *Geriatrics, 49,* 43–50.

Bruno, P., & Craven, R. (1983). Risk factors for falls among the elderly. *The Gerontologist, 23,* 260.

Buchner, D. M., Hornbrook, M. C., Kutner, N. G., Tinetti, M. E., Org, M. G., Mulrow, C. D., Schechtman, K. B., Gerety, M. B., Fiatarone, M. A., Wolf, S. L., Rossiter, T., Arfken, C., Kanten, K., Lipsitz, L. A., Sattin, R. W., DeNiho, L. A., & The

FICSIT Group. (1993). Development of the common data base for the FICSIT trials. *Journal of the American Geriatrics Society, 41,* 297–308.

Buchner, D. M., & Larson, E. B. (1987). Falls and fractures in patients with Alzheimer type dementia. *Journal of the American Medical Association, 257,* 1492–1495.

Burton, L. C., German, P. S., Rovner, B. W., & Brant, L. J. (1992). Physical restraint use and cognitive decline among nursing home residents. *Journal of the American Geriatrics Society, 40,* 811–816.

Byers, V., Arrington, M. E., & Finstuen, K. (1990). Predictive risk factors associated with stroke patient falls in acute care settings. *Journal of Neuroscience Nursing, 22,* 147–154.

Cacha, C. A. (1979). An analysis of the 1976 incident reports of the Carillon nursing home. *Journal of the American Health Care Association, 5,* 29–33.

Calder, C. J., & Kirby, R. L. (1990). Fatal wheelchair-related accidents in the United States. *American Journal of Physical Medicine and Rehabilitation, 69,* 184–190.

Caley, L. M., & Pinchoff, D. M. (1994). A comparison study of patient falls in a psychiatric setting. *Hospital and Community Psychiatry, 45,* 823–825.

Cameron, A. (1991). Community alarm systems in Scotland. *Home Healthcare Services Quarterly, 13,* 149–158.

Campbell, A. J. (1991). Drug treatment as a cause of falls in old age: A review of the offending agents. *Drugs and Aging, 1,* 289–302.

Campbell, A. J., Borrie, M. J., & Spears, G. F. (1989). Risk factors for falls in a community-based prospective study of people 70 years and older. *Journal of Gerontology, 44,* M112–M117.

Campbell, A. J., Borrie, M. J., Spears, G. F., Jackson, S. L., Brown, J. S., & Fitzgerald, J. L. (1990). Circumstances and consequences of falls experienced by a community population 70 years and over during a prospective study. *Age and Ageing, 19,* 136–141.

Campbell, A. J., Reinken, J., Allan, B. C., & Martinez, G. S. (1981). Falls in old age: A study of frequency and related factors. *Age and Ageing, 10,* 264–270.

Campbell, A. J., Spears, G. F., & Borrie, M. J. (1990). Examination by logistic regression modelling of the variables which increase the relative risk of elderly women falling. *Journal of Clinical Epidemiology, 43,* 1415–1420.

Campbell, A. J., Spears, G. F. S., Borrie, M. J., & Fitzgerald, J. L. (1988). Falls, elderly women and the cold. *Gerontology, 34,* 205–208.

Cape, R. (1978). Aging: Its complex management. New York: Harper & Row.

Cape, R. (1983). Freedom from restraints. *Gerontologist, 23,* 217.

Carson, C., Archea, J., Margulis, S., & Carson, F. (1978). *Safety on stairs, BSS 108.* Washington, DC: National Bureau of Standards.

Catchen, H. (1983). Repeaters: Inpatient accidents among the hospitalized elderly. *Gerontologist, 23,* 273–276.

Catz, A., Ron, S., Solzi, P., & Korczyn, A. D. (1994). The vestibulo-ocular reflex and disequilibrium after hemispheric stroke. *American Journal of Physical Medicine and Rehabilitation, 73,* 36–39.

Cauley, J. A., Cummings, S. R., Seeley, D. G., Black, D., Browner, W., Kuller, L. H., Nevitt, M. C., & Study of Osteoporotic Fracture Research Group (1993). Effects of thiazide diuretic therapy on bone mass, fractures, and falls. *Annals of Internal Medicine, 118,* 666–673.

Cauley, J. A., Seeley, D. G., Ensrud, K., Ettinger, B., Black, D., Cummings, S. R., &

Study of Osteoporotic Fracture Research Group (1995). Estrogen replacement therapy and fractures in older women. *Annals of Internal Medicine, 122,* 9–16.

Ceder, L., Thorngren, K. G., & Wallden, B. (1980). Prognstic indicators and early home rehabilitation in elderly patients with hip fractures. *Clinical Orthopedics, 152,* 173–184.

Chandler, J. M., & Duncan, P. W. (1993). Balance and falls in the elderly: Issues in evaluation and treatment. In A. A. Guccione (Ed.), *Geriatric physical therapy* (pp 237–251). St. Louis: Mosby.

Chandler, J. M., Duncan, P. W., & Studenski, S. A. (1990). Balance performance on the postural stress test: Comparison of young adults, healthy elderly, and fallers. *Physical Therapy, 70,* 410–415.

Chao, E. Y., Laughman, R. K., Schneider, E., & Stauffer, R. N. (1983). Normative data of knee joint motion and ground reaction forces in adult level walking. *Journal of Biomechanics, 16,* 219–233.

Chapuy, M. C., Arlot, M. E., Duboeuf, F., Brun, J., Grouzet, B., Arnaud, S., Delmas, P. D., & Meunier, P. J. (1992). Vitamin D3 and calcium to prevent hip fractures in elderly women. *New England Journal of Medicine, 327,* 1637–1642.

Charette, S. I., McEvoy, I., Pyka, G., Snow-Harter, C., Evido, D., Wiswell, R. A., & Marcus, R. (1991). Muscle hypertrophy response to resistance training in older women. *Journal of Applied Physiology, 70,* 1912–1916.

Chen, H. C., Ashton-Miller, J. A., Alexander, N. B., & Schultz, A. B. (1991). Stepping over obstacles: Gait patterns of healthy young and old adults. *Journal of Gerontology, 46,* M196–M203.

Chen Sea, M. J., Henderson, A., & Cermak, S. A. (1993). Patterns of visual spatial inattention and their functional significance in stroke patients. *Archives of Physical Medicine and Rehabilitation, 74,* 355–360.

Chow, R., Harrison, J. E., & Notarius, C. (1987). Effect of two randomized exercise programmes on bone mass of healthy postmenopausal women. *British Medical Journal, 295,* 1441–1444.

Christenson, M. A. (1990). Aging in the designed environment. *Physical and Occupational Therapy in Geriatrics, 8,* 3–30.

Clark, G. (1985). A study of falls among elderly hospitalized patients. *Australian Journal of Advanced Nursing, 2,* 34–44.

Clark, L. P., Dion, D. M., & Barker, W. H. (1990). Taking to bed: Rapid functional decline in an independently mobile older population living in an intermediate-care facility. *Journal of the American Geriatrics Society, 38,* 967–972.

Clark, R. D., Lord, S. R., & Webster, I. W. (1993). Clinical parameters associated with falls in an elderly population. *Gerontology, 39,* 117–123.

Cogan, D. G. (1985). Visual disturbances with focal progressive dementing disease. *American Journal of Ophthalmology, 100,* 68–72.

Colledge, N. R., Cantley, P., Peaston, I., Brash, H., Lewis, S., & Wilson, J. A. (1994). Ageing and balance: The measurement of spontaneous sway by posturography. *Gerontology, 40,* 273–278.

Colling, J., & Park, D. (1983). Home, safe home. *Journal of Gerontological Nursing, 9,* 175–179.

Collopy, B., Boyle, P., & Jennings, B. (1991). *New directions in nursing home ethics: A Hasting Center report.* Briarcliff, NY: Hastings Center.

Connell, B. R. (1993). Patterns of naturally occurring falls among frail nursing home residents. *The Gerontologist, 33* (Special Issue), 58.

Conright, K. C., Evans, J. P., Nassralla, S. M., Tran, M. V., Silver, A. J., & Morley, J. A. (1990). A walking program improves gait and balance in nursing home residents. *Journal of the American Geriatrics Society, 38,* 1267.

Cooper, C., Barker, D. J. P., & Wickman, C. (1988). Physical activity, muscle strength, and calcium intake in fracture of the proximal femur in Britain. *British Medical Journal, 297,* 1443–1446.

Corbett, C., & Pennypacker, B. (1992). Using a quality improvement team to reduce patient falls. *Journal of Hospital Quality, 14,* 38–54.

Coroni-Hantley, J., Brock, D. B., Ostfeld, A., Taylor, J. O., & Wallace, R. B. (Eds.) (1986). *Established populations for epidemiologic studies of the elderly, resource data book.* NIH Pub. No. 86-2443. Bethesda, MD: National Institutes of Health.

Covington, D. L., Maxwell, J. G., & Clancy, T. V. (1993). Hospital resources used to treat the injured elderly at North Carolina trauma centers. *Journal of the American Geriatrics Society, 41,* 847–852.

Craig, G. M. (1994). Clinical presentation of orthostatic hypotension. *Postgraduate Medical Journal, 70,* 638–642.

Crane, M. G., & Harris, J. J. (1976). Effect of aging on renin activity and aldosterone excretion. *Journal of Laboratory and Clinical Medicine, 87,* 947–959.

Crilly, R. G., Richardson, L. D., Roth, J. H., Vandervoort, A. A., Hayes, K. L., & MacKenzie, R. A. (1987). Postural stability and Colles' fracture. *Age and Ageing, 16,* 133–138.

Crilly, R. G., Willems, D. A., Trenholm, K., Vandervoort, A. A., Hayes, K. C., & Delaquerriere-Richardson, L. F. D. (1989). Effect of exercise on postural sway in the elderly. *Gerontology, 351,* 137–143.

Cronin-Golomb, A., Corkin, S., Rizzo, J. F., Cohen, J., Growdon, J. H., & Banks, K. S. (1991). Visual dysfunction in Alzheimer's disease: Relationship to normal aging. *Annals of Neurology, 29,* 41–52.

Cronin-Golomb, A., Corkin, S., & Growden, J. H. (1987). Contrast sensitivity in Alzheimer's disease. *Journal of the Ophthalmology Society of America, 4,* 7.

Crosbie, W. J., Nimmo, M. A., Banks, M. A., Brownlee, M. G., & Meldrum, F. (1989). Standing balance responses in two populations of elderly women: A pilot study. *Archives of Physical Medicine and Rehabilitation, 70,* 751–754.

Cumming, R. G., Kelsey, J. L., & Nevitt, M. C. (1990). Methodologic issues in the study of frequent and recurrent health problems: Falls in the elderly. *Annals of Epidemiology, 1,* 49–56.

Cumming, R. G., & Klineberg, R. J. (1993). Psychotropic, thiazide diuretics and hip fractures in the elderly. *Medical Journal of Australia, 158,* 414–417.

Cumming, R. G., & Klineberg, R. J. (1994a). Case control study of risk factors for hip fractures in the elderly. *American Journal of Epidemiology, 139,* 493–503.

Cumming, R. G., & Klineberg, R. J. (1994b). Fall frequency and characteristics and the risk of hip fractures. *Journal of the American Geriatrics Society, 42,* 774–778.

Cumming, R. G., Miller, J. P., Kelsey, J. L., Davis, P., Arfken, C. L., Birge, S. J., & Peck, W. A. (1991). Medication and multiple falls in elderly people: The St. Louis OASIS study. *Age and Ageing, 20,* 455–461.

Cummings, J. L., & Benson, D. F. (1986). Dementia of the Alzheimer type: An inventory of diagnostic clinical features. *Journal of the American Geriatrics Society, 34,* 12–19.

Cummings, S. R., Black, D. M., Nevitt, M. C., Browner, W. S., Cauley, J. A., Genant, H. K., Mascioli, S. P., Scott, J. C., Seeley, D. G., Steiger, P., Vogt, T. M., & Study of Osteoporotic Fracture Research Group (1990). Appendicular bone density and age predict hip fracture in women: The Study of Osteoporotic Fractures Research Group. *Journal of the American Medical Association, 263,* 665–668.

Cummings, S. R., Black, D., & Rubin, S. M. (1989). Lifetime risks of hip, Colles', or vertebral fracture and coronary heart disease among white postmenopausal women. *Archives of Internal Medicine, 149,* 2445–2448.

Cummings, S. R., Kelsey, J. L., Nevitt, M. C., & O'Dowd, L. J. (1985). Epidemiology of osteoporosis and osteoporotic fractures. *Epidemiology Reviews, 7,* 178–207.

Cummings, S. R., & Nevitt, M. C. (1989). A hypothesis: The cause of hip fracture. *Journal of Gerontology, 44,* 107–111.

Cummings, S. R., & Nevitt, M. C. (1991). Risk factors for fall-related injuries and long lies: Findings from a prospective study. In R. Weindruch, E. C. Hadley, & M. G. Ory (Eds.), *Reducing frailty and falls in older persons* (pp. 90–95). Springfield; IL: Charles C. Thomas.

Cummings, S. R., Nevitt, M. C., & Kidd, S. (1988). Forgetting falls: The limited accuracy of recall in the elderly. *Journal of the American Geriatrics Society, 36,* 613–616.

Cunha, U., Leduc, M., Nayak, U. S. L., & Isaacs, B. (1987). Why do old people stoop? *Archives of Gerontology and Geriatrics, 6,* 363–369.

Curtis, J. R., Geller, G., Stokes, E. J., Levine, D. M., & Moore, R. D. (1989). Characteristics, diagnosis, and treatment of alcoholism in elderly patients. *Journal of the American Geriatrics Society, 37,* 310–316.

Cwikel, J. (1992). Falls among elderly people living at home: Medical and social factors in a national sample. *Israel Journal of Medical Sciences, 28,* 446–453.

Cwikel, J., Fried, A. N., & Galinisky, D. (1989/90). Falls and psychosocial factors among community dwelling elderly persons: A review and integration of findings from Israel. *Public Health Reviews, 17,* 39–50.

Daley, I., & Goldman, L. (1987). A closer look at institutional accidents. *Geriatric Nursing, 8,* 64–67.

Dalsky, G. P., Stocke, K. S., Ehsani, A. A., Slatopolsky, E., Lee, W. C., & Birge, S. J. (1988). Weight bearing, exercise training, and lumbar bone content in postmenopausal women. *Annals of Internal Medicine, 108,* 824–828.

Dalziel, W. B., Kelly, F. A., & Cherkin, A. (1985). *80 do's and 58 don'ts for your safety: A practical guide for eldercare.* Sepulveda, CA: Geriatric Research Education and Clinical Center, Sepulveda VA Medical Center.

Davie, J. W., Blumenthal, M. D., & Robinson-Hawkins, S. (1981). A model of risk of falling for psychogeriatric patients. *Archives of General Psychiatry, 38,* 463–467.

Davies, K. N. (1990). Emergency alarms. *British Medical Journal, 300,* 1713–1715.

de Bruijn, H. P. (1987). The Colles fracture: Review of the literature. *Acta Orthopaedica Scandinavica, 58* (Supp. 223), 7–25.

Dean, E., & Ross, J. (1993). Relationship among cane fitting, function, and falls. *Physical Therapy, 73,* 494–504.

DeHaven, H. (1942). Mechanical analysis of survival in falls from heights of fifty to one hundred and fifty feet. *War and Medicine, 2,* 586–596.

deJaeger, C., Jabourian, A. P., Findji, G., Armenian, G., & Champart-Curie, O.

(1994). Altered cognitive functions in a population of elderly people hospitalized for fall-related fractures. *Journal of the American Geriatrics Society, 42,* 1305.

DeLee, J. C. (1984). Fractures and dislocations of the hip. In C. A. Rockwood & D. P. Green (Eds.), *Fractures in adults* (pp. 1211–1256). Philadelphia: J. B. Lippincott.

Denman, S. J., Ettinger, W. H., Zarkin, B. A., Coon, P. J., & Casani, J. A. (1989). Short-term outcomes of elderly patients discharged from an emergency department. *Journal of the American Geriatrics Society, 37,* 937–943.

Dettman, M. A., Linder, M. T., & Sepic, S. B. (1987). Relationship among walking performance, postural stability, and functional assessments of the hemiplegic patient. *American Journal of Physical Medicine, 66,* 77–90.

DeVincenzo, D. K., & Watkins, S. (1987). Accidental falls in a rehabilitation setting. *Rehabilitation Nursing, 12,* 248–252.

DeVito, C. A., Lambert, D. A., Sattin, R. W., Bacchelli, S., Ros, A., & Rodriguez, J. E. (1988). Fall injuries among the elderly: Community-based surveillance. *Journal of the American Geriatrics Society, 36,* 1029–1035.

Dibner, A. S. (1990). Personal emergency response systems: Communication technology aids elderly and their families. *Journal of Applied Gerontology, 9,* 504–510.

Dibner, A. S. (1991). Personal response services today. *International Journal of Technology and Aging, 4,* 5–7.

Dibner, A. S. (1992). Personal response services present and future. *Home Healthcare Services Quarterly, 13,* 239–243.

Dibner, A. S., Lowy, L., & Morris, J. N. (1982). Usage and acceptance of an emergency alarm system by the frail elderly. *The Gerontologist, 22,* 538–539.

DiFabio, R. P., Badke, M. B., & Duncan, P. W. (1986). Adapting human postural reflexes following localized cerebrovascular lesion: Analysis of bilateral long latency responses. *Brain Research, 363,* 257–264.

Diller, L., & Weinberg, J. (1970). Evidence of accident-prone behavior in hemiplegic patients. *Archives of Physical Medicine and Rehabilitation, 51,* 358–363.

Dimant, J. (1985). Accidents in the skilled nursing facility. *New York State Journal of Medicine, 85,* 202–205.

Discipio, W. J., & Feldman, M. C. (1971). Combined behavior therapy and physical therapy in treatment of a fear of walking. *Journal of Behavior Therapy and Experimental Psychiatry, 2,* 151–152.

DiZio, P., & Lackner, J. R. (1990). Age differences in oculomotor responses to step changes in body velocity and visual surround velocity. *Journal of Gerontology, 45,* M89–M94.

Donaldson, L. J., Parsons, S. L., & Cook, A. J. (1989). Death certification in fractured neck of femur. *Public Health, 103,* 237–243.

Donius, M. G., & Rader, J. (1994). Use of siderails: Rethinking a standard of practice. *Journal of Gerontological Nursing, 20,* 23–27.

Dornan, J., Fernie, G. R., & Holliday, P. J. (1978). Visual input: Its importance in the control of postural sway. *Archives of Physical Medicine and Rehabilitation, 59,* 586–591.

Dove, A. F., & Dave, S. H. (1986). Elderly patients in the accidental department and their problems. *British Medical Journal, 292,* 807–809.

Downton, J. (1987). The problems of epidemiological studies of falls. *Clinical Rehabilitation, 1,* 243–246.

Downton, J. H., & Andrews, K. (1991). Prevalence, characteristics and factors associated with falls among the elderly living at home. *Aging, 3,* 219–228.

Dudley, N. J., Cotter, D. H. G., & Mulley, G. P. (1992). Wheelchair-related accidents. *Clinical Rehabilitation, 6,* 189–194.

Duncan, P. W., Studenski, S., Chandler, J., & Prescott, B. (1992). Functional reach: Predictive validity in a sample of elderly male veterans. *Journal of Gerontology, 47,* M93–M98.

Duncan, P. W., Weiner, D. K., Chandler, J., & Studenski, S. (1990). Functional reach: A new clinical measure of balance. *Journal of Gerontology, 45,* M192–M197.

Dunn, J. E., Rudberg, M. A., Furner, S. E., & Cassel, C. K. (1992). Mortality, disability, and falls in older persons: The role of underlying disease and disability. *American Journal of Public Health, 82,* 395–400.

Eblen, C., & Koeneman, J. B. (1993). A longitudinal evaluation of a four-wheeled walker: Effects of experience. *Topics in Geriatric Rehabilitation, 8,* 65–72.

Eddy, T. P. (1972). Deaths from domestic falls and fractures. *British Journal of Prevention and Social Medicine, 26,* 173–179.

Eddy, T. P. (1973). Deaths from falls and fractures: Comparison of mortality in Scotland and the United States with that in England and Wales. *British Journal of Prevention and Social Medicine, 27,* 247–254.

Edwards, N., Cere, M., & Leblond, D. (1993). A community-based intervention to prevent falls among seniors. *Family and Community Health, 15,* 57–65.

Ehrman, J. (1983). Use of biofeedback to treat incontinence. *Journal of the American Geriatrics Society, 31,* 182–184.

Eisner, A., Fleming, S. A., Klein, M. L., & Mauldin, W. M. (1987). Sensitivities in older eyes with good acuity: Cross-sectional norms. *Investigative Ophthalmology and Visual Science, 28,* 1824–1831.

Ejaz, F. K., Folmer, S. J., Kaufmann, M., Rose, M. S., & Goldman, B. (1994). Restraint reduction: Can it be achieved? *The Gerontologist, 34,* 694–699.

Ejaz, F. K., Jones, J., & Rose, M. (1994). Falls among nursing home residents: An examination of incident reports before and after restraint reduction programs. *Journal of the American Geriatrics Society, 42,* 960–964.

elBanna, S., Raynal, L., & Gerebtzof, A. (1984). Fractures of the hip in the elderly: Therapeutic and medico-social considerations. *Archives of Gerontology and Geriatrics, 3,* 311–319.

Ellis, M. (1988). Choosing easy chairs for the disabled. *British Medical Journal, 296,* 701–702.

Elon, R., & Pawlson, G. (1992). The impact of OBRA on medical practice within nursing facilities. *Journal of the American Geriatrics Society, 40,* 953–963.

Elworth, C. L., Larry, C., & Malmstrom, F. V. (1986). Age, degraded viewing environments, and the speed of accommodation. *Aviation, Space and Environmental Medicine, 57,* 54–58.

Epstein, M., & Hollenberg, N. K. (1976). Age as a determinant of renal sodium conservation in normal man. *Journal of Laboratory and Clinical Medicine, 87,* 411–417.

Era, P., & Heikkinen, E. (1985). Postural sway during standing and unexpected disturbance of balance in random samples of men of different ages. *Journal of Gerontology, 40,* 287–295.

Evans, J. G. (1979). Fractured proximal femur in Newcastle upon Tyne. *Age and Ageing, 8,* 16–24.

Evans, J. G. (1982). Epidemiology of proximal femoral fracture. In B. Isaacs (Ed.), *Recent advances in geriatric medicine, 2,* 201–214. Edinburgh: Churchill Livingstone.

Evans, J. G. (1987). Epidemiology of osteoporosis and fractures of the femoral neck. *Internal Medicine,* Supplement 12, 4–6.

Evans, L. K., & Strumpf, N. E. (1989). Tying down the elderly: A review of the literature on physical restraint. *Journal of the American Geriatrics Society, 37,* 65–74.

Evans, L. K., & Strumpf, N. E. (1990). Myths about elder restraint. *Image: Journal of Nursing Scholarship, 22,* 124–127.

Evans, L. K., & Strumpf, N. E. (1992). Reducing restraints: One nursing home's story. In S. G. Funk, E. M. Tornquist, M. T. Champagne, & R. A. Wise (Eds.), *Key aspects of elder care: Managing falls, incontinence, and cognitive impairment* (pp. 118–128). New York: Springer Publishing Co.

Evans, L. K., Strumpf, N. E., & Williams, C. (1991). Redefining a standard of care for frail older people: Alternatives to routine physical restraint. In P. R. Katz, R. L. Kane, & M. D. Mezey (Eds.), *Advances in long term care* (pp. 81–108). New York: Springer.

Exton-Smith, A. N. (1959). Geriatric emergencies. *Practitioner, 182,* 418–427.

Falbe, W. J. (1990). Falls in the elderly. *U. S. Pharmacist, 4,* 49–62.

Fansler, C. C., Pott, C. C., & Shepard, K. F. (1985). Effects of mental practice on balance in elderly women. *Physical Therapy, 65,* 1332–1338.

Farmer, M. E., White, L. R., Brody, J. A., & Bailey, K. R. (1984). Race and sex differences in hip fracture incidence. *American Journal of Public Health, 74,* 1374–1380.

Feist, R. R. (1978). A survey of accidental falls in a small home for the aged. *Journal of Gerontological Nursing, 4,* 15–17.

Feldman, M. C., & Discipio, W. J. (1972). Integrating Physical therapy with behavior therapy. *Physical Therapy, 52,* 1283–1285.

Felson, D. T., Anderson, J. J., Hannan, M. T., Milton, R. C., Wilson, P. W. F., & Keil, D. P. (1989). Impaired vision and hip fracture: The Framingham study. *Journal of the American Geriatrics Society, 37,* 495–500.

Felson, D. T., Kiel, D. P., Anderson, J., & Kannel, W. B. (1988). Alcohol consumption and hip fractures: The Framingham study. *American Journal of Epidemiology, 128,* 1102–1110.

Felson, D. T., Sloutskis, D., Anderson, J. J., Anthony, J. M., & Kiel, D. P. (1991). Thiazide diuretics and the risk of hip fracture: Results from the Framingham study. *Journal of the American Medical Association, 265,* 370–373.

Fernie, G. R., Gryfe, C. I., Holliday, P. J., & Llewellyn, A. (1982). The relationship of postural sway in standing to the incidence of falls in geriatric subjects. *Age and Ageing, 1,* 11–16.

Fernie, G. R., & Holliday, P. J. (1978). Postural sway in amputees and normal subjects. *Journal of Bone and Joint Surgery, 60,* 895–898.

Ferrandez, A. M., Pailhous, J. & Durup, M. (1990). Slowness in elderly gait. *Experimental Aging Research, 16,* 79–89.

Fethke, C. C., Smith, I. M., & Johnson, N. (1986). Risk factors affecting readmissions of the elderly into the health care system. *Medical Care, 24,* 429–437.

Fiatarone, M. A., Marks, E. C., Ryan, N. D., Meredith, C. N., Lipsitz, L. A., & Evans, W. J. (1990). High-intensity strength training in nonagenarians:

Effects on skeletal muscle. *Journal of the American Medical Association,* *263,* 3029–3034.

Fiatarone, M. A., O'Neill, E. F., Ryan, N. D., Clements, K. M., Solaris, G. R., Nelson, M. E., Roberts, S. B., Kenhayias, J. J., Lipsitz, L. A., & Evans, W. J. (1994). Exercise training and nutritional supplementation for physical frailty in very elderly people. *New England Journal of Medicine, 330,* 1769–1775.

Fife, D. (1987). Injuries and deaths among elderly persons. *American Journal of Epidemiology, 126,* 936–941.

Fife, D. D., Solomon, P., & Stanton, M. (1984). A risk/falls program: Code orange for success. *Nursing Management, 15,* 50–53.

Fife, T. D., & Baloh, R. W. (1993). Disequilibrium of unknown causes in older people. *Annals of Neurology, 34,* 694–702.

Fine, W. (1959). An analysis of 277 falls in hospital. *Gerontologia Clinica, 1,* 292–300.

Finlay, O. E. (1986). Footwear management in the elderly care programme. *Physiotherapy, 72,* 172–178.

Finlay, O. E., Bayles, T. B., Rosen, C., & Milling, J. (1983). The effects of chair design, age and cognitive status on mobility. *Age and Ageing, 12,* 329–335.

Finley, F. R., Cody, K. A., & Finizie, R. V. (1969). Locomotion patterns in elderly women. *Archives of Physical Medicine, 50,* 140–146.

Fisher, N. M., Pendergast, D. R., & Calkins, E. (1991). Muscle rehabilitation in impaired elderly nursing home residents. *Archives of Physical Medicine and Rehabilitation, 72,* 181–185.

Fitzgerald, J. F., & Dittus, R. S. (1990). Institutionalized patients with hip fracture: Characteristics associated with returning to community dwelling. *Journal of General Internal Medicine, 5,* 298–303.

Fitzgerald, J. F., Fagen, L. F., Tierney, W. M., & Dittus, R. S. (1987). Changing patterns of hip fracture care before and after implementation of the prospective payment system. *Journal of the American Medical Association, 258,* 218–221.

Fitzgerald, J. F., Moore, P. S., & Dittus, R. S. (1988). The care of elderly patients with hip fracture: Changes since implementation of the prospective payment system. *New England Journal of Medicine, 319,* 1392–1397.

Fleming, B. E., & Pendergast, D. R. (1993). Physical conditions, activity pattern, and environment as factors in falls by adult care facility residents. *Archives of Physical Medicine and Rehabilitation, 74,* 627–630.

Fleming, B. E., Wilson, D. R., & Pendergast, D. R. (1991). A portable, easily performed muscle power test and its association with falls by elderly persons. *Archives of Physical Medicine and Rehabilitation, 72,* 886–889.

Folman, Y., Gepstein, R., Assaraf, A., & Liberty, S. (1994). Functional recovery after operative treatment of femoral neck fractures in an institutionalized elderly population. *Archives of Physical Medicine and Rehabilitation, 75,* 454–456.

Folmar, S., & Wilson, H. (1989). Social behavior and physical restraints. *The Gerontologist, 29,* 650–653.

Francis, J. (1989). Using restraints in the elderly because of fear of litigation. *New England Journal of Medicine, 320,* 870–871.

Franklin, J. A., & Sheppard, M. C. (1990). Thyroxin replacement treatment and osteoporosis. *British Medical Journal, 300,* 693–694.

Franzoni, S., Rozzini, R., Boffelli, S., Frisoni, E. B., & Trabucchi, M. (1994). Fear of falling in nursing home patients. *Gerontology, 40,* 38–44.

Frengley, J. D., & Mion, L. C. (1986). Incidence of physical restraints on acute general medical wards. *Journal of the American Geriatrics Society, 34,* 565–568.

Fried, A. V., Cwikel, J., Ring, H., & Galinsky, D. (1990). ELGAM—extra-laboratory gait assessment method: Identification of risk factors for falls among the elderly at home. *International Disability Studies, 12,* 161–164.

Friedman, S. M., Denman, S. J., Ankrom, M., Lee, B., Ryan, S., & Williamson, J. D. (1994). Characteristics associated with increased falls in nursing home residents following relocation to a new facility. *Journal of the American Geriatrics Society, 42,* SA18.

Frontera, W. R., Meredith, C. N., O'Reilly, K. P., Knuttgen, H. G., & Evans, W. G. (1988). Strength conditioning in older men: Skeletal muscle hypertrophy and improved function. *Journal of Applied Physiology, 64,* 1038–1044.

Gabell, A., & Nayak, U. S. L. (1984). The effect of age on variability of gait. *Journal of Gerontology, 39,* 662–666.

Gabell, A., Simons, M. A., & Nayak, U. S. L. (1985). Falls in the healthy elderly: Predisposing causes. *Ergonomics, 28,* 965–975.

Gaebler, S. (1993). Predicting which patient will fall . . . and again. *Journal of Advanced Nursing, 18,* 1895–1902.

Galasko, D., Kwo-on-Yuen, P. F., Klauber, R., & Thal, L. J. (1990). Neurological findings in Alzheimer's disease and normal aging. *Archives of Neurology, 47,* 625–627.

Galbraith, S. (1987). Head injuries in the elderly. *British Medical Journal, 294,* 325.

Galbraith, S. L., Murray, W. R., Patel, A. R., & Knill-Jones, R. (1976). The relationship between alcohol and head injury and its effects on the conscious level. *British Journal of Surgery, 63,* 128–130.

Gallagher, J. C., Melton, L. J., Riggs, B. L., & Bergstrath, E. (1980). Epidemiology of fractures of the proximal femur in Rochester, Minnesota. *Clinical Orthopaedics and Related Research, 150,* 163–171.

Garraway, W. M., Stauffer, R. N., Kurland, L. T., & O'Fallon, W. M. (1979). Limb fracutres in a defined population II: Orthopedic treatment and utilization of health care. *Mayo Clinic Proceedings, 54,* 708–713.

Gehlsen, G. M., & Whaley, M. H. (1990a). Falls in the elderly: Part I. Gait. *Archives of Physical Medicine and Rehabilitation, 71,* 735–738.

Gehlsen, G. M., & Whaley, M. H. (1990b). Falls in the elderly: Part II. Balance, strength, and flexibility. *Archives of Physical Medicine and Rehabilitation, 71,* 739–741.

George, J., Binns, V. E., Clayden, A. D., & Mulley, G. P. (1988). Aids and adaptions for the elderly at home: Underprovided, underused, and undermaintained. *British Medical Journal, 296,* 1365–1366.

Gibbs, J., Hughes, S., Dunlop, D., Edelman, P., Singer, R., & Chang, R. (1993). Joint impairment and ambulation in the elderly. *Journal of the American Geriatrics Society, 41,* 1205–1211.

Gibson, M. J. (1987). The prevention of falls in later life. *Danish Medical Bulletin, 34* (supp. 4), 1–24.

Gillis, B., Gilroy, K., Lawley, H., Mott, L., & Wall, J. C. (1986). Slow walking speeds in healthy young and elderly females. *Physiotherapy Canada, 38,* 350–352.

Gitlin, L. N., Levine, R., & Geiger, C. (1993). Adaptive device use by older adults with mixed disabilities. *Archives of Physical Medicine and Rehabilitation, 74,* 149–152.

Glynn, R. J., Sedden, J. M., Krug, J. H., Sahagian, C. R., Chiavelli, M. E., & Campion, E. W. (1991). Falls in elderly patients with glaucoma. *Archives of Ophthalmology, 109,* 205–210.

Gofton, J. P. (1971). Studies in osteoarthritis of the hip: Part IV. Biomechanics and clinical considerations. *Canadian Medical Association Journal, 104,* 1007–1011.

Gooptu, C., & Mulley, G. P. (1994). Survey of elderly people who get stuck in the bath. *British Medical Journal, 308,* 762.

Gordon, J. E. (1949). The epidemiology of accidents. *American Journal of Public Health, 39,* 504–515.

Gosselin, C., Robitaille, Y., Trickey, F., & Maltais, D. (1993). Factors predicting the implementation of home modifications among elderly people with loss of independence. *Physical and Occupational Therapy in Geriatrics, 12,* 15–27.

Grabiner, M. D., Koh, T. J., Lundin, T. M., & Jahnigen, D. W. (1993). Kinematics of recovery from a stumble. *Journal of Gerontology, 48,* M97–M102.

Graham, H. J., & Firth, J. (1992). Home accidents in older people: Role of primary health care team. *British Medical Journal, 305,* 30–32.

Granek, E., Baker, S. P., Abby, H., Robinson, E., Myers, A. H., Sankoff, J. S., & Klein, L. E. (1987). Medication and diagnoses in relation to falls in a long-term care facility. *Journal of the American Geriatrics Society, 35,* 503–511.

Graves, E. J. (1990). 1988 summary: National hospital discharge survey. *Advance Data, 185,* 1–12.

Gray, B. (1966). *Home accidents among older people.* London: Royal Society for the Prevention of Accidents.

Gray-Micelli, D. L., Waxman, H., Cavalieri, T., & Lage, S. (1994). Prodromal falls among older nursing home residents. *Applied Nursing Research, 7,* 18–27.

Gray-Vickery, M. (1984). Education to prevent falls. *Geriatric Nursing, 5,* 179–183.

Greenblatt, D. J., Sellers, E. M., & Shader, R. I. (1982). Drug disposition in old age. *New England Journal of Medicine, 306,* 1081–1088.

Greenspan, S. L., Meyer, E. R., Maitland, L. A., Resnick, V. M., & Hayes, W. C. (1994). Fall severity and bone mineral density as risk factors for hip fracture in ambulatory elderly. *Journal of the American Medical Association, 271,* 128–133.

Greig, C., Butler, F., Skelton, D., Mahmud, S., & Young, A. (1993). Treadmill walking in old age may not reproduce the real life situation. *Journal of the American Geriatrics Society, 41,* 15–18.

Griffin, M. R., Melton, L. J. III, Ray, W. A., Strand, L., & West, R. (1990). Incidence of hip fracture in Saskatchewan, Canada, 1976–1985. *American Journal of Epidemiology, 131,* 502–509.

Griffin, M. R., Ray, W. A., Fought, R. L., & Melton, J. L. III (1992). Black–white differences in fracture rates. *American Journal of Epidemiology, 136,* 1378–1385.

Grimby, G., & Saltin, B. (1983). The aging muscle. *Clinical Physiology, 3,* 209–218.

Grisso, J. A., Kelsey, J. L., Strom, B. L., Chiu, G. Y., Maislin, G., O'Brien, L. A., Hoffman, S., Kaplan, F., & Northeast Hip Fracture Study Group. (1991). Risk factors for falls as a cause of hip fracture in women. *New England Journal of Medicine, 324,* 1326–1331.

Grisso, J. A., Kelsey, J. L. Strom, B. L., O'Brien, L. A., Maislin, G., LaPann, K., Samelson, L., Hoffman, S., & Northeast Hip Fracture Study Group. (1994). Risk factors for hip fracture in black women. *New England Journal of Medicine, 330,* 1555–1559.

Grisso, J. A., Schwarz, D. F., Wishner, A. R., Weene, B., Holmes, J. H., & Sutton, R. L. (1990). Injuries in an elderly inner-city population. *Journal of the American Geriatrics Society, 38,* 1326–1331.

Grisso, J. A., Schwarz, D. F., Wolfson, D., Polansky, M., & LaPenn, K. (1992). The impact of falls in an inner-city elderly African-American population. *Journal of the American Geriatrics Society, 40,* 673–678.

Gross, Y. T., Shimamoto, Y., Rose, C. L., & Frank, B. (1990). Why do they fall? Monitoring risk factors in nursing homes. *Journal of Gerontological Nursing, 16,* 20–25.

Gryfe, C. I., Amies, A., & Ashley, M. J. (1877). A longitudinal study of falls in an elderly population. I. Incidence and morbility. *Age and Ageing, 6,* 201–210.

Guimaraes, R. M., & Isaacs, B. (1980). Characteristics of the gait in old people who fall. *International Rehabilitation Medicine, 2,* 177–180.

Guralnik, J. M., Simonsick, E. M., Ferrucci, L., Glynn, R. J., Berkman, L. F., Blazer, D. G., Scherr, P. A., & Wallace, R. B. (1994). A short performance battery assessing lower extremity function: Association with self-reported disability and prediction of mortality and nursing home admission. *Journal of Gerontology, 49,* M85–M94.

Gurwitz, J. H., Sanchez-Cross, M. T., Eckler, M. A., & Matulis, J. (1994). The epidemiology of adverse and unexpected events in the long-term care setting. *Journal of the American Geriatrics Society, 42,* 33–38.

Haber, P. A. L. (1986). Technology in aging. *The Gerontologist, 26,* 350–357.

Haga, H., Shibata, H., Shichita, K., Matsuzaki, T., & Hatano, S. (1986). Falls in the institutionalized elderly in Japan. *Archives of Gerontology and Geriatrics, 5,* 1–9.

Hageman, P. A., & Blanke, D. J. (1986). Comparison of gait of young women and elderly women. *Physical Therapy, 66,* 1382–1387.

Hale, W. A., Delaney, M. J., & Cable, T. (1993). Accuracy of patient recall and chart documentation of falls. *Journal of the American Board of Family Practice, 6,* 239–242.

Hale, W. A., Delaney, M. J., & McGaghie, W. C. (1990). Predicting elderly patients' mobility using fall history and physician assessment. *Family Medicine, 22,* 383–387.

Hale, W. A., Delaney, M. J., & McGaghie, W. C. (1992). Characteristics and predictors of falls in elderly patients. *Journal of Family Practice, 34,* 577–581.

Hale, W. E., Marks, R. G., & Stewart, R. B. (1980). The Dunedin program: A Florida geriatric screening process: Design and initial data. *Journal of the American Geriatrics Society, 27,* 377–380.

Hale, W. E., May, F. E., Marks, R. G., & Stewart, R. B. (1987). Drug use in an ambulatory elderly population: A five-year update. *Drug Intelligence and Clinical Pharmacy, 21,* 530–535.

Haler, E. M., & Bell, K. R. (1988). Contracture and other deleterious effects of immobility. In J. A. DeLisa (Ed.), *Rehabilitation: Principles and practice* (pp. 448–462). Philadelphia: Lippincott.

Hanger, H. C., Ball, M. C., & Mulley, G. P. (1991). Seating in the outpatient clinic: The elderly patient's perspective. *Clinical Rehabilitation, 5,* 317–321.

Hanson, C. S., Agostinucci, J., Dasler, P. J., & Creel, G. (1992). The effect of short-term, light resistive exercise on well elders. *Physical and Occupational Therapy in Geriatrics, 10,* 73–81.

Hardin, S. B., Magee, R., Stratmann, D., Vinson, M. H., Owen, M., & Hyatt, E. C.

(1994). Extended care and nursing home staff attitudes toward restraints: moderately positive attitudes exist. *Journal of Gerontological Nursing, 20,* 23–31.

Harper, C. M., & Lyles, Y. M. (1988). Physiology and complications of bed rest. *Journal of the American Geriatrics Society, 36,* 1047–1054.

Harris, P. B. (1989). Organizational and staff attitudinal determinants of falls in nursing home residents. *Medical Care, 27,* 737–749.

Harris, T., & Kovar, M. G. (1991). National statistics on the functional status of older persons. In R. Weindruch, E. C. Hudley, & M. G. Ory (Eds.), *Reducing frailty and falls in older persons* (pp. 15–28). Springfield, Illinois: Charles C. Thomas.

Hausdorff, J. M., Forman, D. E., Landin, Z., Goldberger, A. L., Rigney, D. R., & Wei, T. Y. (1994). Increased walking variability in elderly persons with congestive heart failure. *Journal of the American Geriatrics Society, 42,* 1056–1061.

Havlik, R. J. (1986). Aging in the eighties: Impaired senses for sound and light in persons age 65 years and over. *Advance data from Vital and Health Statistics* (DHHS Pub. No. (PHS) 86-1250). Hyattsville, MD: U. S. Department of Health and Human Services.

Hawe, P., Gebski, V., & Andrews, G. (1986). Elderly patients after they leave hospital. *Medical Journal of Australia, 145,* 251–254.

Hayes, K. C. (1982). Biomechanics of postural control. *Exercise and Sport Sciences Reviews, 10,* 363–391.

Hayes, W. C., Myers, E. R., Morris, J. N., Gerhardt, T. N., Yett, H. S., & Lipsitz, L. A. (1993). Impact near the hip dominates fracture risk in elderly nursing home residents who fall. *Calcified Tissue International, 52,* 192–198.

Health Care Financing Administration. (1992). HCFA Interpretive Guidelines (Rev. 250.) *Part II. Guidelines to surveyors for long-term care facilities.* Tag number F 221-222, pp 76, F 320, pp 131–132.

Hedlund, R., & Lindgren, U. (1987). Trauma type, age and gender as determinants of hip fracture. *Journal of Orthopedic Research, 5,* 242–246.

Heidrich, F. E., Stergachis, A., & Gross, F. M. (1991). Diuretic drug use and the risk of hip fracture. *Annals of Internal Medicine, 115,* 1–6.

Heislein, D. M., Harris, B. A., & Jette, A. M. (1994). A strength training program for postmenopausal women: A pilot study. *Archives of Physical Medicine and Rehabilitation, 75,* 198–204.

Helling, D. K., Lemke, J. H., Semla, T. P., Wallace, R. B., Lipson, D. P., & Cononi-Hutley, J. (1987). Medication use characteristics in the elderly: The Iowa 65 + Rural Health Study. *Journal of the American Geriatrics Society, 35,* 4–12.

Hendrich, A. L. (1988). An effective unit based fall prevention plan. *Journal of Nursing Quality Assurance, 3,* 28–36.

Hendriksen, C., Lund, E., & Stromgard, E. (1989). Hospitalization of elderly people: A 3-year controlled trial. *Journal of the American Geriatrics Society, 37,* 117–122.

Hernandez, M., & Miller, J. (1986). How to reduce patient falls. *Geriatric Nursing, 7,* 97–102.

Heslin, K., Towers, J., Leckie, C., Thornton-Lawrence, H., Perkin, K., Jacques, M., Mullin, J., & Wick, L. (1992). Managing falls: identifying population specific risk factors and prevention strategies. In S. G. Funk, E. M. Tornquist, M. T. Champagne, & R. A. Wiese (Eds.), *Key aspects of elder care: Managing falls, incontinence, and cognitive impairment* (pp. 70–88). New York: Springer.

Higgins, K. E., Jaffe, M. J., Caruso, R. C., & de Monasterio, F. M. (1988). Spatial contrast sensitivity: Effects of age, test-retest, and psychophysical method. *Journal of the Optical Society of America, 5,* 2173–2180.

Himann, J. E., Cunningham, D. A., Rechnitzer, P. A., & Paterson, D. H. (1988). Age-related changes in speed of walking. *Medicine and Science in Sports and Exercise, 20,* 161–166.

Hingson, R., & Howland, J. (1987). Alcohol as a risk factor from accidental falls: A review of the literature. *Journal of Studies on Alcohol, 48,* 212–219.

Hirsch, C. H., Sommers, L., Olsen, A., Muller, L., & Winograd, C. H. (1990). The natural history of functional morbidity in hospitalized older patients. *Journal of the American Geriatrics Society, 38,* 1296–1303.

Ho, S. C., Bacon, W. E., Harris, T., Looker, A., & Maggi, S. (1993). Hip fracture rates in Hong Kong and the United States, 1988 through 1989. *American Journal of Public Health, 83,* 694–697.

Hodkinson, H. M. (1962). A study of falls and getting up from the floor in the aged. *Practitioner, 189,* 207–209.

Hogue, C. C. (1980). Epidemiology of injury in older age. In *Epidemiology of aging: Proceedings of the second conference. National Institute of Health, NIH Publication No. 88-969.* Bethesda, MD: U.S. Department of Health and Human Services.

Hogue, C. C. (1982a). Injury in late life: I. Epidemiology. *Journal of the American Geriatrics Society, 30,* 182–190.

Hogue, C. C. (1982b). Injury in late life: II. Prevention. *Journal of the American Geriatrics Society, 30,* 276–280.

Hogue, C. C. (1991). A person-environment model for understanding fall risk. In R. Weindruch, E. C. Hadley, & M. G. Ory (Eds.), *Reducing frailty and falls in older persons* (pp. 96–105). Springfield, IL: Charles C. Thomas.

Holmberg, S., Conradi, P., & Falen, R. (1986). Mortality after cervical hip fracture: 3002 patients followed for 6 years. *Acta Orthopaedica Scandinavica, 57,* 8–11.

Hongladarum, G. C. (1977). Analysis of the causes and prevention of injuries attributed to falls. A study for the USPHS Center for Disease Control, Contract no. 200-76-0635. Olympia, Washington, pp 160–165.

Hope, T., Tilling, K. M., Gedling, K., Keene, J. M., & Cooper, S. D. (1994). The structure of wandering in dementia. *International Journal of Geriatric Psychiatry, 9,* 149–155.

Hopkins, D. R., Murich, B., Hoeger, W. W. K., & Rhodes, R. C. (1990). Effect of low-impact aerobic dance on the functional fitness of elderly women. *Journal of Gerontology, 30,* 189–192.

Hornbrook, M. C., Stevens, V. J., Wingfield, D. J., Hollis, J. F., Greenlick, M. R., & Ory, M. E. (1994). Preventing falls among community-dwelling older persons: Results from a randomized trial. *The Gerontologist, 34,* 16–23.

Hornbrook, M. C., Wingfield, D. J., Stevens, V. J., Hollis, J. F., & Greenlick, M. R. (1991). Falls among older persons: antecedents and consequences. In R. Weindruch, E. C. Hadley, & M. G. Ory (Eds.), *Reducing frailty and falls in older persons* (pp. 106–125). Springfield, IL: Charles C. Thomas.

Howell, T. H. (1955). Old folk who fall. *Practitioner, 175,* 56–58.

Hoxie, R. E., Rubenstein, L. Z., Hoeing, H., & Gallagher, B. R. (1994). The older pedestrian. *Journal of the American Geriatrics Society, 42,* 444–450.

Hu, M. H., & Woollacott, M. H. (1994a). Multisensory training of standing balance in older adults: I. Postural Stability and one-leg Stand balance. *Journal of Gerontology, 49,* M52–M61.

Hu, M. H., & Woollacott, M. H. (1994b). Multisensory training of standing balance in older adults: II. Kinematic and electromyographic postural responses. *Journal of Gerontology, 49,* M61–M71.

Hughes, J., Clark, P., & Klenerman, L. (1990). The importance of the toes in walking. *Journal of Bone and Joint Surgery, 72B,* 245–251.

Hughes, S. L., Edelman, P. L., Singer, R. H., & Chang, R. W. (1993). Joint impairment and self-reported disability in elderly persons. *Journal of Gerontology, 48,* S84–S92.

Hulley, S. B., Furberg, C. D., Gurland, B., McDonald, R., Perry, H. M., Schnaper, H. W., Schoenberger, J. A., Smith, W. M., & Vogt, I. M. (1985). Systolic hypertension in the elderly program (SHEP): Antihypertensive efficacy of chlorthalidone. *American Journal of Cardiology, 56,* 913–920.

Hyer, K., & Rudick, L. (1994). The effectiveness of personal emergency response systems in meeting the safety monitoring needs of home care clients. *Journal of Nursing Administration, 24,* 39–44.

Imms, F. J., & Edholm, O. G. (1981). Studies of gait and mobility in the elderly. *Age and Ageing, 10,* 147–156.

Inglin, B., & Woollacott, M. (1988). Age-related changes in anticipatory postural adjustments associated with arm movements. *Journal of Gerontology, 43,* M105–M113.

Innes, E. M. (1985). Maintaining fall prevention. *Quality Review Bulletin, 11,* 217–221.

Institute of Medicine. (1990). Osteoporosis. In R. L. Berg & J. S. Cassells (Eds.), *The second fifty years: Promoting health and preventing disability* (pp. 76–100). Washington, DC: National Academy Press.

Ions, G. K., & Stevens, J. (1987). Prediction of survival in patients with femoral neck fractures. *Journal of Bone and Joint Surgery, 68B,* 384–387.

Isaacs, B. (1978). Are falls a manifestation of brain failure? *Age and Ageing, 7*(Supplement), 97–111.

Isaacs, B. (1985). Clinical and laboratory studies of falls in old people: Prospects for prevention. *Clinics in Geriatric Medicine, 1,* 513–524.

Jackson, G., Pierscianowski, T. A., Mahon, W., & Condon, J. (1976). Inappropriate antihypertensive therapy in the elderly. *Lancet, 2,* 1317–1318.

Jacobsen, B., Goldberg, J., Miles, T. P., Brody, J. A., Stiers, W., & Rimm, A. A. (1990). Hip fracture incidence among the old and very old: A population-based study of 745,435 cases. *American Journal of Public Health, 80,* 871–873.

James, B., & Parker, A. W. (1989). Active and passive mobility of lower limb joints in elderly men and women. *American Journal of Physical Medicine and Rehabilitation, 68,* 162–167.

Janelli, L. M., Kanski, G. W., & Neary, M. A. (1994). Physical restraints: Has OBRA made a difference? *Journal of Gerontological Nursing, 20,* 17–21.

Janken, J. K., & Reynolds, B. A. (1987). Identifying patients with the potential for falling. In A. McLane (Ed.), *Classification of nursing diagnosis* (pp. 136–143). St. Louis: Mosby.

Janken, J. K., Reynolds, B. A., & Swiech, K. (1986). Patient falls in the acute care setting: Identifying risk factors. *Nursing Research, 35,* 215–219.

Jansen, E. C., Vittas, D., Hellberg, S., & Hansen, J. (1982). Normal gait of young and old men and women. *Acta Orthopaedica Scandinvica, 53,* 193–196.

Jansen, R. W. M. M., & Hoefnagels, W. H. L. (1991). Hormonal mechanisms of postprandial hypotension. *Journal of the American Geriatrics Society, 39,* 1201–1207.

Jansen, R. W. M. M., Peters, T. L., Lenders, J. W. M., van Lier, H. J. J., Laar, A., & Hoefnagels, H. L. W. (1989). Somatostatin analogue octreotide (SMS 201-995) prevents the decrease of blood pressure after oral glucose loading in the elderly. *Journal of Clinical Endocrinology and Metabolism, 68,* 752–756.

Jansen, R. W. M. M., Penterman, B. J. M., van Lier, H. L. L., Willibrord, H. L., & Hoefnagels, M. D. (1987). Blood pressure reduction after oral glucose loading and its relation to age, blood pressure and insulin. *American Journal of Cardiology, 60,* 1087–1091.

Jantti, P. (1993). Falls in the elderly. *Acta Universitatis Tamperensis, 365,* 3–64.

Jantti, P. O., Pyykko, V. I., & Hervonen, A. L. J. (1993). Falls among elderly nursing home residents. *Public Health, 107,* 89–96.

Jensen, J. S., Nielsen, L. H., Lyhne, N., Hallas, J., Brosen, K., & Gram, L. F. (1991). Drugs and femoral neck fractures: A case-controlled study. *Journal of Internal Medicine, 229,* 29–33.

Jette, A. M., Harris, B. A., Cleary, P. D., & Campion, E. W. (1987). Functional recovery after hip fracture. *Archives of Physical Medicine and Rehabilitation, 68,* 735–740.

Johnell, O., Nilsson, B., Obrant, K., & Sernbo, I. (1984). Age and sex patterns of hip fracture: Changes in 30 years. *Acta Orthopaedica Scandinavica, 55,* 290–292.

Johnson., C., & Keltner, J. (1986). Incidence of visual field loss in 20,000 eyes and its relationship to driving performance. *Archives of Ophthalmology, 101,* 371–375.

Johnson, D. (1991). Make your own chair bound alternatives. *Geriatric Nursing, 12,* 18–19.

Johnson, S. H. (1990). The fear of liability and the use of restraints in nursing homes. *Law, Medicine and Health Care, 18,* 263–273.

Joint Commission on Accreditation of Healthcare Organizations. (1993). Limitations on hospital patient movement that constitute restraint. *Joint Commission Perspectives,* 11–12.

Jones, D. (1992). Characteristics of elderly people taking psychotropic medications. *Drugs and Aging, 2,* 389–394.

Jones, W. J., & Smith, A. (1989). Preventing hospital incidents: What we can do. *Nursing Management, 20,* 58–60.

Jonsson, B. Gardsell, P., Johnell, O., Redlund-Johnell, I., & Sernbo, I. (1994). Remembering fractures: Fracture registration and proband recall in southern Sweden. *Journal of Epidemiology and Community Health, 48,* 489–490.

Jonsson, P. V., Lipsitz, L. A., Kelly, M., & Koostner, J. (1990). Hypotensive responses to common daily activities in institutionalized elderly. *Archives of Internal Medicine, 150,* 1518–1524.

Joyce, B. M., & Kirby, L. (1991). Canes, crutches and walkers. *American Family Physician, 43,* 535–542.

Judge, J. O., King, M. B., Whipple, P., Clive, J., & Wolfson, L. I. (1995). Dynamic balance in older persons: Effects of reduced visual and proprioceptive input. *Journal of Gerontology, 50A,* M263–M270.

Judge, J. O., Lindsey, C., Underwood, M., & Winsemius, D. (1993). Balance improvements in older women: Effects of exercise training. *Physical Therapy, 73,* 254–262.

Judge, J. O., Underwood, M., & Gennosa, T. (1993). Exercise to improve gait velocity in older persons. *Archives of Physical Medicine and Rehabilitation, 74,* 400–406.

Kanis, J. A., Johnell, O., Gullberg, B., Allander, E., Dilsen, G., Gennari, C., Lopes Vaz, A. A., Lyritis, G. P., Mazzuoli, G., Miravet, L., Passeri, M., Can0, R. P., Rapado, A., & Rib0t, C. (1992). Evidence for efficacy of drugs affecting bone metabolism in preventing hip fracture. *British Medical Journal, 305,* 1124–1128.

Kapoor, W. N. (1994). Syncope in older persons. *Journal of the American Geriatrics Society, 42,* 426–436.

Kapp, B. (1992). Nursing home restraints and legal liability. Merging the standard of care and industry practice. *The Journal of Legal Medicine, 13,* 1–32.

Katz, B., & Rimmer, S. (1989). Ophthalmologic manifestations of Alzheimer's disease. *Survey of Ophthalmology, 34,* 31–43.

Kayser-Jones, J. S., Wiener, C. L., & Barobaccia, J. C. (1989). Factors contributing to the hospitalization of nursing home residents. *The Gerontologist, 29,* 502–510.

Kelly, J. G., & O'Malley, K. (1992). Principles of altered drug handling in the elderly. *Reviews in Clinical Gerontology, 2,* 11–19.

Kelsey, J. L., Browner, W. S., Seeley, D. G., Nevitt, M. C., Cummings, S. P., & Study of Osteoporotic Fracture Group. (1992). Risk factors for fractures of the distal forearm and proximal humerus. *American Journal of Epidemiology, 135,* 477–489.

Kelsey, J. L., & Hoffman, S. (1987). Risk factors for hip fracture. *New England Journal of Medicine, 516,* 404–406.

Kenzora, J. E., McCarthy, R. E., Lowell, J. D., & Sledge, C. B. (1984). Hip fracture mortality: Relation to age, treatment, preoperative illness, time of surgery, and complications. *Clinical Orthopaedics and Related Research, 186,* 45–56.

Kerman, M., & Mulvihill, M. (1990). The role of medication in falls among the elderly in a long-term care facility. *The Mount Sinai Journal of Medicine, 57,* 343–347.

Kiel, D. P. (1994). New strategies to prevent hip fracture. *Hospital Practice, 29,* 47–54.

Kiel, D. P., Felson, D. T., Anderson, J. J., Wilson, P. W., & Moskowitz, M. A. (1987). Hip fracture and the use of estrogens in postmenopausal women: The Framingham study. *New England Journal of Medicine, 317,* 1169–1174.

Kiel, D. P., O'Sullivan, P., Teno, J. M., & Mori, V. (1991). Health care utilization and functional status in the aged following a fall. *Medical Care, 29,* 221–228.

Kirby, R. L., Ackroyd-Stolarz, S. A., Brown, M. G., Kirkland, S. A., & MacLeod, D.A. (1994). Wheelchair-related accidents caused by trips and falls among noninstitutionalized users of manually propelled wheelchairs in Nova Scotia. *American Journal of Physical Medicine and Rehabilitation, 73,* 319–330.

Kirchner, C. (1985). *Data on blindness and visual impairment in the U.S.: A resource manual on characteristics, education, employment, and service delivery* (pp. 20–37). New York: American Foundation for Blind.

Kirshen, A. J., Cape, R. D. T., Hayes, H. C., & Spenser, J. D. (1984). Postural sway and cardiovascular parameters associated with falls. *Journal of Clinical and Experimental Gerontology, 6,* 291–307.

Klein, W. M., Taylor, B., Tsai, T., & Tideiksaar, R. (1992). Reliability of a performance-oriented environmental mobility screen. *Journal of the American Geriatrics Society, 40,* SA27.

Kohn, D., Sinoff, G., Strulov, A., Ciechanover, M., & Wei, J. Y. (1991). Long-term follow-up of patients aged 75 years and older admitted to an acute care hospital. *Aging, 3,* 279–285.

Kokmen, E., Bossemeyer, R. W., & Williams, W. J. (1978). Quantitative evaluation of joint motion sensation in an aging population. *Journal of Gerontology, 33,* 62–67.

Koller, W. C., Glatt, S., Vetere-Overfield, B., & Hassanein, R. (1989). Falls and Parkinson's disease. *Clinical Neuropharmacology, 12,* 98–105.

Kosinski, M., & Ramcharitar, S. (1994). In-office management of common geriatric foot problems. *Geriatrics, 49,* 43–47.

Kosorok, M. R., Omenn, G. S., Diehr, P., Koopsell, T. D., & Patrick, D. L. (1992). Restricted activity days among older adults. *American Journal of Public Health, 82,* 1263–1267.

Krall, E. A., & Dawson-Hughes, B. (1994). Walking is related to bone density and rates of bone loss. *American Journal of Medicine, 96,* 20–26.

Kramer, J. D. (1994). Reducing restraint use in a nursing home. *Clinical Nurse Specialist, 8,* 158–162.

Krolner, B., & Toft, B. (1983). Vertebral bone loss: An unheeded side effect of therapeutic bed rest. *Clinical Science, 64,* 541–546.

Kutner, N. G., Schechtman, K. B., Ory, M. G., Baker, D. L., & FICSIT Group. (1994). Older adults' perceptions of their health and functioning in relation to sleep disturbances, falling, and urinary incontinence. *Journal of the American Geriatrics Society, 42,* 757–762.

Lach, H. W., Reed, A. T., Arfken, C. L., Miller, P., Paige, G. D., Birge, S. J., & Peck, W. A. (1991). Falls in the elderly: Reliability of a classification system. *Journal of the American Geriatrics Society, 39,* 197–202.

LaCroix, A. Z., Wienpahl, J., White, L. R., Wallace, R. B., Scherr, P. A., George, L. K., Coroni-Huntley, J., & Ostfeld, A. M. (1990). Thiazide diuretic agents and the incidence of hip fracture. *New England Journal of Medicine, 322,* 286–290.

Lake, M., & Biro, G. (1989). Survey of falls of inpatients at the Ryde hospital in 1986. *Australian Clinical Review, 8,* 242–246.

Lampert, J., & Lapolice, D. J. (1995). Functional considerations in evaluation and treatment of the client with low vision. *American Journal of Occupational Therapy, 49,* 885–890.

Larish, D. D., Martin, P. E., & Mungiole, M. (1988). Characteristic patterns of gait in the healthy old. *Annals of the New York Academy of Sciences, 515,* 18–31.

Lau, E. M. C., & Donnan, S. P. B. (1990). Falls and hip fracture in Hong Kong Chinese. *Public Health, 104,* 117–121.

Lau, E. M. C., Donnan, S. P. B., Baker, D. J. P., & Cooper, C. (1988). Physical activity and calcium intake in fracture of the proximal femur in Hong Kong. *British Medical Journal, 297,* 1441–1443.

Lauritzen, J. B., & Askrgaard, V. (1992). Protection against hip fractures by energy absorption. *Danish Medical Bulletin, 39,* 91–93.

Lauritzen, J. B., Peterson, M. M., & Lund, B. (1993). Effect of external hip protectors on hip fractures. *Lancet, 341,* 11–13.

Lauritzen, J. B., Schwarz, P., Lund, B., McNair, P., & Transbol, I. (1993). Changing incidence and residual lifetime risk of common osteoporosis-related fractures. *Osteoporosis International, 4,* 127–132.

Lauritzen, J. B., Schwarz, P., McNair, P. Lund, B., & Transbol, I. (1993). Radial and humeral fractures as predictors of subsequent hip, radial or humeral fractures in women, and their seasonal variations. *Osteoporosis International, 3,* 133–137.

Lawrence, J. I., & Maher, P. L. (1992). An interdisciplinary falls consult team: A collaborative approach to patient falls. *Journal of Nursing Care Quality, 6,* 21–29.

Lawton, M. P. (1982). Competence, environmental press, and the adaption of older people. In M. P. Lawton, P. G. Windley, & T. O. Byers (Eds.), *Aging and the environment* (pp. 33–59). New York: Springer Publishing Co.

Leary, P. R. (1982). Walking sticks used by elderly patients. *British Medical Journal, 285,* 58.

Lee, A, Deming, L., & Sahgal, V. (1988). Quantitative and clinical measures of static standing balance in hemiparetic and normal subjects. *Physical Therapy, 68,* 970–976.

Leibowitz, H. W., Rodemer, C. S., & Dichgans, J. (1979). The independence of dynamic spatial orientation from luminance and refractive error. *Perception and Psychophysiology, 25,* 75–79.

Levine, D., & Tideiksaar, R. (1993). Factors associated with compliance of personal emergency response systems in older persons. *Journal of the American Geriatrics Society, 41,* SA29.

Levine, D. N., Lee, J. M., & Fisher, M. (1993). The visual variant of Alzheimer's disease: A clinicopathologic case study. *Neurology, 43,* 305–313.

Levine, J. M. (1993). Rhabdomyolysis in association with acute pressure sore. *Journal of the American Geriatrics Society, 41,* 870–872.

Levine, R. M. (1991). The prevention of osteoporosis. *Hospital Practice, 26,* 77–80, 83–86, 91–94.

Lewis, D. A., Campbell, M. J., Terry, R. D., & Morrison, J. H. (1987). Laminer and regional distribution of neurofibrillary tangles and neuritic plaques in Alzheimer's disease: A quantitative study of visual and auditory cortices. *Journal of Neuroscience, 7,* 1799–1808.

Lichtenstein, M. J., Burger, M. C., Shields, S. L., & Shiavi, R. G. (1990). Comparison of biomechanics platform measures of balance and video-taped measures of gait with a clinical mobility scale in elderly women. *Journal of Gerontology, 45,* M49–M54.

Lichtenstein, M. J., Shields, S. L., Shiavi, R., & Burger, M. C. (1988). Clinical determinants of biomechanical platform measures of balance in aged women. *Journal of the American Geriatrics Society, 36,* 996–1002.

Lichtenstein, M. J., Shields, S. L., Shiavi, R. G., & Burger, M. C. (1989). Exercise and balance in aged women: A pilot controlled clinical trial. *Archives of Physical Medicine and Rehabilitation, 70,* 138–143.

Lindley, C. M., Tully, M. P., Paramsothy, V., & Tallis, R. C. (1992). Inappropriate medications is a major cause of adverse drug reactions in elderly patients. *Age and Ageing, 21,* 294–300.

Lipsitz, L. A. (1985). Abnormalities in blood pressure homeostasis that contribute to falls in the elderly. *Clinics of Geriatric Medicine, 1,* 637–648.

Lipsitz, L. A. (1989). Altered blood pressure homeostasis in advanced age. *Journal of Gerontology, 44,* M179–M183.

Lipsitz, L. A. (1991). Cardiovascular risk factors for falls in older persons. In R. Weindruch, E. C. Hadley, & M. G. Ory (Eds.), *Reducing frailty and falls in older persons* (pp. 67–75). Springfield, IL: Charles C. Thomas.

Lipsitz, L. A., & Fullerton, K. J. (1986). Postprandial blood pressu
in healthy elderly. *Journal of the American Geriatrics Society, 34*

Lipsitz, L. A., Jonsson, P. V., Kelley, M. M., & Koestner, J. S. (1991). Cau
relates of recurrent falls in ambulatory frail elderly. *Journal of Gerc*
M112–M122.

Lipsitz, L. A., Nyquist, R. P. Jr., Wei, J. Y., & Rowe, J. W. (1983). Po.
reduction in blood pressure in the elderly. *New England Journal of*
309, 81–83.

Lipsitz, L. A., Pluchino, F. C., Wei, J. Y., & Rowe, J. W. (1986). Syncope ii
tionalized elderly: The impact of multiple pathological conditions a
ational stresses. *Journal of Chronic Disease, 39,* 619–630.

Liu, L., Gauthier, L., & Gauthier, S. (1991). Spatial disorientation in p
with early senile dementia of the Alzheimer type. *American Jou*
Occupational Therapy, 45, 67–74.

Lofgren, R. P., MacPherson, D. S., Granieri, R., Myllenbeck, S., & Spraf.
(1989). Mechanical restraints on the medical wards: Are protective de\
safe? *American Journal of Public Health, 79,* 735–758.

London Borough of Hillingdon (1976). *Domiciliary services evaluation. II. i*
types of aid in common use. London: Social Services Research.

Lord, S. R. (1990). Falls in the elderly: Admissions, bed use, outcome and p.
jections. *Medical Journal of Australia, 153,* 117–118.

Lord, S. R., Caplan, G. A., & Ward, J. A. (1993). Balance, reaction time, and mu.
cle strength in exercising and non-exercising older women: A pilot study
Archives of Physical Medicine and Rehabilitation, 74, 837–839.

Lord, S. R., & Castell, S. (1994). Physical activity for older persons: Effect on
balance, strength, neuromuscular control, and reaction time. *Archives of*
Physical Medicine and Rehabilitation, 75, 648–652.

Lord, S. R., Clark, R. D., & Webster, I. W. (1991a). Postural stability and associated physiological factors in a population of aged persons. *Journal of*
Gerontology, 46, M69–M76.

Lord, S. R., Clark, R. D., & Webster, I. W. (1991b) Visual acuity and contrast sensitivity in relation to falls in an elderly population. *Age and Ageing, 20,* 175–181.

Lord, S. R., McLean, D., & Stathers, G. (1992). Physiological factors associated
with injurious falls in older people living in the community. *Gerontology,*
38, 338–364.

Lord, S. R., Ward, J. A., Williams, P., & Anstey, K. J. (1993). An epidemiological
study of falls in older community-dwelling women: The Randwick falls and
fracture study. *Australian Journal of Public Health, 17,* 240–245.

Lord, S. R., & Webster, I. W. (1990). Visual field dependence in elderly fallers
and non-fallers. *International Journal of Aging and Human Development, 31,*
267–277.

Louis, M. (1983). Falls and their causes. *Journal of Gerontological Nursing, 9,*
143–149.

Lowenstein, S. R., Crescenzi, C. A., Kern, D. C., & Steel, K. (1986). Care of the elderly in the emergency department. *Annals of Emergency Medicine, 15,* 528–535.

Luchies, C. W., Alexander, N. B., Schultz, A. B., & Ashton-Miller, J. (1994).
Stepping responses of young and old adults to postural disturbances:
Kinematics. *Journal of the American Geriatrics Society, 42,* 506–512.

Lucht, U. (1971). A prospective study of accidental falls and injuries in the
home among elderly people. *Acta Socio Medica Scandinavica, 3,* 105–120.

ıcy, S. D., & Hayes, K. C. (1985). Postural sway profiles: Normal subjects and subjects with cerebellar ataxia. *Physiotherapy Canada, 37,* 140–148.

Lukert, B. P., & Raisz, L. G. (1990). Glucocorticoid-induced osteoporosis pathogenesis and management. *Annals of Internal Medicine, 112,* 352–364.

Lundgren-Linquist, B., Aniansson, A., & Rundgren, A. (1983). Functional studies in 79-year-olds: Walking performance and climbing capacity. *Scandinavian Journal of Rehabilitation Medicine, 15,* 125–131.

Luukinen, H., Koski, L., Hiltunen, L., & Kivela, S. L. (1994). Incidence rate of falls in an aged population in northern Finland. *Journal of Clinical Epidemiology, 47,* 843–850.

Lu-Yao, G. L., Baron, J. A., Barrett, J. A., & Fisher, E. S. (1994). Treatment and survival among elderly Americans with hip fractures: A population-based study. *American Journal of Public Health, 84,* 1287–1291.

Macdonald, J. B. (1985). The role of drugs in the elderly. *Clinics in Geriatric Medicine, 1,* 621–636.

MacDonald, M., & Butler, A. (1974). Reversal of helplessness: Producing walking behavior in nursing home wheelchair residents using behavior modification procedures. *Journal of Gerontology, 29,* 97–100.

Maciorowski, L. F., Bruno, B., Dietrick-Gallagher, M., McNew, C., Sheppard-Hinkel, E., Wanich, C., & Regan, P. (1988). A review of the patient fall literature. *Journal of Nursing Quality Assurance, 3,* 18–27.

MacLennan, W. J., Timothy, J. I., & Hall, M. R. P. (1980). Vibration sense, proprioception and ankle reflexes in old age. *Journal of Clinical and Experimental Gerontology, 2,* 159–171.

Mader, S. L. (1989). Aging and postural hypotension: An update. *Journal of the American Geriatrics Society, 37,* 129–137.

Mader, S. L., Josephson, K. R., & Rubenstein, L. Z. (1987). Low prevalence of postural hypotension among community-dwelling elderly. *Journal of the American Medical Association, 258,* 1511–1514.

Madhok, R., & Bhopal, R. S. (1992). Coping with an upper limb fracture? A study of the elderly. *Public Health, 106,* 19–28.

Madhok, R., & Green, S. (1993). Longer term functional outcome and societal implications of upper limb fracture in the elderly. *Journal of the Royal Society of Health, 8,* 179–180.

Magaziner, J., Simonsick, E. M., Kashner, T. M., Hebel, J. R., & Kenzora, J. E. (1989). Survival experience of aged hip fracture patients. *American Journal of Public Health, 79,* 274–278.

Magaziner, J., Simonsick, E. M., Kashner, T. M., Hebel, J. R., & Kenzora, J. E. (1990). Predictors of functional recovery one year following hospital discharge for hip fracture: A prospective study. *Journal of Gerontology, 45,* 101–107.

Magee, R., Hyatt, E. C., Hardin, S. B., Straatmann, D., Vinson, M. H., & Owen, M. (1993). Institutional policy: Use of restraints in extended care and nursing homes. *Journal of Gerontological Nursing, 19,* 31–39.

Maguire, P. A., Taylor, I. C., & Stout, R. W. (1986). Elderly patients in acute medical wards: Factors predicting length of stay in hospitals. *British Medical Journal, 292,* 1251–1253.

Mahoney, J., Euhardy, R., & Carnes, M. (1992). A comparison of a two-wheeled walker and a three-wheeled walker in a geriatric population. *Journal of the American Geriatrics Society, 40,* 208–212.

Mahoney, J., Sager, M., Dunham, N. C., & Johnson, J. (1994). Risk of falls after hospital discharge. *Journal of the American Geriatrics Society, 42,* 269–274.

Maki, B. E., Holliday, P. J., & Topper, A. K. (1991). Fear of falling and postural performance in the elderly. *Journal of Gerontology, 46,* M123–M131.

Maki, B. E., Holliday, P. J., & Topper, A. K. (1994). A prospective study of postural balance and risk of falling in an ambulatory and independent elderly population. *Journal of Gerontology, 49,* M72–M84.

Malmberg, B., Martin, E., & Nilsson, B. (1980). Walking aids for elderly people. *International Journal of Rehabilitation Research, 3,* 66–67.

Malmivaara, A., Heliovaara, M., Knekt, P., Revnanen, A., & Aromaa, A. (1993). Risk factors for injurious falls leading to hospitalization or death in a cohort of 19,500 adults. *American Journal of Epidemiology, 138,* 384–394.

Malone, M. L., Rozario, N., Gavinski, M., & Goodwin, J. (1991). The epidemiology of skin tears in the institutionalized elderly. *Journal of the American Geriatrics Society, 39,* 591–595.

Manchester, D., Woollacott, M., Zederbauer-Hylton, N., & Marin, O. (1989). Visual, vestibular and somatosensory contributions to balance control in the older adult. *Journal of Gerontology, 44,* 118–127.

Mancia, G., Grossi, G., Berdinieri, G., Ferri, A., & Zanchetti, A. (1984). Arterial baroreceptor control of blood pressure in man. *Journal of the Autonomic and Nervous System, 11,* 115–124.

Mankovskii, N. B., Mints, A. Y., & Lysenyuk, V. P. (1980). Regulation of the preparatory period for complex voluntary movement in old and extreme old age. *Human Physiology, 6,* 46–50.

Marcus, E. L., Rudensky, B., & Sonnenblick, M. (1992). Occult elevation of CPK as a manifestation of rhabdomyolysis in the elderly. *Journal of the American Geriatrics Society, 40,* 454–456.

Markham, C. H. (1987). Vestibular control of muscular tone and posture. *Canadian Journal of Neurological Sciences, 14,* 493–496.

Marks, I., & Bebbington, P. (1976). Space phobia: Syndrome or agoraphobic variant? *British Medical Journal, 2,* 345–347.

Marks, W. (1992). Physical restraints in the practice of medicine: Current concepts. *Archives of Internal Medicine, 152,* 2203–2206.

Marottoli, R. A., Berkman, L. F., & Cooney, L. M. (1992). Decline in physical function following hip fracture. *Journal of the American Geriatrics Society, 40,* 861–866.

Marx, C. W., Dailey, G. E., III, Cheney, C., Vint, V. C., II, & Muchmore, D. B. (1992). Do estrogens improve bone mineral density in osteoporotic women over age 65? *Journal of Bone and Mineral Research, 329,* 1141–1146.

Marx, M. S., Cohen-Mansfield, J., & Werner, P. (1990). Agitation and falls in institutionalized elderly persons. *Journal of Applied Gerontology, 9,* 106–117.

Marx, M. S., Werner, P., Cohen-Mansfield, J., & Feldman, R. (1992). The relationship between low vision and performance of activities of daily living in nursing home residents. *Journal of the American Geriatrics Society, 40,* 1018–1020.

Mass, M. (1988). Management of patients with Alzheimer's disease in long-term care facilities. *Nursing Clinics of North America, 23,* 57–58.

Massachusetts Department of Health. (1987). *Injuries in Massachusetts: A status report.* Boston: Department of Health.

Mathias, S., Nayak, U. S. L., & Isaacs, B. (1986). Balance in elderly patients: The "get-up and go" test. *Archives of Physical Medicine and Rehabilitation, 67,* 384–389.

Mayo, N., Korner-Bitensky, N., Becker, R., & Georges, P. C. (1989). Preventing falls among patients in a rehabilitation hospital. *Canadian Journal of Rehabilitation, 2,* 235–240.

Mayo, N. E., Korner-Bitensky, N., & Levy, A. R. (1993). Risk factors for fractures due to falls. *Archives of Physical Medicine and Rehabilitation, 74,* 917–921.

McClaran, J., Forette, F., Hervy, M. P., & Bouchacourt, P. (1991). Two faller risk functions for geriatric assessment unit patients. *Age, 14,* 5–12.

McConnell, E. S., & Matteson, M. A. (1988). Psychosocial problems associated with aging. In M. A. Matteson & E. S. McConnell (Eds.), *Gerontological nursing* (pp. 481–520). Philadelphia: W. B. Saunders.

McHutchion, E., & Morse, J. M. (1989). Releasing restraints: A nursing dilemma. *Journal of Gerontological Nursing, 15,* 35–40.

McMurdo, M. E. T., & Gaskell, A. (1991). Dark adaptation and falls in the elderly. *Gerontology, 37,* 221–224.

McMurdo, M. E. T., & Rennie, L. (1993). A controlled trial of exercise by residents of old peoples' homes. *Age and Ageing, 22,* 11–15.

McMurdo, M. E. T., & Rennie, L. M. (1994). Improvements in quadriceps strength with regular seated exercise in the institutionalized elderly. *Archives of Physical Medicine and Rehabilitation, 75,* 600–603.

McVey, L., Becker, P. M., Saltz, C. C., Feussner, R., & Cohen, H. J. (1989). Effects of a geriatric consult team on functional status in elderly hospitalized patients. *Annals of Internal Medicine, 110,* 78–84.

Meadows, S. E., Zuckerman, J. D., Sakales, S. R., & Frankel, V. H. (1991). Ambulatory ability after hip fracture: A prospective study in geriatric patients. *Orthopedic Transactions, 15,* 700.

Melton, L. J. (1988). Epidemiology of fractures. In B. L. Riggs & L. J. Melton (Eds.), *Osteoporosis: Etiology, diagnosis, and management* (pp. 133–154). New York: Raven Press.

Melton, L. J., Beard, M. C., Kokmen, E., Atkinson, E. J., & O'Fallon, W. M. (1994). Fracture risk in patients with Alzheimer's disease. *Journal of the American Geriatrics Society, 42,* 614–619.

Melton, L. J., Chao, E. Y. S., & Lane, J. (1988). Biomechanical aspects of fractures. In B. L. Riggs & L. J. Melton (Eds.), *Osteoporosis: Etiology, diagnosis, and management* (pp. 111–131). New York: Raven Press.

Messier, S. P., Loeser, R. F., Hoover, J. L., Semble, E. L., & Wise, C. M. (1992). Osteoarthritis of the knee: Effects on gait, strength, and flexibility. *Archives of Physical Medicine and Rehabilitation, 73,* 29–36.

Meyer, J. S., & Shaw, T. G. (1984). Cerebral blood flow in aging. In M. C. Albert (Ed.), *Clinical neurology of aging* (pp. 178–196). New York: Oxford University Press.

Meyer, R. M., Kraenzle, D. K., Gettman, J., & Morley, J. E. (1994). The effect of reduction in restraint use on falls and injuries in two nursing homes. *Nursing Home Medicine, 2,* 23–26.

Miles, S. H., & Irvine, P. (1992). Deaths caused by physical restraints. *The Gerontologist, 32,* 762–766.

Miller, M. B., & Elliott, D. F. (1979). Accidents in nursing homes: Implications for patients and administrators. In M. B. Miller (ed.), *Current issues in clinical geriatrics* (pp. 97–137). New York: Tiresias Press.

Mion, L. C. (1994). Reducing use of physical restraints in the acute care setting. *Untie the Elderly, 6,* 1–3.

Mion, L. C., Frengley, J. D., Jakovcic, C. A., & Marino, J. A. (1989). A further exploration of the use of physical restraints in hospitalized patients. *Journal of the American Geriatrics Society, 37,* 949–956.

Mion, L. C., Gregor, S., Buettner, M., Chwirchak, D., Lee, O., & Paras, W. (1989). Falls in the rehabilitation setting: Incidence and characteristics. *Rehabilitation Nursing, 14,* 17–22.

Mion, L. C., & Mercurio, A. T. (1992). Methods to reduce restraints: Process, outcomes, and future directions. *Journal of Gerontological Nursing, 18,* 5–11.

Mion, L. C., Strumpf, N., & Nurses Improving Care to the Hospitalized Elderly (NICHE) Faculty. (1994). Use of physical restraints in the hospital setting: Implications for the nurse. *Geriatric Nursing, 15,* 127–131.

Mitchell-Pedersen, L., Edmond, L., Fingerote, E., & Powell, C. (1985). Let's untie the elderly. *Quarterly Journal of Long Term Care, 21*(10), 10–14.

Morey, M. C., Cowper, P. A., Feussner, J. R., DiPasquale, M. S., Crowley, G. M., & Sullivan, R. J. (1991). Two-year trends in physical performance following supervised exercise among community-dwelling older veterans. *Journal of the American Geriatrics Society, 31,* 549–554.

Morfitt, J. M. (1983). Falls in old people at home: Intrinsic versus environmental factors in causation. *Public Health, 97,* 115–120.

Morgan, V. R., Mathison, J. H., Rice, J. C., & Clemmer, D. I. (1985). Hospital falls: A persistent problem. *American Journal of Public Health, 75,* 775–777.

Morris, E. V., & Isaacs, B. (1980). The prevention of falls in a geriatric hospital. *Age and Ageing, 9,* 181–185.

Morris, J. L., Rubin, E. H., Morris, E. J., & Mandel, S. A. (1987). Senile dementia of the Alzheimers type: An important risk factor for serious falls. *Journal of Gerontology, 42,* 412–417.

Morse, J. M. (1993). Nursing research on patient falls in health care institutions. *Annual Review of Nursing Research, 11,* 299–316.

Morse, J. M., Black, C., Oberle, K., & Donahue, P. (1989). A prospective study to identify the fall-prone patient. *Social Sciences and Medicine, 28,* 81–86.

Morse, J. M., & Morse, R. M. (1988). Calculating fall rates: Methodological concerns. *Quality Review Bulletin, 14,* 369–371.

Morse, J. M., Prowse, M. D., Morrow, N., & Federspeil, G. (1985). A retrospective analysis of patient falls. *Canadian Journal of Public Health, 76,* 116–118.

Morse, J. M., Tylko, S. J., & Dixon, H. A. (1985). The patient who falls and falls again. *Journal of Gerontological Nursing, 11,* 15–18.

Morse, J. M., Tylko, S. J., & Dixon, H. A. (1987). Characteristics of the fall-prone patient. *The Gerontologist, 27,* 516–522.

Morton, D. (1989). Five years of fewer falls. *American Journal of Nursing, 89,* 204–205.

Morton, D. J., Barrett-Connor, E. L., & Edelstein, S. L. (1994). Thiazides and bone mineral density in elderly men and women. *American Journal of Epidemiology, 139,* 1107–1115.

Mossey, J. M. (1985). Social and psychosocial factors related to falls among the elderly. *Clinics in Geriatric Medicine, 1,* 541–553.

Mossey, J. M., Knott, K., & Craik, R. (1990). The effects of persistent depressive symptoms on hip fracture recovery. *Journal of Gerontology, 45,* M163–M168.

Mossey, J. M., Mutran, E., Knott, K., & Craik, R. (1989). Determinants of recovery 12 months after hip fracture: The importance of psychosocial factors. *American Journal of Public Health, 79,* 279–286.

Mulley, G. P. (1988). Provision of aids. *British Medical Journal, 296,* 1317–1318.

Mulley, G. P. (1990). Walking frames. *British Medical Journal, 300,* 925–927.

Mulley, G. P. (1992). Aids for old people living at home. *Reviews in Clinical Gerontology, 2,* 157–169.

Mulley, G. P. (1994). Rehabilitative technology: Equipment for the disabled elderly. In B. J. Vellas, J. L. Albarede, & P. J. Garry (Eds.), *Facts and research in gerontology: 1994* (pp. 139–148). Paris: Serdi.

Mulrow, C. D., Gerety, M. B., Kanten, D., Cornell, J. E., DeNino, L. A. Chioda, L., Aguilar, C., O'Neill, M. B., Rosenberg, J., & Solis, R. M. (1994). A randomized trial of physical rehabilitation for very frail nursing home residents. *Journal of the American Medical Association, 271,* 519–524.

Murphy, J., & Isaacs, B. (1982). Post-fall syndrome: A study of 36 patients. *Gerontology, 28,* 265–270.

Murray, M. P. (1967). Gait as a total pattern of movement. *American Journal of Physical Medicine, 46,* 290–333.

Murray, M. P., Kroy, R. C., & Clarkson, B. H. (1969). Walking patterns in healthy old men. *Journal of Gerontology, 24,* 169–178.

Murrell, P., Cornwall, M. W., & Doucet, S. K. (1991). Leg-length discrepancy: Effects on amplitude of postural sway. *Archives of Physical Medicine and Rehabilitation, 72,* 646–648.

Myers, A. H., Baker, S. P., VanNatta, M. L., Abbey, H., & Robinson, E. G. (1991). Risk factors associated with falls and injuries among elderly institutionalized persons. *American Journal of Epidemiology, 133,* 1179–1190.

Myers, M. G., Kearns, P. M., Kennedy, D. S., & Fisher, R. H. (1978). Postural hypotension and diuretic therapy in the elderly. *Canadian Medical Association Journal, 119,* 581–585.

Nankhonya, J. M., Turnbull, C. T., & Newton, J. T. (1991). Social and functional impact of minor fractures in elderly people. *British Medical Journal, 303,* 1514–1515.

Nashner, L. M. (1971). A model describing vestibular detection of body sway motion. *Acta Otolaryngologica, 72,* 429–436.

National Center for Health Statistics. (1986). *Vital statistics of the United States, 1982* (Vol. II, part A). Hyattsville, MD: U.S. Public Health Service.

National Center for Health Statistics (1987). Current estimates from the national Health Interview Survey: United States, 1986. *Vital and Health Statistics: Series 10 (164)* (pp. 16–52). Washington, DC: U. S. Government Printing Office.

National Center for Health Statistics (1988). 1987 summary: National Hospital Discharge Survey. *Vital and Health Statistics* (No. 159, rev.). Washington, DC: U. S. Government Printing Office.

National Center for Health Statistics (1989). *Health, United States, 1988.* (DHHS publication no. (PHS) 89-1232). Washington, DC: U. S. Government Printing Office.

National Safety Council. (1990). *Accident facts.* Chicago: National Safety Council.

Naylor, R., & Rosen, A. J. (1970). Falling as a cuase of admission to a geriatric unit. *Practitioner, 205,* 327–330.

Neary, M. A., Kanski, G., Janelli, R., Scherer, Y., & North, N. (1991). Restraints as nurse's aides see them. *Geriatric Nursing, 12,* 191–192.

Nelson, D. E., Sattin, R. W., Langlois, J. A., DeVito, C. A., & Stevens, J. A. (1992). Alcohol as a risk factor for fall injury events among elderly persons living in the community. *Journal of the American Geriatrics Society, 40,* 658–661.

Nelson, M. E., Fiatarone, M. A., Morganti, C. M., Trice, I., Greenberg, R. A., & Evans, W. J. (1994). Effects of high-intensity strength training on multiple risk factors for osteoporotic fractures: A randomized controlled trial. *Journal of the American Medical Association, 272,* 1909–1914.

Neufeld, R. R., Tideiksaar, R., Yew, E., Brooks, F., Young, J., Browne, G., & Hsu, M. A. (1991). A multidisciplinary falls consultation service in a nursing home. *The Gerontologist, 31,* 120–123.

Nevitt, M. C. (1990). Falls in older persons: Risk factors and prevention. In R. L. Berg & J. S. Cassells (Eds.), *The second fifty years: Promoting health and preventing disability* (pp. 263–290). Washington, DC: National Academy Press.

Nevitt, M. C., Cummings, S. R., Browner, W. S., Seeley, D. G., Cauley, T. A., Vogt, T. M., & Black, D. M. (1992). The accuracy of self-report of fractures in elderly women: Evidence from a prospective study. *American Journal of Epidemiology, 135,* 490–499.

Nevitt, M. C., Cummings, S. R., & Hudes, E. S. (1991). Risk factors for injurious falls: A prospective study. *Journal of Gerontology, 46,* M164–M170.

Nevitt, M. C., Cummings, S. R., Kidd, D., & Black, D. (1989). Factors for recurrent nonsyncopal falls: A prospective study. *Journal of the American Medical Association, 261,* 2663–2668.

Nevitt, M. C., Cummings, S. R., & the Study of Osteoporotic Fractures Research Group. (1993). Type of fall and risk of hip and wrist fractures: The study of osteoporotic fractures. *Journal of the American Geriatrics Society, 41,* 1226–1234.

Newbern, V. B., & Lindsey, I. H. (1994). Attitudes of wives toward having their elderly husbands restrained. *Geriatric Nursing, 15,* 135–138.

Nigg, B. M., & Sklerk, B. N. (1988). Gait characteristics of the elderly. *Clinical Biomechanics, 3,* 79–87.

Nolan, L., & O'Malley, K. (1988). Prescribing for the elderly: Part II. Prescribing patterns: Differences due to age. *Journal of the American Geriatrics Society, 36,* 245–254.

Noltie, K., & Denham, M. J. (1981). Subdural hematoma in the elderly. *Age and Ageing, 10,* 241–246.

Nutt, J. G., Marsden, C. D., & Thompson, P. D. (1993). Human walking and higher-level gait disorders, particularly in the elderly. *Neurology, 43,* 268–279.

O'Day, B. L., & Cororan, P. J. (1994). Assistive technology: Problems and policy alternatives. *Archives of Physical Medicine and Rehabilitation, 75,* 1165–1169.

Odetunde, Z. (1982, February 24). Fell walking. *Nursing Mirror,* pp. 33–36.

Olney, R. K. (1985). Age-related changes in peripheral nerve function. *Geriatric Medicine Today, 4,* 76–78.

O'Loughlin, J. L., Robitaille, Y., Boivin, J. F., & Suissa, S. (1993). Incidence of and risk factors for falls and injurious falls among the community-dwelling elderly. *American Journal of Epidemiology, 137,* 342–354.

O'Loughlin, J. L., Robitaille, Y., Boivin, J. F., & Suissa, S. (1994). Falls among the elderly: Distinguishing indoor and outdoor risk factors in Canada. *Journal of Epidemiology and Community Health, 48,* 488–489.

Omnibus Reconciliation Act, PL 100–203 (1987).

Ory, M. G., Schechtman, K. B., Miller, J. P., Hadley, E. C. Fiatarone, M. A., Provience, M. A., Arfken, C. L., Morgan, D., Weiss, S., Kaplan, M., & The FIC-SIT Group. (1993). Frailty and injuries in later life: The FICSIT trials. *Journal of the American Geriatrics Society, 41,* 283–296.

Over, R. (1966). Possible visual factors in falls by old people. *Gerontologist, 6,* 212–214.

Overstall, P. W. (1985). Epidemiology and pathophysiology of falls. In M. S. Kataria (ed.), *Fits, faints and falls in old age* (pp. 15–26). Lancaster, England: MTP Press Limited.

Overstall, P. W., Exton-Smith, Imms, F. J., & Johnson, A. L. (1977). Falls in the elderly related to postural imbalance. *British Medical Journal, 1,* 261–264.

Owen, D. H. (1985). Maintaining posture and avoiding tripping: Optical information for detecting and controlling orientation and locomotion. *Clinics in Geriatric Medicine, 1,* 581–599.

Pablo, R. Y. (1977). Patient accidents in a long-term care facility. *Canadian Journal of Public Health, 68,* 237–247.

Palmer, R. M., Landefeld, C. S., Kresevic, D., & Kowal, J. (1994). A medical unit for the acute care of the elderly. *Journal of the American Geriatrics Society, 42,* 545–552.

Palmer, R. M., Saywell, R. M., Jr., Zollinger, T. W., Erner, B. K., LaBov Freund, D. A., Garber, J. E., Misamore, G. W., & Throop, F. B. (1989). The impact of the prospective payment system on the treatment of hip fractures in the elderly. *Archives of Internal Medicine, 149,* 2237–2241.

Pardo, R. D., Deathe, A. B., & Winter, D. A. (1993). Walker user risk index: A method for quantifying stability in walker users. *American Journal of Physical Medicine and Rehabilitation, 72,* 301–305.

Parker, M. J., & Anand, J. K. (1991). What is the true mortality of hip fractures? *Public Health, 105,* 443–446.

Parker, M. G., & Thorsland, M. (1991). Use of technical aids among community-based elderly. *American Journal of Occupational Therapy, 45,* 712–718.

Parrish, H. M., & Weil, T. P. (1958). Patient accidents occurring in hospitals: Epidemiologic study of 614 accidents. *New York State Journal of Medicine, 58,* 838–846.

Pastalan, L. (1982). Environmental design and adaptations to the visual environment of the elderly. In R. Sekuler, D. Kline, & K. Dismukes (eds.), *Aging and human visual functioning.* New York: Alan R. Liss.

Pastalan, L., Mautz, R., & Merrill, J. (1973). The simulation of age-related sensory losses: A new approach to the study of environmental barriers. In W. F. E. Preiser (Ed.), *Environmental design research.* Stroudsburg, PA: Dowden, Hitchinson, & Ross.

Paulus, W. M., Straube, A., & Brandt, T. (1984). Visual stabilization of posture. *Brain, 107,* 1143–1168.

Paulus, W. M., Straube, A., & Brandt, T. H. (1987). Visual postural performance after loss of somatosensory and vestibular function. *Journal of Neurology, Neurosurgery and Psychiatry, 50,* 1542–1545.

Peck, W. A., Riggs, B. L., Bell, N. H., Wallace, R. B., Johnston, C. G., Gordon, S. L., & Shulman, L. E. (1988). Research directions in osteoporosis. *American Journal of Medicine, 84,* 275–282.

Peh, C. A., Horowitz, M., Wishart, J. M., Need, A. G., Morris, H. A., & Nordin, B.

E. C. (1993). The effect of chlorothiazide on bone-related biochemical variables in normal post-menopausal women. *Journal of the American Geriatrics Society, 41,* 513–516.

Peitzman, S. J., & Berger, S. R. (1989). Postprandial blood pressure decrease in well elderly persons. *Archives of Internal Medicine, 149,* 286–288.

Pemberton, J. (1988). Are hip fractures underestimated as a cause of death? The influence of coroners and pathologists on death rate. *Community Medicine, 29,* 117–123.

Pentland, B., Jones, P. A., Roy, C. W., & Miller, J. D. (1986). Head injury in the elderly. *Age and Ageing, 15,* 193–202.

Perry, B. C. (1982). Falls among the elderly in high-rise apartments. *Journal of Family Practice, 14,* 1069–1073.

Perry, H. M., Dickneite, S., Boesch, J., Kraenzle, D., Liano, E., Hierro, M., & Morley, J. E. (1994). Falls in wheelchair dependent individuals in nursing homes: Utility of a sitting balance scale. *Nursing Home Medicine, 2,* 171–197.

Petera, R. J., & Black, F. O. (1990). Age-related changes in human posture control: Sensory organization tests. *Journal of Vestibular Research, 1,* 73–85.

Phillips, C. D., Hawes, C., & Fries, B. E. (1993). Reducing the use of physical restraints in nursing homes: Will it increase costs? *American Journal of Public Health, 83,* 342–348.

Podsiadlo, D., & Richardson, S. (1991). The timed "up and go": A test of basic functional mobility for frail elderly persons. *Journal of the American Geriatrics Society, 39,* 142–148.

Poster, E. C., Pelletier, L. R., & Kay, K. (1991). A retrospective cohort study of falls in a psychiatric inpatient setting. *Hospital and Community Psychiatry, 42,* 714–720.

Potempa, K., Carvalho, A., Hahn, J., & LeSage, J. (1990). Containing the cost of patient falls: A risk management model. *Topics in Geriatric Rehabilitation, 6,* 69–78.

Potvin, A. R., Syndulko, K., Tourtellotte, W. W., et al. (1980). Human neurologic function and the aging process. *Journal of the American Geriatrics Society, 28,* 1–9.

Potvin, A. R., & Tourtellotte, W. W. (1975). The neurological examination: Advancements in its quantification. *Archives of Physical Medicine and Rehabilitation, 56,* 425–437.

Powell, C., Mitchell-Pedersen, L., Fingerote, E., & Edmund, L. (1989). Freedom from restraint: Consequences of reducing physical restraints in the management of the elderly. *Canadian Medical Association Journal, 141,* 561–564.

Powell, L. E., & Myers, A. M. (1995). The activities-specific balance confidence (ABC) scale. *Journal of Gerontology, 50A,* M28–M34.

Probst, C. (1989). *The influence of hip abduction strength on postural sway in elderly females.* Unpublished master's thesis. University of Pittsburgh.

Province, M. A., Hadley, E. C., Hornbrook, M. C., Lipsitz, C. A., Miller, J. P., Mulrow, C. D., Ory, M. G., Sattin, P. W., Tinetti, M. E., Wolf, S. L., & FICSIT Group. (1995). The effects of exercise on falls in elderly patients: A preplanned meta-analysis of the FICSIT trials. *Journal of the American Medical Association, 273,* 1341–1347.

Prudham, D., & Evans, J. (1981). Factors associated with falls in the elderly: A community study. *Age and Ageing, 10,* 141–146.

Pruzansky, M. E., Turano, M., Lucky, M., & Senie, R. (1989). Low body weight as a risk factor for hip fracture in both black and white women. *Journal of Orthopedic Research, 7,* 192–197.

Public Health Service. (1991). *Healthy people 2000: National health promotion and disease preventive objectives: A full report, with commentary* (DHHS Pub. No. (PHS) 91–50212). Washington, DC: U. S. Government Printing Office.

Puetz, K. (1988). Development of an incident reporting system. *Quality Review Bulletin, 14,* 245–250.

Pyka, G., Lindenberger, E., Charette, S., & Marcus, R. (1994). Muscle strength and fiber adaptations to a year-long resistance training program in elderly men and women. *Journal of Gerontology, 49,* M22–M27.

Pynoos, J., Cohen, E., Davis, L., & Bernhart, S. (1987). Home modifications: Improvements that extend independence. In V. Regnier & J. Paynoos (Eds.), *Housing the aged: Design directives and policy considerations* (pp. 277–303). New York: Elsevier Science Publishing.

Pyykko, I., Jantti, P., & Aalto, H. (1990). Postural control in elderly subjects. *Age and Ageing, 19,* 215–221.

Quigley, M. E., Martin, P. L., Burnier, A. M., & Brooks, P. (1987). Estrogen therapy arrests bone loss in elderly women. *American Journal of Obstetrics and Gynecology, 156,* 1516–1523.

Quinlan, W. C. (1994). The liability risk of patients who fall. *Journal of Healthcare Risk Management, 14,* 29–33.

Raab, D. M., Agre, J. C., McAdam, M., & Smith, E. L. (1988). Light resistance and stretching exercise in elderly women: Effects upon flexibility. *Archives of Physical Medicine and Rehabilitation, 69,* 268–272.

Rabin, D. L., & Stockton, P. (1987). *Long-term care for the elderly: A fact book.* New York: Oxford University Press.

Radebaugh, T. S., Hadley, E., & Suzman, R. (Eds.). (1985). Falls in the elderly: Biologic and behavioral aspects. *Clinics in Geriatric Medicine, 1,* 497–697.

Randall, P., Burkhardt, S. S. J., & Kutcher, J. (1990). Exterior space for patients with Alzheimer's disease and related disorders. *American Journal of Alzheimer's Care and Related Disorders Research, 5,* 31–37.

Rapport, L. J., Webster, J. S., Flemming, K. L., Lindberg, J. W., Godlewski, M. C., Brees, J. E., & Abadee, P. S. (1993). Predictors of falls among right-hemisphere stroke patients in the rehabilitation setting. *Archives of Physical Medicine and Rehabilitation, 74,* 621–626.

Rashiq, S., & Logan, R. F. A. (1986). Role of drugs in fracture of the femoral neck. *British Medical Journal, 292,* 861–863.

Ray, W. A., & Griffin, M. R. (1990). Prescribed medications and the risk of falling. *Topics in Geriatric Rehabilitation, 5,* 12–20.

Ray, W. A., Griffin, M. R., & Downey, W. (1989). Benzodiazepines of long and short elimination half-life and the risk of hip fracture. *Journal of the American Medical Association, 262,* 3303–3307.

Ray, W. A., Griffin, M. R., Downey, W., & Melton, L. J. (1989). Long-term use of thiazide diuretics and risk of hip fracture. *Lancet, 1,* 687–690.

Ray, W. A., Griffin, M. R., & Malcolm, E. (1991). Cyclic antidepressants and the risk of hip fracture. *Archives of Internal Medicine, 151,* 754–756.

Ray, W. A., Griffin, M. R., Schaffner, W., & Melton, L. J., III. (1987). Psychotropic drug use and the risk of hip fracture. *New England Journal of Medicine, 316,* 363–369.

Raz, T., & Baretich, M. F. (1987). Factors affecting the incidence of patient falls in hospital. *Medical Care, 25,* 185–195.

Read, S., Bagheri, A., & Strickland, P. (1991). Are restraints all bad? *Journal of the American Geriatrics Society, 39,* 223.

Reid, R. I., & Ashby, N. A. (1982). Ulnar nerve palsey and walking frames. *British Medical Journal, 285,* 778.

Reinsch, S., MacRae, P., Lachenbruch, P. A., & Tobis, J. S. (1992a). Attempts to prevent falls and injury: A prospective community study. *The Gerontologist, 32,* 450–456.

Reinsch, S., MacRae, P., Lachenbruch, P. A., & Tobis, J. S. (1992b). Why do healthy older adults falls? Behavioral and environmental risks. *Physical and Occupational Therapy in Geriatrics, 11,* 1–15.

Reschovsky, J. D., & Newman, S. J. (1990). Adaptations for independent living by older frail households. *The Gerontologist, 30,* 543–552.

Rice, D. P., Mackenzie, E. J., & Associates. (1989). *Cost of injury in the United States: A report to Congress.* San Francisco: Institute for Health and Aging, University of California, and Injury Prevention Center, The Johns Hopkins University.

Richardson, J. K., Ching, C., & Hurvitz, E. A. (1992). The relationship between electromyographically documented peripheral neuropathy and falls. *Journal of the American Geriatrics Society, 40,* 1008–1012.

Riggs, J. E. (1993). Mortality from accidental falls among the elderly in the United States, 1962–1988: Demonstrating the impact of improved trauma management. *Journal of Trauma, 35,* 212–219.

Ring, C., Nayak, U. S. L., & Isaacs, B. (1988). Balance function in elderly people who have and who have not fallen. *Archives of Physical Medicine and Rehabilitation, 69,* 261–264.

Ring, C., Nayak, U. S. L., & Isaacs, B. (1989). The effect of visual deprivation and proprioceptive changes on postural sway in healthy adults. *Journal of the American Geriatrics Society, 37,* 745–749.

Robbins, A. S., Rubenstein, L. Z., Josephson, K. R., Schulman, B. L., Osterweil, D., & Fine, G. (1989). Predictors of falls among elderly people: Results of two population-based studies. *Archives of Internal Medicine, 149,* 1628–1633.

Robbins, L. J. (1986). Restraining the elderly patient. *Clinics in Geriatric Medicine, 2,* 591–599.

Robbins, L. J., Boyko, E., Lane, J., Cooper, D., & Jahnigen, D. W. (1987). Binding the elderly: A prospective study of the use of mechanical restraints in an acute care hospital. *Journal of the American Geriatrics Society, 35,* 290–296.

Robbins, S., Gouw, G. J., & McClaran, J. (1992). Shoe sole thickness and hardness influence balance in older men. *Journal of the American Geriatrics Society, 40,* 1089–1094.

Roberts, B. L. (1989). Effects of walking on balance among elders. *Nursing Research, 38,* 180–183.

Roberts, B. L. (1993). Is a stay in an intensive care unit a risk for falls? *Applied Nursing Research, 6,* 135–136.

Rockwood, P. R., Horne, J. G., & Cujer, C. (1990). Hip fractures: A future epidemic? *Journal of Orthopedic Trauma, 4,* 388–393.

Rodgers, S. (1994). Reducing restraints in a rehabilitation setting: A safer environment through team effort. *Rehabilitation Nursing, 19,* 274–276.

Rodriquez, J., Herrara, A., Canales, V., & Serrano, S. (1987). Epidemiologic factors, morbidity and mortality after femoral neck fracture in the elderly. *Acta Orthopaedica Belgica, 53,* 472–479.

Rodriquez, J. G., Sattin, R. W., DeVito, C. A., Wingo, P. A., & the Study to Assess Falls Among the Elderly Group. (1991). Developing an environmental hazards assessment instrument for falls among the elderly. In R. Weindruch, E. C. Hadley, & M. G. Ory (Eds.), *Reducing frailty and falls in older persons* (pp. 263–276). Springfield, IL: Charles C Thomas.

Rodstein, M. (1964). Accidents among the aged: Incidence, causes, and prevention. *Journal of Chronic Disease, 17,* 515–526.

Rose, J. (1987). When the care plan says restrain. *Geriatric Nursing, 8,* 20–21.

Rosenfeld, V., Lerman, Y., & Habot, B. (1993). Acute stooped position in elderly with Alzheimer's disease. *Journal of the American Geriatrics Society, 41,* 468.

Rosenhall, U., & Rubin, W. (1975). Degenerative changes in the human vestibular sensory epithelia. *Acta Otolaryngologia, 79,* 67–80.

Ross, J. E. R., Mass, M., Huston, J. C., Kundel, C. J., Woodward, P. J., Gyldenvard, T. A., Modarressi, L., Heffner, M., Daly, J., Casselman, M., Sellberg, M. S., Tunink, P., Smith, J. C., Woodworth, G., & Kruckeberg, T. (1992). Evaluation of two interventions to reduce falls and fall injuries: The challenge of hip pads and individualized elimination rounds. In S. G. Funk, E. M. Tornquist, M. T. Champagne, & R. A. Wiese (Eds.), *Key aspects of elder care: Managing falls, incontinence, and cognitive impairment* (pp. 97–103). New York: Springer Publishing Co.

Rothman, S. A. (1990). Minimizing fall injuries to older patients. *Contemporary Senior Health, 263,* 2021–2023.

Rozzelle, C. J., Wofford, J. L., & Branch, C. L. (1995). Predictors of hospital mortality in older patients with subdural hematoma. *Journal of the American Geriatrics Society, 43,* 240–244.

Rubenstein, H. S., Miller, F. H., Postel, S., & Evans, H. B. (1983). Standards of medical care based on consensus rather than evidence: The case of routine bedrail use for the elderly. *Law, Medicine and Health Care, 11,* 271–276.

Rubenstein, L. Z., Josephson, K. R., & Robbins, A. S. (1994). Falls in the nursing home. *Annals of Internal Medicine, 121,* 442–451.

Rubenstein, L. Z., Robbins, A. S., Josephson, K. R., Schulman, B. L., & Osterweil, D. (1990). The value of assessing falls in an elderly population: A randomized clinical trial. *Annals of Internal Medicine, 113,* 308–316.

Rubenstein, L. Z., Robbins, A. S., Schulman, B. L., Rosado, J., Osterweil, D., & Josephson, K. R. (1988). Falls and instability in the elderly. *Journal of the American Geriatrics Society, 36,* 278–288.

Rubin, B. S., Dube, A. H., & Mitchell, E. K. (1993). Asphyxial deaths due to physical restraints. *Archives of Family Medicine, 2,* 405–408.

Rubin, S. M., & Cummings, S. R. (1992). Results of bone densitometry affect women's decisions about taking measures to prevent fractures. *Annals of Internal Medicine, 116,* 990–995.

Ruthazer, R., & Lipsitz, L. A. (1993). Antidepressants and falls among elderly people in long-term care. *American Journal of Public Health, 83,* 746–749.

Ryan, J. W., Dinkel, J. L., & Petrucci, K. (1993). Near falls incidence: A study of older adults in the community. *Journal of Gerontological Nursing, 19,* 23–28.

Ryynanen, O. P. (1994). Health, functional capacity, health behavior, psychological factors and falling in old age. *Public Health, 108,* 99–110.

Ryynanen, O. P., Kivela, S. L., Honkanen, R., & Laippala, P. (1992a). Falls and lying helpless in the elderly. *Zeitschrift Fur Gerontologie, 25,* 278–282.

Ryynanen, O. P., Kivela, S. L., Honkanen, R., & Laippala, P. (1992b). Recurrent elderly fallers. *Scandinavian Journal of Primary Health Care, 10,* 277–283.

Ryynanen, O. P., Kivela, S. L., Honkanen, R., Laippala, P., & Saano, V. (1993). Medications and chronic diseases as risk factors for falling injuries in the elderly. *Scandinavian Journal of Social Medicine, 4,* 264–271.

Sainsbury, R., & Mulley, G. P. (1982). Walking sticks used by the elderly. *British Medical Journal, 284,* 1751.

Salive, M. E., Guralnik, J., Christen, W., Glynn, P. J., Colsher, P., & Ostfeld, A. M. (1992). Functional blindness and visual impairments of older adults from three communities. *Ophthalmology, 99,* 1840–1847.

Salive, M. E., Guralnik, J., Glynn, R. J., Christen, W., Wallace, R. B., & Ostfeld, A. M. (1994). Association of visual impairment with mobility and physical function. *Journal of the American Geriatrics Society, 42,* 287–292.

Sanders, A. B., & Morley, J. E. (1993). The older person and the emergency department. *Journal of the American Geriatrics Society, 41,* 880–882.

Sattin, R. W. (1992). Falls among older persons: A public health perspective. *Annual Review of Public Health, 13,* 489–508.

Sattin, R. W., Lambert Huber, D. A., DeVito, C. A., Rodriguez, J. A., Ros, A., Bacchelli, S., Stevens, J. A., & Waxweiler, R. J. (1990). The incidence of fall injuries in a defined population. *American Journal of Epidemiology, 131,* 1028–1037.

Sauvage, L. R., Myklebust, B. M., Crow-Pan, J., Novak, S., Millington, P., Hoffman, M. D., Hartz, A. J., & Rudman, D. (1992). A clinical trial of strengthening and aerobic exercise to improve gait and balance in elderly male nursing home residents. *American Journal of Physical Medicine and Rehabilitation, 71,* 333–342.

Saywell, R. M., Woods, J. R., Rappaport, S. A., & Allen, T. L. (1989). The value of age and severity as predictors of costs in geriatric head trauma patients. *Journal of the American Geriatrics Society, 37,* 625–630.

Scharf, S., & Christophidis, N. (1993). Prescribing for the elderly: I. Relevance of pharmacokinetics and pharmacodynamics. *Medical Journal of Australia, 158,* 395–402.

Schelp, L., & Svanstrom, L. (1986). One year incidence of home accidents in a rural Swedish municipality. *Scandinavian Journal of Social Medicine, 14,* 75–82.

Schieber, C. J., Poullier, J. P., & Greenwald, L. M. (1992). U. S. health expenditure performance: An international comparison and data update. *Health Care Financing Review, 13,* 1–15.

Schleenbaker, R. E., McDowell, S. M., Moore, R. W., Costich, J. F., & Prater, G. (1994). Restraint use in inpatient rehabilitation: Incidence, predictors, and implications. *Archives of Physical Medicine and Rehabilitation, 75,* 427–430.

Schneider, E. L., & Guralnik, J. M. (1990). The aging of America: Impact on health care costs. *Journal of the American Medical Association, 263,* 2335–2340.

Schnelle, J. F., MacRae, P. G., Simmons, S. F., Uman, G., Ouslander, J. G., Rosenquist, L. L., & Chang, B. (1994). Safety assessment for the frail elderly: A comparison of restrained and unrestrained nursing home residents. *Journal of the American Geriatrics Society, 42,* 586–592.

Schorr, R. I., Griffin, M. R., Daugherty, J. R., & Ray, W. A. (1992). Opioid analgesics and the risk of hip fracture in the elderly: Codeine and propoxyphene. *Journal of Gerontology, 47,* M111–M115.

Schulz, R., Visintainer, P., & Williamson, G. M. (1990). Psychiatric and physical morbidity effects of caregiving. *Journal of Gerontology, 45,* P181–P191.

Scott, C. J. (1976). Accidents in hospital with special reference to older people. *Health Bulletin, 34,* 330–335.

Scott, R. (1954). Accidents to old people. *Practitioner, 172,* 642–648.

Seedham, B. B., & Terayama, K. (1976). Knee forces during activity of getting out of a chair with and without armrests. *Biomedical Engineering, 11,* 278–282.

Sehested, P., & Severin-Nielsen, T. (1977). Falls by hospitalized patients: Causes, prevention. *Geriatrics, 32,* 101–108.

Seiler, H. E., & Ramsay, C. B. (1954). Home accidents. *Practitioner, 172,* 628–636.

Sexson, S. B., & Leher, J. T. (1987). Factors affecting hip fracture mortality. *Journal of Orthopedic Trauma, 1,* 298–305.

Shamash, K., O'Connell, K., Lowy, M., & Katona, C. L. E. (1992). Psychiatric morbidity and outcome in elderly patients undergoing emergency hip surgery: A one-year follow-up study. *International Journal of Geriatric Psychiatry, 7,* 505–509.

Shapiro, E. (1988). Hospital use by elderly Manitobans resulting from an injury. *Canadian Journal of Aging, 7,* 125.

Sharma, J. C., & MacLennan, W. J. (1988). Causes of ataxia in patients attending a falls laboratory. *Age and Ageing, 17,* 94–102.

Sheldon, J. H. (1948). *The social medicine of old age.* London: Oxford University Press.

Sheldon, J. H. (1960). On the natural history of falls in old age. *British Medical Journal, 4,* 1685–1690.

Shepherd, J., Lutz, L. J., Miller, R. S., & Main, D. S. (1992). Patients presenting to family physicians after a fall: A report from the Ambulatory Sentinel Practice Network. *Journal of Family Practice, 35,* 43–48.

Shimada, K., Kitazumi, T., Ogura, H., Sadakane, N., & Ozawa, T. (1986). Differences in age-independent effects of blood pressure on baroreflex sensitivity between normal and hypertensive subjects. *Clinical Science, 70,* 489–494.

Shuren, J., & Heilman, K. M. (1993). Visual field loss in Alzheimer's disease. *Journal of the American Geriatrics Society, 41,* 1114–1115.

Silver, J. H., Gould, E. S., Irvine, D., & Culliman, T. R. (1978). Visual acuity at home and in eye clinics. *Transactions of the American Ophthalmological Society, 98,* 262–266.

Silverman, S. L., & Madison, R. E. (1988). Decreased incidence of hip fractures in Hispanics, Asians, and blacks: California hospital discharge data. *American Journal of Public Health, 78,* 1482–1483.

Simoneau, G. G., Cavanagh, P. R., Ulbrecht, J. S., Leibowitz, H. W., & Tyrrell, R. A. (1991). The influence of visual factors on fall-related kinematic variables during stair descent by older women. *Journal of Gerontology, 46,* M188–M195.

Simpson, J. M., & Mandelstam, H. (1993). Not all elderly people who fall are able or willing to be taught how to get up again. *Age and Ageing, 22,* 34.

Simpson, J. M., & Salkin, S. (1993). Are elderly people at risk of falling taught how to get up again? *Age and Ageing, 22,* 294–296.

Sjorgen, H., & Bjornstig, U. (1989). Unintentional injuries among elderly people:

Incidence, causes, severity, and costs. *Accident Analysis and Prevention, 21,* 233–242.

Sjorgen, H., & Bjornstig, U. (1991). Injuries among the elderly in the home environment. *Journal of Aging and Health, 3,* 107–125.

Skinner, H. B., Barrack, R. L., & Cook, S. D. (1984). Age-related decline in proprioception. *Clinical Orthopedics and Related Research, 184,* 208–211.

Sloane, P. D., Baloh, R. W., & Honrubia, V. (1989). The vestibular system in the elderly: Clinical implications. *American Journal of Otolaryngology, 10,* 422–428.

Sloane, P. D., Papougenis, D., & Blakeslee, J. A. (1992). Alternatives to physical and pharmacologic restraints in long-term care. *American Family Physician, 45,* 763–769.

Smith, E. L. (1995). The role of exercise in the prevention and treatment of osteoporosis. *Topics in Geriatric Rehabilitation, 10,* 55–63.

Smith, E. L., Gilligan, C., Shea, M. M., Ensign, P., & Smith, P. E. (1989). Deterring bone loss by exercise intervention in postmenopausal women. *Calcified Tissue International, 44,* 312–321.

Snell, W. E. (1956). Accidents to patients in hospital. *Lancet, 2,* 1202–1203.

Snow, R., Williams, K., & Holmes, G. (1992). The effects of wearing high-heeled shoes on pedal pressure in women. *Foot and Ankle, 13,* 85–92.

Sorock, G. S. (1983). A case control study of falling incidents among the hospitalized elderly. *Journal of Safety Research, 14,* 47–52.

Sorock, G. S., Bush, T. L., Golden, A. L., Fried, C. P., Brewer, B., & Hale, W. E. (1988). Physical activity and fracture risk in a free-living elderly cohort. *Journal of Gerontology, 43,* M134–M139.

Sorock, G. S., & Labiner, D. M. (1992). Peripheral neuromuscular dysfunction and falls in an elderly cohort. *American Journal of Epidemiology, 136,* 584–591.

Sorock, G. S., & Shimkin, E. (1988). Benzodiazepine sedatives and the risk of falling in a community-dwelling elderly cohort. *Archives of Internal Medicine, 148,* 2441–2444.

Spar, J., LaRue, A., Hewes, C., & Fairbanks, L. (1987). Multivariate prediction of falls in elderly inpatients. *International Journal of Geriatric Psychiatry, 2,* 185–188.

Speechley, M., & Tinetti, M. E. (1991). Falls and injuries in frail and vigorous community elderly persons. *Journal of the American Geriatrics Society, 39,* 46–52.

Spellbring, A. M., Gannon, M. E., Kleckner, T., & Conway, K. (1988). Improving safety for hospitalized elderly. *Journal of Gerontological Nursing, 14,* 31–37.

Spencer, H., Rubin, N., Rubio, E., Indreika, M., & Seitan, A. (1986). Chronic alcoholism: Frequently overlooked cause of osteoporosis in men. *American Journal of Medicine, 80,* 393–396.

Spirduso, W. W., MacRae, H. H., MacRae, P. G., Prewitt, J., & Osborne, L. (1988). Exercise effects on aged motor function. *Annals of the New York Academy of Sciences, 515,* 363–373.

Stamford, B. A. (1988). Exercise and the elderly. In K. Pandolf (Ed.), *Exercise and Sports Sciences Reviews* (Vol. 76, pp. 341–381). New York: Macmillan.

Stauffer, R. N., Chao, E. Y. S., & Gyory, A. N. (1977). Biomechanical gait analysis of the diseased knee joint. *Clinical Orthopaedics and Related Research, 126,* 246–255.

Steffes, R., & Thralow, J. (1987). Visual field limitation in the patient with dementia of the Alzheimer's type. *Journal of the American Geriatrics Society, 35,* 198–204.

Steinberg, F. U., & Roettger, R. F. (1993). Exercise in prevention and therapy of osteoporosis. In L. A. Avioli (Ed.), *The osteoporotic syndrome* (pp. 171–184). New York: Wiley-Liss.

Stelmach, G. E., Phillips, J., DiFabio, R. P., & Teasdale, N. (1989). Age, functional postural reflexes, and voluntary sway. *Journal of Gerontology, 44,* B100–B161.

Stelmach, G. E., & Sirica, A. (1987). Aging and proprioception. *Age, 9,* 99–103.

Stelmach, G. E., & Worringham, C. J. (1985). Sensorimotor deficits related to postural stability: Implications for falling in the elderly. *Clinics in Geriatric Medicine, 1,* 679–694.

Stelmach, G. E., Zelaznik, H. N., & Lowe, D. (1990). The influence of aging and attentional demands on recovery from postural instability. *Aging, 2,* 155–161.

Stevens, G. L., Walsh, R. A., & Baldwin, B. A. (1993). Family caregivers of institutionalized and noninstitutionalized elderly individuals. *Nursing Clinics of North America, 28,* 349–362.

Stewart, R. B., Moore, M. T., May, F. E., Marks, R. G., & Hale, W. E. (1992). Nocturia: A risk factor for falls in the elderly. *Journal of the American Geriatrics Society, 40,* 1217–1220.

Stone, S. P., Halligan, P. W., & Greenwood, R. J. (1993). The incidence of neglect phenomena and related disorders in patients with an acute right or left hemisphere stroke. *Age and Ageing, 22,* 46–52.

Stowe, J. (1990). Stairlifts. *British Medical Journal, 301,* 865–867.

Strain, J. J., Lyons, J. S., Hammer, J. S., Fahs, M., Lebovits, A., Paddison, P. L., Snyder, S., Strauss, E., Burton, R., Nuber, G., Abernathy, M. A., Sacks, H., Nordlie, J., & Sacks, C. (1991). Cost offset from a psychiatric consultation-liaison intervention with elderly hip fracture patients. *American Journal of Psychiatry, 148,* 1044–1049.

Strandgaard, S., Olesen, J., Skinhoj, E., & Lassen, N. A. (1973). Autoregulation of brain circulation in severe arterial hypertension. *British Medical Journal, 1,* 507–510.

Strumpf, N. E., & Evans, L. K. (1988). Physical restraint of the hospitalized elderly: Perceptions of patients and nurses. *Nursing Research, 37,* 132–137.

Strumpf, N. E., & Tomes, N. (1993). Restraining the troublesome patient: A historical perspective on a contemporary debate. *Nursing History Review, 1,* 3–24.

Strumpf, N. E., Wagner, J., Evans, L. K., & Patterson, J. E. (1992). *Reducing restraints: Individual approaches to behavior; A teaching guide.* New York: Geriatric Research and Training Center.

Struyk, R. J. (1987). Housing adaptations: Needs and practices. In V. Regnier & J. Paynoos (Eds.), *Housing the aged: Design directives and policy considerations* (pp. 259–275). New York: Elsevier.

Struyk, R. J., & Katsura, M. (1987). Aging at home: How the elderly adjust their housing without moving. *Journal of Housing for the Elderly, 4,* 1–185.

Studenski, S., Duncan, P. W., & Chandler, J. (1991). Postural responses and effector factors in persons with unexplained falls: Results and methodologic issues. *Journal of American Geriatrics Society, 39,* 229–234.

Sudarsky, L. (1990). Geriatrics: Gait disorders in the elderly. *New England Journal of Medicine, 322,* 1441–1446.

Sundel, M., Garrett, R. M., & Horn, R. D. (1994). Restraint reduction in a nursing home and its impact on employee attitudes. *Journal of the American Geriatrics Society, 42,* 381–387.

Sutton, J. C., Standen, P. J., & Wallace, W. A. (1994). Unreported accidents to patients in hospital. *Nursing Times, 90,* 46–49.

Svanstrom, L. (1974). Falls on stairs: An epidemiologic study. *Scandinavian Journal of Social Medicine, 2,* 113–120.

Svensson, M. L., Rundgren, A., Larsson, M., Oden, A., Sund, V., & Landahl, S. (1991). Accidents in the institutionalized elderly: A risk analysis. *Aging, 3,* 181–192.

Svensson, M. L., Rundgren, A., & Landahl, S. (1992). Falls in 84- to 85-year-old people living at home. *Accident Analysis and Prevention, 24,* 527–537.

Svensson, M. L., Rundgren, A., Larsson, M., & Landahl, S. (1992). Accidents in the institutionalized elderly: Injuries and consequences. *Aging: Clinical and Experimental Research, 4,* 125–133.

Swartzbeck, E. M., & Milligan, W. L. (1982). A comparative study of hospital incidents. *Nursing Management, 13,* 39–43.

Swift, C. G. (1984). Postural instability as a measure of sedative drug response. *British Journal of Clinical Pharmacology, 18,* 87S.

Swift, C. G., Ewen, J. M., & Stevenson, I. H. (1985). Responsiveness to oral diazepam in the elderly: Relationship to total and free plasma concentrations. *British Journal of Clinical Pharmacology, 20,* 111–118.

Swift, C. G., & Stevenson, I. H. (1983). Benzodiazepines in the elderly. In E. Costa (Ed.), *The benzodiazepines: From molecular biology to clinical practice* (pp. 225–236). New York: Raven Press.

Swift, C. G., Swift, M. R., Hamley, Y. J., Stevenson, I. H., & Crooks, J. (1989). Side effect "tolerance" in elderly long-term care recipients of benzodiazepine hypnotics. *Age and Ageing, 13,* 335–343.

Swift, C. G., & Tiggs, E. J. (1987). Clinical pharmacokinetics. In C. G. Swift (Ed.), *Clinical pharmacology in the elderly.* New York: Marcel Dekker.

Tack, K. A., Ulrich, B., & Kehr, C. (1987). Patient falls: Profile for prevention. *Journal of Neuroscience Nursing, 19,* 83–89.

Taggart, H. M. (1988). Do drugs affect the risk of hip fracture in elderly women? *Journal of the American Geriatrics Society, 36,* 1006–1010.

Talmage, R. U., Stinnett, S. S., Landwehr, J. T., Vincent, L. M., & McCartney, W. H. (1986). Age-related loss of bone mineral density in non-athletic and athletic women. *Journal of Bone and Mineral Research, 1,* 115–125.

Teasdale, N., Bard, C., LaRue, J., & Fleury, M. (1993). On the cognitive penetrability of postural control. *Experimental Aging Research, 19,* 1–13.

Teasdale, N., Stelmach, G. E., & Breunig, A. (1991). Postural sway characteristics of elderly persons under normal and altered visual and support surface conditions. *Journal of Gerontology, 46,* B238–B244.

Teno, J., Kiel, D. P., & Mor, V. (1990). Multiple stumbles: A risk factor for falls in community-dwelling elderly: A prospective study. *Journal of the American Geriatrics Society, 38,* 1321–1325.

Teri, L., Larson, E. B., & Reifler, B. V. (1988). Behavioral disturbances in dementia of the Alzheimer's type. *Journal of the American Geriatrics Society, 36,* 1–6.

Tideiksaar, R. (1986). Preventing falls: Home hazard check lists to help older patients protect themselves. *Geriatrics, 41,* 26–28.

Tideiksaar, R. (1989). *Falling in old age: Its prevention and treatment.* New York: Springer Publishing Co.

Tideiksaar, R. (1990). The biomechanical and environmental characteristics of slips, stumbles, and falls. In B. E. Gray (Ed.), *Slips, stumbles, and falls:*

Pedestrian footwear and surfaces (pp. 17–27) (ASTM–STP 1103). Philadelphia: American Society for Testing and Materials.

Tideiksaar, R. (1992). Falls among the elderly: A community prevention program. *American Journal of Public Health, 82,* 892–893.

Tideiksaar, R. (1993a). Falls in older persons. *The Mount Sinai Journal of Medicine, 60,* 515–521.

Tideiksaar, R. (1993b). *Falls in older persons: Prevention and management in hospitals and nursing homes.* Boulder, CO: Tactilitics.

Tideiksaar, R. (1993c). Treatable falls in dementia. *International Journal of Geriatric Psychiatry, 8,* 615–616.

Tideiksaar, R. (1993d). A comparison of a two-wheeled walker and a four-wheeled walker in a geriatric population. *Journal of the American Geriatrics Society, 41,* SA32.

Tideiksaar, R. (1993e). Unpublished data.

Tideiksaar, R. (1994a). The compliance of older persons with external hip protectors: A device to prevent hip fractures. In J. Vossoughi (Ed.), *Biomedical engineering recent developments* (pp. 567–570). Washington, DC: Engineering Research Center, University of the District of Columbia.

Tideiksaar, R. (1994b). Falls. In B. P. Bunder & M. B. Wagner (Eds.), *Functional performance in older adults* (pp. 224–239). Philadelphia: F. A. Davis.

Tideiksaar, R. (1995a). Reducing the risk of falls and injury in older persons: Contribution of a falls and immobility clinic. *Falls in the Elderly, Facts and Research in Gerontology,* (Supplement), 129–148.

Tideiksaar, R. (1995b). Falls in older persons. In B. S. Spivack (Ed.), *Evaluation and management of gait disorders* (pp. 243–266). New York: Marcel Dekker.

Tideiksaar, R., Feiner, C. F., & Maby, J. (1993). Falls prevention: The efficacy of a bed alarm system in an acute-care setting. *The Mount Sinai Journal of Medicine, 60,* 522–527.

Tideiksaar, R., & Kay, A. (1986). What causes falls? A logical diagnostic procedure. *Geriatrics, 41,* 32–50.

Tideiksaar, R., & Osterweil, D. (1989). Prevention of bed falls: The Sepulveda GRECC method. *Geriatric Medicine Today, 8,* 70–78.

Tielsch, J. M., Sommer, A., Witt, K., Katz, J., & Royall, R. M. (1990). Blindness and visual impairment in an American urban population. *Archives of Ophthalmology, 108,* 286–290.

Tinetti, M. E. (1986). Performance-oriented assessment of mobility problems in the elderly. *Journal of the American Geriatrics Society, 34,* 119–126.

Tinetti, M. E. (1987). Factors associated with serious injury during falls by ambulatory nursing home residents. *Journal of the American Geriatrics Society, 35,* 644–648.

Tinetti, M. E. (1994). Prevention of falls and fall injuries in elderly persons. *Preventive Medicine, 23,* 756–762.

Tinetti, M. E., Claus, E., & Liu, W. L. (1992). Risk factors for fall-related injuries among community elderly: Methodological issues. In B. Vellas, M. Toupet, L. Rubenstein, J. L. Albarde, & Y. Christen (Eds.). *Falls, balance and gait disorders in the elderly* (pp. 6–19). Paris: Elsevier.

Tinetti, M. E., & Ginter, S. F. (1988). Identifying mobility dysfunctions in elderly patients: Standard neuromuscular examination or direct assessment? *Journal of the American Medical Association, 259,* 1190–1193.

Tinetti, M. E., & Ginter, S. F. (1990). The nursing home life-space diameter: A measure of extent and frequency of mobility among nursing home residents. *Journal of the American Geriatrics Society, 38,* 1311–1315.

Tinetti, M. E., Liu, W. L., & Claus, E. B. (1993). Predictors and prognosis of inability to get up after falls among elderly persons. *Journal of the American Medical Association, 269,* 65–70.

Tinetti, M. E., Liu, W. L., & Ginter, S. F. (1992). Mechanical restraint use and fall-related injuries among residents of skilled nursing facilities. *Annals of Internal Medicine, 116,* 369–374.

Tinetti, M. E., Liu, W. L., Marottoli, R. A., & Ginter, S. F. (1991). Mechanical restraint use among residents of skilled nursing facilities: Prevalence, patterns and predictors. *Journal of the American Medical Association, 265,* 468–471.

Tinetti, M. E., Mendes de Leon, C. F., Doucette, J. T., & Baker, D. I. (1994). Fear of falling and fall-related efficacy in relationship to functioning among community-living elders. *Journal of Gerontology, 49,* M140–M147.

Tinetti, M. E., & Powell, L. (1993). Fear of falling and low self-efficacy: A cause of dependency in elderly persons. *Journal of Gerontology, 48* (Special Issue), 35–38.

Tinetti, M. E., Richman, D., & Powell, L. (1990). Falls efficacy as a measure of fear of falling. *Journal of Gerontology, 45,* P239–P243.

Tinetti, M. E., & Speechley, M. (1989). Prevention of falls among the elderly. *New England Journal of Medicine, 320,* 1055–1059.

Tinetti, M. E., Speechley, M., & Ginter, S. F. (1988). Risk factors for falls among elderly persons living in the community. *New England Journal of Medicine, 319,* 1701–1707.

Tinetti, M. E., Williams, T. F., & Mayewski, R. (1986). A fall risk index for elderly patients based on number of chronic disabilities. *American Journal of Medicine, 80,* 429–434.

Tinker, A. (1991). Alarms and telephones in personal response: Research from the United Kingdom. *International Journal of Technology and Aging, 4,* 21–25.

Tinker, G. M. (1979). Accidents in a geriatric department. *Age and Ageing, 8,* 196–198.

Tobis, J. S., Block, M., Steinhaus-Donham, C., Reinsch, S., Tamaru, K., & Weil, D. (1990). Falling among the sensorially impaired elderly. *Archives of Physical Medicine and Rehabilitation, 71,* 144–147.

Tobis, J. S., Nayak, L., & Hoehler, F. (1981). Visual perception of verticality and horizontality among elderly fallers. *Archives of Physical Medicine and Rehabilitation, 62,* 619–622.

Topp, R., Mikesky, A., Wigglesworth, J., Holt, M., & Edwards, J. E. (1993). The effect of a 12-week dynamic resistance strength training program on gait velocity and balance of older adults. *The Gerontologist, 33,* 501–506.

Trewin, V. F., Lawrence, C. J., & Veitch, G. B. A. (1992). An investigation of the association of benzodiazepines and other hypnotics with the incidence of falls in the elderly. *Journal of Clinical Pharmacy and Therapeutics, 17,* 129–133.

Trickey, F., Maltais, D., Gosselin, C., & Robitailley, Y. (1993). Adapting older persons' homes to promote independence. *Physical and Occupational Therapy in Geriatrics, 12,* 1–14.

Tse, S. K., & Bailey, D. M. (1992). Tai Chi and postural control in the well elderly. *American Journal of Occupational Therapy, 46,* 295–300.

Tutuarima, J. A., deHann, R. J., & Limburg, M. (1993). Number of nursing staff and falls: A case-control study on falls by stroke patients in acute care setting. *Journal of Advanced Nursing, 18,* 1101–1105.

Vaitkevicius, P. V., Esserwein, D. M., Maynard, A. K., O'Connor, F. C., & Fleg, J. L. (1991). Frequency and importance of postprandial blood pressure reduction in elderly nursing-home patients. *Annals of Internal Medicine, 115,* 865–870.

Vandervoort, A. A., Hayes, K. C., & Belanger, A. Y. (1986). Strength and endurance of skeletal muscle in the elderly. *Physiotherapy Canada, 38,* 167–173.

van Dijk, P. T. M., Meulenberg, O. G. R. M., van de Sande, H. J., & Habbema, J. D. F. (1993). Falls in demented patients. *The Gerontologist, 33,* 200–204.

Vellas, B., & Albarede, J. L. (1993). Sleep disorders and falls in healthy elderly persons. In J. L. Albarede, J. E. Morley, T. Roth, & B. J. Vellas (Eds.), *Facts and Research in Gerontology: Vol 7. Sleep disorders and insomnia in the elderly* (pp. 77–87). Paris: Serdi.

Vellas, B., Cayla, F., Bocquet, H., dePemille, F., & Albarede, J. L. (1987). Prospective study of restriction of activity in old people after falls. *Age and Ageing, 16,* 189–193.

Vellas, B. J., Garry, P. J., Wayne, S. J., Baumgartner, R. N., & Albarede, J. L. (1992). A comparative study of falls, gait and balance in elderly persons living in North American (Albuquerque, NM, USA) and Europe (Toulouse, France): Methodology and preliminary results. In B. Vellas, M. Toupet, L. Rubinstein, J. L. Albarede, & Y. Christen (Eds.), *Falls, balance and gait disorders in the elderly* (pp. 93–116). Paris: Elsevier.

Vellas, B. Toupet, M., Rubenstein, L., Albarede, J. L., & Christen, Y. (Eds.) (1992). *Falls, balance and gait disorders in the elderly.* Paris: Elsevier.

Venglarik, J. M., & Adams, M. (1985). Which client is a high risk? *Journal of Gerontological Nursing, 11,* 28–30.

Versluysen, M. (1985). Pressure sores in elderly patients: The epidemiology related to hip operations. *Journal of Bone and Joint Surgery, 67B,* 10–13.

Vetter, N. J., & Ford, D. (1989). Anxiety and depression scores in elderly fallers. *International Journal of Geriatric Psychiatry, 4,* 159–163.

Vetter, N. J., Lewis, P. A., & Ford, D. (1992). Can health visitors prevent fractures in elderly people? *British Medical Journal, 304,* 888–890.

Visser, H. (1983). Gait and balance in senile dementia of Alzheimer's type. *Age and Ageing, 12,* 296–301.

Vlahov, D., Myers, A. H., & Al-Ibrahim, M. S. (1990). Epidemiology of falls among patients in a rehabilitation hospital. *Archives of Physical Medicine and Rehabilitation, 71,* 8–12.

Vogt, M. T. (1995). Risk factors for osteoporotic fractures in elderly women. *Clinical Geriatrics, 3,* 36–48.

Wagner, E. H., LaCroix, A. Z., Grothaus, L., Leveille, S. G., Hect, J. A., Artz, K., Odle, K., & Buchner, D. M. (1994). Preventing disability and falls in older adults: A population-based randomized trial. *American Journal of Public Health, 84,* 1800–1806.

Wahlin, T. B. R., Backman, L., Wahlin, A., & Winblad, B. (1993). Visuospatial functioning and spatial orientation in a community-based sample of healthy old persons. *Archives of Gerontology and Geriatrics, 17,* 165–177.

Walker, J. E., & Howland, J. (1991). Falls and fear of falling among elderly persons living in the community: Occupational therapy interventions. *American Journal of Occupational Therapy, 45,* 119–122.

Wallace, R. B., Ross, J. E., Huston, J. C., Kundel, C., & Woodworth, G. (1993). Iowa FICSIT trial: The feasibility of elderly wearing a hip joint protective garment to reduce hip fractures. *Journal of the American Geriatrics Society, 41,* 338–340.

Waller, J. A. (1974). Injury in the aged: Clinical and epidemiological implications. *New York State Journal of Medicine, 74,* 2200–2208.

Waller, J. A. (1978). Falls among the elderly—human and environmental factors. *Accident Analysis and Prevention, 10,* 21-23.

Walshe, A., & Rosen, H. (1979). A study of patients' falls from bed. *Journal of Nursing Administration, 9,* 31–35.

Warsaw, G., Moore, J., Friedman, W., Currie, C., Kennie, D., Kane, W., & Means, P. (1982). Functional disability in the hospitalized elderly. *Journal of the American Medical Association, 248,* 847–850.

Wasnich, R. D., Ross, P. D., Heilbrun, L. K., Vogel, J. M., Yano, K., & Benfante, R. J. (1986). Differential effects of thiazide and estrogen upon bone mineral content and fracture prevalence. *Obstetrics and Gynecology, 67,* 457–462.

Watson, J. P., Gaind, R., & Marks, I. M. (1971). Prolonged exposure: A rapid treatment for phobias. *British Medical Journal, 1,* 13–15.

Watzke, J. R., & Kemp, B. (1992). Safety for older adults: The role of technology and the home environment. *Topics in Geriatric Rehabilitation, 7,* 9–21.

Weatherall, M. (1994). One-year follow up of patients with fracture of the proximal femur. *New Zealand Medical Journal, 107,* 308–309.

Webster, J. S., Cottam, G., Gouvier, W. D., Blanton, P., Beissel, G. F., & Wofford, J. (1989). Wheelchair obstacle course performance in right cerebral vascular accident victims. *Journal of Clinical and Experimental Neuropsychology, 11,* 295–310.

Weick, M. D. (1992). Physical restraint: An FDA update. *American Journal of Nursing, 92,* 11, 74, 76–78, 80.

Weiner, D. K., Long, R., Hughes, M. A., Chandler, J., & Studenski, S. (1993). When older adults face the chair-rise challenge. *Journal of the American Geriatrics Society, 41,* 6–10.

Weller, G., Humphrey, S. J. E., Kirollos, C., Bowes, S. G., Charlett, A., Dobbs, S. M., & Dobbs, R. J. (1992). Gait on a shoestring: Falls and foot separation in Parkinsonism. *Age and Ageing, 21,* 242–244.

Werner, J. S., Peterzell, D. H., & Sheetz, A. J. (1990). Light, vision, and aging. *Optometry and Vision Science, 67,* 214–229.

Werner, P., Cohen-Mansfield, J., Braun, J, & Marx, M. S. (1989). Physical restraints and agitation in nursing home residents. *Journal of the American Geriatrics Society, 37,* 1122–1126.

Werner, P., Cohen-Mansfield, J., Green, P. M., Pasis, S., & Gerber, B. (1993). Families' perceptions of the use of physical restraints in the nursing home. *Clinical Gerontologist, 13,* 45–57.

Werner, P., Koroknay, V., Braun, J., & Cohen-Mansfield, J. (1994). Individualized care alternatives used in the process of removing physical restraints in the nursing home. *Journal of the American Geriatrics Society, 42,* 321–325.

Whanger, A. D., & Wang, H. S. (1974). Clinical correlates of the vibratory sense in elderly psychiatric patients. *Journal of Gerontology, 29,* 39–45.

Whedon, M. B., & Shedd, P. (1989). Prediction and prevention of patient falls. *Image: Journal of Nursing Scholarship, 21,* 108–114.

Whipple, R. H., Wolfson, L. I., & Amerman, P. M. (1987). The relationship of knee and ankle weakness to falls in nursing home residents: An isokinetic study. *Journal of the American Geriatrics Society, 35,* 13–20.

White, E. G., & Mulley, G. P. (1989). Footwear worn by the over 80's: A community survey. *Clinical Rehabilitation, 3,* 23–25.

White, M. W., Karam, S., & Cowell, B. (1994). Skin tears in frail elders: A practical approach to prevention. *Geriatric Nursing, 15,* 95–99.

Wickman, C. A. C., Walsh, K., Cooper, C., Barker, D. J. D., Marqetts, B. M., Morris, J., & Bruce, S. A. (1989). Dietary calcium, physical activity, and risk of hip fracture: A prospective study. *British Medical Journal, 299,* 889–892.

Wild, D., Nayak, U. S. L., & Isaacs, B. (1981a). How dangerous are falls in old people at home? *British Medical Journal, 282,* 266–268.

Wild, D., Nayak, U. S. L., & Isaacs, B. (1981b). Prognosis of falls in old people at home. *Journal of Epidemiology and Community Health, 35,* 200–204.

Wild D., Nayak, U. S. L., & Isaacs, B. (1981c). Description, classification and prevention of falls in older people. *Rhumatology and Rehabilitation, 20,* 153–159.

Williams, C. C. (1989). Liberation: Alternatives to physical restraints. *The Gerontologist, 29,* 585–586.

Williams, M. A., Oberst, M. T., & Bjorklund, B. C. (1994). Early outcomes after hip fracture among women discharged home and to nursing homes. *Research in Nursing and Health, 17,* 175–183.

Willmott, M. (1986). The effects of a vinyl floor surface upon walking in elderly hospital inpatients. *Age and Ageing, 15,* 119–120.

Winograd, C. H., Lemsky, C. M., Nevitt, M. C., Nordstrom, T. M., Stewart, A. L., Miller, C. J., & Bloch, D. A. (1994). Development of a physical performance and mobility examination. *Journal of the American Geriatrics Society, 42,* 743–749.

Winter, D. A., Patla, A. E., Frank, J. S., & Walt, S. E. (1990). Biomechanical walking pattern changes in the fit and healthy elderly. *Physical Therapy, 70,* 340–347.

Wister, A. V. (1989). Environmental adaptation by persons in their later life. *Research on Aging, 11,* 267–291.

Wolf-Klein, G. P., Silverstone, F. A., Basavaraju, N., Foley, C. T., Pascarv, A., & Ma, P. H. (1988). Prevention of falls in the elderly population. *Archives of Physical Medicine and Rehabilitation, 69,* 689–691.

Wolfson, L. I., Whipple, R., Amerman, P., & Kleinberg, A. (1986). Stressing the postural response: A quantitative method for testing balance. *Journal of the American Geriatrics Society, 34,* 845–850.

Wolfson, L. I., Whipple, R., Amerman, P., & Tobin, J. N. (1990). Gait assessment in the elderly: A gait abnormality rating scale and its relation to falls. *Journal of Gerontology, 45,* M12–M19.

Wolfson, L. I., Whipple, R., Derby, C. A., Amerman, P., & Nasher, L. (1994). Gender differences in the balance of healthy elderly as demonstrated by dynamic posturography. *Journal of Gerontology, 49,* M160–M167.

Wolinsky, F. D., & Fitzgerald, J. F. (1994). the risk of hip fracture among noninstitutionalized older adults. *Journal of Gerontology, 49,* S165–S175.

Wolinsky, F. D., Johnson, R. J., & Fitzgerald, J. F. (1992). Falling, health status, and the use of health services by older adults. *Medical Care, 30,* 587–597.

Woodhouse, K. W., & James, O. F. W. (1990). Hepatic drug metabolism and ageing. *British Medical Bulletin, 46,* 22–35.

Woodhouse, P., Briggs, R., & Ward, D. (1983). Falls and disability in old people's homes. *Journal of Clinical and Experimental Gerontology, 5,* 309–321.

Woodhull-McNeal, A. P. (1992). Changes in posture and balance with age. *Aging and Clinical Experimental Research, 4,* 219–225.

Woollacott, M. H. (1990). Changes in posture and voluntary control in the elderly: Research findings and rehabilitation. *Topics in Geriatric Rehabilitation, 5,* 1–11.

Woolacott, M. H., Shumway-Cook, A., & Nasher, L. M. (1982). Postural reflexes and aging. In J. A. Mortimer, F. J. Pirozzolo, & G. J. Maletta (Eds.), *The aging motor system* (pp. 98–119). New York: Praeger.

Woollacott, M., Inglin, B., & Manchester, D. (1988). Response preparation and posture control: Neuromuscular changes in the older adult. *Annals of the New York Academy of Science, 515,* 42–53.

Woollacott, M. H., & Manchester, D. L. (1993). Anticipatory postural adjustments in older adults: Are changes in response characteristics due to changes in strategy? *Journal of Gerontology, 48,* M64–M70.

Woollacott, M. H., Shumway-Cook, A., & Nasher, L. M. (1986). Aging and posture control: Changes in sensory organization and muscular coordination. *International Journal of Aging and Human Development, 23,* 97–114.

World Health Organization (1984). *Working group in cooperation with the International Center for Social Gerontology: Medical and social aspects of accidents among the elderly.* Paris: WHO.

World Health Organization. (1986). Vital statistics. *Annual statistical report,* 1986.

Wright, B. A., Aizenstein, S., Vogler, G., Rowe, M., & Miller, C. (1990). Frequent fallers: Leading groups to identify psychological factors. *Journal of Gerontological Nursing, 16,* 15–19.

Wyke, B. (1979). Cervical articular contributions to posture and gait: Their relation to senile disequilibrium. *Age and Ageing, 8,* 251–257.

Wykle, M. L. (1994). The physical and mental health of women caregivers of older adults. *Journal of Gerontological Nursing, 20,* 48–49.

Yasumura, S., Haga, H., Nagai, H., Suzuki, T., Amano, H., & Shibata, H. (1994). Rate of falls and correlates among elderly people living in an urban community in Japan. *Age and Ageing, 23,* 323–327.

Yip, B. Y., & Cumming, R. G. (1994). The association between medications and falls in Australian nursing-home residents. *Medical Journal of Australia, 160,* 14–18.

Young, A. (1986). Exercise physiology in geriatric practice. *Acta Medica Scandinavica, (suppl. 711),* 227–232.

Young, A., Stokes, M., & Crowe, M. (1984). Size and strength of the quadriceps muscles of old and young women. *European Journal of Clinical Investigation, 14,* 282–287.

Young, J. B., Belfield, P. W., Mascie-Taylor, B. H., & Mulley, G. P. (1985). The neglected hospital wheelchair. *British Medical Journal, 291,* 1388–1389.

Young, S. W., Abedzadeh, C. B., & White, M. W. (1989). A fall-prevention program for nursing homes. *Nursing Management, 20,* 80Y–80FF.

Zattara, M., & Bouisset, S. (1986). Chronometric analysis of the posturo-kinetic programming of voluntary movement. *Journal of Motor Behavior, 18,* 215–223.

Zeman, F. D. (1948). Accident hazards of old age: The physician's role in a program of prevention. *Geriatrics, 3,* 15–25.

Zimmer, Z., & Chappell, N. L. (1994). Mobility restriction and use of devices among seniors. *Journal of Aging and Health, 6,* 185–208.

Zook, J., Savicks, S. F., & Moore, F. D. (1980). Repeated hospitalization for the same disease: A multiplier of national health costs. *Millbank Fund Quarterly/Health and Society, 58,* 454–471.

Zuckerman, J. D., Skovron, M. L., Fessel, K., Cohen, H., & Frankel, V. A. (1992–1993). The role of surgical delay in the long-term outcome of hip fractures in geriatric patients. *Orthopedic Transactions, 16,* 750.

Index